MARGARET FULLER

*From Transcendentalism
to Revolution*

RADCLIFFE BIOGRAPHY SERIES

MARGARET FULLER

From Transcendentalism to Revolution

Paula Blanchard, 1936–

A Merloyd Lawrence Book
DELACORTE PRESS / SEYMOUR LAWRENCE

A Merloyd Lawrence Book

Published by
Delacorte Press / Seymour Lawrence
1 Dag Hammarskjold Plaza
New York, New York 10017

Manufactured in the United States of America
First printing
Designed by MaryJane DiMassi

LIBRARY OF CONGRESS CATALOGING IN PUBLICATION DATA

Blanchard, Paula.
Margaret Fuller: from Transcendentalism
to revolution.

(Radcliffe biography series)
"A Merloyd Lawrence book."
Bibliography: p.
Includes index.
1. Ossoli, Sarah Margaret Fuller, marchesa d',
1810–1850—Biography.   2. Authors, American—
19th century—Biography.   I. Series.
PS2506.B57   818'.03'09   78-739

ISBN 0-440-05314-5

FOREWORD

Radcliffe College is pleased and proud to sponsor the Radcliffe Biographies, a series of lives of extraordinary American women.

Each volume of the Radcliffe Biographies serves to remind us of two of the values of biographical writing. A fine biography is first of all a work of scholarship, grounded in the virtues of diligent and scrupulous research, judicious evaluation of information, and a fresh vision of the connections between persons, places, and events.

Beyond this, fine biographies give us both a glimpse of ourselves and a reflection of the human spirit. Biography illuminates history, inspires by example, and fires the imagination to life's possibilities. Good biography can create for us lifelong models. Reading about others' experiences encourages us to persist, to face hardship, and to feel less alone. Biography tells us about choice, steadfastness, and chance.

The women whose lives are told in the Radcliffe Biographies have been teachers, adventurers, writers, scholars. The lives of some of them were hard pressed by poverty, cultural heritage, or physical handicap. Some of the women achieved fame; the victories and defeats of others have been unsung. Some of the women lived and died years ago; others are our contemporaries. We can learn from all of them something of ourselves. In sponsoring this series, Radcliffe College is responding to the renewed interest of our society in exploring and understanding the experience of women.

The Radcliffe Biographies project found its inspiration in the publication in 1971 of *Notable American Women,* a scholarly encyclopedia sponsored by Radcliffe's Schlesinger Library on the History of Women in America. We became convinced that some of the encyclopedia's essays should be expanded into full-length biographies, so that a wider audience could grasp the many contributions women have made to American life—an awareness of which is as yet by no means universal. It seemed appropriate that an institution dedicated to the higher education of women should initiate such a project, to hold a mirror up to the lives of particular women, to pay tribute to them, and so to deepen our understanding of them and of ourselves.

We have been joined in this project by two distinguished publishing houses and by a remarkable group of writers. I am grateful to them and to the editorial board—and particularly to Deane Lord who first proposed the series, both in concept and in detail. Finally, I am happy to present this volume of the Radcliffe Biographies.

MATINA S. HORNER
President

Radcliffe College
Cambridge, Massachusetts

AUTHOR'S NOTE

Because the Fuller manuscripts are fragmented and in many cases exist in one or more copies as well as in an original, it is difficult to achieve textual accuracy. I have tried to use original sources whenever possible, but have not always been successful. Robert N. Hudspeth's *Calendar of the Letters of Margaret Fuller,* a manuscript copy of which he generously sent me, was extremely helpful; but it reached me at a fairly late stage in my writing and I was not able to use it as fully as I wished. Such success as I had in finding the most reliable sources I owe largely to the "Calendar." The shortcomings are entirely my own.

I have taken a few editorial liberties with the manuscript quotations, deleting ampersands, adding punctuation where absolutely necessary, and occasionally joining paragraphs.

Many people have helped me over the past several years. I owe a great deal to Jane Cohen and the members of her 1971 Radcliffe Seminar and to my editor, Merloyd Lawrence, for their early and warm encouragement. And I would like to express my thanks to Daphne Ehrlich, Robert N. Hudspeth, Joel Myerson, and Terence Mullen—each of whom helped me in a particularly important way—and to the unfailingly patient librarians at Houghton Library, Harvard University, and the Boston Public Library Department of Rare Books and Manuscripts.

I would also like to thank Willard P. Fuller, Jr. for pictures of Margaret Fuller and the Fuller family, and for permission to examine and quote from the Fuller papers; the Houghton Library, Harvard University, for permission to quote from the Fuller and Ward-Barker papers; the Trustees of the Boston Public Library for permission to quote from the Fuller papers in their possession; the Massachusetts Historical Society and Mrs. Lewis F. Perry for permission to quote from the Margaret Fuller 1844 Commonplace Book; Joel Myerson and the Harvard Library Bulletin for permission to quote from ''Margaret Fuller's 1842 Journal''; the Trustees of the Ralph Waldo Emerson Association and Houghton Mifflin Co. for permission to quote from *The Journals of Ralph Waldo Emerson;* the same Trustees and Columbia University Press for permission to quote from *The Letters of Ralph Waldo Emerson*; Mrs. Peggy Laible and Mrs. Jayne Gordon of Orchard House, Concord, and Mrs. Marcia Moss of the Concord Free Public Library for their assistance in obtaining illustrations; and librarians at the Princeton University Library, the New York Public Library, the Pennsylvania State University Library, and the Bancroft Library of the University of California for sending me copies of letters in their possession.

There is no adequate way to acknowledge the steady moral support I received from my husband, Byron, and four close friends: Wynne Skolnikoff, Bobby Siegal, Karen Polenske, and Lydia Breed. I think they know that (for better or worse) this book would not have been written without them.

CONTENTS

	Foreword	vii
	Author's Note	ix
	Introduction	I
I.	The Fullers	7
II.	Childhood	16
III.	School Days	36
IV.	Cambridge	48
V.	Groton	73
VI.	Emerson and Alcott	98
VII.	Providence	118
VIII.	Conversations and the *Dial*	139
IX.	Vicissitudes	163
X.	Hawthorne and Margaret Fuller	187
XI.	The West	196
XII.	*Woman in the Nineteenth Century*	213
XIII.	New York	225

XIV.   Britain and France   245
XV.   Italy, 1847   264
XVI.   Spring and Summer, 1848   280
XVII.   The Siege of Rome   296
XVIII. Rieti and Florence   314
XIX.   Voyage of the *Elizabeth*   331
        EPILOGUE   338
        NOTES   343
        BIBLIOGRAPHY   353
        INDEX   361

Illustrations follow page 148.

INTRODUCTION

Biographies of Margaret Fuller have been written in the past, and the question might well be asked, "Why write another?" There are several answers. First of all, most women still have never heard of her. Those who have, remember her as an insufferably egocentric bluestocking who once announced, "I accept the Universe." Insufferable, even ludicrous, she often was, but she was also a remarkably sensitive and complex woman, with a breadth of sympathy that matched the considerable breadth of her mind. The complexity was largely ignored, even during her lifetime, by all but a few people, and the "Margaret Myth," or what she herself once called the "phantom Margaret," had by the time of her death already obscured the true outlines of her personality. Bell Gale Chevigny's new anthology, *The Woman and the Myth* (The Feminist Press, 1976), has done much to clarify the difference between the real and the phantom Margarets. I hope my own biography, written independently but from a similar point of view, will contribute to a deeper understanding both of why Margaret Fuller became the kind of woman she was and why the public image of her became so distorted.

Though she gave a strong impetus to the women's movement, for many New England daughters of later generations Margaret Fuller was held up as a dreadful example of the Presumptuous Woman. The intensity of the dislike directed against her sometimes bordered on frenzy. It originated not only with people who knew her slightly, like Poe, Hawthorne, and Lowell (all of whom, by the way, nursed a fierce antagonism toward strong women in general), but with people who apparently did not know her at all, like the *New Quarterly* writer quoted on p. 341. To so distant an acquaintance as the elder brother of a former student, who happened to be in Florence when she arrived there in 1849, her marriage was an occasion for malicious sniping: "What a strange story, is it not? Now that the scornful, manhating Margaret of 40 has got a husband, really no old maid need despair, while there is life in her body." [1]

The belief that because Margaret competed intellectually with men she must have hated them was both widespread and untrue, and it provided, as did the notion that she had "unsexed" herself by her choice of a literary vocation, a convenient excuse for outbursts against intellectual women in general. In her own time, Margaret Fuller became a legendary bogeywoman, symbolizing a threat not only to the male ego but to the family, and thus to the social order. The contrast between the harpy of the legend and the private personality revealed in her letters and journals is striking. It suggests the enormity of her transgression and the depth of opposition it aroused. In spite of the efforts of previous biographers, the "Margaret Myth" still persists, 125 years after her death, and it seems to be time once more to try to lay it to rest.

Beyond that, this book is an attempt to view Margaret Fuller's life through the eyes of another woman, living in the 1970s with an awareness of the questions raised about women in the past decade. In other words, this is not an unbiased biography, though I have tried to do justice to the full variety and subtlety of Margaret's personality. Setting aside Joseph Jay Deiss's detailed partial biography, *The Roman Years of Margaret Fuller,* the best of the existing biographies is *Margaret Fuller: Whetstone of Genius,* by Mason Wade. But Wade's book was written over thirty-

five years ago. His allusions to what he terms Margaret's "feminization" betray a Freudian point of view which many women today
would find objectionable, and he does not discuss some of the difficulties in her life to which the feminist movement has sensitized
us.

One such difficulty was the ambiguous nature of her education.
In the past, biographers have discussed Margaret Fuller's education chiefly in terms of the tremendous early demands it placed on
her, to the detriment of her physical and social development. This
is the way she herself discusses it in the *Memoirs*. But there is
another factor which, from a feminist point of view, has not received enough attention: that is the dramatic change in educational
goals that took place when she reached the age of ten or eleven, so
that the primary end of her education suddenly became the ac-
quirement of qualities that would enhance her attractions as prospective wife and mother. Inevitably the achievements most valued
in this new, "feminine" education conflicted with those that had
been most prized before. The contradiction became an internal
one, siphoning off energy which a man could have used in a
direct, uncomplicated way to reach his life goals.

I think, too, that her particular isolation has not been stressed
enough. Of course, all the women who strove for any kind of recognition were fighting a lonely battle. But most of them, like
Lydia Maria Child, were primarily moral rather than intellectual
leaders, and they had at least the dubious precedent of woman's
traditional role as guardian of religious and moral values. In aim-
ing for a "life of letters," Margaret set herself somewhat apart,
and it could be argued that she had even more resistance to overcome. She was the only woman in the Transcendentalist group to
be given a leading role, and the support she received from those
around her was mixed. Even the most liberal of Americans were
confused, as they still are, about how to reconcile domestic tranquility and vocational freedom for women. Her father reversed her
education in midstream; Eliza Farrar tried vainly to teach her to let
the gentlemen be right, even when they were not; Emerson's journals reveal how deeply he felt that an intelligent woman who
makes a public show of her intelligence becomes less of a woman

than one who holds her tongue. James Freeman Clarke, in his section of the *Memoirs,* has to explain Margaret's tormenting ambition as no more than the Goethean striving for "self-culture," thus unconsciously portraying his friend in accordance with his own ideal of womanliness:

> Margaret's life *had an aim* . . . [which was] distinctly apprehended and steadily pursued by her from first to last. It was a high, noble one, wholly religious, almost Christian . . . [It was] SELF-CUL-TURE. If she ever was ambitious of knowledge and talent, as a means of excelling others, and gaining fame, position, admiration,—this vanity had passed before I knew her, and was replaced by the profound desire for a full development of her whole nature, by means of a full experience of life.[2]

But Clarke, if he had not been blinded by preconceptions, might have known that Margaret's passion for "self-culture," adopted in the early years of their friendship partly because no other course was open to her, developed into a need for recognition every bit as strong as Emerson's or Lowell's. He dismisses any such notion as "vanity," unwilling to acknowledge in a woman what would have been only natural to acknowledge in a man. Nevertheless, like all Margaret's close friends, Clarke believed that intellectually she was equal or superior to anyone he knew.

The Margaret of the "Myth" is notable for a self-confidence which amounts to self-reverence, and certainly the real Margaret was largely responsible for this. But we should ask how much of her much-vaunted arrogance was defensive, and how much inner doubt it masked. She very early developed a remarkable ability to keep her emotional life to herself, and her private papers show that her self-confidence was often shaken by doubt. She was sure of the intellectual equality of women, but not sure of their equality as artists. On a personal level, she wondered whether her own failings as a writer had to do with being female, and also whether her ambition was worth the price she felt it demanded, which was total celibacy. Only a few of her friends knew the amount of sacrifice demanded by her apparently steadfast dedication to a single life.

As long as she lived in America she could see marriage and an "outside" vocation only as mutually exclusive. After she went to Europe, both sex outside of marriage and writing within marriage became possible for her. But to those of us born before 1950 her dilemma is not at all quaint, though the authorities invoked to keep us in our place have been psychologists rather than prophets and theologians.

She was temperamentally more active than contemplative, and I have tried to show her life as bridging the gap between Transcendentalism and social activism. The recognition of this must be implicit in any biography of Margaret Fuller, but I think the preciousness of Transcendentalism sometimes disguises its relationship to nineteenth-century movements for social and political reform. It is almost as easy to make fun of Emerson in his "crystal cell" (Emerson's term) as it is to make fun of Margaret Fuller, but the Emersonian concern for the integrity of the individual deeply influenced many of the humanitarian movers and shakers of his time. Margaret herself never discarded her early beliefs, though she carried them far beyond the point where she picked them up. One would be hard pressed to say where the development of her political consciousness began: whether in Liverpool, or in New York, or with the writing of *Woman in the Nineteenth Century,* or with the trip West, or with Emerson's doctrine of self-reliance and Channing's spiritual egalitarianism, or with her father's admiration for Jefferson and Adams and his stiffnecked disregard of Boston federalist opinion.

Finally, I have tried to bring out the level-headed, "classical" side of her nature, while not neglecting the passionately emotional side which is so abundantly documented in the *Memoirs.* In doing so I have felt, as any biographer of Margaret's must, the full weight of Whitman's line, "I am large, I contain multitudes." But though the classical and the romantic are inextricably mixed in her character, her more visible faults and virtues are those of a romantic, lived out with *élan* to the point where they are larger than life. It is partly because so much in her life is writ large—in capital letters with underlining and exclamation points—that we may be able to recognize those elements that affect our own lives in ways which are harder to identify now. By examining the life of a woman who in the past fought, on a heroic scale, against the open and hidden forces that worked against her in our society, we may be able to gain better insight into the subtle and pervasive ways those forces, now buried under several more layers of social history, still work against women today.

I

The Fullers

Massachusetts at the end of the eighteenth century already had a strong sense of history, but the history of Massachusetts and of the country was still measured in generations, not centuries. New England's oldest families—those who might have begun to constitute a leisured class had Americans been able to contemplate such a thing—had been in this country five, perhaps six generations. One such family were the Fullers, descended from Thomas Fuller (probably a blacksmith, although one or two of his descendents refer to him genteelly as an ''agriculturalist''), who settled in Salem, Massachusetts in 1629, married a native-born girl, bought himself some land and set up a farm and a forge. He begat sons and daughters with the enthusiasm usual to the times, and those children begat children who begat children, one of whom was Timothy Fuller born in 1739, three years after the first centennial of Harvard University. At that already venerable institution he eventually prepared himself for the ministry, graduating in 1760. He was ordained and pursued his vocation, apparently without incident, for several years before entering into an agreement with the

new community of Princeton, in western Massachusetts, whereby
he agreed to be their minister for an indefinite length of time, and
they agreed to pay him a modest annual salary and to grant him
500 acres of land at the foot of Mount Wachuset. Here he brought
his bride, Sarah Williams, in 1771, and here he determined to
settle and raise his family; and as the town of Princeton later found
out to its sorrow, it was as difficult to pry Timothy Fuller loose
from such a resolution as to dislodge Mount Wachuset itself.

During the next few years republican sentiments in Princeton
and elsewhere heated rapidly. Timothy Fuller was perhaps less
combustible than most; in any case, by 1775 he was defending
himself against charges of Toryism brought by some townspeople
who complained that, among other offenses, he did not call a fast
day when the British blocked Boston harbor. It is difficult, from
today's cool vantage point, to see anything wrong with Timothy
Fuller's patriotism. He agreed wholeheartedly that the colonies
ought to go to war, and he even offered to join the army himself as
a chaplain. But his accusers held firm, and one day he found himself forcibly barred from preaching in his own pulpit. He announced that he would hold services that day in his own home,
and so he did, then and for six months thereafter. Eventually he
and his family moved to Martha's Vineyard, where he accepted
the pastorate of the Chilmark church. Princeton meanwhile hired a
new minister and probably thought the matter closed.

But Timothy did not want to live in Martha's Vineyard; he
wanted to live on his own 500-acre farm in Princeton. And he did
not want to be known as one of the King's men. There ensued a
succession of letters from Timothy Fuller to the Princeton Town
Committee, in which he exhorted them to live up to their original
agreement and scolded them for breach of faith—always reminding them at the end that he was ready to resume his ministerial
duties in a spirit of Christian love. But as any shepherd knows, the
way to catch a flock of runaway sheep is not to bound after them,
hallooing and waving your crook. Several years went by, the
peace with Britain was won, Fuller children were born and weaned
and taught their letters, while Princeton remained unrepentant. In
1781 the family moved back to their farm—it is hardly likely that

they were received kindly—and the following year they lived for a while in the family homestead near Salem so that Timothy could file suit against Princeton from another county (as the law required) for breach of contract. In 1783 they returned to Princeton, there to remain for the next thirteen years. Although Timothy Fuller did not regain his pulpit, apparently he was restored to the good graces of the townspeople, for in 1787 he was sent to Philadelphia as a delegate to the Constitutional Convention. There he once again defied popular opinion by refusing to ratify the Constitution because it condoned slavery. Several years later the Fullers left Princeton, this time on their own terms, and moved to a farm in Merrimac, New Hampshire, not far from the Massachusetts border.

His almost fanatical adherence to principle and his stoic endurance—if not positive enjoyment—of public criticism must have made a strong impression on all of Timothy Fuller's eleven children. Timothy Jr., the eldest son, developed into a stiff and earnest young man, resolutely self-sufficient, not without humor or affection but incapable of expressing them except in cramped and quirky ways that were frequently misconstrued. Like his four brothers after him, he decided to prepare himself for the bar rather than the pulpit. Entering Harvard in 1797 at the relatively advanced age of eighteen, he exercised his love of dispute and rhetoric before the Hasty Pudding Club, was elected to Phi Beta Kappa, and gained himself something of a reputation as a gadfly, leading student protests against arbitrary college rules concerning student posture and the saying of grace before meals. In politics and religion he conspicuously took the unpopular side. Dr. Channing, that white knight of Unitarianism, had not yet entered the lists in 1798, and though Harvard was even now becoming more receptive to liberal religion, it would not for another decade become that nest of Unitarians to which Julia Ward Howe's New York neighbors refused to send their sons.[1] Young Fuller was not only a Unitarian among Congregationalists, he was a republican among Federalists and an abolitionist among the sons of Massachusetts merchants who had much to thank the South for. His campus radicalism almost cost him his "part" in the 1801 Commencement (he delivered one of the two forensic addresses), and his politics cost him the prospect of a teaching job in Roxbury after graduation.

Notwithstanding his humanitarian ideals, his capacity for empathy was small. His opinions were based on early religious training and an intellectual apprehension of "correct" moral principles, rather than on any real imaginative sympathy with the oppressed. There are in his diary very few of those small details that would show an understanding of the everyday suffering that people around him endured; yet he always tries to be tolerant and kind. His words of praise are general, and of an Augustan moderation: people are "amiable," "judicious," "sensible," "agreeable," or (especially if they are women) "modest." Once he gave an oration before the Hasty Pudding Club in which he maintained that the "instinct" of beasts is akin to human reason and partakes in a limited way of the divine; he saw no basis for denying that animals may have their own kind of souls. This is endearing, but at the same time it is difficult to picture him stopping to pat a stray dog or give a cart horse a lump of sugar.

The point is worth pursuing because young Timothy Fuller, in his role of father, is often portrayed as a bully, an altogether joyless authoritarian, and an insufferable prig. He could be all of those, but he was also capable of loving, if not with sympathy, at least with loyalty and tenderness. Outwardly rigid and vain, he was inwardly vulnerable. He was chary of bestowing praise but had an immoderate need of it himself, and it was his own misfortune, as well as other people's, that he had to set about earning it in such a peculiarly cold-blooded and laborious way. Riding in a stage, shortly after graduation from college, he made an effort to be attentive to each of his fellow passengers in turn, especially a little girl who suffered from motion sickness. "This behavior," he noted later in his diary, "turned favorable and partial eyes upon me; and as far, as I could judge, I have reason to think, I appeared, what I have so long wished, *amiable*." [2] Syntax aside, the combination of pomposity and wistfulness is characteristic; even at the age of twenty-two Timothy Fuller, Jr. was forever trying to crack his way out of his own shell.

He had early taken on some responsibility for the education of his younger brother Elisha, correcting the spelling in the child's letters and advising him to spend his Sundays "reading good books." This role would be much amplified after the death of his father. While he was still at Harvard he worked between terms as a tutor or assistant schoolmaster in various Boston suburbs, and immediately after graduation he became an English preceptor at Leicester Academy, near Princeton. Leicester was coeducational, and his pupils were girls in their early to mid-teens. At this time of his life Timothy Fuller's views on the education of women, while not exactly conservative, were only a little to the left of center. It is true that after he reached Leicester he read Mary Wollstonecraft's *Vindication of the Rights of Women* without comment. (He would read it again, with somewhat more enthusiasm, later in life.) He fretted over his father's neglect of his sisters' education. He was disappointed when a delectable girl at a party turned out to be lacking in "understanding." But he never questioned the universal belief that a woman's education prepared her only to be a wife and mother, or at most a governess should she be so unlucky as to be deprived of male support. He shared the contempt of bluestockings usual to men of the time. Of an erudite spinster he met at a friend's house, he observes that she is

> about thirty, rather plain, has read considerable, which makes her both pedantic and dogmatical; by frequenting Boston company she has contracted a kind of politeness which shews itself in all she says and does; it consists in her conviction of her own superior sense and breeding, and she deems it condescension to be civil. Notwithstanding this, and a certain moroseness approaching to misanthropy, she is a pretty good companion.[3]

Good companionship was not really what Timothy wanted from a woman, or at least it was fairly far down the list. At Leicester he was rather a Don Juan, within the limits of decorum. He buzzed from girl to girl, no sooner making a conquest than bored with it, and the abundant descriptions of his amours in his diary convey an accurate picture of what his ideal woman was like. There was Miss Frink ("modesty, good sense, and loveliness are thy attributes"); [4]

Miss White, who "recommends herself not less by her understanding, than by her amiable modesty and quick sense of obligation"; [5] Miss Tucker, with her "innocence and inbred modesty"; [6] and Miss Plimpton, who had shown him "every attention" in anticipating his wants at the tea table, and who had the "mildness and sweetness of an angel." [7] And of one of his sisters, he once wrote, "Debby is a very judicious girl; but the quality most valuable and most uncommon, which she possesses in a high degree, is docility; docility without surrendering her own judgment too far. She is also distinguished by an innocent simplicity, becoming [to] the heroine of a novel. Few can discern or justly appreciate such qualities." [8]

At the end of a year he left Leicester Academy in order to read law in Boston. He left under a small cloud: he had, in fun, broken the seal of a letter addressed to Miss Plimpton (she of the tea table) and pretended to read it. That he had not actually done so is beyond question, for he had such an excruciating sense of honor that he would agonize for hours over telling a social lie. But there was a scene, and the other students seem to have taken Miss Plimpton's part. A ball given the last night of the term held no appeal for him, and instead of noting in his diary, as he usually did, which girls were the prettiest or the most modest and amiable, he remarks sulkily, "Few of the Belles were calculated to excite interest or even attention." [9] The incident is typical of the way Timothy's heavy-handed attempts at humor often misfired. The sulking too is characteristic; it would always be extremely difficult for him to admit a fault, and his defense against even a hint of blame would always be to play the injured party.

The next few years were spent living in various boardinghouses, while he read law and eventually opened his own Court Street office. He was making himself heard in the Republican party, for his political scrappiness had now been directed toward a specific goal, and he would before long run successfully for the state legislature. He was active socially, making the rounds of the balls and dinner parties as became a fledgling politician, but he made few close friends and took no particular pleasure in his socializing. Years later he would be surprised when two of his colleagues in the U.S. Senate accused him of being unsociable, but they were perfectly right. His descriptions of these affairs have a dismaying sameness to them (the evening is "pleasant" or "enjoyable"; Miss _____, who has a "pleasing shape," consents to sing), and while he undertook a strenuous social schedule, and probably even preferred partying to staying in his bachelor rooms, this period must have been lonely and cheerless. His friends from Harvard were drifting away, geographically and emotionally (his two closest friends had become strong Federalists), and increasingly he began to miss his family. "Though I have at the moment of writing this been absent from them several days," he writes in 1803 after a visit home, "I am melted in tenderness and affection at the recollection." [10] But he assumed the role of elder brother in a manner that belied his feelings, especially after his father died in 1805. There were small rebellions and occasional real quarrels as his sisters and brothers began to assert their independence, and the little Eden in Merrimac took on a distinct chill. The love between brother and sister, Timothy complained to his mother in 1807, should resemble that between parent and child, which was the "nearest of any thing conceivable, to the true love which unites God and his saints and his saints to each other." [11] This was a standard which Mrs. Fuller herself, let alone the ten young Fullers, could hardly be expected to match, and eventually Timothy began to look elsewhere for his celestial kind of love. When he was nearing thirty he bought a house in Cambridgeport, and two years later he brought to it Margarett Crane, the daughter of Major Peter Crane of Canton.

Beside the angular silhouette of her husband's personality, which lends itself only too well to caricature, Margarett Crane Fuller* has come down to us as a shadowy figure. Contemporary descriptions of her are both vague and cloying, emphasizing the saintliness of her disposition, an apparently endless capacity for self-sacrifice, and that "delicacy" of health which in the last century was so often taken to mean that a woman was altogether too good for this world. Those of her letters which survive show her as

* Margarett Crane Fuller preferred to spell her name with two *t*'s. After her daughter's birth this practice was followed with her name as well, but with decreasing frequency as she grew older.

an even-tempered, undemanding, affectionate, thoroughly domestic woman, very much involved in day-to-day social intercourse,
more at ease with people than her husband (though she was a little
shy), completely unaffected in her manners and without any intellectual pretensions. She had taught school briefly before her marriage, but she accepted gratefully her place as the consort of an
overprotective, domineering husband. In later life, after she lost
his protection, she leaned heavily on her children; but there was
never any trace of the martyr in her dependence, and she kept her
remarkably cheerful temper until her death. Above all she was
profoundly religious, though not in a carping or proselytizing way.

Fair and blue-eyed, rather above average height, with a beauty
that has been described as madonna-like, Margarett Crane Fuller
came very close to embodying Timothy's ideal woman. She
danced well, she had a slender figure, she loved pretty clothes only
less than she loved flowers, and she had the requisite measure of
"docility." She drew forth all Timothy's long-pent devotion: the
letters he wrote her from Washington eight years after their marriage, during his first term in Congress, are as playful and anxious
as those of a bridegroom; and though some resurgence of early affection was natural under the circumstances, still the gentle court-
liness of this austere man to his wife, now four times a mother, is
remarkable. Except for his children while they were very young,
she was the only person to whom he could unabashedly confess
weakness or express affection, and when the children began to
grow older she became the mediator through whom love and praise
could be conveyed from father to child. "Give my love to my dear
little ones," he would write, and in the context of his letters to her
the message would become believable, as it never was in the little
homilies that occasionally arrived signed, "Yr affectionate father."

Docile though she was, Margarett Crane Fuller did have a mind
of her own. She was not above resorting to the traditional expedient of the dutiful wife confronted with a blustering husband—she
assented to his demands and quietly went her own way. Her husband blustered more and more as he grew older (although his letters to her never lost their uniquely tender tone) and his almost obsessive concern with detail, evident even in his early youth,

became even more pronounced. His anxiety about the postal service was a case in point: After he was elected to the Senate he spent every winter in Washington, and while he was there he worried incessantly about the mail, which in fact was quite reliable.* He insisted that his wife date her letters precisely, down to the time of day; that she mail them immediately after sealing; that she number each one, and acknowledge each of his by number. There are periods when almost every letter he wrote to her (and he wrote every day) would include some admonition about the mail. But it had very little effect. She usually remembered to date her letters, but she often posted them a day or two later. She almost always forgot to number hers and acknowledge his, and—as her children grew more numerous—she often forgot to write at all.

These were the parents of Sarah Margaret Fuller, born in the Cambridgeport house on May 23, 1810.

* Letters from Boston to Washington took four days in good weather, longer when the roads were muddy. Few seem to have been lost.

II

Childhood

The heart of Cambridge in 1810 was a cluster of four brick buildings set in an open field at the intersection of the roads to Boston, Concord, and Watertown. From the windows of those buildings the students of Harvard, who presumably were as given to staring out windows as students everywhere always have been, could watch the cows as they shuffled, drooling and clanking, twice a day across the road to and from their pasture on the common. Beyond the cows and the common they could see the mansions of Tory Row, and beyond those the quiet water and cattail marshes of the Charles River, where, God willing, they would go rowing as soon as examinations were over.

A few hundred feet away the large, spare presence of the First Parish Church called the faithful to worship twice every sabbath. Most of the 2,300 inhabitants of the town lived within easy walking distance of the square, but nevertheless many parishoners arrived in carriages and chaises so that the ladies could say their prayers in dry slippers and clean gowns. The unpaved roads were scarcely more suitable for driving than for walking: in winter they froze into ruts that never quite corresponded to the width of the vehicle one was riding in; in spring they softened to the consistency of porridge; and in summer they baked hard and flat, and a fine haze of dust spun up behind the wheels of each carriage, hanging in the air to sting the eyes of the horses pulling the ones behind, and drifting into dooryards, where it mingled with the dust of the previous day which the housemaids were trying vainly to shake out of their mops.

As one moved away from the square in any direction the houses became more scattered, but a mile or more to the east, separated from the main village by marshland, pasture, and an occasional farm, was the new settlement of Cambridgeport, established in a futile attempt to have Cambridge compete as a port with the commercial giant across the river. ''The Port'' was a distinctly unfashionable part of town, but it was a convenient place to live for those whose business took them across the bridge to Boston. The house Timothy Fuller had chosen to buy there was an ugly, square, yellow building on the corner of Cherry and Eaton streets. Its only redeeming features were a small garden behind it and the two young elm trees which Timothy, to celebrate the birth of his first child, planted in the narrow strip of grass between the front door and the road.

It has been said that Timothy immediately usurped much of his wife's role in the rearing of his daughter, supervising every detail of her existence down to the choosing of her infant dresses. That he took an intense interest in the baby, and that in this as in almost everything else he was something of a busybody, is certainly true. But his law practice and the political connections he was beginning to cultivate kept him away all day long, and in any case he was too much in love with his wife to have seriously interfered in her early relationship with the child. Besides, both Timothy and Margarett Crane Fuller were openly, physically demonstrative with all their children while they were babies. Margaret was petted and played with by her parents, her grandparents, and her many aunts and uncles, and it is reasonable to assume that she had a happy and uncomplicated infancy and that she was not set to learning her alphabet or anything else until she was ready for it. But since she was extraordinarily bright, she was ready for it by the age of three. By then her rapidly unfolding intelligence had attracted her father's attention and wakened those pedagogical instincts which had been more or less dormant since the days of Leicester Academy and the brotherly notes to little Elisha. Timothy set up a lesson plan for the child, which his wife helped her to follow during the day, and when he came home in the evening he would ask for a report of how she had spent the day and what she had learned. By the time she visited her grandparents in Canton, Massachusetts, in the spring of her fourth year, her father's affection had become firmly associated in her mind with intellectual achievement, and he was closing his letters to his wife with such conditional endearments as, "My love to the little Sarah Margarett. I love her if she is a good girl and learns to read." [1]

Just as this rigorous education began, there occurred a loss in her life which became her first conscious memory of anything. Her sister Julia Adelaide, two years younger than she, suddenly died:

> I remember coming home and meeting our nursery-maid, her face streaming with tears. That strange sight of tears made an indelible impression. . . . She took me by the hand and led me into a still and dark chamber,—then drew aside the curtain and showed me my sister. I see yet that beauty of death! The highest achievements of sculpture are only the reminder of its severe sweetness. Then I remember the house all still and dark,—the people in their black clothes and dreary faces,—the scent of the newly-made coffin,—my being set up in a chair and detained by a gentle hand to hear the clergyman,—the carriages slowly going, the procession slowly doling out their steps to the grave. But I have no remembrance of what I have since been told I did,—insisting, with loud cries, that they should not put the body in the ground. I suppose that my emotion was spent at the time, and so there was nothing to fix that moment in my memory. [2]

Her sense of desolation and bewilderment must have been keen; at three-and-a-half she would have been old enough to ask some painful questions about her sister's death, but too young to make use of the religious explanations with which her elders comforted themselves. Aside from the shock and grief, this event would affect her life in two far-reaching ways. The first was that for the next two years there would be no other child in the family to shade her occasionally from the full glare of her father's attention. The second was that she had lost the companionship of another little girl, which she needed not so much now as later on: "Her character, if that fair face promised right, would have been soft, graceful and lively; it would have tempered mine to a gentler and more gradual course."[3] Margaret is guilty here of some characteristic hyperbole—her sister was, after all, only eighteen months old—but any sister this close to her in age, graceful and lively or not, would have made the next dozen years or so a great deal more bearable. Now, although there would be eight other children born to her mother, the next in line would be a full five years younger than she, male, and no help at all when she began to blunder through the mazes of an especially difficult adolescence.

During these early years Margaret and her mother were together all day long, and Margaret learned to read, to sew and cook, to sing and to do simple household tasks. At no time would they be temperamentally more alike or more likely to enjoy one another's company; they would drift apart as more babies arrived, Mrs. Fuller's health deteriorated, and Margaret gradually withdrew into the private concerns of a sensitive, precocious child. T. W. Higginson remembers Margarett Crane Fuller as "one of the sweetest and most self-effacing wives ever ruled by a strong-willed spouse,"[4] and she is dismissed by some biographers as having had virtually no influence in the lives of her children. One needs only to look at the kind of people her children became, as compared with their father, to realize that this must be an oversimplification. But her influence in the family, which ran directly counter to her husband's, was subtle and nonverbal, and therefore is difficult to describe. She may be justly accused of being too much involved in trivia—in the measurement of silk and the dispensation of clean handkerchiefs—but her trivia was, for her children, a cool relief from her husband's incessant concern with matters of law, commerce, and social propriety.

The one interest she had which was hers alone, and which did not revolve around family or community, was gardening. She gave it every moment she could spare, and whenever the family moved (eight times during her life) she carefully dug up her lilies, pinks, and violets and transplanted them. We have occasional vignettes which throw light not only on her own personality but on the softening effect it had on her husband's, such as Richard's delightful picture of his parents driving slowly to Canton with him on a sunny day, resting the horse on the hills, picking up children who were trudging along the road, and singing hymns all the way.[5]

On the whole, she did not take Timothy very seriously. She politely asked his advice, but if it clashed with her own judgment she occasionally circumvented or ignored it. As Margaret grew older, her mother's ability to draw out the hidden gentleness in her father, and her relative lack of awe in his presence, must have done much to reduce him to merely mortal dimensions in the child's eyes.

Margarett Crane Fuller was a truly pious woman, believing unquestioningly in a personal God and accepting death as a translation to bliss. Her letters remind us how intimately people lived with death in the early nineteenth century, and indeed in so large a family as hers it was a mark of good fortune to lose, as she did, only two children in infancy. To have her family come safely through one of their periodic bouts with the ordinary diseases of childhood was the occasion of real thanksgiving, and it was quite characteristic of her to speculate on just what form a recently departed friend's soul would take in heaven.

When Margaret was five her brother Eugene arrived to claim much of her mother's time, and the early bond between mother and daughter began to weaken. It would have even without the competitive presence of a little brother, for by now the early drudgery of learning her letters was behind her, and reading had changed from a chore to a pleasure that far outweighed all others. By the age of five she could, according to her father, read "tolerably in any common book,"[6] and by the time she was six she was progressing so well in Maria Edgeworth's *Parents' Assistant* that her father decided she was ready to learn Latin. It took her only a few weeks to master the elements of grammar, and then she began memorizing daily passages from Virgil. Her father insisted on hearing her recite personally; so after he had finished his evening tea, Margaret would be called into the drawing room. Since he was now a member of the state legislature as well as an attorney, his working day was long and these recitations kept the child up far beyond her normal bedtime. Afterward, overtired and still wrought up from the strain of having to produce a perfect recitation (her father would accept nothing less), her head crammed with violent images of the Greek wars and the horrors of Hades, she would be sent off to bed. Not surprisingly, she began to suffer from nightmares. She would dream she was slowly drowning in pools of blood, or that herds of horses were about to trample her to death. Hideous faces advanced out of the darkness, and sometimes eyes would detach themselves from the faces and converge on her. Once she dreamed her mother had died and she was following her coffin as she had her sister's. She became terrified of going to bed at all and would plead to be allowed to stay up a few minutes longer, causing her aunts to shake their heads and cluck their tongues over the shockingly bad upbringing Timothy was giving his eldest child. After a while another fear was added to that of the nightmares; she began to walk in her sleep. She would wake up, or be shaken awake, in the middle of the night in unfamiliar surroundings, certain to be scolded for having given way to morbid fancies in her sleep, and twice she was found in convulsions, apparently after having had nightmares. She did not outgrow the nightmares and the somnambulism until adulthood, and the excruciating headaches from which she now began to suffer would plague her all her life. Years later, looking back at her childhood, she would remark with dubious accuracy that the nightmares checked her growth.[7] Although she may have lost her appetite temporarily and become thin and fatigued, there is no evidence that her physical growth was ever checked: on the contrary, by the age of nine or ten she was as tall as the average thirteen-year-old. If anything, the remark tells us more about a subsequent adult confusion of physical and emotional pain than it does about Margaret's health as a child. But regardless of physical effect, or lack thereof, the direct psychological damage inflicted by the regimen and the choice of reading matter was undeniable.

Timothy Fuller imposed on his daughter not only his standards of achievement (which in themselves she was capable of reaching) but also his own relentlessly logical thought processes, which were quite another thing:

> Trained to great dexterity in artificial methods, accurate, ready, with entire command of his resources, he had no belief in minds that listen, wait, and receive. He had no conception of the subtle and indirect motions of imagination and feeling. His influence on me was great, and opposed to the natural unfolding of my character, which was fervent, of strong grasp, and disposed to infatuation, and self-forgetfulness.[8]

Obviously this influence, so foreign to her own temperament, would have been far less powerful if Timothy had been the unmitigated tyrant he is sometimes pictured as being. But he was also, in his sporadic way, an affectionate father, and the bond between him and his daughter was strong and complex. At no time was Margaret totally deprived of her father's love and praise, but at no time did she get enough of it.

Her early education was unusual only for a girl. Many of the Cambridge and Boston boys her own age were reading Virgil at the age of six; when they were nine they were customarily handed over to the untender tutorship of the masters at the Cambridgeport Private Grammar School or the Boston Latin School, who speedily prepared them for college. Frederick Henry Hedge, son of Harvard philosophy professor Levi Hedge, entered Harvard at the age of thirteen, and James Freeman Clarke at fifteen. In her father's generation, William Ellery Channing was a Harvard freshman at fourteen, and among her younger brothers' friends, T. W. Higginson would enter at thirteen. There were examples even among girls (though not in Cambridge) of an education almost as demanding as Margaret's: Julia Ward Howe, born in New York in 1809, was reading fluently in French, Latin, Italian, and German by the age of sixteen; and in England, Harriet Martineau received the same education as her brothers and recited in Latin for four hours every Saturday at the age of eleven. But the impersonality of any schoolmaster, even a brutal one, can be a blessing. The peculiar inter-mixture of Margaret Fuller's intellectual achievement with her emotional life is perhaps comparable only to that of John Stuart Mill, although in Margaret's case it received an extra psychological twist from the fact that she was a girl.

From Virgil, Margaret went on to read Plutarch, with a growing delight that kept her reading long after she had fulfilled her assignments. From this early introduction to the Plutarchian hero, whose sandalled feet were placed so firmly on the ground, she derived a code by which she learned to withstand patiently all kinds of discomfort, including her father's displeasure, and a standard by which she would always measure herself and other people—though happily not as inflexibly as she did at this age. The word "Roman" came to mean for her the man of "heroic common sense,"[9] the austere, self-sacrificing, nonliterary, non-philosophical Roman warrior or political figure. "In vain for me are men more, if they are less, than Romans," she wrote.[10] She admired the strength and endurance of the Romans, the direct, un-complicated way they translated thought into action, and their preference for the active over the contemplative life: "The history of Rome abides in mind, of course, more than the literature. It was degeneracy for a Roman to use the pen; his life was in the day."[11] One cannot help noticing, as Margaret herself apparently did not, how opposite the Roman character is to the character she describes as her own, and how closely it resembles that of her father.

Her admiration for the Greeks, at least at this age, was less. She seems to have turned to them purely for relaxation rather than for any positive counterpoise to her Romans. She had not yet learned the language, and Greek mythology was available to her primarily through Ovid. "I wish I had learned as much of Greece as of Rome,—so freely does the mind play in her sunny waters, where there is no chill, and the restraint is from within out; for these Greeks, in an atmosphere of ample grace, could not be impetuous, or stern, but loved moderation as equable life always must, for it is the law of beauty."[12]

The man she did find to keep the Romans "in their place"[13] was Shakespeare. She first discovered him when she was eight,

while looking in a desultory way through the drawing-room book-
case one Sunday afternoon for a book that was serious enough for
the sabbath and interesting enough to keep her from falling asleep.
(The Unitarian Fullers kept the sabbath scrupulously. Margaret
customarily spent Sunday morning listening, with much inner rebellion, to one of the local minister's seemingly endless sermons.
Afternoons were spent in quiet occupations or in reading religious
books.) Probably her father's edition of Shakespeare was a one-
volume *Complete Works,* in which case the sheer bulk of it would
have made it look innocent enough, and shortly she was well into
Romeo and Juliet. When her father, noticing her complete absorption, asked what the book was, she was reprimanded for indulging
in frivolous reading on the sabbath and ordered to put it away. She
did, but as the afternoon wore on she was drawn back to it so
strongly that, in a rare act of open defiance, she took the book
down again. When she was caught the second time her astonished
father sent her straight to bed. After a while he came into her
room, thinking to find her contrite, but instead found her still so
engrossed in the story, which would not leave her mind, that she
hardly heard anything he said to her:

> He felt it right, before going to rest, to reason with me about my dis-
> obedience, shown in a way, as he considered, so insolent. I listened,
> but could not feel interested in what he said, nor turn my mind from
> what engaged it. He went away really grieved at my inpenitence,
> and quite at a loss to understand conduct in me so unusual.[14]

Not all the books were kept in the drawing room. There was no
library, but upstairs, adjoining her father's room, was what she
calls a "closet," evidently a small room with three walls of book-
shelves and a bay window. Here her father kept his collection of
lighter works, chiefly from the Queen Anne period (one wonders
why Shakespeare was not here too, rather than down among the
sermons), and here she discovered Smollett, Fielding, Molière,
and Cervantes. She was free to read anything she wished. It was
characteristic of the Fullers and their neighbors to combine liberalism and puritanism in unexpected ways. An author's works might

be earthy, even bawdy, so long as his or her life was unexceptionable; but New Englanders avoided the works of any writer whose life was tinged with scandal,* such as Goethe, George Sand, or Mary Wollstonecraft (whose views on education Timothy found "sensible and just" even while he doubted the propriety of allowing women to read them).[15] Thus Timothy Fuller's mother—daughter and wife of ministers though she was—read with gusto the works of Fielding, who she said "treated the world as it deserved."[16] No one minded eight-year-old Margaret reading Fielding, or Shakespeare either for that matter, except on the sabbath. In any case, although she was given free rein there seems to have been no danger of her being corrupted by the more worldly writers in her father's library. Of Fielding and Smollett she remarks primly that they "deal too broadly with the coarse actualities of life."[17] Cervantes and Molière were more to her taste, and with Shakespeare taught her most of what she learned about human nature at this age: "They loved the *natural history* of Man. Not what he should be, but what he is, was the favorite subject of their thought."[18] She was allowed to read some lyric poetry— Goldsmith, Cowper, probably Thompson and Gray. She apparently did not read Wordsworth until some years later. Scott, that genial comforter of other bleak nineteenth-century childhoods, was for some reason not among her favorites, although she did read and enjoy his works. But both narrative poetry and novels would come to be discouraged by her father on the grounds that narrative of any kind was "false" and only worth reading for the sake of the writer's style and use of imagery. A request to read William Sotheby's translation of Wieland's *Oberon* was put off when she was nine because the story was so interesting as to completely distract her from the merits of the prosody.[19]

Obviously, almost all of Margaret's esthetic experience was literary. She had almost no opportunity to explore the world directly, through her own senses. "Nature" was all around her, but her encounters with it were limited to weekend drives in the country with her parents and walks over the bridge to watch the light on

* A possible exception was Byron, who managed to offend on both counts.

the river. But she did have available to her a tiny, domesticated bit of nature in her mother's garden. Here, in the absence of any other kind of companionship, she would bury her face in the petals of her mother's flowers and talk to them. She was fond of watching the sun set through the garden gate, "a wooden gate made of boards, in a high, unpainted board wall, and embowered in the clematis creeper. . . . Beyond this black frame I did not step, for I liked to look at the deep gold behind it."[20] The garden was a unifying bond in the Fuller family. Even Timothy found time to dig in it in the spring; it reminded him of his boyhood home in Princeton, to which he dreamed of returning in his less practical moments.

If Margaret had been willing, as the neighborhood boys were, to climb fences and to bluff her way through encircling herds of near-sighted, curious cattle, there were raspberries, blackberries, and blueberries to be had for the picking in the fields beyond the gate. But since she had no wish to venture so far, her physical activity was very limited. Once in a while, when she was cramped from hours of sitting over books, sitting over meals, and sitting over embroidery, she would want to run around so much that she would go outdoors and join some other children in a street game. They would allow her to play, but their acceptance of her and hers of them was an expedient of the moment. She was not only awkward and shy, she did not know how to talk to other children; she had learned her vocabulary from Plutarch and Shakespeare (chiefly, one suspects, from Coriolanus). Moreover, partly as a result of nearsightedness she was beginning to develop a habit of half-closing her eyes whenever she looked at anyone. These mannerisms effectively shut off communication with other children, and when the game was over she would come indoors alone. She continued to rely for companionship on her books, her mother's flowers, and her immediate family, until a few months before her eighth birthday when she made friends with an adult woman.

While she was in church on Sunday, looking around at the congregation (she never listened to the sermon), she noticed a delicately pretty young woman sitting with some acquaintances. There was something vaguely foreign about her clothes and her expression, and Margaret decided immediately that she would like to meet her. As it happened, the Fullers did stop to talk with the woman's friends afterward, and she was introduced to them as Ellen Kilshaw, the daughter of a wealthy Liverpool manufacturer. She was visiting America for several months, her sister having married an American. All the Fullers were much taken with her, and she responded to Margaret's admiration with a kindness that grew into real friendship, despite—or perhaps because of—the difference in their ages and backgrounds. Timothy and his wife strongly encouraged the attachment, seeing in Ellen a model of feminine accomplishment. Her British manners were a study in grace and tact; she played the harp and painted in oils. Margaret writes of Ellen:

> She did not say much to me—not much to anyone. She spoke in her whole being rather than by chosen words. Indeed, her proper speech was dance or song, and what was less expressive did not greatly interest her. . . . To the mind she brought assurance that there was a region . . . whose object, fulfilled or not, was to gratify the sense of beauty, not the mere utilities of life.[21]

One small but significant measure of the understanding between them was that Ellen was the first adult to yield to the child's request that she be called simply by her middle name, Margaret, and not by her full name, Sarah Margaret, which she detested.

After only a few months Ellen had to return to England. Her correspondence with all the Fullers lasted two more years, but it was more active with the parents than with the daughter. It is in keeping with Margaret's remark about the unimportance of words in their friendship that, although she was desolated by Ellen's departure, she had to be prodded to write to her after the first few months. Ellen's letters were inevitably less interesting than her physical presence, and in the face of Timothy's frequent reminders to "write to our dear Ellen," what originally had been a delight must have become a chore.

From one of Ellen's letters to Margaret's mother we have a rare picture of her at the age of seven:

I can give [family and friends] no idea of what my dear Margaret is. She is so surprising for her years, and expresses herself in such appropriate language upon subjects that most of twice her age do not comprehend. I was really astonished when she first conversed with me; for her manners are quite childish: I remember when I first called upon you; after the pleasant evening I had passed at your house, she was at the window, she flushed (as I have reason to flatter myself with pleasure) at my approach; and opened the door; but after opening it, ran, and concealed herself behind your chair; the simplicity of the child, triumphing over her maturer understanding.[22]

Ellen's direct influence on Margaret, while she was in America, was all in the direction of conventional feminine propriety. But the vicissitudes she underwent during the next two years, and her reaction to them, probably had a more complex effect. To begin with, Ellen was uneasy about the status of women in society. She had strong domestic inclinations, and she writes with clearly genuine admiration of the affection between Timothy Fuller and his wife. Her dislike of "masculine women" was no less genuine,[23] and she cautioned Margaret that "the acquirements of a female are not for the world, unless she be a public character they are for the private domestic circle."[24] But her letters are much concerned with the unequal relationship between the sexes, and especially with the plight of women who enter into a loveless marriage (or any marriage, for that matter) and are afterward neglected or abandoned by their husbands.[25] She speaks only half-playfully of women as the "superior sex" and of men as the "lordly sex"; she hopes very much that Mrs. Fuller's next child will be a girl. (It was; Ellen Kilshaw Fuller was born in September 1820.) Her observations on the subject could be taken for no more than drawing-room banter, and perhaps on the conscious level they were, but in some of her letters she hardly writes about anything else. She was acutely conscious of her own position as a marketable virgin, and after she reached England her doubts on the subject were put to a real test. Her father's fortune, which had begun to slide during Ellen's visit to the United States, was all but destroyed in the depression of 1819. He was no longer able to provide dowries for his remaining daughters, and in fact was barely able to support them. In the midst of this family crisis Ellen received a proposal from a wealthy gentleman for whom she had only moderately "amiable" feelings. There is something of the Jane Austen heroine in the way she agonized over her decision for several weeks. She actually had brought herself to the point of entering one of those loveless marriages she so much feared, when the gentleman's Catholic mother, learning of Ellen's firm Unitarianism, prevented the match. Her embarrassment over the whole affair is evident in her subsequent letters. She tries to make clear to her friends that she had *some* regard for the man, and that she would not marry *merely* for money.[26] But it seems clear that her primary motive had been to do her duty as society prescribed it, even against her own principles. Soon after this she resolved on an alternative which was only less painful because presumably less permanent: she decided to go out as a governess, as her sister had before her, although the prospect of being subjected to the humiliations commonly suffered by governesses, such as not being allowed to speak in company, filled her with "almost horror."[27] She received several offers, and after delaying as long as she could, accepted one from Lord Gosford. This meant sailing to Ireland, where she could not see her family and could not even accept letters from her American friends, since the postage would be higher than she could afford.* After some further mishaps, including a near-shipwreck, she reached Ireland. Except for one letter the correspondence ceased after that until 1835, when she wrote to say that she was married, had several children, and had grown "enormously fat."[28]

Both Timothy Fuller and his wife frequently expressed admiration for Ellen during her ordeal, and Timothy went so far as to suggest that she return to America, with the help of her friends here, and open a seminary for girls. Ellen declined, possibly because of the amount of money involved. Of Margaret's thoughts we have no record, but if Ellen was a model of grace, beauty, and gentleness, she was also a model of what use grace, beauty, and gentleness were to a woman in the early nineteenth century.

* Postage was usually paid by the recipient of a letter.

Three weeks after Ellen sailed for England, Timothy Fuller left for Washington to serve the first of four terms in Congress. From now until Margaret was fifteen he would be absent from home three to five months of every year. This meant that the pressure on her to achieve was somewhat lessened in intensity, although by no means removed. Her father demanded a scrupulous account of how her studies were progressing and sent her little assignments from time to time. If she or her mother neglected to answer a question, Timothy would peck away at it in letter after letter until he was satisfied. But fortunately he had many other things on his mind besides his daughter's education. The diaries he kept during this period reflect the duality of his life; they are almost totally concerned with social obligations and political debate and rarely mention his family. At the same time, he writes to his wife—and there seems no reason to doubt his sincerity—that he is embarrassed to show in front of his colleagues the emotion he feels at receiving one of her letters.[29] His letters home are gossipy and playful, full of concern for his wife and children: "Did my dear Sarah Margarett inquire if I sent a kiss to her—I sent two for her this time—this [kiss] and this [kiss] —both these places I kissed this moment on purpose for my girl."[30]

In order to fully understand the relationship of Margaret to her father during these Washington years it is necessary to read Timothy's letters to her in the context of his letters to his wife, and it must be remembered that Mrs. Fuller either read those letters to the children or repeated anything that had to do expressly with them. This three-sided relationship shows itself clearly in the matter of the tooth. When Timothy left for Washington, Margaret was suffering from a painful broken baby-tooth, the root of which was thought to be impeding the growth of the tooth beneath it. Just as he left it was advised that the root be extracted, and after he arrived in Washington his wife, with characteristic (and perhaps defiant) negligence, did not write to him for almost three weeks. Frantic with worry about them all, he pleaded with her by mail: "Now listen a moment to my fears —You are sick—or Sarah Margarett, dear child of mine, has been in some peril and some pain, and very much anxiety with her tooth."[31] But earlier, writing to Margaret herself, he had betrayed no sympathy at all. On the contrary, he only mentions her pain in order to urge her to bear it with Roman—or puritan—fortitude. Now and then her father did make an effort to tell her that he was "pleased" or "gratified" at something she had done, but having said this much his vocabulary of praise would creak into silence, and the well-worn wheels of exhortation would begin to hum. To assume that he was never sympathetic, or never pleased with her, or that Margaret didn't know he was, would be wrong. But the manner in which his praise was conveyed to her, through the mediation of his wife, probably set off its own kind of psychological reverberations.

Margaret's depression at the loss of Ellen's companionship, accompanied by severe headaches, gradually hardened into a permanent change in her behavior. She withdrew further and further into her books and became outwardly cold and uncommunicative. By the age of nine she was behaving like a moody adolescent. "Sarah Margarett forgot to send her love," Timothy writes his wife in December 1819. "I suppose she was *bending* over some tale of woe or mystery, and so forgot it. I forgive the little girl and expect her recollection will come to her in time."[32] And writing on Christmas Day (which, being a good American, he ignores) he recalls that she used to greet him when he walked in the door, but no longer does.

> She is a good and affectionate child, but I have sometimes wished she would have continued to show pleasure on my return, instead of being absorbed in reading. Tho' I have no doubt of her affection, yet it is particularly engaging to have any one greet your entrance into the room with those expressive actions of pleasure, that spring unbidden from the heart.[33]

Probably reacting in kind to her coldness, her parents themselves became more distant, concentrating their affection on their two little boys, both endearingly dependent and of fortunately normal intelligence: "You have hardly mentioned [Sarah Margarett] for a long time; but I hope she pursues her studies,"[34] Timothy writes in January. And, a few months later, "Sarah Margarett seems quite a stranger, so little is said of her."[35] He still sends "2 kisses each," and sometimes real raisins, to his two little boys; but his daughter, along with his sister-in-law Abigail, is remembered simply with "love."

Her fondness for reading, far from remaining a source of pride to her parents, now has become a source of anxiety. Her father cautions her against "immoderate indulgence" in reading; intemperance in anything, he advises, leads to "vice and crime." [36] He begs his wife to exercise some control over Margaret's reading lest further eyestrain exacerbate her habit of partially closing her eyes. She has been studying Cicero and reciting 500 lines of Virgil to her uncle every week; she is also expected to progress in household affairs and sewing, penmanship, music, Greek, and French. But it is her manners and her appearance which most concern her father. "How does Sarah Margarett improve in *ease and grace?*— I hope rapidly." [37] He visits an acquaintance who, concerned about his daughters' posture, has bought them a big drum which they carry suspended from a strap while they beat it for a certain amount of time each day. The daughters have "profited" from this exercise, and Timothy offers to buy Margaret a drum too, softening the suggestion as best he can by making the exercise seem a kind of game which she can share with her little brothers. [38] Margaret apparently resisted this suggestion with some vigor; it is one of those rare subjects which her father, having mentioned once, does not mention again.

Mrs. Fuller spent the winter of 1818, the first of her husband's absence, in Canton with her parents and her sister Abigail. The family returned to Cambridgeport in the spring when the congressional session was over and remained there the following winter; Abigail stayed with them. Margaret attended Mr. Dickinson's school in Cambridge for at least a quarter term, in addition to studying Greek with her Uncle Elisha, music with Mr. Taylor, and penmanship with the writing-master, Mr. Gould. Her penmanship improved, but both her writing style and her speech became even more formal and stilted than they had been before. Asking her Grandmother Fuller to write to her, she says, "The great entertainment and instruction I have received from your letters to my father and mother has induced me also to request that I may be favored with a correspondence with my grandmother.''[39] This style, which reads like a parody of her father at his most self-righteous, found its counterpart in the manners she assumed in person, which can only be described as regal. This was partly a conscious role-playing, for one of her favorite daydreams was that she was a queen, a royal foundling left on the doorstep of that depressingly ugly house on Cherry Street. In a letter written to Ellen but never sent, she carried on a game that was understood between them and discussed the propriety of betrothing her little brother William Henry to Ellen's niece:

> I have heard of a French princess who was married at ten years and a prince betrothed at six months. . . . I am William Henrys elder sister and as he is so young I take the charge of inquiring into these things myself. I doubt not if Wm Henry were to see her he would be charmed with her. As to nobility of blood our family needs no ennobling [for] I as you well know am a queen. William Henry unites a prince and king in his single person and Eugene is prince of Savoy. I am besides being a queen duchess of Marlborough. But I remember I told you over all our titles in a former letter so I shall dwell upon this no longer.[40]

It was at about this age that she found courage to ask her family to agree, as Ellen already had long ago, not to address her by her first name, but to drop it in favor of her middle name. Her father, whose mother's name was Sarah, was predictably enraged, and asked to know "what whim" had made Sarah Margaret drop her first name in writing to him. "That," he remarked heavily to his wife, "cannot be done without an act of General Court—is she willing to petition for the alteration?"[41] He eventually came around so far as to address her, at least in writing, as "S. Margarett."

By 1820 all trace of the childish spontaneity Ellen remembered in Margaret had disappeared. She had become a moody, silent, priggish, indolent, forgetful, untidy ten-year-old who could not converse with her peers and preferred not to converse with most adults, whose shoulders were rounded from bending over books and who had acquired a facial mannerism which tipped the balance of her neutral looks toward plainness. In company she combined haughtiness with absolute candor (for she had been taught always to tell the truth regardless of the consequences), so that she was capable of blurting out some embarrassingly frank remark on a subject that everyone else present was wise enough to avoid.

Her parents decided that Margaret's education could no longer be left to Mr. Dickinson and her uncle; it needed the leavening influence of other girls her own age. They wished very much that Ellen Kilshaw would come to Cambridge, open a seminary and marry Timothy's brother Abraham. But since this was not to be, they looked around for a school in which to enroll Margaret. Timothy insisted that the school offer a good course in music, and since none in Cambridge met this requirement it was decided to send her across the river to Dr. Park's school in Boston, where her cousin Susan Williams was already enrolled. Margaret herself seems to have felt a mixture of happiness and fear at the prospect, but above all she was anxious to please her father:

> I am sorry my dear sir you write to me so seldom. Has your affection decreased? I fear it has; I have so often pained you but I hope you still love me. I should be most happy to be Dr. Park's scholar. I will endeavor to gratify all your wishes.[42]

But she was not altogether unconscious of the change she had undergone since Ellen's departure: " 'Men grow wiser every day,' but in reality I find difficulty in imagining myself an infant."[43]

In the fall of 1821, Mrs. Fuller, yielding at last to her husband's wish that she accompany him to Washington, sent the two little boys and baby Ellen to Canton. Margaret went to live with her Uncle Henry and his wife in Boston and attended Dr. Park's school. The first phase of her education was over, and from now on the emphasis would increasingly shift from the intellectual sphere to the social. From infancy her education had been more complicated than a boy's, but little boys were also taught to be polite and not to slurp their soup, and the time she had spent over sewing and cooking lessons was small; it was only in the "accomplishment" of music that any significant extra burden had been placed upon her. As she approached her teens the intellectual momentum of her early years was not only slowed but deliberately deflected. Before, she had been encouraged to be competitive, outspoken, candid, and abstractly idealistic; she would now be told to make herself less conspicuous, not to compete, not to speak her mind boldly, and to pay more attention to the practical details of everyday life. Virgil and Cicero were still very important, but they now claimed only part of her attention, while the rest would be directed to a new, often contradictory, set of priorities.

III

School Days

If we believed only what Margaret wrote to her mother soon after entering Dr. Park's school, we would have to conclude that the experience was everything she had hoped it would be:

> Tell Papa that I do not believe I shall be happy if I leave school soon. Ask him mamma whether I shall not stay more than a year. Oh I hope I shall for I love the Dr so much, and my companions seem so amiable that I long to stay. I talk about this too much perhaps but it is uppermost in my thoughts.[1]

There seems little doubt that she means it—at least at the moment. But reality as Margaret wanted it to be, and reality as it was, were quite different. In fact, her schoolmates reacted to this stiff, bookish child from across the river, who could not play games and spoke like a lesson out of Blair's *Rhetorick,* in just the way they might be expected to. To make matters worse, she set out immediately to take top honors away from a popular girl, Susan Channing, thereby adding to her sins in the eyes of her contemporaries, if not of her father. Susan's brother William Henry Channing, who became Margaret's close friend some ten years later, describes the attitude of her peers toward her at this age:

> At that period she was considered a prodigy of talent and accomplishment; but a sad feeling prevailed, that she had been overtasked by her father, who wished to train her like a boy, and that she was paying the penalty for undue application, in nearsightedness, awkward manners, extravagant tendencies of thought, and a pedantic style of talk, that made her a butt for the ridicule of frivolous companions.[2]

No inkling of this appears in the few letters that remain that were written by Margaret during this period. But it seems clear that she must have felt very much alone, especially during the first few months, while both her parents were away and she had to live in the relatively uncongenial atmosphere of her uncle's home. Her manners were modified not at all during the year she spent at the school, and she made no close friends. Her cousin, Susan Williams, who might have served as an intermediary between Margaret and the other girls, became ill early in the year and had to leave school.

Aside from the Pyrrhic victory of winning top honors away from Susan Channing, Margaret did achieve one small but satisfying triumph this year in gaining her parents' consent to attend dancing school. The New England attitude toward dancing, carried down from colonial days, was something of an anomaly, as was the attitude toward alcohol. The Fullers did their best to discourage their daughter from indulging in other amusements which seem equally harmless. Cautioning her daughter against reading novels and playing cards, Margaret's mother writes, "You well know my dear child your father's *views* and *wishes* on this subject, and your accountability to your Maker for the faithful improvement of your talents, and your duty to your parents."[3] But dancing was considered a "graceful and healthy exercise"[4] and an essential part of everyone's education. After some token demurrals, lest Margaret think she had won their consent too cheaply, they agreed to send her to dancing school twice a week. She enjoyed it tremendously;

she was, she said, "passionately fond of dancing." [5] Privately her parents hoped that it would succeed where many admonitions and the abortive idea of the drum had failed, in helping her to overcome her bookworm slouch.

The Fullers had hardly arrived and settled into their life at Washington when word arrived from the Crane household, where the younger children were staying, that they all had measles. Mrs. Fuller immediately returned to Canton and remained there until March, when she returned to Cambridge. It must have been a relief to Margaret to leave her uncle's home and move back to her own. At the same time, her responsibilities increased. Her mother gave birth to her fifth living child, third son, that summer and was unwell that fall and winter with an ulcerous sore or cyst in the breast which understandably caused her and her husband a good deal of anxiety; it was only after several months that it was definitely pronounced to be healing. Margaret undertook many of her mother's usual household duties and helped to watch and tutor her brothers and sister. She continued her lessons on the pianoforte with Mr. Taylor (Dr. Park's music course seems not to have proved adequate after all), went to her dancing classes, and continued to win top grades at school.

In December her father decided to take her out of Dr. Park's school, for reasons which are not clear. He authorized his brother to give her money so that she might buy presents for some of her classmates, and warned her to be discreet: "As you will soon part from some, to whom you may perhaps feel considerable attachment, and who may continue some time at the school, I advise you not to say that you never expect to return to the school; still less to suggest any dissatisfaction on *my part* with Dr. P.'s arrangements." [6] He goes on to discuss their plans for her to attend the school in Cambridge run by Mr. Frost, which her brother Eugene already attended. She must take care, her father warns, to be prudent and not to display her attainments too soon. To his wife he was even more explicit, after Margaret apparently had been rather rude to Mr. Frost in a friend's house: "She should not take too great liberty with Mr. F[rost], as he may make reprisals with the ferule, when she is his scholar." [7]

In the end she did not enroll in Mr. Frost's school after all, probably because her nearsightedness seemed worse than it had been and her father wished to give her a respite from intensive studying for a while. Instead she remained at home, studying only for short periods at a time, and increasingly she began to accompany her mother out into society. Soon after leaving Dr. Park's school she gave a party, to which she invited her former schoolmates from Boston as well as a great many people from Cambridge: in fact, she sent out some ninety invitations in all, most of them to adults. (This mixture in the ages of the guests was not unusual for the time, though the number does seem excessive for a twelve-year-old girl.) In spite of Timothy's repeated questions, it was some time before either Margaret or her mother would tell him how the party had gone, except for one laconic observation by Mrs. Fuller that it was "well over." Finally Margaret wrote that it had been a success, but she confined her description to a brief list of those particular friends who had come and those who had not. According to T. W. Higginson, Margaret's attempt to introduce her Boston classmates to the people she knew in Cambridge was "disastrous; she had little natural tact, and her endeavors to pay, as was proper, the chief attention to the stranger guests brought upon her the general indignation of her little world in Cambridge." [8]

In spite of this inauspicious beginning, Margaret went into company the following year with increasing frequency. She was received as an adult, although her awkwardness and affected manners excited much unfavorable comment. She was precocious physically as well as mentally, and at thirteen was already rather above average in height and had a well-developed figure. She had inherited her mother's broad forehead and strawberry blond hair, but unlike her mother and sister she was generally thought to be plain. Her blue eyes were expressive when her face was animated, but when she spoke to anyone she almost always kept them half-closed. She had unusually well-shaped hands and a graceful way of inclining her head which Oliver Wendell Holmes once said put one in mind of a swan or a snake, depending on her mood (or depending, perhaps, on whether one liked Margaret; Holmes did not). Her complexion, which would later take on the delicate col-oring of her mother's, was for a few years marred by what Margaret terms "a determination of blood to the head,"[9] which may have been a case of normal adolescent acne. While it lasted it worried her father almost as much as her eyes, and he regularly sent advice on how to treat it, favoring especially "rhubarb and calomel twice a week," together with "abstinence in diet."[10] Margaret herself was much upset by it, but as she later wrote, "I recovered, and made up my mind to be bright and ugly."[11]

In fact she managed to enjoy herself heartily at parties, though not in the approved manner. Most of the young men she met were her own age or a little older, and having undergone the customary intellectual force-feeding of young Cambridge males were either already enrolled at Harvard or were about to be. Some of them, like Holmes and William Henry Channing, were repelled by her queenly self-assurance and by a talent for mimicry and repartee which often turned to sarcasm, but those who would listen to her were openly appreciative of her talent for argument. She had never been the center of so much flattering male attention, but she was attracting it at the expense of violating the acknowledged rules of female behavior.

Women, to Timothy Fuller, were the charming ornaments of an otherwise austere and frequently dull society, and heaven knows ornaments of any kind were rare enough in his life. Some time before, when he had begun to realize how very far from ornamen-tal his elder daughter was, the emphasis in her education had begun to shift. She had been encouraged to go out to parties and receptions, in the hope that just by observing other people she would learn the proper way to behave. But now it was clear she was lamentably backward in this phase of her education. Word began to filter back to him that his daughter's manners were still decidedly *outré,* and presently Timothy began to hint to his wife that it would be best to keep Margaret more at home: "Abraham says S. Margarett is no *small* child, and Mr. Fay in his letter recv'd yesterday, says he hears much of her being in company, etc. Perhaps we may think it best for her to keep more at the domestic hearth for a few years yet."[12] And, "How did you send S. Margarett to Boston and bring her home? I hope the good girl danced moderately and returned early; that is the way to preserve health and obtain the approbation of the wise. She has too much sense I trust to wish to cheapen her value by too frequent appearance in company.''[13] In the spring he hopes the cotillions are over, but if they are not he is sure that ''S. Margarett must be too discreet to wish to attend.''[14] He asks often about domestic pursuits: ''What are Sarah M.'s *employments* and studies? The needle and the arrangement of her chamber are not forgotten I hope.''[15] He hopes that ''while S. Margt. remains at home . . . she has not neglected her musick, and that she has assisted in teaching Lydia [the new nursemaid] to read and spell.''[16] He approves buying her a new bonnet ''if her improvements in *neatness* and in all other respects merit it, as I hope they do.''[17] He has by no means forgotten her studies (''Does Sarah Margt. study Greek?—does she teach Eugene Latin?''),[18] but he is increasingly aware of how little use Greek is to a lady of marriageable age. He sympathizes, only half-jokingly, with poor Major P., who has *''four daughters,* of whom only one is handsome,'' and who has been so imprudent as to send them all into society together: he has ''produced his whole *stock in trade* at once,'' which must ''spoil the chance of them all.''[19]

By the spring of 1824 Margaret was dissatisfied with the slow progress she was making in her lessons, particularly in Greek, without the help of an instructor. Two months earlier she had asked to be allowed to attend young Ralph Waldo Emerson's school in Boston. Her father agreed that she should attend school, but he had a different purpose in mind. On the advice of the Fuller aunts and uncles, who had been watching Margaret's excursions into society with increasing alarm, he had decided to send her to school in the country, where the aunts and uncles thought she should stay for four years. He chose Miss Prescott's School for Young Ladies in Groton, forty miles northwest of Boston and not far from his childhood home of Princeton. When Margaret protested, he simply fell altogether silent on the subject. Finally, in April, she capitulated, although only (as she thought) for the summer:

I thank you most sincerely for the assurances of your continued affection, which have set my heart at ease. I shall willingly go to Groton for the summer, at your pleasure, though nothing else could in the least reconcile me to it. I shall entirely depend upon an immediate visit from you according to your promise. . . . How much I regret to leave this charming place, where I am beloved and go to one where I am an entire stranger and where I must behave entirely by rule. . . . I hope *you* are not quite so anxious to get rid of your *little* daughter.[20]

Her father retorted:

Your reluctance to go "among strangers" cannot too soon be overcome; and the way to overcome it, is not to remain *at home,* but to go among them and resolve to *deserve* and obtain the love and esteem of those, who have never before known you. With them you have a fair opportunity to *begin the world anew,* to avoid the mistakes and faults, which have deprived you of *some esteem,* among your present acquaintances.[21]

In another letter he reminded her how much her parents' pleasure depended on her acquiring

modesty, [and] unassuming deportment. These qualities are indispensable to endear any one, especially a young lady to her friends, and to obtain the "world's good word." . . . I would not willingly suppose you inferior to Harriet Fay or Elizabeth Ware in good sense, discretion, and *observation;* but I should be VERY much gratified to find your *deportment* exhibit as much true *tact,* as theirs. . . . Depend upon my undiminished affection, as long as you continue dutiful.[22]

In May, accompanied by her Uncle Elisha, Margaret set off for Groton in a stagecoach. She found the school set in a picture-book village, in the heart of the Massachusetts apple country. The orchards were in full bloom, and below the town a sleepy river wound its way off into the rolling, forested countryside. This was her father's boyhood home, and he was waiting impatiently for her letter describing the delights of nature. Margaret did her best to oblige. She wrote as cheerful a letter as she could, praising the beauty of the setting, but although this pleased her father it is not a recurring theme in subsequent letters. The first letter goes on in a resolutely positive vein. She congratulates her parents on the arrival of another son (Richard), and tells them the names of her roommates: "Miss Caroline Eames is my chum, and I have likewise in the room with me a Miss Wood [a very disagreeable girl]." The bracketed words, and some others, are carefully inked out.

They study, she says, "Hedge's Logick, Blair's Rhetorick and Colburn's Arithmetick. I feel myself rather degraded from Cicero's Oratory to one and two are how many. It *is* rather a change is it not?"[23] Her father, who after all was not totally indifferent to her continuing intellectual growth even though he now believed that the acquisition of "female *propriety*"[24] was far more important, agreed to consult with Miss Prescott and set up a study plan that was geared to Margaret's needs. With the sympathetic help of that lady she continued to progress at her own level. She slowly began, too, to change her behavior in order to conform to her father's wishes. This was, in its way, a task no less impossible than the recitations from Virgil she was expected to memorize perfectly at the age of six. Two of Timothy's first letters to her have much to say on the need to combine perfect candor with perfect kindness, and to entertain only "benevolent and charitable feelings" toward her schoolmates.[25] It was not enough to refrain from mentioning that Miss Wood was a disagreeable girl; she must believe from the moment she met Miss Wood that she was agreeable in every way. Whatever her success in controlling her emotions at the source may have been, her success in reforming her outward behavior, at least with adults, was such that at the end of several months she was able to write impeccably courteous notes to her uncles Henry and Abraham (both of whom she disliked), demonstrating her ability to fill a whole page or more with polite gossip and detailed inquiries after her correspondents' health.

Her schoolmates' reactions to her appear to have been mixed. These girls, older than those at Dr. Park's school, were better able to tolerate eccentricity, and among some of them her need to be at the center of any group, her fondness for exaggeration and talent for sarcasm, the sheer volume of her learning and the brilliant use she made of it in conversation, aroused some reluctant admiration. She chafed at the restrictions imposed on her, but she was far less unhappy than she had been at Dr. Park's school. She apparently took on the role of class rebel with some zest.

In *Summer on the Lakes* there is a curious account, written when she was an adult, of the experiences at boarding school of a girl named Mariana. It has often been taken to be autobiographical, but her brother cautions against reading it this way, and Perry Miller suggests that it "is more revealing as a psychological disclosure than as a piece of autobiography. It is one among several efforts of plain Margaret to act out the role of a beautiful and foredoomed heroine."[26] Nevertheless there are several traceable bits of autobiography in it, and no one really knows how far they go.

The episode concerns a beautiful, brilliant, haughty, eccentric, impulsive, affectionate, rebellious girl who is (not surprisingly) connected with the Spanish aristocracy.[27] Her schoolmates find her both captivating and irritating. They are much taken with her "love of wild dances and sudden song, her freaks of passion and wit," and she is very loving, though very demanding of love in return. But she is often moody and silent, given to sudden withdrawals which she expects the other girls to understand, as indeed she understands and respects their less widely fluctuating moods. She is an insomniac and a sleepwalker and has suffered from convulsions in childhood. She has a taste for costume and fancy dress and becomes the leading star in the school's dramatic productions. The school routine seems to her almost unbearably stifling, and more than once, when the funereal silence of study hour has lasted longer than she can stand, she has jumped up and whirled around in the middle of the room until she was dizzy, then chanted "weird verses" until she was sure everyone was thoroughly shaken awake.

Torn between admiration and envy, the other girls decide to humble her a little. Her theatrical tastes have given her a weakness for rouge. She keeps a pot of it on her dressing table and faithfully applies it twice a day. One evening, arriving late to dinner (which she detests, as she does everything done by rule), she finds that every other girl at the long table has painted two brilliantly red, perfectly round spots on her cheeks. They are all watching her, waiting for her to react, and the teachers and servants are clearly in on the prank. She responds with the composure "which, in a better cause, had made the Roman matron say of her death wound, 'It is not painful Poetus.' . . . She swallowed her dinner . . . [and] made remarks to those near her, as if she had no eyes." But afterward she goes straight to her room, where an alarmed mistress finds her later in convulsions.

After that "Mariana, born for love . . . hated all the world." Outwardly subdued, she sets about her revenge by spreading vicious rumors and causing general discord among the girls. Eventually she is found out and called to account by the headmistress. At first she denies it all, and then when she sees that she is caught, she throws herself down on the floor, dashing her head against the iron hearth. Put to bed, she refuses to eat, until a compassionate teacher tells her about a deeply painful and embarrassing incident in her own life, which she has had to live down. The revelation brings about the desired result, and Mariana goes home a "wonderfully instructed being."

The head injury is undeniably fiction (although the tendency for Mariana to become ill or injured in an emotional crisis is noteworthy, given Margaret's later history of ill health). The sleepwalking, the dramatic productions, the whirling dervish behavior, the convulsions, and the bizarre taste in clothes are all taken from Margaret's own experience. That *something* traumatic happened while she was at Miss Prescott's School is suggested by the fact that letters exchanged with her parents between March 1825 and September 1826 are missing, and by a letter published in the *Memoirs,* written in 1830 and almost certainly addressed to Susan Prescott:

> You need not fear to revive painful recollections. I often think of those sad experiences. True, they agitate me deeply. But it was best so. They have had a most powerful effect on my character. I tremble at whatever looks like dissimulation. The remembrance of that evening subdues every proud, passionate impulse. My beloved supporter in those sorrowful hours, your image shines as fair to my

mind's eye as it did in 1825, when I left you with my heart overflowing with gratitude for your singular and judicious tenderness.
Can I ever forget that to your treatment in that crisis of youth I owe
the true life,—the love of Truth and Honor?[28]

In the very proper letters she sent home during her two years in
Groton—at least in those that were not destroyed—there is no hint
of eccentricity, or of any upheaval in her emotional life, unless it
be found in her persistent love of hyperbole, which marred her
writing style then and for many years afterward. Her father vainly
tried to interest her in a decent set of Augustan caliphers: "Let
your approbation and *affection* be so measured and adjusted as to
have its *proper* place."[29]

Margaret returned from school in September of her sixteenth
year. Of that inner quality of docility which her father so much admired there was little evidence, but she had at least learned to
moderate her outward behavior, to be more gentle and to speak her
mind, when she had to, in a softer way. Her formal education was
over; she was now free to direct her own studies, which she did
with firm resolution. The boys her own age whom she began to
meet once again in Cambridge were graduating from Harvard, and
most of them had their sights fixed on the ministry or the bar. Her
own goal, a "life of letters," was far less clearly defined than
theirs, though no less deeply desired. She had no American models to follow. In the America of 1826 women did not undertake a
life of letters. Men did not either, for that matter, any more than
they do today, but commonly combined a literary career with one
of a more practical or lucrative kind, as Dr. Holmes and Professor
Longfellow did. But the ministry, law, medicine, politics, and university teaching were all closed to women. Margaret was reading
Mme de Staël at this age, but she must have realized that no
woman had ever come remotely near achieving that kind of intellectual recognition in America. To teach young children (an occupation for which she felt temperamentally unsuited); to marry
and subordinate her intellectual life to the demands of a husband
and an indeterminate number of babies; to imitate Ellen Kilshaw
and go out as a governess—these were the alternatives open to her.

If she thought about them at all realistically at sixteen, she kept her thoughts to herself.

Nor does Timothy Fuller seem to have wondered, when he first set about educating his small daughter, what possible advantage her mind and education could be in the round of parties and domestic duties with which Cambridge matrons occupied their time. One was obliged to develop one's intellectual powers, since they were a gift of God; to what end one developed them was a question best not asked by mortal minds. When Margaret began to approach the age of puberty, he belatedly realized that the education he had been at such pains to provide had equipped her not at all for the world in which she would have to live. So he set about superimposing another kind of education on the one she had already received. From requiring her to be the perfect scholar, he shifted to requiring her to be the perfect lady. In the end she was neither, and both the intellectual education of her early childhood and the social education of her adolescence, in many other ways contradictory to one another, had served to discourage any legitimate expression of her emotional life.

IV

Cambridge

The Cambridge to which Margaret returned in 1826 was one of those fragile communities, unique to the nineteenth century, which some of us occasionally believe we would give our souls, not to mention our plumbing, to live in. Families lived in comfortable frame houses, surrounded by gardens and orchards. They kept chickens, cows, and pigs, and even among the workers at the "Soap Works" in Cambridgeport, no one was really poor. The sounds of the business day in Harvard Square were no louder than the jingling and snorting of horses and the soft, regular thudding of their feet; the creak and rumble of wheels and the sound of voices in quiet conversation; the barking of dogs, the shouting of children on the common, the clucking of hens and the occasional bellow of a lovesick bull. Over them all the sea gulls mewed a soothing continuo, as they still do today if anyone could hear them. On quiet evenings people could listen to the surf breaking on the rocks twenty miles away.

Pre-urban existence exacted its price. People died of cholera, typhoid, tuberculosis, or of unnamed, mystifying ailments (James

Russell Lowell's two little daughters died of complications of teething). When they survived sickness, they did so in spite of the medical science of the day, which prescribed fasting, purgatives, leeches, and surgery without anesthetic or antiseptic. And there were lesser dangers, like the occasional flood tide which surged up the Charles and compelled the Fullers to take refuge in the upper floors of their Cambridgeport house. Working hours were long, and ordinary tasks like doing the laundry consumed a whole day. Still, if one escaped calamity and kept one's patience, life in Cambridge had its amenities, and it was far from primitive. Delicacies like ice cream, pineapple, oranges, coconut, and champagne were available to everyone in this seaport town. Women dressed themselves in everyday gowns of finely woven, embroidered cambric or lawn and ballgowns of silk brocade; they shod their feet in Italian kid slippers and warmed their shoulders with cashmere shawls from the far east. They did without polyester and dairyfreeze, but they had parasols, sleigh rides, handmade quilts, bedwarmers, and afternoon tea.

In this bucolic setting there was perhaps more intellectual ferment taking place per square mile than in any other place in the whole, yeasty New World. Having devoted itself for 200 years to training young men in the classics (with a cursory nod to English composition, mathematics, and geography), Harvard College was being prodded into the new century by a number of innovative, gifted men. Edward Everett was revitalizing the study of Greek, and Edward Tyrrel Channing was doing the same for English rhetoric. The new law school was expanding under the leadership of Judge Joseph Story. The botanical garden had recently been opened and natural science was becoming a respectable field of study under the eminent British naturalist Thomas Nuttall. George Bancroft, who had just been appointed tutor at Harvard, was about to open up the field of modern history. George Ticknor, who like Everett and Bancroft had studied at Göttingen, had come home determined to establish a modern language department at Harvard and had succeeded despite vigorous resistance from some members of the Board of Overseers. Among the students at Harvard were the members of the renowned class of 1829, the class of Oliver

Wendell Holmes, Wendell Phillips, Charles Sumner, and James Freeman Clarke—all men who would in their various ways help their country shake herself free of her old colonial identity.

On a larger scale, in areas seemingly unrelated to each other, change was quietly building under the surface of things. On July 4, 1826, John Adams, in Quincy, and Thomas Jefferson, in Monticello, died peacefully within hours of each other, while in Washington, Andrew Jackson mustered his political allies in preparation for the presidential election of 1828. In October 1826, young Ralph Waldo Emerson was approbated to preach. The publication of James Fenimore Cooper's third and best-known novel, *The Last of the Mohicans,* confirmed the fact that America could produce novelists whose works deserved a place on the shelf beside those of Sir Walter Scott. In Germany, Henry Wadsworth Longfellow was studying at Göttingen before coming to Harvard to teach under Bancroft; at Elmwood, on Tory Row, six-year-old James Russell Lowell was learning his Virgil.

The established verities were being questioned on all levels: educational, economic, social, and religious. On the economic level, New England had discovered to her pain, during the Embargo of 1807 and the subsequent war, that the cherished ideal of an agrarian economy supplemented by trade with the Old World must give way before America's need to become more self-sustaining and less dependent on the goodwill of England and Europe. With some reluctance, New Englanders had turned to manufacturing. Textile and shoe mills had been established in the coastal towns and along the interior river valleys. Built in the midst of new, planned communities which were equipped with attractive living quarters, libraries, and lyceums, they were designed to prevent the occurrence in America of the urban squalor which industrialization had brought to England. By the 1820s the mills were flourishing, and New England was riding the crest of her second wave of prosperity. Parallel to the shift to manufacturing was an intensified interest in transporting goods to the rapidly expanding interior. An ambitious system of canals had already been completed, but now it was railroads that caught the attention of the more far-seeing men. In Boston the editor of the *Daily Advertiser,* Nathan Hale, was arguing for the construction of a railroad from Boston to Worcester. It would eventually be built, though not in time to prevent the spectacular growth of New York at the expense of Boston. In the meantime, a horse-drawn railroad, the first in the country, was completed in 1826 near the Quincy home of the Adams family.

In the area of social change, a small but increasing number of New Englanders believed that the institution of slavery could no longer be tolerated. Young William Lloyd Garrison, now barely in his twenties, was not yet making his voice heard; but sentiment was rising, and in Massachusetts it met with bitter opposition from those whose continued prosperity depended upon the unimpeded flow of raw materials from the South.

Few phenomena were so disturbing to the status quo in Massachusetts, or so illustrative of the new, questioning spirit of post-Jeffersonian democracy, as the Unitarian controversy. The movement was centered in Cambridge and Boston, and its most prominent spokesman was the gentle, ascetic William Ellery Channing. Colonial America had been a theocracy, its ruling Calvinist creed best expressed by men like Cotton and Increase Mather and Jonathan Edwards: Every man was irrevocably stained by original sin and doomed to everlasting fire, unless he was saved by the mysterious gift of grace—a gift that was ultimately beyond anyone's power to earn, although one was obliged to try anyway. During the eighteenth century, mainly under the influence of John Locke, David Hartley, and other English rationalists, a schism began to grow quietly within the American Congregational church. The doctrine of man's depravity became more and more difficult to reconcile with the ideals of democracy, which depended upon each person's assuming active responsibility for his own welfare and that of his country. In order to assume responsibility, one has to believe that one is free to choose among alternatives, and that one's own life and the nation's depends on these choices. But what choices can one make in a universe in which everything is predetermined? Moreover, Calvinism taught that life on this earth was beset with evil and suffering, while the blessings of capitalism in the 1820s made such a belief seem downright ungrateful. Congregations, especially in Massachusetts, had become increasingly restive under the conflict between their political-economic systems and the teachings of the church, and more and more ministers found it convenient to omit all mention of original sin from their sermons. But the schism widened as rationalism was brought to bear on one doctrine after another, including the Trinity itself.

In Timothy Fuller's youth the term ''Unitarian'' was not used except pejoratively, and to openly avow oneself a Unitarian as he did was to invite censure even from those whose own Calvinism had long since been tacitly abandoned. But by 1820 the dispute had broken out into the open and the entire left wing of the established church, under Channing's leadership, was adopting the name ''Unitarian.'' The movement was limited almost entirely to Massachusetts, but within the state hundreds of churches were bitterly divided between those members who wanted to remain within the fold and those who wanted to leave. Heated battles were fought in the courts over who kept the church buildings and the communion silver. In 1826 Lyman Beecher, one of the most persuasive orators in the conservative camp, was assigned to Boston's Hanover Street Church to try to staunch the flow of liberals from the church, but by then there was little even he could do. In Cambridge that year, Abiel Holmes still strode across the square twice on Sundays to warn a too-complacent congregation that hell yawned below for every sinner, whether or not he kept a carriage. But by 1829 he would be dismissed from his pulpit by a rebellious majority of his parishioners, and sixty more would leave with him to establish a new church.

It was Channing who first breathed some life into the skeleton of ''pale negations'' [1] that was Unitarian belief. American Unitarians were anxious to dissociate themselves from their English counterparts: that was why they had been so reluctant to adopt the name. English Unitarianism was associated in their minds with necessitarian philosophy, which while it relieved every human being from the burden of damnation, left him literally blank at birth, a *tabula rasa,* to be formed for good or ill by stimuli from his environment. There was no room in such a philosophy for anything innate, mysterious, and unique to the individual soul—if indeed there was a soul. God was seen as the benevolent but distant source of all good.

In his sermons Channing brought God back into the affairs of men as an active force, a constant paternal presence—which was hardly a revolutionary idea except in the context of the times. "We maintain," he wrote in 1819, "that God's attributes are intelligible, and that we can conceive as truly of his goodness and justice as of these qualities in men. In fact, these qualities are essentially the same in God and man, though differing in degree, in purity, and in extent of operation." [2] It is, he taught, the responsibility of every individual to discover and develop that part of his own spirit which is closest to the divine; then the precept of Jesus, "Be thou perfect," can indeed be realized on this earth.

Such a doctrine can give rise to an exaggerated optimism, as indeed it did in Channing's own writings and later in those of Emerson, but it can also give rise to reform movements and good works of all kinds. Prison reform, reform in education and the care of the insane, the temperance movement, the women's rights movements, and the abolitionist movement would all receive a healthy impetus from the Unitarian belief in the perfectibility of man (although, at least in the latter case, the tardiness of Massachusetts Unitarians in joining their countrymen argues that in practice the perfectibility of one's own pocketbook was all too likely to take precedence over any other kind).

The rise of Unitarianism cannot be separated from the intellectual climate of Massachusetts in the 1820s and 1830s; it was, in fact, at the very center of it. Channing and his younger disciples in the Unitarian church—among them Theodore Parker, George Ripley, and Ralph Waldo Emerson—would be among the earliest moving spirits of the American Romantic movement, assuming a role similar to that of Coleridge twenty years before in England. Moreover, Emerson and Ripley and many other young ministers just assuming the pulpit in the 1820s would quickly find—again like Coleridge—that Unitarianism itself was hardening into orthodoxy, and that even its wide boundaries were too confining.

So the Cambridge to which Margaret returned combined the pastoral beauty of a country village with an intellectual atmosphere that was alive with inquiry and change. Few things were taken for granted. The questions of the day—economic, political, social, and religious—were argued in pamphlets and articles, in public forums and in private meeting rooms. And since Cambridge was so small and closely knit, and one's opponent in debate was likely to be a cousin or an in-law, brisk and spirited exchanges took place over tea and gingerbread. To Margaret, returning from her Groton cloister, the Cambridge air must have seemed unbelievably fresh.

The year she returned, the family left the ugly house in Cambridgeport and moved to the beautiful Dana mansion. Built in 1785 by Judge Francis Dana, it was set on a hill overlooking the college, the river, and the surrounding countryside, in the midst of acres of landscaped grounds. Here Timothy Fuller gave a ball for President Adams in 1826*—one is tempted to wonder whether he moved to the house in order to have a proper setting for his party—and here Margaret, appropriately enough, began a new and rich phase of her life. Not only did she think and learn more in the next few years than she had ever been able to before, but she began to discover, possibly to her own surprise and certainly to her family's, that she had an extraordinary talent for friendship. To have made friends at all after such a solitary childhood would have been an entirely new experience; but the depth and endurance of the friendships she now formed, as well as their sheer numbers, testifies not only to a deeply affectionate nature but to a rare breadth of human understanding. Most people meeting her for the first time were still repelled by her audacious manners, but an increasing number of young people, initially drawn to her by her wit, remained to form a deep emotional bond which lasted, in many instances, as long as she or they lived. In the midst of a group she seemed, as one friend expressed it, to be on "intellectual stilts." But when they met her alone, few people could resist confiding in her. "She could not make a journey," Emerson wrote, "or go to an evening party, without meeting a new person, who wished presently to impart his history to her."[3] Like her semifictional Mariana she would tolerate no reserve; but neither did she set up any herself. She both gave and expected (with those who could tolerate it) total loyalty.

* Or at least a dinner; Adams left before the dancing began.

James Freeman Clarke, perhaps her closest friend during this period, describes the determination with which she disarmed prospective friends:

> Such a prejudice against her had been created by her faults of manner, that the persons she might most wish to know often retired from her and avoided her. But she was "sagacious of her quarry," and never suffered herself to be repelled by this. She saw when any one belonged to her, and never rested till she came into possession of her property. I recollect a lady who thus fled from her for several years, yet, at last, became most nearly attached to her.[4]

The variety of her friendships speaks for the fact that intellect was not what she valued most. She looked for integrity, sensitivity, and idealism in her friends. Her closest woman friend during these years was Elizabeth Randall, about whom we know nothing except that she was the daughter of the family physician. Another early friend was Lydia Maria Francis, later Lydia Maria Child, whose dry, no-nonsense, Yankee reserve complemented Margaret's exuberance. Among the other young people who joined the circle forming around her was Frederick Henry Hedge, whom she had known slightly two years before. Somewhat older than Margaret, Hedge had entered Harvard at the age of thirteen, and following graduation had gone abroad to study at Göttingen. Having returned full of enthusiasm for all things German, he was now about to enter the Unitarian ministry. Margaret's cousin George Davis, a law student, was another frequent visitor. James Freeman Clarke, another cousin, was a close friend as was, somewhat later, his sister Sarah. Dr. Channing's nephew William Henry Channing was drawn into Margaret's orbit; so was Elizabeth Peabody. Both Clarke and Channing were members of the Harvard class of '29, and during this period they both enrolled in the Divinity School. Elizabeth Peabody, teaching in Roxbury and Brookline, was already forming her advanced views on elementary education.

It was within this group that Margaret's skill at conversation, which had begun to be evident two years before, reached maturity. It was a double-sided talent, as any true conversationalist's must be, showing the same finely tuned sensitivity to the nuances of personality that strengthened her talent for friendship. On the one hand, she was able to light directly upon the central idea in a discussion and enlarge upon it at length, with great clarity and precision. But this in itself would have made her only a good monologuist, as she was often called by her critics, with more malice than justice. Her reputation as a conversationalist rested equally on her brilliance as a speaker and her gift for sensing what others were thinking and tossing the ball to each of them at just the right moment, so that the shyest among them had no choice but to catch it.

It was primarily as a conversationalist, rather than as a writer, that Margaret Fuller was known during her own lifetime, and for this reason much of what was best and most admirable about her remains out of reach of any modern biographer. We have only a few recorded fragments of her conversations, and those are incomplete not simply in content but in all those other intangible qualities—voice, facial expression, gesture—that make the great conversationalists of the nineteenth century worthy of the epitaph of Keats.* We must fall back on contemporary descriptions, most of them written by friends. Despite their eulogistic tone, they are the best we have. Here is one by Hedge:

> Her conversation, as it was then, I have seldom heard equalled. It was not so much attractive as commanding. Though remarkably fluent and select, it was neither fluency, nor choice diction, nor wit, nor sentiment, that gave it its peculiar power, but accuracy of statement, keen discrimination, and a certain weight of judgment, which contrasted strongly and charmingly with the youth and sex of the speaker. I do not remember that the vulgar charge of talking "like a book" was ever fastened upon her, although, by her precision, she might seem to have incurred it. The fact was, her speech, though finished and true as the most deliberate rhetoric of the pen, had always an air of spontaneity which made it seem the grace of the moment,—the result of some organic provision which made finished sentences as natural to her as blundering and hesitation are to most of us.[5]

* "Here lies one whose name was writ in water."

Hedge's chivalrous scruples cause him to slide over those aspects of her conversation which drove as many people out of Margaret Fuller's company as were attracted to it. While her ordinary manners had become more polished during the two years she spent under the eye of Miss Prescott, they were forgotten—or transcended—when her mind was fully engaged. In these early years she was capable of merciless satire, and even without satire her ability to completely demolish an opponent with one sure thrust must have been disconcerting. Tolerant as Cambridge people thought themselves, the old prejudice against bluestockings was very much alive. One can detect it in Hedge's comment, in his surprise at the weight and force of the intellect which contrasts so "charmingly" with Margaret's youth and sex. Jane Austen had the sense to hide her writing under the blotting paper, and Emily Dickinson and the Brontës hid their whole selves. But Margaret Fuller, partly because of the sheer ebullience of her mind, partly because her own stern code of truth would never allow her to hide her light under a bushel, seemed to all except a few close friends to be the archetypal bluestocking, the aggressively intelligent woman who wants to out-Herod Herod. People of both sexes found this impossible to forgive. She was keenly aware of the censure directed against her and withstood it with firmness and ironic good humor, though not without pain. A letter to a woman friend, written in 1830, shows her resilience and, incidentally, shows that side of her nature which had nothing at all to do with literature, the arts, or the Mysteries of the Universe:

> Many things have happened since I echoed your farewell laugh. Elizabeth and I have been fully occupied. She has cried a good deal, fainted a good deal, and played the harp most of all. I have neither fertilized the earth with my tears, edified its inhabitants by my delicacy of constitution, nor wakened its echoes to my harmony,—yet some things have I achieved in my own soft, feminine style. I hate glare, thou knowest, and have hitherto successfully screened my virtues therefrom. I have made several garments fitted for the wear of American youth; I have written six letters, and received a correspondent number; I have read one book,—a piece of poetry entitled "Two Agonies," by M. A. Browne, (pretty caption, is it not?) and

J. J. Knapp's trial; I have given advice twenty times,—I have taken
it once; I have gained two friends, and recovered two; I have felt admiration four times,—honor once, and disgust twice; I have been a
journey [*sic*], and shewed my penetration in discovering the beauties
of Nature through a thick and never-lifted shroud of rain; I have
turned two new leaves in the book of human nature; I have got a
new pink bag, (beautiful!). I have imposed on the world time and
again, by describing your Lynn life as the perfection of human
felicity, and adorning my visit there with all sorts of impossible adventure,—thus at once exhibiting my own rich invention and the
credulous ignorance of my auditors (light and dark, you know, dear,
give life to a picture). I have had tears for others' woes, and patience
for my own,—in short, to climax this journal of many-colored deeds
and chances, so well have I played my part, that in the self-same
night I was styled by two several persons "a sprightly young lady",
and "a Syren!!" Oh rapturous sound! I have reached the goal of my
ambition; Earth has nothing fairer or brighter to offer. *"In-
telligency"* was nothing to it. A "supercilious," "satirical," "affected," "pedantic" "Syren" !!!! Can the olla-podrida of human
nature present a compound of more varied ingredients, or higher
gusto?[6]

Even the admiration of her friends was tinged with attitudes
which, unless they had grown up in a vacuum, they could not entirely escape. The complexity of Hedge's feelings toward
Margaret, in which there is a hint of residual prejudice despite his
efforts to overcome it, is echoed in a passage from the *Memoirs* by
William Henry Channing. He remembers first meeting her when
she was a schoolmate of his sisters' at Dr. Park's school. In those
days, Channing admits, he was repelled by her "saucy sprightli-
ness."

About 1830, however, we often met in the social circles of Cambridge, and I began to observe her more nearly. At first, her viva-
city, decisive tone, downrightness, and contempt of conventional
standards, continued to repel. She appeared too *intense* in expression, action, emphasis, to be pleasing, and wanting in that *retenue*
which we associate with delicate dignity. Occasionally, also, words
flashed from her of such scathing satire, that prudence counselled the

keeping at safe distance from a body so surcharged with electricity. Then, again, there was an imperial—shall it be said imperious?—air, exacting deference to her judgments and loyalty to her behests, that prompted pride to retaliatory measures. She paid slight heed, moreover, to the trim palings of etiquette, but swept through the garden-beds and into the doorway of one's confidence so cavalierly, that a reserved person felt inclined to lock himself up in his sanctum.[7]

The liberal-minded Channing, a close friend and later one of Margaret's biographers, surely would have resented any suggestion that he did not in the course of time overcome his initial reservations and accept Margaret on terms equal with himself. And of course her undeniable eccentricity would have put people off in any time and place. But Channing's choice of words does suggest the double barrier Margaret, or any woman, would have to cross to gain acceptance and recognition. One wonders inevitably how successful even so good a friend as Channing was in overcoming his own early bias. Would he have found a similarly gifted and similarly deviant member of his own sex wanting in the *"retenue* which we associate with delicate dignity,'' and would another man so quickly have "prompted pride to retaliatory measures"? Channing says it was only gradually that he was won over by "the sagacity of her sallies, the profound thoughts carelessly dropped by her on transient topics, the breadth and richness of culture manifested in her allusions or quotations, her easy comprehension of new views, her just discrimination, and, above all, her *truthfulness.*'' In a sentence striking for its sexual imagery, he describes how he finally became her friend one evening during a tête-à-tête, when she "laid bare her secret hope of what Woman might be and do, as an author in our Republic."[8] His sympathy with her ambition is real and undeniable, but he expresses it in a way that makes Margaret's confession seem a kind of sexual submission. At the same time, normal sexual relationships (meaning, of course, those usual to the times) were denied her by the men around her.

There is no better example of the sexual-asexual ambiguity of her relationships with men at this time than her friendship with James Freeman Clarke. Their personalities complemented one another. Having spent much of his boyhood on the Newton farm of his grandfather, Dr. James Freeman,* Clarke had become bookish and introspective, as Margaret had. But his grandfather had provided him with an education that was the exact opposite of Margaret's, encouraging him to inquire into all sides of a question and to acknowledge complexities, whereas Margaret had been encouraged to arrive quickly at a firm, unqualified opinion. It is difficult to say whether this effect of Clarke's education contributed much to his relatively severe difficulties with the crises of young adulthood, but at any rate he often found himself all but paralysed, Hamlet-like, by his own powers of ratiocination. He found in Margaret's decisiveness, energy, and capacity for self-discipline a source of strength, and in return helped her learn to tolerate ambiguities and provided, as time went on, some valuable critiques of her murky, highly colored writing style.

With Clarke, as with all her friends, Margaret would permit no reserve, and to this stipulation the ordinarily reserved Clarke agreed enthusiastically:

> You cannot think how full of gratitude my heart was when I read your last note. I said to myself that I had found something more valuable than anything else on earth—something which I hardly imagined to exist before—a heart joined to an intellect in such just proportion that its fervour should not displease the taste by being ill-directed, nor its wisdom freeze by being too abstract, and she who possessed this nature, desirous of joining it to mine in friendship. My first feeling, I have said, was great joy and gratitude; I said, there has come an aera, a wonderful epoch in my life; I shall now begin to live out of my own soul, and I went, everywhere ruminating on my approaching happiness.[9]

The language is close to that of a lover, even for those days of passionate friendships, and one wonders what sort of emotions it may have stirred in the recipient. But their friendship always remained on a platonic level. Margaret became Clarke's confidant in affairs of the heart, a role she assumed often, with friends of both sexes.

* Pastor of Kings Chapel, the first church in Massachusetts to call itself Unitarian.

He spoke and wrote to her in anguished detail of his unrequited love for two of her friends, one of whom was Elizabeth Randall, and he repeatedly described his ideal sexual partner as everything Margaret could never be: a gentle, silent, utterly helpless creature who is intellectually his inferior, who will listen to him talk without ever contradicting him, a "loved and loving one, twining her arms about me and gazing in my face with eyes full of passion and dependence." [10]

In this context an otherwise inexcusable act of Margaret's becomes at least more understandable: ostensibly because she had decided that the couple was ill-matched, she intercepted an important letter from James to Elizabeth, causing a permanent rupture between them. It seems possible that she may have been unconsciously retaliating against Clarke; for even if she was not attracted to him as a lover, the lesson he and her other male friends were teaching her was a painful one. An intellectual woman ran a strong risk of being thought of as absolutely sexless, even while she was welcomed as a friend and equal. The price of being one of the boys was to be one of the boys.

Physically Margaret Fuller has been described as plain, but as with the contemporary descriptions of her personality, it is difficult to know how much of what is said is colored by envy or malice. Several portraits exist from different periods, but they vary so widely as to be hardly recognizable as the same person. It is certain, though, that at the age of sixteen she was no beauty. She was slightly above average in height, rather stout, and still red in the face. She wore her reddish-blond hair tightly curled, possibly in emulation of her friend Harriet Fay, a Cambridge beauty whose curls were nature's own. Her habit of partially closing her eyes had become permanent. She was still fond of brightly colored, conspicuous clothes, and she took advantage of the fashion for tight lacing to try to disguise her stoutness, succeeding only in redistributing it and making herself very uncomfortable.

But by the time she reached the age of twenty her appearance had changed much for the better, thanks to her friendship with Eliza Farrar, the English-born wife of a Harvard professor. Mrs. Farrar undertook that part of Margaret's education in which her mother and Miss Prescott had obviously failed. She was well able to cope with the task: in 1836 she would publish a book titled *The Young Lady's Friend,* intended to guide young women through the years between school and marriage. She supervised Margaret's hairdresser and seamstress, took her visiting and traveling, and succeeded so well in reforming the appearance of her protégée that in a few years Margaret had earned a reputation for irreproachable taste in clothes. The tight curls were abandoned in favor of a smooth, simple style with a part in the middle, the excess pounds were shed, and the awkward, sudden movements were transformed into the graceful carriage remarked on by everyone who knew her in later years.

Mrs. Farrar did not accomplish this metamorphosis without help. Anna Barker, a young cousin from New Orleans who was living with the Farrars, became a close friend and, without being pointed out as the model of everything a young woman should be, inevitably was just that. Higginson writes of Anna Barker that her "gifts and graces have . . . won affectionate admiration in two continents."[11] He apparently exaggerates only slightly, for Anna was by all accounts an extraordinarily beautiful woman. Margaret's feeling for her was somewhat similar in kind and intensity to her early love for Ellen Kilshaw. It was probably of Anna that Margaret wrote,

> I loved _____ for a time with as much passion as I was then strong enough to feel. Her face was always gleaming before me, her voice was echoing in my ear, all poetic thoughts clustered round the dear image. This love was for me a key which unlocked many a treasure which I still possess; it was the carbuncle (emblematic gem!) which cast light into many of the darkest corners of human nature. She loved me, too, though not so much, because her nature was "less high, less grave, less large, less deep"; but she loved more tenderly, less passionately. She loved me, for I well remember her suffering when she first could feel my faults, and knew one part of the exquisite veil rent away.[12]

"It was," Higginson remarks, "Madame de Staël and Madame Récamier in a schoolroom."[13] Certainly he is not deliberately alluding to a homosexual element in either relationship, but the existence of such an element in both Mme de Staël's feelings for her friend and in Margaret's seems probable. It may account for the intensity of Margaret's love for Anna Barker and some of her other woman friends, although it always remained well below the conscious level.

Eliza Farrar was so successful in revising Margaret's standards of appearance that it is only natural to ask if she influenced other areas of her life. Presumably they discussed Margaret's future and the role of women in general, since this was a subject that was much in Margaret's thoughts and on which Mrs. Farrar had decided views. An intelligent woman, she directed the full force of her intellect into making the most of the role assigned to her sex. If woman was confined to a narrow space, she must make that space supremely habitable, supremely pleasant and civilized, rather than spend her energies chipping away at the walls.

Eliza Farrar's book was being formed in her mind during the height of her friendship with Margaret Fuller. It has been called a book on etiquette, but this is something of an understatement. The author anticipates most of the situations a young woman is likely to encounter, from nursing the sick to refusing a proposal, and tells her how to steer through them without causing the least ripple in her surroundings. In a manner reminiscent of Castiglione, she advises women to guide every aspect of their behavior by a consideration for other people, although she concedes that some personal needs (exercise, for example) may be motivated by a healthy self-love. There is much in the book that is sensible (she deplores the fashions of tight lacing and hoops); a few things that are faddish and amusing (Mrs. Farrar, like many of her contemporaries, is a true believer in the miraculous virtue of cold baths); and occasionally something that is actually harmful (she insists that people should reduce their liquid intake to almost nothing, since "man is one of those animals which require very little drink").[14] Domestic responsibilities have unquestioned priority in the life of any woman, married or single:

> If a woman does not know how the various work of a house should be done, she might as well know nothing, for that is her express vocation; and it matters not how much learning, or how many ac-

complishments, she may have, if she is wanting in that which is to fit her for her peculiar calling.[15]

Paradoxically, domestic tasks must be done quickly and efficiently; one must spend as little time as possible on them. The central theme of the book is, in fact, that a young woman must organize her days according to a well-planned schedule and not fritter away her time on housekeeping, personal adornment, or frivolous socializing. About what to do with the time thus saved the author is vague: it should be devoted to reading, to drawing, to serious discussion, to music, to "self-culture." But except for some discreet private philanthropy, perhaps, a woman may not use her free time in any way which could expose her to comment. And if she must write, she had best do it as Mrs. Farrar does, anonymously.

In all this, of course, Eliza Farrar is the spokeswoman for the society in which she and Margaret both lived. In her advocacy of "self-culture," a concept popular in a time when people were increasingly turning their attention from the next world to this, she strengthened Margaret's resolution to study and absorb all her mind could hold. But in going beyond this, and in setting her sights firmly on a "life of letters," Margaret swam against the influence of society and of this admired older friend.

Soon after she arrived home in 1826 she wrote Miss Prescott describing a typical day:

> You keep me to my promise of giving you some sketch of my pursuits. I rise a little before five, walk an hour, and then practise on the piano, till seven, when we breakfast. Next I read French,—Sismondi's Literature of the South of Europe,—till eight, then two or three lectures in Brown's Philosophy. About half-past nine I go to Mr. Perkins's school* and study Greek till twelve, when, school being dismissed, I recite, go home, and practise again till dinner, at two. Sometimes, if the conversation is very agreeable, I lounge for

---

* The Cambridgeport Private Grammar School, where Margaret studied Greek during her first year home. Oliver Wendell Holmes and Richard Henry Dana were her classmates here according to most authorities, although this is rather a puzzling statement since Holmes graduated from Harvard in 1829.

half an hour over the dessert, though rarely so lavish of time. Then, when I can, I read two hours in Italian, but I am often interrupted. At six, I walk, or take a drive. Before going to bed, I play or sing, for half an hour or so, to make all sleepy, and, about eleven, retire to write a little while in my journal, exercises on what I have read, or a series of characterictics which I am filling up acording to advice. Thus, you see, I am learning Greek, and making acquaintance with metaphysics, and French and Italian literature.[16]

It should not be supposed that Margaret was able to maintain such an orderly regimen over an extended period, although apparently she did so for a while after her return. Gradually the obligations of domestic duties and the distractions of a full social life began to compete for her time. Nevertheless she continued to read at an astonishing rate, although not always according to any particular plan. Fortunately several of her friends' libraries were at her disposal, offering a wide variety of books. At one point in the spring of her sixteenth year, in addition to de Staël, she was reading Epictetus, Milton, Racine, and a smattering of Castilian ballads. Early in 1828 she reports, "I am reading Sir William Temple's works, with great pleasure. . . . I have also read . . . Russell's Tour in Germany. . . . I have passed a luxurious afternoon, having been in bed from dinner till tea, reading Rammohun Roy's book, and framing dialogues aloud on every argument beneath the sun. . . . Did you ever read the letters and reflections of Prince de Ligne, the most agreeable man of his day? I have just had it."[17] One relatively coherent course of study she set herself was a careful reading of the major Italian poets, chiefly Dante, but also Petrarch, Tasso, Berni, Ariosto, Alfieri, and Manzoni.

During this period of voracious reading and active thinking, her mother's health, never robust, became more fragile with every pregnancy. There were six younger children in the family now; Eugene, the eldest, was eleven in 1826. The baby, James Lloyd, was already beginning to show symptoms of his later emotional disturbance and was subject to violent tantrums. Like most middle-class women, Mrs. Fuller employed one or two woman servants, but they were young girls from the country who, after the custom of domestic "help" in democratic America, left as soon as they could find better-paying jobs in the textile mills. Then the responsibility for finding and training a new girl, if her mother was not well, would naturally fall on the shoulders of an adult, unmarried daughter. She would also be expected to help with the general housework until a new servant was found, and to help with the family sewing (children's clothes were made at home), and she was often called upon to be a hostess and companion for her father. She found time for it all without visibly faltering, though the headaches which had bothered her since childhood were becoming more severe. Speaking for other girls her age, Higginson remarks, "It does not seem to have been their impression that she neglected her home duties for the sake of knowledge; such was her conceded ability that she was supposed equal to doing everything at once. It was currently reported that she could rock a cradle, read a book, eat an apple, and knit a stocking, all at the same time." [18] All credit to Margaret, but it is no wonder that other girls found her example disheartening.

Gradually, under the influence of her growing circle of friends, Margaret's reading became less haphazard. According to James Freeman Clarke, the members of Margaret's circle read Lamb, Browne, Wordsworth, Coleridge, and Carlyle together, and through the latter two writers they became aware of the large and important body of philosophical and artistic literature being produced in Germany. They had not been totally ignorant of it before: Dr. Follen had been teaching German to small but enthusiastic groups of students since 1825, and George Ticknor, George Bancroft, Edward Everett, Frederick Henry Hedge, and President Adams himself had all studied in Germany. But in the early 1830s it was all but impossible to buy a German book in an American bookstore. It was not until Coleridge's *Friend, Biographia Literaria,* and *Aids to Reflection* had been published in America in 1829, and Carlyle's essays on Schiller, Goethe, and Richter had appeared in the English periodicals, that Margaret Fuller and James Freeman Clarke began to listen seriously to Hedge's encomiums on German literature and his repeated offers to put his library at their disposal. But once having begun to listen, they decided that the rewards of reading the new literature would be sufficient to justify learning the language. Beginning in 1830, they pursued this commitment with single-minded determination, meeting every evening to read Goethe or Schiller together. When they could not meet they wrote out translations and exchanged them for criticism.

Although their systems of thought and modes of expression varied, the German writers offered these children of puritanism an affirmative warmth and a sense of spiritual discovery which the Unitarian movement was unable to give them. It was not enough to have abolished the gloom and terrors of Calvinism and the cold mechanics of rationalism; it was not enough to believe (in Arthur W. Brown's words) that "a man's salvation depend[s] on his obedience to God's will, an obedience consisting of both faith and righteousness, and within the power of everyone." [19] This was a reasonable and kindly faith, but it gave one too little to reach for. It was pedestrian. It lacked passion, mystery, and poetry.

In 1781 the great German philosopher Immanuel Kant, in his *Critique of Pure Reason,* had shaken the foundations of rationalistic philosophy by maintaining that the mind is not a blank slate, passively accumulating sense impressions from the external world. Mind, said Kant, is a free, actively creative force born into each human being. It forms its own consciousness by selecting and arranging the sense impressions available to it. It cannot be explained by science or theology; like God, it simply exists. Kant called the mysterious selective power of the mind "transcendental" knowledge because it transcends all rational attempts to analyze it.

This liberating, terrifying thesis gave rise to a new generation of philosophers in Germany, among them Fichte, Schelling, and Hegel. It also nourished a new generation of poets known as the German Romantics, including Novalis, Richter, Schiller, and Goethe. Differing in the ways they interpreted the new faith, these writers were united in a sense of the awesome responsibility of the individual for his own moral development; a joyful acceptance of the ultimate mysteriousness of an orderly universe; and a search for new ways to explain God's relationship to creation. They shared a belief that God was intimately related to man and nature, and a sense that the unfolding of human consciousness, or soul, must be to some degree divinely assisted from within. Turning from the traditional search for God through scriptural revelation, they looked to nature and humanity instead and, despite the imperfections of both, were not disappointed.

Around the turn of the century the new Romanticism reached England. There its high priests were Wordsworth and Coleridge, both of whom wrote poetry vibrant with faith in a benevolent, immanent God. Wordsworth had gained his faith primarily on his own, with little knowledge of his spiritual kinship with the Germans. It was Coleridge who, by adopting German philosophy into his own prose writings (with and without acknowledgments), made it accessible to readers in England and America. In his theory of the poetic imagination and his passionate belief in an innate and indestructible core of consciousness in everyone, Coleridge firmly laid to rest the necessitarianism which he himself had briefly embraced as a young man.

After another twenty-year lapse the new literature reached America. The young people of Cambridge found in the English and German poets the emotional richness which was conspicuously lacking in their own Unitarian faith. At the same time, it strengthened their newfound belief in the dignity and significance of all forms of life. It was above all to Goethe, who had been adopted universally as the spokesman of the German Romantic movement, that Margaret Fuller and James Freeman Clarke were drawn during their first year of reading together. A complex man who was at once scientist, poet, and public servant, he was much misunderstood by people who insisted on making one side of his character represent all. But it was precisely because he was all these things that he was able to translate the abstractions of philosophy into art. In Goethe's poetry, nature and man are regarded as extensions of the divine; leaves, insects, and people all have a unique nucleus of identity which as a scientist he explored and as an artist he celebrated. Because all life was a continuously awe-inspiring gift, no one moment in a person's life should be slurred over. The best lives, he believed, were lived actively, and no experience, however painful or monotonous, was worthless. One made the best of what was at hand.

Goethe himself lived up to this view, frankly enjoying fame and worldly position and in the course of his life becoming involved in several romantic liaisons, each of which he abandoned when it threatened to become too confining. For this he was, of course, roundly condemned, and nowhere more vociferously than in America, where German thought in any case was associated with an untidy and vaguely immoral enthusiasm. He was accused of being a dangerous influence, an opportunist, and a sham.

But to Margaret and Clarke, Goethe offered a new sense of freedom as well as a bolstered confidence in their ability to overcome the obstacles they saw ahead of them. The immediate future seemed formidable to both. Margaret knew what she wanted, but did not know how to achieve it. Clarke had on him all the pressures of male freedom with too many options. Goethe, with his insistence that if one did the duty nearest—the future would take care of itself, became a sort of prophet to them both. By the end of the year Margaret had translated Goethe's *Tasso,* and Clarke had translated the first act of *Die Jungfrau von Orleans* and passages from *Hermann und Dorothea.* According to Clarke, Margaret's reading this year included

> Goethe's *Faust, Tasso, Iphigenia, Hermann and Dorothea, Elective Affinities,* and *Memoirs;* Tieck's *William Lovel, Prince Zerbino,* and other works; Körner, Novalis, and something of Richter; all of Schiller's principal dramas, and his lyric poetry. Almost every evening I saw her, and heard an account of her studies. Her mind opened under this influence, as the apple-blossom at the end of a warm week in May. The thought and beauty of this rich literature equally filled her mind and fascinated her imagination."[20]

In 1832 the Fuller family moved once more, this time into the pre-Revolutionary house built by Colonel Brattle, now owned by Timothy's brother Abraham. Though not as large as Dana House, it too was something of a showplace, surrounded by gardens and wooded grounds. Here, in a journal entry written early in 1833,

Margaret took stock of her achievements and shut out distractions with a Goethean strength of purpose:

> I have settled the occupations of the coming six months. Some duties come first,—to parents, brothers, and sister,—but these will not consume above one sixth of the time; the family is so small now, mother will have little need of my sewing; we shall probably see very little company. The visits required of me by civility will be few. When the Farrars return, I hope to see them frequently,—and E. Woodward I may possibly know, if she comes. But I shall not, of free-will, look out of doors for a moment's pleasure. I shall have no one to stay here for any time except E. [Elizabeth Randall]. I love her, and she is never in the way. All hopes of travelling I have dismissed. All youthful hopes, of very kind, I have pushed from my thoughts. I will not, if I can help it, lose an hour in castle-building and repining,—too much of that already. I have now a pursuit of immediate importance: to the German language and literature I will give my undivided attention. I have made rapid progress for one quite unassisted. I have always hitherto been too constantly distracted by childish feelings to acquire anything properly, but have snatched a little here and there to feed my restless fancy therewith. Please God now to keep my mind composed that I may store it with all that may be hereafter conducive to the best good of others. Oh keep me steady in an honorable ambition; favored by this calm, this obscurity of life, I might learn everything, did not feeling lavish away my strength. Let it be no longer thus. Teach me to think justly and act firmly. Stifle in my breast those feelings which, pouring forth so aimlessly, did indeed water but the desert, and offend the sun's clear eye by producing weeds of rank luxuriance. Thou art my only Friend! Thou hast not seen fit to interpose one feeling, understanding breast between me and a rude, woful world. Vouchsafe then thy protection, that I may hold on in courage of soul![21]

As may be inferred, there is more behind this than an interest in German literature. The "hopes of travelling" probably involved a half-promised trip to Europe. In earlier years, Timothy Fuller had looked for an ambassadorship as a reward for his loyal support of John Quincy Adams, and he may have told Margaret that even if this hope failed he could afford to send her abroad by herself. But the expected plum had not been forthcoming, and when Jackson's victory in 1828 dimmed Fuller's political hopes outside his own state, the family's finances became more straitened.

But the "repining" and the feelings that "water the desert" have to do with the first serious love of her life, her witty but somewhat superficial cousin George Davis. During his law school days he had been a constant visitor at Dana House and, on Margaret's side at least, cousinship rapidly deepened into something else. Davis was either unaware of this or did not know how to make a graceful exit. He suddenly announced his engagement to an out-of-town girl and forthwith left Cambridge to set up housekeeping and a law practice in western Massachusetts. Margaret suffered the pangs of despised love, and it is perhaps no coincidence that around this time she had an acute and prolonged attack of headache, for which she was bled. For the next several weeks she spent long hours every day sleeping.

Even setting aside the impact of this loss, the diary entry shows that she had reached a crucial point in her life. There is a new sense of urgency and an underlying impatience at the lack of focus in her life and the dissipation of her energies. Her male contemporaries had finished their education and were moving into other, well-defined stages in their lives: Davis was a lawyer; young Channing had gone west to found a Unitarian church in Cincinnati; Hedge would soon accept a pastorate in Bangor, Maine. Clarke remained, his studies having been interrupted for a year, but he too would probably leave within the next few months. To continue in her "honorable ambition," unsustained by any example from members of her own sex (at least in America), was a lonely and difficult course. And although she had written earlier that if she failed she would find her consolation in "useful employment," she knew, if the memory of Ellen Kilshaw had not reminded her, just how limiting that employment would be. She now knew, too, as the passage above clearly shows, that marriage was all but impossible, and that she would have to live out her life within the emotional and financial limbo assigned to New England spinsters.

Nevertheless, Cambridge was a solid comfort, and a few friends remained. It was a devastating blow, therefore, to be told that once again she was to be banished to the country. In 1832, after a bitter and dirty campaign, Jackson was reelected and John Quincy Adams's presidential hopes were permanently dashed. Timothy Fuller, disillusioned with politics, decided to act on his old dream of rural retirement. Entirely oblivious to the pleas of his eldest child that he not separate her from her own natural environment once more, he made the change doubly painful by choosing as his retreat her old school town of Groton.

V

Groton

Timothy Fuller's ideal of pastoral life was hardly of the vine-covered-cottage variety. Augustan to his bones, he had a clear perception not only of where nature (delightful as it was) ended and man began, but where man-as-farmer ended and man-as-honored-public-servant began. This was not so much snobbery in the European sense, as an extension of Timothy's need for order. In America, after all, one's place in the world was not established by birth but by one's own efforts; nevertheless, one had a sort of obligation to live up to it. A gentleman-farmer was no less a gentleman for being a farmer, and it is not difficult to imagine Timothy Fuller hoeing his turnips in a coat and tie.

And so the house at Groton, in spite of the family's reduced income, still expressed Timothy's sense of his own status. Much smaller than the old Judge Dana mansion in Cambridge, it nevertheless managed with its high setting, its tall front windows and handsome fanlight door, to impress a visitor with a sense of austere dignity, if not opulence. The house still stands today, somewhat altered by the addition of a wide porch and an extended left wing. Like the Cambridge house it had been built by a Judge Dana—this one Judge Samuel Dana, who had served with Timothy in the Massachusetts House. And like the other Dana house it overlooked a fine view, which to Timothy was all but sanctified by the purple silhouette, visible from the upper windows, of Mount Wachuset. After all those strenuous years in Washington, separated from his family for months at a time and mewed up in boardinghouses, drawing rooms, and the grandly impersonal halls of Congress itself, Timothy Fuller had come back to the childhood idyl he had always kept in mind as the place where God and man were most likely to meet, if they met anywhere on this earth.

That none of the members of his family except the younger boys shared his enthusiasm for farming he found regrettable but not surprising. He set it down to the inferiority of their judgment and the narrowness of their experience, and trusted that they would soon discover for themselves the compensations of rural life. To the sullenness of William Henry (Eugene was at Harvard), the forced cheerfulness and martyred sighs of his wife, and the tight-lipped silence of his elder daughter he was impervious. He looked forward to helping his sons learn the satisfactions of hard manual labor, though at the same time he did not intend to neglect their education. He could, in fact, think of no better way for Sarah Margaret to employ her time than by tutoring her younger brothers and sister and one or two of the neighbors' children, thereby saving the expense of tuition elsewhere and at the same time gaining the teaching experience she would need if (as seemed very likely) she did not marry.

He saw no reason for the women to be lonely. There was a stage to Boston once a day, on which he himself would frequently travel, since although his law practice was much diminished he could not bring himself to give it up altogether. If his wife and daughters wanted to come along they were welcome, and the Farrars and Randalls would always be glad to have them visit for a week or two. Eventually they would make friends here. Margaret's old teacher Susan Prescott had married and moved to Lowell, but Groton was full of respectable people, including a disproportionate number of Harvard graduates and their families. In the handsome, spacious houses that lined the main street lived more Danas and more Prescotts, as well as Lawrences and Farnsworths—sound people all, some of them even Unitarians. He had always envied the apparent ease with which women made new acquaintances.

But to Margaret the banishment was complete, and visiting her old friends was only a temporary palliative. She quickly found that in Groton society there was no place for her to shine; she would be expected to hold her tongue. Intellectual discussions were rare even among men, and though people seemed to be universally kind and disinclined to gossip, she constantly felt compelled to subdue her active mind. To lose the ready access to books she had enjoyed was a deprivation she had prepared for, filling the shelves next to her bed with volumes of Goethe, Richter, and Novalis borrowed from Hedge. But without conversation she was afraid that books would be largely wasted on her. She needed to strike her sparks against another mind, otherwise she felt she was only studying, not thinking for herself. She knew people who, for lack of better company, could talk to a blank page, but she was not one of them. To her, writing was a result of conversation, not a substitute for it. "Going into mental solitude is desperately trying," she would warn Hedge when he moved to Maine in 1835. "To me the expression of thought and feeling is to the mind what respiration is to the lungs and much suffering and probable injury will ensue from living in a thick and harsh atmosphere."[1]

Apart from her sense of isolation, she was now forcibly confronted with an image of what her future life would be if she did not succeed in changing it by her own efforts. The full restrictions and responsibilities of womanhood, whether married or unmarried, were far more starkly revealed in this rural setting, and she could vividly imagine how they might continue indefinitely in such a place as Groton. Her life there began with domestic tragedy: when she arrived, having lingered in Cambridge after the rest of the family had left, she found that her ten-year-old brother Arthur had had an accident with a farm tool and was likely to lose an eye. He was in great pain and had a high fever. Their mother was all but prostrated by anxiety and fatigue, and Margaret took on the larger share of nursing her brother until his life was pronounced out of danger. Nothing could save the sight in his eye. At about the same time the baby Edward sickened. Margaret sat with him half of every night, but after a few weeks of wasting illness he died in her arms. In the face of her mother's helpless grief Margaret trained the new servant and saw to the feeding of eight or nine people three times a day. Thirteen-year-old Ellen was not much help, though she could be set to watching Lloyd, who was even less tractable and more unpredictable than most three-year-olds.

Crisis gradually resolved itself into a numbing routine. Margaret spent five to eight hours a day tutoring her sister, her brothers Arthur and Richard, and three other children, accepting this task with no enthusiasm but with as good a will as she could summon. Her pupils, even more bored than she was, found her fair game. "When we recited," her brother Richard writes, "we had certain nervous ways of moving about which annoyed her inexpressibly. I laughingly remember a habit of insistent movement of the hands, as if clutching at succor, in our recitations when we were drowning in the deep pools of Virgil."[2]

To her friend Almira Barlow she described her life at Groton when she had been there about a year:

> I will tell you how I pass my time, without society or exercise. Even till two o'clock, sometimes later, I pour ideas into the heads of the little Fullers; much runs out;—indeed I am often reminded of the chapter on home-education, in the New-Monthly. But the few drops which remain mightily gladden the sight of my father. Then I go downstairs and ask for my letters from the Post; this is my only pleasure; according to the ideas most people entertain of pleasure. Do you write me an excellent epistle by return of mail, or I will make your head ache by a minute account of the way in which the remaining hours are spent.[3]

The remaining hours were spent largely on housework and needlework, although she managed to save three evenings a week and odd hours during the day for her studies. In spite of her reservations about studying on her own, she burned her way fiercely through the books her friends sent her; Emerson once remarked that her reading rate during these years was comparable to that of

Gibbon. By the end of the first winter she had finished a self-prescribed course of study which included the remaining works of Goethe, works by Alfieri and Schiller, extensive reading in European history and in the elements of architecture, and the life and letters of Thomas Jefferson. This last project was shared with her father, and it was probably the only interest they had genuinely shared since her childhood. It mitigated somewhat the habitual coldness between them, and it brought them together by centering in one personality Timothy's earnest but chilly political liberalism and Margaret's Germanized Unitarian belief that *Alle Menschen werden Brüder*—a belief as detached in its way as her father's from the realities of poverty and gross injustice, neither of which she had ever seen.*

But housework was the most pressing demand on her free time. The Fullers' reduced income allowed them to hire only one servant to help care for a large house and family. Margaret's mother was often ill, either with recurrent colds which everyone always seemed convinced were incipient consumption, or with chronic stomach trouble which Margaret terms "bilious colic." Margaret's grandmother stayed with them for a long period at Groton, and she too was ill. At such times Margaret nursed both of them as well as helping the servant with the household chores. In January 1835 the servant gave notice, and in so remote a town they had difficulty finding another one. Eventually one was hired; but as long as she lived with her family, Margaret's own work would have to give way to the higher priority accorded household duties.

The day-to-day details of housekeeping in the first half of the last century have largely slipped out of memory and record, and most of us have little idea of the way in which women spent their lives, except for a vague realization that they "worked hard," augmented by our own experiences with power failures and country outhouses. Specifically, then, a woman's daily or weekly work included planning menus; ordering food; cooking on open hearths or (if she were lucky and prosperous) on the wood ranges

---

* Probably Margaret, leafing through Jefferson's admirable statements on the equality of man, did not come across his remark that "American women have the good sense to value domestic happiness above all other, and the art to cultivate it beyond all other."

which were just coming into use; heating water and washing dishes (in a succession of pans); baking breads, pies, cakes, and puddings; keeping the kitchen fireplace and those in the other rooms stoked; dusting; sweeping and scrubbing floors; beating or shaking carpets; scouring iron utensils (which, of course, rusted) with sand; rubbing brass ones with flannel and rum; cleaning, filling, and trimming oil lamps; salting and/or smoking meat, or storing it in brine; storing other perishables, such as butter, vegetables, fruit, and eggs, each after its kind (eggs were sometimes kept in barrels of limewater); sewing clothes, bedding, and table linen without machines or ready-made patterns; making feather beds (they had to be shaken); mending; laundry (an entire day); ironing (most of a day); and keeping the children from falling in the well.

Chores performed seasonally or infrequently included: washing windows; blacking boots and shoes; scrubbing hearths and marble mantlepieces; polishing silver; dyeing clothes (colors were not fixed); removing stains; making soap (hard for laundry, soft for floors); tending the garden; nursing the sick; making preserves; knitting and embroidery. Most household concoctions, such as cleaning agents, medicines, and insect poisons, were either made at home or had to undergo some processing after they were purchased. If the family was very poor or lived far from an urban center, women also made candles, starch, and yeast, churned butter, and dried their own herbs.

How many of these duties were actually performed by the housewife depended on how many daughters she had and whether she could afford to hire one or more servants. The middle-class wife with two or three domestics might have only supervising, nursing, and fine handwork to do in addition to spending as much or as little time as she liked with her children. But in a day when fortunes were made and lost overnight and servants were becoming more and more independent, even this pampered creature had to be ready to assume the total workload of her house at any time. The women in a home like the Fullers', where there was only one servant, had to share the housework among them even in the best of times.

Two informative books on the period are *A Treatise on Domes-*

tic Economy by Catherine E. Beecher and *The American Frugal Housewife* by Lydia Maria Child. This excerpt from Mrs. Child's book is a reminder of what winter was like in the kitchen:

> In winter, always set the handle of your pump as high as possible, before you go to bed. Except in very frigid weather, this keeps the handle from freezing. When there is reason to apprehend extreme cold, do not forget to throw a rug or horse-blanket over your pump; a frozen pump is a comfortless preparation for a winter's breakfast.

Summer, on the other hand, was hardly more pleasant:

> There is a difference in wood in giving out heat; there is a great difference in the construction of ovens; and when an oven is extremely cold, either on account of the weather, or want of use, it must be heated more. Economical people heat ovens with pine wood, fagots, brush, and such light stuff. If you have none but hard wood, you must remember that it makes very hot coals, and therefore less of it will answer. A smart fire for an hour and a half is a general rule for common sized family ovens, provided brown bread and beans are to be baked. An hour is long enough to heat an oven for flour bread. Pies bear about as much heat as flour bread; pumpkin pies will bear more. If you are afraid your oven is too hot, throw in a little flour, and shut it up for a minute. If it scorches black immediately, the heat is too furious; if it merely browns, it is right. Some people wet an old broom two or three times, and turn it round near the top of the oven till it dries; this prevents pies and cakes from scorching on the top.[4]

Meats were roasted or boiled two to three hours, vegetables boiled about an hour. Baking took several hours, each food being cooked in turn as the heat became less intense, beginning with pies and ending with brown bread.

Mrs. Child recommends beginning one's laundry the night before by sorting the clothes. White clothes were then soaked overnight. The next day they were washed in a tub of suds, often with lye or soda added; then boiled in a huge pot; then rinsed, wrung out, put in blueing and (just before hanging out) dipped in previously boiled starch. Colored clothes were never soaked, but were washed in lukewarm suds to which beef gall (made at home by soaking beef liver) was added. Grease stains had been previously removed with French chalk, starch, magnesia, or "Wilmington clay." Starch for colored clothes was made with coffee-water, and Mrs. Child cautions never to allow them to freeze while drying.

Ironing involved long skirts, laces, and lots of ruffles. An ironing board was just that—a board laid over the backs of two chairs, covered with a blanket and a sheet. Two or three irons were kept heating on the hearth all the time, and were used alternately. They smoked, so beeswax was rubbed on them from time to time. Mrs. Child recommends that three irons per worker be provided, as well as clothes-frames, a special board on which to iron shirt-bosoms, another one for skirts, and a fluting iron for ruffles. Since the fire had to be kept hot, one presumably could choose on a summer day between ironing in the same room with it or running back and forth between rooms to change irons.

And so on.

The point is not that the Fuller women necessarily followed Mrs. Child's procedure for laundry and ironing, or for other housekeeping tasks; every woman had her short cuts then as now. Very likely they bought their bread instead of baking it, and they even may have hung their calicoes out on frosty days. But even so the sheer number of exhausting, repetitive, mind-numbing chores for which women were responsible was indeed formidable. When Catherine Beecher claimed that American women became old before their time because of the demands of housework, she was not speaking only of pioneer women, but also of urban, middle-class wives who could afford to hire a servant. Even families who had very little money would do without all but the barest necessities in order to hire "help." But with the advent of the textile mills the servants were leaving the drudgery of housework, for which they were paid $1 a week plus board, for the comparative ease of working seventy hours a week in a mill, for which they were paid twice as much.

Not infrequently Margaret would be all but overwhelmed by the prospect of permanent spinsterhood in her father's house. In the early months especially her chief buttress against these waves of despair was Goethe's teaching that one's life was a changing, organic thing in which no experience was wasted. She found a strong ally in James Clarke, who had his own exile to face, having accepted the pastorate of a young Unitarian church in the rough frontier town of Louisville. They exhorted one another to take Wilhelm Meister as their model. One did not sit down and let adversity wash over one; one used it in the end, no matter how painful it was for the moment, and the important thing was not only to come through, but to come through with spirit. In April 1833, while wagonloads of Fuller household goods followed one another to Groton, Margaret heard Clarke preach in Cambridge on Goethe's favorite biblical text: "Whatsoever thy hand findeth to do, do it with thy might."

In the first months, too, she was heartened somewhat by the visits and letters from her friends, who she had been afraid might forget her. Clarke stopped on his way to Louisville; Hedge wrote faithfully and kept her supplied with books; and Sarah Clarke, Elizabeth Randall, and Anna Barker all found their way to Groton. Margaret in turn was able to escape to Cambridge whenever her mother's health permitted. But as winter came on her exile was sealed by snowdrifts which made travel by stagecoach all but impossible. The roads were given over to farmers who loaded their sledges with the year's produce and drove them in convoys to market, armed with shovels for mutual aid. To anyone unwilling to drive to town perched on a load of squashes and dressed hogs, these months were a time of solitude broken only by the small talk of neighbors and the annual New Year's Eve ball at the inn.

In November 1834 she was encouraged by seeing her own words in print for the first time. In the *North American Review* the historian George Bancroft had published an article in which he dealt rather harshly with Brutus. At her father's urging Margaret wrote a reply, which was printed in the *Daily Advertiser* as a letter signed simply *J*. As Margaret wrote to Hedge,

It was responded to (I flatter myself by some big-wig) from Salem. He detected some ignorance in me. Nevertheless as he remarked that

I wrote with "ability" and seemed to *consider me* as an elderly gentleman *I considered* the affair as highly flattering and beg you will
keep it in mind and furnish it for my memoirs as such after I am
dead.[5]

Spurred on by this modest success, she found time during that
second winter to write articles on Hannah More, Edward Bulwer-
Lytton, George Crabbe, and Henry Taylor's drama *Philip Van Artevelde,* and submitted them for publication to a Boston periodical,
probably *The Christian Examiner.** They were promptly rejected,
and inquiries concerning the publication of her *Tasso* translation,
though they seemed to meet with some interest at first, also ended
in discouragement.

During the first year at Groton she began seriously to consider
teaching, although she felt it would divert her from her chosen
course and she saw little chance that she would find the teaching of
strangers any more satisfying than the teaching of her own siblings. Apparently wishing to make a clean break with her family,
she wrote to Clarke asking about the possibility of coming to
Louisville to teach. She had no illusions about what she would
find there: to Margaret, and no one else, Clarke had unsparingly
described the brutal ugliness of the treeless, muddy frontier city.
The people there had received him politely, but except for a few
members of the congregation (which included George Keats,
brother of the poet), they had made plain that what they expected
from their preacher was solid, unexceptionable, orthodox doctrine,
unleavened with any speculations as to First Principles or the nature of the soul. Clarke was bitterly disappointed, as well as plain
homesick, but so far he had been able to swallow his Germanisms
and preach the kind of sermons he thought his congregation
wanted to hear. However, if Kentucky was not ready for this
mildly liberal young minister, it was certainly not ready for a phe-
nomenally learned young woman whose extravagance of sentiment
was matched only by her extravagance of manner, and who was

---

* Hannah More was an English writer and religious reformer of the Johnsonian era (d.
1833); *Philip Van Artevelde* is a romantic blank verse drama about a scholarly, noble-
minded man who was thrust into political leadership in a fourteenth-century revolt against
the Earl of Flanders.

unwilling, and often unable, to modify either of them for the sake of anyone else's benighted sensibilities.

His reply was flatly discouraging:

> You would find teaching in Kentucky intolerable, on account of the utter disrespect and lawlessness of the children here. Several years must pass before a school can be brought into decent discipline. . . . Duels, dirkings, shootings, beatings to death, etc., happen here every day, and no one troubles themselves about them. There is an indifference here which would shock New Englanders as regards human life.

He says that Cincinnati is the only fit place for her purpose, provided she can assure herself of a situation before coming. But even about that he is evasive:

> If you wish to come to Cincinnati, I shall be able, I think, to get the arrangements made. Mrs. Hentez keeps a large school there. However, I think it will do to talk about that when I see you face to face. . . .[6]

Since this was February, and he would not see her "face to face" until summer, the iron (which was never very hot to begin with) would be stone cold before it was struck.

Busy nursing her mother and grandmother when his letter arrived, she had no time to sort out her mingled feelings of relief and disappointment at not having actually to go to Kentucky. But the future weighed heavily on her mind, and she met her family obligations in a mood of silent rebellion not unlike her withdrawal during early adolescence. After the twin spring scourges of mud and blackflies receded, she retreated with her books, when she could, to a grove of hazel trees where no one would disturb her. In a blank verse journal entry probably written during this summer she writes of having spent five days

> Uncheered by friendly voice, oppressed
> By doubt, and fear, and bitter introspection,
> Performing duties, or pursuing studies
> With cold reluctance . . .

She reproaches herself for being vain and selfish, and describes the healing effect of the river and the birds, but it is typical of Margaret's feelings toward nature that its soothing influence was only superficial. She herself knew that she was incapable of any deep, Wordsworthian communion with the natural world, and she was aware of the reasons:

> . . . Might but the years of childhood,
> Which a precocious growth of mind stole from me,
> Come to me now! Some years of mere sensation;
> I cannot *feel* this thing . . .
> My mind too early filled,—the outward sense neglected,
> I know each object, having seen its picture;
> Feelings, from the descriptions I have read . . .[7]

The emotion, if not the poetry, is reminiscent of Coleridge's "Ode to Dejection," but Coleridge was lamenting the loss of a mystical sense of universal harmony which he had really experienced, while Margaret is lamenting the fact that she has never attained it at all. It was only through other people that she was able to reach beyond herself.

In late summer of 1834 her father rewarded her diligence by sending her off to spend a month in Newport, Rhode Island, with Anna and the Farrars. It was diverting, but a month of light summer society was not what she craved. In an October letter to Mrs. Barlow she speaks of her recently renewed depression in words which, although they show her egotism in its least becoming light, are nevertheless tinged with typically self-conscious irony:

> Surely the intercourse I used to have with you and other friends of my youth, was penetrating, was satisfying, compared with that I have with people now. I am more and more dissatisfied with this world, I *cannot* find a home in it. Outward things how vain! when we lean on them merely, and Heaven knows I have striven enough to make my mind its own place. I have resolution for the contest, and will not shrink or faint, but I know not, just at this moment, where to turn.
>
> I have been wandering about somewhat since I saw you last; one

month in Rhode-Island, where I was so happy! Had you seen me then I could have flashed and sparkled, and afforded you some amusement. I had many little stories to tell, ludicrous and pathetic, and many ideas, not very deep, 'tis true, but tasteful and brilliant, which I had been throwing from right to left, to people who would hardly trouble themselves, and would give me nothing in return, except experience.

Experience! Why cannot I value thee, and make thee my peculiar household deity, as did our master, Goethe? I suppose I could, if I had the same reproducing power: but, as it is, Experience only gives me "Byron head-ache." [8]

It is to Margaret's credit that however much Byronic anger and self-pity she felt, she was never capable of Byronic misanthropy, nor did she ever evade her responsibilities. That she performed them with an ill grace is certainly true. The flagrant beauty of the maple trees that October not only left her unmoved, but must have further alienated her from a natural world so detached from human unhappiness and so comfortably regulated by the predictable cycle of the seasons. Even Goethe was failing her; she could not see that doing the duty nearest at hand was leading to anything except more of the same. She could not have helped but reflect that "experience" for Goethe in the Weimar court, or for Carlyle in his snug den warmed by a fire made with Jane's own hands, was radically, hopelessly different from her own. It is easier to turn the rejections of critics or the sting of a broken love affair into a positive, forward thrust in one's life than it is to do the same with the beating of carpets and the mending of stockings.

Increasingly aware of how threadbare a protection this secular stoicism was against the chill reality of the coming winter, and increasingly angry with herself and guilty over what she saw as a preoccupation with her own needs at the expense of others, she followed the example of millions of other women and turned to religion. She had always been contemptuous of formal Unitarianism, but her objections were directed toward the dullness and the superficiality of the sermons and the social proprieties of church-going rather than toward Christianity itself. In actual belief she had never strayed very far from the Channingite wing of the church, accepting Jesus as a perfect ethical model, neither God nor man but something in between, and believing in a personal God and a future life. She had flirted briefly with a kind of Deism at the age of nineteen, when she said she believed simply in "Eternal Progression."[9] Two years later, when the futility of her love for George Davis and the uncertainties of her future were becoming painfully clear, she had had a vivid religious experience. It was Thanksgiving Day, 1831, and the rather facile optimism of the sermon had jarred even more heavily than usual upon her mood: "I felt within myself great power, and generosity, and tenderness; but it seemed to me as if they were all unrecognized, and as if it was impossible that they should be used in life. I was only one-and-twenty; the past was worthless, the future hopeless, yet I could not remember ever voluntarily to have done a wrong thing, and my aspiration seemed very high."

Hurrying away over the bleak fields after the service, she finally sat down next to a dark pool in the woods: "Suddenly the sun shone out with that transparent sweetness, like the last smile of a dying lover, which it will use when it has been unkind all a cold autumn day." She experienced what can only be called a kind of mystical transcendence: "I saw there was no self; that selfishness was all folly, and the result of circumstance; that it was only because I thought self real that I suffered; that I had only to live in the idea of the All, and all was mine. This truth came to me, and I received it unhesitatingly; so that I was for that hour taken up into God."[10]

Such total self-abnegation could not be sustained in so assertive a nature as Margaret's, but the memory of it and the wish to regain it persisted at Groton. In 1834 she began a systematic study of the Bible, supplemented by commentaries recommended by Clarke and Hedge, to see if she could recapture the faith in Divine Providence she had had as a child. Eventually she did work her way through to a profound acceptance of everything in her life, both good and evil, as part of a divine plan, and since she was incapable of superficial belief this was to lend great solidity to the patience and perseverance which already were strong qualities in her nature. It was in this sense of embracing one's experience as a whole that she later made the famous statement, "I accept the Universe"—at which Carlyle reportedly remarked, "By Gad, she'd better!" The fact that this is sometimes the only thing people know about her reflects the way anecdotes told about her both during her life and after her death have distorted beyond all measure the shell of egotism which was necessary to her survival. She meant the remark in the Emersonian sense, as an affirmation of faith not in the least arrogant, but simply total. She meant (to borrow Carlyle's own terms) that she would say an Everlasting Yea to whatever circumstances were visited on her, and not avoid the world by renouncing it. A journal entry, probably dating from 1835, enlarges on this:

> This is my ideal—the soul that, capable of the most delicate and strongest emotions, can yet look upon the world as it is with a free and eagle gaze, and, without any vain optimism or weak hope of a peculiar lot can . . . *accept life.* That is the true Stoicism not to be insensible but superior to pain. How noble to rush to battle like the Spartan youth without a buckler.[11]

She differed from Emerson in other ways, notably in her inability to identify deeply with nature and her need to personify God as Father (which undoubtedly has its roots in her emotional life), but in this central belief she and the sage of Concord were on common ground.

As for meeting Emerson himself, Margaret looked forward to it with confidence, although for the time being various things prevented it. In 1834 she wrote to Mrs. Barlow of a visitor at the Farrars who had spoken "with due admiration of the Rev. W. Emerson, that only clergyman of all possible clergymen who eludes my acquaintance. Mais n'importe! I keep his image bright in my mind."[12] Emerson, now thirty-one, had left the ministry and was lecturing in Boston and delivering guest sermons at those churches liberal enough to invite him. The eloquent force with which he explained his unconventional views on the relationship of man, nature, and God were gaining him a sizable following, especially among young people. He was a friend of Hedge, who did all he could to promote a meeting with Margaret, including sending Emerson her *Tasso* and asking for comments. Nothing came of this, nor (at first) of Margaret's suggestion to Mr. Robinson, the Groton pastor, that Emerson be invited to preach. Nevertheless, it seemed inevitable to her that she should meet him sooner or later: "I cannot think I should be disappointed in him as I have been in others to whom I have hoped to look up, the sensation one experiences in the atmosphere of his thought is too decided and peculiar." [13]

Spring of 1835 brought some brightening of her mood, and she wrote out an ambitious plan of literary projects for the coming year, including a series of "Hebrew romances" and one of "German tales." Meanwhile Hedge wrote from the cultural outlands of Bangor with what to Margaret were unaccountably good spirits. He was, he said, planning to launch a new "Transcendental" periodical, which would give admirers of Carlyle and the Germans a forum denied them by the established publications. Would Margaret like to write for it? Still absorbed in her Old Testament studies, she replied that she would be glad to, but feared she was only "Germanico" and not "Transcendental"; if she were to write an article now she would choose "the character of King David aesthetically considered" for her subject. [14] This was not the response Hedge had in mind, and his other friends seem to have been equally unhelpful. The project was dropped for the time being.

But another request came from Clarke, who had assumed the coeditorship of a new Unitarian journal called the *Western Messenger*. Margaret sent him the articles she had written the previous winter (which may have been too literary for Hedge), and Clarke printed them, though not without some judicious editorial comments on the loftiness and obscurity of the style. These were defects she would never entirely correct, but Clarke was one of several friends whose comments helped her writing gain in tautness and economy over the years. What was important in her essays was content, not style. In the early one on *Philip Van Artevelde* she was already moving toward the establishment of objective critical standards, at a time when reviews written on both

sides of the Atlantic alternated between the bland and the vituperative and were generally characterized by much heat and very little
light.

The publication of her articles gave impetus to another project,
so daring that she had only considered it tentatively. Goethe had
died in 1832, and no biography had yet been written. The public
was still sharply divided in its opinion of him, those who could not
excuse his morals denouncing him as a hypocrite, and those who
admired him lauding him as the greatest literary genius since
Shakespeare. In the preface to her later translation of *Eckermann's
Conversations with Goethe,* Margaret lists some of the reasons for
her admiration of Goethe. He is a necessary corrective to the spirit
of the age, believing "more in man than men, effort than success,
thought than action, nature than providence"; she adds that she
does not necessarily agree with him, but likes to see the world
from this perspective occasionally. Then he is one of the finest
lyric poets of the times, "the best writer of the German language," an unsurpassed critic, and a keen observer of nature,
human and otherwise. Finally, she admires him "as a mind which
has known how to reconcile individuality of character with univer-
sality of thought; a mind which, whatever be its faults, ruled and
relied on itself alone." [15] In this last can be seen, I think, one of
the strongest reasons for an identification powerful enough to
impel her to write a biography. Goethe, as a member of the German school, believed that one should trust one's God-given inner
voice. Like Emerson, he was an example par excellence of the
person who can draw strength from within, but unlike Emerson he
was able to also remain active in the world. This kind of ability to
balance involvement in the world and inner integrity was a personal trait Margaret highly valued.

Other reasons can be inferred: Goethe's insistence on the importance of duty, renunciation, and patience while fashioning one's
own life, like Wilhelm Meister, through a slow and painful process of growth; his peculiar blend of classical moderation with a
rather unruly and (as Margaret admitted) irresponsibly passionate
temperament. And, on a more personal level still, his unhappy
childhood experiences with a cold, authoritarian father in a

bourgeois environment uncongenial to the needs of a highly intelligent, sensitive child.

Disciple though she was, Margaret believed she was not blind to Goethe's faults and could write a balanced biography. She had begun quietly to gather information from books and from American scholars who had met him abroad, but she was handicapped not only by distance from her materials but by the extraordinary squeamishness of her male acquaintances in discussing Goethe's liaisons. Of all the men she knew, only Clarke would discuss sex more or less frankly with her; and Clarke, alas, knew nothing about Goethe that she didn't know herself. In reply to her letter asking for information, he told her a story about a Western gentleman who, in carving a fowl, had tried to think of a way to offer a lady a thigh without actually offering her a thigh. It was highly entertaining, but it had nothing to do with her question.

But in June, during a visit to the Farrars, she suddenly was made happier than she had ever been before by gaining the friendship of the first literary woman she had ever met and glimpsing the possibility of actually researching her book on Goethe's home ground. The new friend was Harriet Martineau, an English writer of semifictional books on social reform who was visiting the United States for two years and was spending some weeks with the Farrars. Eight years older than Margaret, she had overcome formidable obstacles, many of them similar to those in Margaret's own life. She had been born into a liberal Unitarian family and had been educated with her brothers, but she had been a clumsy, morbidly fearful child, haunted by nightmares conjured up by a Calvinist nurse's graphic descriptions of hell. Rejected and ridiculed in her own family, in adolescence she had developed several vaguely defined ailments—chronic indigestion, "languor," "muscular weakness," and depression—and one specifically defined one, deafness, which obliged her to use an ear trumpet. When she was twenty-four her father had died, leaving his family destitute, and Harriet, her mother and sisters supported themselves by taking in needlework. Harriet had been forced to do her writing late at night, because her mother disapproved and because it brought in no money. When at length she finished her *Illustrations on Political Economy* it had been rejected by every publisher to whom she submitted it, but she had somehow found the money to publish it on her own, under her own name. It was an instant success, and she stood before Margaret as living proof that Margaret's own ambition was not an impossible one.

They became friends, though their temperaments were very dissimilar and the friendship lacked the passionate intensity of some of Margaret's others. Besides determination and a sometimes excessive regard for truth at all costs, they had little in common. Miss Martineau was a necessitarian and a social reformer, with little esthetic feeling and no tolerance of the more speculative flights of philosophy and literature. Her chief interest in the United States was the abolition of slavery, and she made a determined effort to bring Margaret into the abolitionist party. But Margaret, like her father, belonged to the group which called itself "antislavery" rather than "abolitionist," and which advocated the gradual phasing out of slavery. Nevertheless, their discussions sharpened Margaret's awareness of social issues, and in Miss Martineau and the women abolitionists of Boston she saw members of her sex assuming leadership, defying social convention, and facing down real physical danger in a totally new kind of role.

The new friendship led to an opportuinty that hardly seemed real. For years Margaret had wished above all else to go to Europe, believing that only in this way could she compensate for her lack of a college degree and compete with men in the world of letters. The move to Groton and her father's political eclipse had obliged her to put Europe out of her mind. But the door had not been entirely closed, and lately an understanding had developed that means might be found for Margaret to go in return for teaching the younger children. Now Miss Martineau, who was planning to return to England the following year, and Mrs. Farrar, who was sailing with her, asked Margaret to accompany them. To her delight, her father consented. She would complete her education and see the England of Carlyle, Wordsworth, and Coleridge, the Greece of Homer, and the Rome of Virgil and Plutarch. She would visit Weimar and talk to people who had known Goethe; she would turn on them the full battery of that persuasiveness she knew she possessed, and they would be unable to resist telling her all they knew about their revered national poet.

In this transported state she set off on an August excursion up the Hudson with the Farrars and a group of their friends. To someone who had rarely been outside of Massachusetts, it was a fitting prelude to a European tour, and in fact the wild and picturesque scenery along the upper Hudson was sometimes likened to that along the Rhine. In a mood to appreciate fully everything she saw and everyone she met, she found herself especially appreciative of a Harvard senior, several years younger than she, named Samuel Gray Ward.* The son of a banker, Sam Ward wanted only to be an artist and study in Europe; needless to say, he found in Margaret a sympathetic listener. They looked at Trenton Falls by moonlight together, and he taught her to see them with a painterly eye. By the time she returned to Groton she had added another to her list of ambiguously ardent friendships.

At home she found an older friendship temporarily disrupted, entirely by her own fault. A short story she had written the previous winter had found its way into print. Margaret's writing ability was entirely of an expository or critical nature, and the story was a thinly disguised account of a flirtation between Harriet Russell, now George Davis's wife, and a man who had passed through Boston during her engagement. Margaret had naively thought that no one would recognize the characters, and that if anyone did, no harm would be done since Harriet had done the honorable thing and married George after all. Understandably, the Davises took a different view, and Margaret was all but overcome with mortification. Within a few days she became ill with severe pains in the head—not in themselves unusual for her, but this time accompanied by a high fever which lasted for nine days. It seems open to question whether this was a "real" illness or conversion hysteria, as has been suggested,[16] but her life was thought to be in danger, and the fear of losing her brought from her father the strongest words of praise she had ever heard from him. "My dear," he said, standing beside her bed, "I have been thinking of you in the night, and I cannot remember that you have any *faults*. You have defects, of course, as all mortals have, but I do not know that you have a

* Not to be confused with Julia Ward Howe's brother of the same name.

single fault.''[17] The strange, stiff words, coming so unwillingly from her father's lips, moved her to tears.

She had not fully recovered when, on September 30, her father looking rather pale and unsteady, came in from ditching one of the lower meadows. Shortly afterward he was seized with a violent fit of retching. Within hours it was clear that he had been stricken by some deadly disease, probably cholera. He survived one more day and died on the morning of October 2.

Margaret's grief was sharpened, as grief almost always is, by guilt, and she immediately began to idealize her father's memory:

> My father's image follows me constantly, whenever I am in my room he seems to open the door and to look on me with a complacent tender smile. What would I not give to have it in my power, to make that heart beat once more with joy. The saddest feeling is the remembrance of little things, in which I have fallen short of love and duty. I never sympathized in his liking for this farm, and secretly wondered how a mind which had for thirty years been so widely engaged in the affairs of men could care so much for trees and crops. But now, amidst the beautiful autumn days, I walk over the grounds and look with painful emotions at every little improvement. He had selected a spot to place a seat where I might go to read alone, and had asked me to visit it. I contented myself with ''where you please Father,'' but we never went; what would I not now give, if I had fixed a time, and shown more interest.[18]

Guilt fueled the spirit of renunciation with which she now resolved to devote herself above all to the welfare of her family. In the absence of so dominant a figure as Timothy Fuller, no one else seemed able to act. Her mother, whose air of sweet, graceful dependency had always captivated all who knew her, was as handicapped for conducting her own life, let alone raising her children, as if her feet had been bound from birth. Some years later Margaret would write that the ideal woman was one who could, if her husband died, be both father and mother to her children. This role now fell not to Margaret's mother, but to Margaret herself, while her mother leaned on her as heavily as did her four younger siblings. The two oldest boys were both absent, Eugene in a tutoring job in Virginia and William Henry (who in any case was too young to help) in Boston, where he was working in a store.

Margaret's first duty, although she had neither experience nor aptitude in business, was to try to disentangle her father's affairs. It was a shock to realize that Timothy's methodical habits had been abandoned when it came to financial management. His cash income had been much reduced since his retirement and most of his assets were tied up in unproductive real estate scattered around the state, some of it needing repairs, some tenants, some both. The total estate amounted to about $20,000, but for the foreseeable future there was almost no money. Margaret found that the receipts and journals which she had assumed her father kept in meticulous order were either filed haphazardly or missing altogether. Uncle Abraham, hired as an attorney to help manage the estate, took advantage of what he believed to be his authority as senior male of the family to try to impose his will on his sister-in-law and especially on his niece, whose unwomanly forwardness he now saw a chance to chastise.

Winter returned and the succeeding months dragged on. Ellen was sent to Cambridge on a prolonged visit to the Randalls, and Mrs. Fuller went there herself for frequent visits, leaving Margaret to run the farm. In November both Mrs. Fuller and Richard were ill. Except for the small and uncertain income from the rental properties they were almost without funds, and Abraham's recalcitrance in providing for their future was alarming. In exchange for each dollar he allowed them for present living expenses he tried to exact a promise that they would adopt the way of life he chose for them. He insisted, piously invoking the name of his dead brother, that all plans for continuing the children's education be canceled, that Ellen be sent out as a governess and that one of the younger boys be given for adoption to a farmer who had expressed an interest in him. Margaret fought him doggedly, and her mother backed her up. They slaughtered a cow and two hogs for the winter, and hoped for the best. It was hardly likely that Abraham would let them starve, but he was determined to humble them all, and the prospects of buying other necessities, let alone educating the children, looked bleak. Added to it all was the continual trial, seldom mentioned by any of them, of Lloyd's mental instability.

In February Margaret wrote to Almira Barlow:

> I have turned over some dark pages since we met. Were I with you I
> could speak, but it is not easy to write of their lore. You know that I
> looked upon Death very near, nor at the time should I have grieved
> to go. I thought there never could come a time when my departure
> would be easier to myself, or less painful to others. I felt as I
> thought I should feel at that awful season. It was not to be so, and I
> returned into life to bear a sorrow of which you know the heaviness.
> But my hard-won faith has not deserted me, and I have so far pre-
> served a serenity which might seem heartlessness to a common ob-
> server. It was indeed sad when I went back, in some sort, into the
> world, and felt myself fatherless. Yet I gave no sign, and hope to
> preserve more or less fortitude. I cannot now tell you much about
> myself. My plans are various, but all undecided. I feel however that
> the crisis is approaching, and my prayer is that I may now act with
> wisdom and energy; and that since I *was* called back to this state of
> things, it may be to perform some piece of work which another
> could not do.[19]

It is not easy to tell what she means by the last phrase, and in
fact at this point she did not know herself. Writing her book was
work that only she, "this Margaret Fuller," could do; but support-
ing her family was also work which, for the moment, only she
could do. In a letter to Clarke written early in the year her resolution to continue with her book seemed firm, and he replied encour-
agingly with some information about the influence of German transcendentalism on Goethe's thinking. But if she were to earn
money by writing—a dubious undertaking for anyone—she would
have to concentrate her energies on journal articles, leaving only
odd moments for her book. She wrote two journal articles during
these months, one on Heinrich Heine and one on Sir James Macintosh, which were published in a Massachusetts periodical the following summer. But the small remuneration she received was not
encouraging, and her confidence in her writing ability, never very
high, was at a low ebb. She decided to try it for a few months, but
she was almost certain she would have to abandon writing and
teach for an indefinite period in order to keep the family together.
She dreaded it, and she resented society's assumption that all

women, *qua* women, must find joy in a profession for which many of them felt no calling whatever.

But her own religious crisis had indeed brought about a change in the way she perceived her own needs and those of other people, especially since the Christian ethical code did not contradict that of Goethe and Carlyle, but reinforced it with supernatural authority. For better or worse, she was able to put aside her own ambition with less conflict than she would have felt three years before:

> I shall be obliged to give up selfishness in the end. May God enable me to see the way clear, and not to let down the intellectual, in raising the moral tone of my mind. Difficulties and duties became distinct the very night after my father's death, and a solemn prayer was offered then, that I might combine what is due to others with what is due to myself. The spirit of that prayer I shall constantly endeavor to maintain. What ought to be done for a few months is plain, and, as I proceed, the view will open.[20]

The earliest and most difficult test came in having to give up the trip to Europe, which at first she believed might still be possible. Her mother, brothers, and sister urged her to borrow on the estate and go, but she felt uneasy at leaving them even for a few months and postponing her efforts at breadwinning. Her brother Richard says she spent long hours wrestling with her decision, reading the New Testament with "her sympathizing friend Miss Martineau"— referring presumably to Miss Martineau's sympathy with Margaret and not with the New Testament. By May she had firmly decided against going:

> Circumstances have decided that I must not go to Europe, and shut upon me the door, as I think, forever, to the scenes I could have loved. Let me now try to forget myself, and act for others' sakes. What I can do with my pen, I know not. At present, I feel no confidence or hope. The expectations so many have been led to cherish by my conversational powers, I am disposed to deem ill-founded. I do not think I can produce a valuable work. I do not feel in my bosom that confidence necessary to sustain me in such undertakings,—the confidence of genius. But I am now but just recovered

from bodily illness, and still heart-broken by sorrow and disappointment. I may be renewed again, and feel differently. If I do not soon, I will make up my mind to teach. I can thus get money, which I will use for the benefit of my dear, gentle, suffering mother,—my brothers and sister. This will be the greatest consolation to me, at all events.[21]

One other great consolation was waiting for her, in the form of her friendship with Ralph Waldo Emerson.

VI

Emerson and Alcott

In the summer of 1836 Emerson had been married less than a year to his second wife, "Lidian," the former Lydia Jackson of Plymouth. On the day of their wedding he had brought her to Concord, where his family had lived for generations and where he himself had lived from time to time in his boyhood. Here he hoped to find that balance of solitude and society which he would always guard jealously and which was necessary to the development of his particular genius. Having turned his back on a career in the ministry, he hoped to support himself and his family by a combination of lecturing and writing, and for such a life Concord was ideal. The intellectual currents of the city flowed easily this far into the hinterland, and although the inhabitants of Concord were as concerned as farmers up-country with guarding their maple sugar buckets from marauding bears and keeping the deer out of their cornfields, it was possible to drive to Boston in two or three hours, accomplish whatever business there was to do, and be home in time for tea at six.

The Emerson house, nicknamed "Coolidge Castle" after the

previous owners, stood at the junction of the Cambridge Turnpike and the Lexington-Boston road. It was a simple, comfortable New England farmhouse, built on the traditional plan of four rooms on the ground floor grouped around a generous hallway and central staircase, with four rooms above and an attic on the third floor. A wing extending back from the main house contained the kitchen and servants' quarters, and Emerson had recently enlarged this by adding two rooms, anticipating the marriage of his brother Charles and Elizabeth Hoar. To the left and a little behind the house stood the barn, and to the left of that the kitchen garden where Emerson, rather to his own surprise, successfully raised vegetables for the family table. If he was in a solitary mood, a few minutes' walk through the woods brought him to the steep banks overlooking Walden Pond; or he could walk along the Concord River, drowsing among its weeds and duck nests with scarcely enough current to carry a leaf.

The long period of stability which people associate with Emerson's life had just begun. In the course of the previous few years he had painfully renounced the career in the church for which he had prepared, lived abroad for twenty-two months, and suffered three wrenching losses: the death of his beloved first wife, Ellen, in 1831; the death of his brother Edward, in 1834; and the death, in the spring of this first year in Concord, of his favorite brother, Charles. He needed all the resources of his philosophy not to succumb to bitterness under this final blow. Charles had been his closest and most necessary friend, bringing the world and its "holy hurrahs" (among them abolitionism) home to his elder brother. Ungraciously as he sometimes received this favor, no one knew better than Waldo how sterile his thinking could become if he allowed himself to lose touch with other people.

Outwardly he recovered his equilibrium quickly—it was always a source of shame to him that one's life went on much as usual after such a loss—but he made an effort to cement old friendships more firmly and to form new ones. The first of these was with A. Bronson Alcott, ex-pedlar and radical educator, in whose saintly and single-minded idealism, so close to his and formed under very different conditions, Emerson found support for his own approach to the old philosophical problem of the dualism of matter and spirit. In Alcott's mind, less subtle than his own and less trammeled by an inconvenient affection for the world of matter, Emerson saw a colder, purer idealism than he could ever attain. In moments of unqualified admiration he called Alcott "the highest genius of the time."[1]

But his delight in "the meal in the firkin, the milk in the pan; the ballad in the street; the news of the boat; the glance of the eye; the form and gait of the body"[2] helped to strengthen that healthy sense of reality which gave muscle and tension to his thinking. Margaret Fuller, arriving fortuitously at the height of his enthusiasm for Alcott, provided another important counterinfluence. Urban and social as he was not, possessed of a vitality and spontaneity which he lacked, and convinced that the life of the emotions was no less important than the life of the intellect, she would not let him withdraw from society either personally or philosophically; she constantly prodded and coaxed him to allow himself to feel and express affection, reminded him of the barrenness of the purely contemplative life, challenged his opinions when no one else would, and brought her frank and critical judgment to bear on his enthusiasm for the thinking of other men, notably Alcott and Carlyle. Lacking his creative ability, she possessed a remarkable flexibility of intellect which allowed her to form opinions, as she approached people, each separately and without preconceptions. It was a quality which could only be appreciated over a long period of time, by people who knew her best: "You cannot predict her opinion," Emerson would write of her in 1843. "She sympathizes so fast with all forms of life, that she talks never narrowly or hostilely, nor betrays, like all the rest, under a thin garb of new words, the old droning cast-iron opinions or notions of many years' standing."[3] She helped Emerson keep his own mind from settling into too comfortable a mold.

Socially too she broadened his experience, bringing to Concord a choice succession of those friends whom, Elizabeth Hoar said, she wore like "a necklace of diamonds about her neck."[4] With three of them, Samuel Gray Ward, Anna Barker, and Caroline Sturgis, Emerson formed lifelong friendships of his own. There is no doubt that without Margaret, Emerson's life would have been a good deal more insulated and narrow. Like his brother Charles, she was a bridge to the outer world.

He for his part provided a steadying influence, a source of motivation and encouragement, and a sparring partner (one of many, but probably the best). He deepened her appreciation of solitude and nature, and on a practical level provided a helping hand at times when she needed one to gain entrance into the male literary world. His serenity reinforced her native common sense and patience, and helped restrain those powerful emotional forces which propelled her toward a sentimental effusiveness. (He began during her first visit by reminding her that adjectives come in degrees, of which the superlative is only one; but in order really to succeed at this he would have had to exorcise the lean, determined ghost of Timothy Fuller, with its everlasting adjuration to "let approbation and *affection* be so measured and adjusted as to have its *proper* place.")

Their educations complemented one another, his having been the traditional classical one provided at Harvard, augmented by his own extensive reading in English literature. Margaret, on the other hand, was immensely well read in German, French, and Italian literature, but lacked a thorough knowledge of the literature of her own language. The exchange was salutary for both of them: in the first few months of their acquaintance she lent him some of her biographical books on Goethe: he lent her, among other things, Coleridge's *Literary Remains* and volumes of Milton, Ben Jonson, and Carlyle. He persuaded her to read Chaucer, Herbert, and more Browne, and widened her acquaintance with Shakespeare, thus adding a much-needed dash of Anglo-Saxon salt to her heavy literary diet. She encouraged him to read more appreciatively the writers of Germany and France, particularly Goethe (whom he regarded with a mixture of admiration and puritanical distrust), and she introduced him to the works of George Sand.

Emerson found the emotional fervor which Margaret poured into their relationship rather threatening, and there were periods of mutual exasperation as well as benefit. Biographers have puzzled over the effect Emerson's friendship with Margaret must have had on his wife, who was of a sober and religious temperament and who remains a curiously indistinct figure in his life. But Lidian's place, though narrow, was evidently secure. The two women were friendly, though not intimate, and except for one incident (see chapter 9), Lidian seems to have been able to accept Margaret's close relationship with Waldo as no more exclusive of herself than Alcott's or Carlyle's. Insofar as the Fuller-Emerson friendship involved a female sensibility both passionate and suppressed, and insofar as it pitted "female" commitment against "male" independence, it was, as Perry Miller has termed it, a "sexual duel."[5] But to go beyond that, as at least one modern scholar has done, and suggest that Margaret was in love with Emerson,[6] is to risk perpetrating one of our twentieth-century vulgarities. In the first place, other friends of Emerson, including Caroline Sturgis and George and Sophia Ripley, complained of his inability to commit himself in friendship. In the second place, Margaret had learned to sublimate her sexual feelings early in life, and this lent additional intensity to her friendships with people of both sexes. Her relationship with Emerson in this respect was little different from several others, notably those with James Freeman Clarke and Anna Barker.

Margaret's long-awaited meeting with Emerson was finally brought about by the intercession of several friends—Hedge, Elizabeth Peabody, and Miss Martineau—but the timing was probably Miss Martineau's. She may have asked Emerson, as a particular kindness, to invite Margaret to Concord when she and Mrs. Farrar set sail for England. At any rate, that is when Margaret came, to spend a fortnight which lengthened into three weeks. The visit began inauspiciously, with misgivings on the part of the Emersons, who had heard the usual rumors about Margaret's "disdain" for other people. Emerson's first sight of her was not reassuring:

> She had a face and frame that would indicate fulness and tenacity of life. She was rather under the middle height;* her complexion was fair, with strong fair hair. She was then, as always, carefully and

* Emerson's is the only description I have seen in which Margaret is said to be shorter than average.

becomingly dressed, and of ladylike self-possession. For the rest, her appearance had nothing prepossessing. Her extreme plainness,— a trick of incessantly opening and shutting her eyelids,—the nasal tone of her voice,—all repelled; and I said to myself, we shall never get far.

Margaret had long been accustomed to this initial repulsion in people she met, and if she really set about overcoming it she invariably succeeded. Resorting now to that talent for satire which had intrigued and scandalized Cambridge a few years before, she soon had Emerson laughing "more than he liked." (He did not like laughing at all; he had an odd idea that it made him lose control over the muscles in his face.) By the end of the afternoon he had been unwillingly but irrevocably won over:

> I was, at that time, an eager scholar of ethics, and had tasted the sweets of solitude and stoicism, and I found something profane in the hours of amusing gossip into which she drew me, and, when I returned to my library, had much to think of the crackling of thorns under a pot.[7]

But he concluded, when he knew her better, that there was little real malice in her mimicry:

> This rumor was spread abroad, that she was sneering, scoffing, critical, disdainful of humble people, and of all but the intellectual. I had heard it whenever she was named. It was a superficial judgment. Her satire was only the pastime and necessity of her talent, the play of superabundant animal spirits.[8]

Her satire was indeed a "superabundance of animal spirits"— more so, one suspects, than Emerson could comprehend. He did see that it was one facet of an extraordinarily generous and many-sided nature, which people of more stolid and predictable temperament insisted on characterizing by a single trait. The opposite side of her satire was that sensitivity which made her "the wedding guest, to whom the long-pent story must be told."[9] Total strangers would confide the half-buried tragedies of their lives to her after an hour's acquaintance, sensing the breadth of her sympathy. Her reputation for satire was closely linked to her reputation for intellectual pride, of which she was certainly guilty. But what Emerson called "Margaret's mountainous ME" was in part a consciously adopted defense. She had to value herself too much if she were to succeed in a society which valued women so little, and it would be interesting to know how many of the rumors about her coldness toward others originated with those whom she had bested in an argument.

Emerson, tolerant as he was, had his own prejudices about women, which like Mrs. Farrar's are significant of the steady undercurrent of opposition she encountered in even her most valued friends. It should be remembered, too, that Emerson was the most important influence in her life except for her father. Unlike Timothy Fuller, Emerson did like women of intelligence and spirit, and he found "docility" rather boring. There were two remarkably accomplished women in his own family, Sarah Alden Ripley and Mary Moody Emerson; but he admired Mrs. Ripley's reticence almost as much as he admired her intellect, and his attitude toward Aunt Mary as the years went by became tinged with exasperated indulgence accorded eccentric old ladies. It was, of course, a basic article of his philosophical creed that all human beings should be allowed to develop in perfect freedom, but on a personal level he did not like to be anticipated in a discussion, receiving ideas that should have been his own from the mouths of others. This must have irritated him doubly in a woman: "A woman's strength," he writes, "is not masculine, but is the unresistible might of weakness." [10] He believed that the male mind was essentially active and creative, the female merely passive, and that the best and brightest female minds would always be inferior to the best and brightest male minds. He believed, too, that women's minds or emotions (both, probably) had less substance and staying power ("The man loves hard wood, the woman loves pitch-pine"),[11] and that "women have less accurate measure of time than men." [12] After Margaret left in August he mused, "How rarely can a female mind be impersonal. Sarah R[ipley] is wonderfully free from egotism of place and time and blood. Margaret F. by no means so free. . . . What shall I say of Aunt Mary?''[13] What is important here is not so much the observation on Margaret's egotism, but the fact that he expected to encounter it, along with various other negative traits, in every woman he met.

But Emerson's prejudices, of which Margaret was only partially aware, did not prevent her from making him a ''saint in her oratory.'' And thanks to Lidian's hospitality, the Concord household became an invaluable retreat for her. Lidian was an efficient manager, and she did not have to stint. Better off than the Fullers, the Emersons employed three servants, and in a house with no children (Lidian was pregnant with her first baby), this meant that all the domestic apparatus was practically out of sight. At six in the morning Waldo retired to his study with his coffee, and Margaret too was free to work undisturbed in her own room, drawing freely on the well-stocked library which contained, among other things, a fifty-volume set of Goethe. Dinner for four (Emerson's mother lived with them) was served at one or two, and the rest of the afternoon might be spent in walking, visiting, or reading aloud. After early evening tea there would be several hours of spirited conversation, in which they might be joined by Elizabeth Hoar, the cool, clear-minded girl who had been Charles Emerson's fiancée, or by Emerson's step-grandfather, Ezra Ripley, who was the Unitarian pastor.

On August 2 Emerson invited Bronson Alcott to spend the day. Golden-haired and blue-eyed, he arrived like some Old World holy man, shaking the dust of Boston from his feet, and carrying some of the iniquities of Boston on his shoulders. His Temple School was regarded with increasing suspicion, and murmurings were being heard against him. Two years earlier it had been welcomed by Boston liberals as an alternative to the available schools, which were conducted in the old-fashioned recite-by-rote method, with liberal use of the ferule. But Alcott's educational method was far more radical than his supporters had realized. It was based on a belief that children were the purest of all human beings, having come so recently from God (Wordsworth's ''Ode to Immortality'' was a frequent topic of discussion in Alcott's classroom). It was the priestly duty of the schoolmaster, Alcott believed, to encour-

age this spark of divinity by allowing children to express themselves freely, and so classes were conducted by a conversational
method, and no topic was banned. Boston parents were beginning
to wonder what depths of corruption this could lead to, and the
fact that most of the discussions were based on the Bible was far
from reassuring. The growing criticism bothered Alcott not at all;
he had an angelic disregard for opinions that differed from his
own. But now Elizabeth Peabody, who had worked as his assistant
since 1834 and who had recorded many of the conversations for
his forthcoming book, had begun to worry over the effect of the
rumors on her future teaching career and her maidenly reputation,
and in a fit of panic had resigned.* This was a real setback, for he
did not see how he could find anyone else brave enough to replace
her.

Unlike most people who encountered Alcott face to face,
Margaret did not take him for either a saint or a fool. She could
not help but admire his gentleness, his courage, and his faith in
human nature, unshakable despite the fact that he had been
hounded out of several school districts already and must suspect
that there would be no permanent home for him in Boston. She
could not but applaud his theory, although she felt it to be imperfect. Even with its imperfections it opposed all that had stifled and
baffled her in her own childhood. Before Alcott returned to Boston
he had asked her to take Miss Peabody's place; realizing that if she
had to teach, there was no better place to do it, she agreed. It was
arranged that she would come to Boston in December, so that she
could spend the autumn in Groton helping her mother prepare for
winter.

At home she was partially relieved of her heavy responsibilities
by the arrival of Eugene, who had left his tutoring job and decided
to read law. Despite Uncle Abraham, enough money was found to
send young Arthur to Leicester Academy, where his father had
taught thirty-five years before. Ellen was sent to Cambridge, and
Richard was persuaded to remain at home for a while, with the
promise that eventually means would be found to complete his ed-

---

* She and Alcott remained on good terms, and she subsequently published her own book
about the school, *Record of a School,* in the hope of vindicating both Alcott and herself.

ucation. Margaret saw Emerson again only briefly, if at all, during these months. In September the Groton pastor, with a seeming perversity born more of indifference than malice, for the second time invited Emerson to preach while she was away. ("While I was with you you very justly corrected me for using too strong expressions on some subjects," she wrote to Emerson, "but there is no exaggeration in saying—I *must* be allowed to say that I *detest* Mr. Robinson at this moment.")[14]

In December Margaret took rooms in Boston at her Uncle Henry's home, where she had briefly lived while she attended Dr. Park's school, and undertook her duties at the Temple School. The first few weeks were very difficult. Her headaches seldom left her, and she was puzzled and hurt by the sudden coldness of several old friends, who may have been expressing their disapproval of her association with Alcott. She found herself trying to overcome a wave of distaste for her favorite authors, now that she was forced to talk about them for profit. Nevertheless, she adhered to a rigorous schedule.

Every morning she taught languages to the thirty-seven boys and girls at the school. Sarah Clarke, a gifted painter whose independence of mind resembled Margaret's own, joined her to teach drawing. In the afternoon she sat to one side of the classroom and recorded as much as she could of the conversations, as Elizabeth Peabody and her sister Sophia had before her. These records would be published as *Conversations with Children on the Gospels,* Volume I appearing in December as Margaret began teaching. Volume 2 would be published in February.

The atmosphere and physical setting were remarkably like those of a modern progressive school. Particular attention was paid to abolishing the visual dreariness of the typical classroom. The room was carpeted, with white wainscotting and tall, arched windows. Scattered about in niches were plaster busts of Socrates, Shakespeare, Milton, and Sir Walter Scott, casts of "Silence," "A Child Aspiring," and—oddly enough—Bacchus riding a barrel. A bas-relief of Christ hung over the master's desk. There were bookcases and pictures and a sofa for visitors. The students' desks, arranged around the perimeter facing the walls, had movable chairs so that the children could gather in a semicircle around the teacher.

Some subjects, like arithmetic and geography, had to be taught mostly by conventional methods, but free discussion was used whenever possible. A typical language arts lesson might begin with reading aloud a passage from the Bible or *Pilgrim's Progress*. The children would then be asked to spell and define some of the words, and conversation would proceed from there. Of course, the "spontaneity" of which Alcott was so proud was relative. The teacher's bias was perfectly evident to the children, who produced, to his unfailing delight, statements of the most severe Platonic-Christian asceticism: "In the Bible some one says, *I die daily*," said Alcott. "Do you understand that?" "Yes," piped the children, "it means you daily go more and more away from the senses, into the inward life." [15] But even with this reservation, Margaret was impressed by the free atmosphere of the classroom, and by the alertness of the children as compared with her own brothers and sister, to whom learning had been a wasteland of boredom which no enthusiasm of her own could animate.

But it was the conversational teaching of adults, not children, which really interested her. Before coming to Boston she had decided to supplement her income by giving evening lessons to women in her own rooms, reading in translation the German and Italian poets. In the advertisement Margaret prepared for these courses she says that she has been impeded in her own studies by lack of oral instruction, but hopes to be able to relieve other women of similar embarrassments. She offers a course of twenty-four lessons, two a week, for a total charge of $15.[16] This is the first evidence of that concern for women's education which would lead to the more famous Conversations of 1839–42 and the writing of *Woman in the Nineteenth Century*. With a sadness and resentment sharpened by her own experience, she saw all around her women struggling to acquire, alone and in odd hours, the knowledge of languages, literature, and history which was available almost as a matter of course to men of the same aptitude and background. She saw them slip farther and farther behind, their tentative self-confidence undermined by the solitude and the difficulty of their task, eventually to give up and reinforce the preju-

dice common even among women themselves that the smaller size
of their skulls meant that their brains were inferior. Now and then
a rare woman succeeded in spite of all obstacles: in Massachusetts
one of these was Sarah Alden Ripley, wife of Emerson's step-
uncle Samuel Ripley. She helped her husband keep a school in
Waltham and was thought by Emerson to be one of the two or
three best Greek scholars in the country. But for every Sarah
Ripley there were a hundred anonymous women with a capacity
for learning no less than hers, who fell by the wayside. Even Mrs.
Ripley's scholarship gained her nothing but the grudging respect of
the local *cognoscenti,* and it is perhaps worth noting that the
Ripleys' school was open only to boys.

But the eighteenth century was gone, with its paradoxical tendency to ignore, even while the new wave of humanism crested
into revolution, the vestigial existence of medieval hierarchies of
all kinds: social, religious, and sexual. In the new century the
movement to abolish one of the grossest abuses of humanity led
slowly to a recognition of others. The abolitionist movement was
gaining strength, and a great proportion of that strength came from
the persistence and courage of women. This had nothing to do
with education per se, but it had a great deal to do with men's respect for women and women's respect for themselves. In 1836 the
Grimké sisters, Angelina and Sarah, overcoming scruples im-
planted by a lifetime spent in southern polite society, were beginning to speak out against slavery in larger and larger gatherings, and
in the following year they would tour Massachusetts, braving public ridicule and leaving the air behind them murky with barroom
epithets. Women were learning that they had the strength and intelligence to change the established order, but with rare exceptions
institutions of higher learning remained closed to them.*

With her German literature class Margaret read works of Schiller, Goethe, Lessing, Tieck, and Richter. With the class in Italian
literature she read Tasso, Petrarch, Ariosto, and all of the *Divine*

---

* Mt. Holyoke, which would open the following year, would offer courses on the collegiate
level but would still be called a seminary. It would not gain full collegiate status until 1893.
Oberlin, founded in 1833 and open to all, would in 1837 with great reluctance free women
students from the requirement that they take a special, less demanding course carefully
designed for their weak little heads. See Eleanor Flexner, *Century of Struggle,* pp. 29–36.

Comedy. Of all her students she required that they be able to discuss in some depth what they had read. In addition she taught a reading knowledge of German to one class, counting herself well satisfied when, at the end of three months, they could easily read twenty pages at a session. And she found time for several individual private pupils, including one blind boy to whom she taught Latin orally, supplementing the language instruction with readings from Shakespeare's histories and the works of various British historians. She did this every day for ten weeks and pronounced it interesting but fatiguing, as well she might.

One evening a week she devoted to translating aloud, directly from the original, the works of de Wette and Herder for Dr. Channing, whose eyesight was failing and whose knowledge of German was imperfect. She had known Channing before only slightly, and had always been slightly in awe of him. She had been warned, too, that she would find him difficult to talk to, withdrawn behind a courteous reserve. But she found him free and approachable in his manner and unbiased in his opinions—indeed, she thought, fair-minded to a fault. It was not altogether in a complimentary spirit that she observed:

> Dr. C[hanning] takes in subjects more deliberately than is conceivable to us feminine people, with our habits of ducking, diving, or flying for truth. Doubtless, however, he makes better use of what he gets, and if his sympathies were livelier he would not view certain truths in so steady a light.[17]

It was a comment not only on "masculine" and "feminine" thinking, but on two eras. Timothy Fuller had belonged to the worst of the previous century, as Channing belonged to the best of it, but Margaret belonged to a time when the value of "feminine" thought—that part of the consciousness variously termed "intuition," "reason" (in the Coleridgean sense), or "imagination"—was being accorded a new respect by poets and philosophers alike. It was only now becoming possible for an Emerson to maintain, as none of his forebears would have dared, that "a foolish consistency is the hobgoblin of little minds," and to many readers of Emerson's essays the phrase "ducking, diving, or flying for truth" seems apt. Margaret Fuller regarded herself as a classicist and had no patience with any kind of intellectual sloppiness, but her remark on Channing shows her awareness of the disadvantages of traditional inductive thought. There is a strong implication that Channing should *both* possess "livelier sympathies" and retain his ability to "view certain truths" in a steady light. Margaret looked for an androgynous balance of sensibility and discipline in the minds she met, and she was equally critical of an excess of one or the other. That she was able to bring this perceptiveness to bear on literature would be the particular strength of her best criticism, in a time when the elderly survivors of the Enlightenment and the young ragtag-and-bobtail of Romanticism were drawn into opposing camps, leaving the middle ground very sparsely defended.

Margaret's reading sessions with Channing went on slowly, for the good preacher never closed his door to visitors, and he and Margaret were constantly interrupted. She could not regret this. Emerson, who was delivering a series of lectures on "The Philosophy of History," was a frequent guest. Alcott came, talking indefatigably for hours on one single, endlessly polished theme and confirming Margaret's early impression of him:

> I wish I could define my distrust of Mr. Alcott's mind; I constantly think him one-sided, without being able to see where the fault lies. There is something in his view of every subject, something in his philosophy which revolts either my common-sense or my prejudices, I cannot be sure which.[18]

Lydia Maria Child—eight years older than Margaret, an established writer and deeply committed abolitionist—was a close friend of Channing's at this time. Elizabeth Peabody was often there, as was George Ripley, a Unitarian minister somewhat older than Margaret who was finding the pulpit too confining, as Emerson had before him, and who was about to venture into publishing. She met the mercurial, often bearish nineteen-year-old poet William Ellery Channing (one of the doctor's nephews; another, William Henry, had long been a friend). She became better acquainted with Channing's colleague at the Federal Street Church, Jonathan Phillips, and was introduced to Richard Henry Dana the elder, whose literary views she no doubt would have found too subjective even if he had not called Goethe a "coxcombical pretender." [19]

Conversation at Channing's ranged over topics that would soon be associated with "Transcendentalism," although the term was not yet in general use in America. They included the nature of immortality and the personality of God; the new interest in astrology and the occult; the relative merits of the English Lake poets; the lack of inspiration among the New England clergy; and the esthetic backwardness of the New England people, which Henry Hedge termed their "want of a secular religion." Channing himself was usually on the conservative side in these discussions. His early sermons, which had shaken the Unitarian church to its very toes, were now regarded as rather stuffy by men like Ripley and Theodore Parker, and he had outraged the abolitionists by his advocacy of gradualism in the elimination of slavery. Margaret realized, though, that most of these men (except Alcott, who had sprung full-blown, so to speak, from the hills of Connecticut) owed to Channing both their ideas and the churches in which they expressed them. She blamed Ripley and the other young radicals for their occasional impatient mutterings against the older man. Channing himself seemed scarcely aware of their disaffection and went on dispensing his own sane and balanced views to anyone who came, foreseeing among other things the dissolution of the Union and the annexation of Texas, and lamenting that his young country was being forced into a false and unseasonable maturity.

Besides teaching five days and two or three evenings a week and translating for Channing, Margaret attended Emerson's lectures and heard a variety of other speakers, renewed her acquaintance with her old Boston friends, and went to as many concerts (sometimes two an evening) as possible. Not surprisingly, her headaches plagued her more than they had before. It is difficult to tell from her letters and journals how often they occurred, but they followed the invigorating conversations she loved, and there were periods in her life when they lasted for weeks at a time. They were severe, usually causing her to take to her bed at least temporarily. Her brother Richard says that at times she could barely keep from screaming.[20] But on the other hand, she seldom seems to have lost much time from her customary activities, and even when she was in bed she would read and converse with the feverish brilliance of an opera heroine picturesquely expiring from consumption. She herself believed that "pain [gave] tension to her powers."[21]

It seems unlikely that the headaches were caused by her near-sightedness, since they were usually brought on by conversation, not by reading. Margaret herself referred to them as "nervous" and blamed the psychological and intellectual rigors of her education and the fact that she never had enough fresh air and exercise as a child. Psychosomatic illness was common in the mid-nineteenth century, as evidenced by the various ailments of Coleridge, both the Carlyles, Miss Martineau, Mrs. Browning, and (probably) Margaret's own mother. But here and there among her papers are hints of a possible organic origin: the headaches were sometimes accompanied by nosebleeds and were actually relieved by the medical practice of bloodletting, however barbarous that may seem. Margaret associates their onset with that "determination of blood to the head" which spoiled her complexion in adolescence. She had occasionally suffered from childhood convulsions. Frequently in later years her headaches migrated to her spine. Two acquaintances, Caroline Healey Dall[22] and Georgianna Bruce Kirby,[23] claim that Margaret had a curvature of the spine. Mrs. Kirby asserts that the curvature was caused by Margaret's Groton illness (which she says was typhoid), and that it was cured in 1845 by the mesmerist Theodore Léger. Afterward, she says, Margaret was three inches taller and her shoulders were "perfectly flat and similar." Margaret herself once referred to the relief Léger brought to "the distorted bones."[24] But it is strange that no one else mentions it.

From such a tangle it is difficult to extract the truth, but possibly a modern physician might recognize a physical disorder in the more verifiable of Margaret's symptoms. Regardless of their cause, the headaches were a handicap throughout her adult life. She tried to maintain toward them the attitude one takes toward an unavoidable nuisance: "It is but a bad head,—as bad as if I were a great man!'' she wrote in the spring of 1837. ''I am not entitled to so bad a head by anything I have done.''[25]

She had in fact done a great deal that winter, but the thing she most wanted to do, the book on Goethe, remained almost untouched. ''But,'' she wrote, ''I have studied and thought about it much. It grows in my mind with everything that does grow there. My friends in Europe have sent me the needed books on the subject, and I am now beginning to work in good earnest.''[26] But a series of events was under way which would upset her plans for remaining in Boston. With the publication of *Conversations on the Gospels,* the feeling against Alcott had risen to a crescendo. The fact that he habitually referred to Christ simply as Jesus, together with several mild hints to the children that babies were born by women and not found under cabbage leaves, had set up a righteous clamor even among Unitarians. A scathing review in Nathan Hale's *Daily Advertiser* was followed by another in the *Courier* in which the editor declared *Conversations* the most obscene and indecent book yet published in America and suggested that Alcott be prosecuted for blasphemy. The most telling malediction came from the Rev. Andrews Norton, high priest of the old-style Unitarianism and arch-foe of Channing and Emerson. Norton pronounced the book ''one-third absurd, one-third blasphemous, and one-third obscene.''[27]

Able defenses written by Orestes Brownson, Ralph Waldo Emerson, James Freeman Clarke, and Elizabeth Peabody could not save Alcott from the brimstone wrath that now descended on him. Emerson wrote to offer comfort: ''I hate to have all the little dogs barking at you, for you have something better to do than to attend to them; but every beast must do after its kind, and why not these? And you will hold by yourself and presently forget them.''[28] Margaret could not defend him in the press, but she did defend him privately against people who should have known better. One of these was Henry Hedge:

> Why is it that I hear you are writing a piece to ''cut up'' Mr. Alcott? I do not believe you are going to cut up Mr. Alcott. There are plenty of fish in the net created solely for markets, etc.;—no need to try your knife on a dolphin like him. . . . If you were here I am sure

that you would feel as I do, and that your wit would never lend its patronage to the ugly blinking owls, who are now hooting from their snug tenements, overgrown rather with nettles than with ivy, at this star of purest ray serene.[29]

Another attack had come from an equally unsuspected and far more damaging source. Harriet Martineau, returning to England, had written an account of her visit to the United States titled *Society in America*. It was not without insight into American life, but it was distorted by her pet biases, necessitarianism and abolitionism. As an abolitionist Alcott might have merited Miss Martineau's sympathy, but his mystical idealism offended her to her heart's core. Having spent only one afternoon in his school, she wrote:

[Alcott] presupposes his little pupils possessed of all truth in philosophy and morals, and [believes] his business is to bring it out into expression, to help the outward life to conform to the inner light and especially to learn of these enlightened babes with all humility. Large exposures might be made of the mischief this gentleman is doing to his pupils by relaxing their bodies, pampering their imaginations, over-stimulating the consciences of some and hardening those of others, and by his extraordinary management, offering them every inducement to falsehood and hypocrisy.[30]

The rebuke Margaret sent, though temperate, was characteristically frank. It damaged her friendship with Harriet Martineau far more than she realized at the time.

A want of soundness, of habits of patient investigation, of completeness, of arrangement, are felt throughout the book; and, for all its fine descriptions of scenery, breadth of reasoning and generous daring, I cannot be happy in it, because it is not worthy of my friend, and I think a few months given to ripen it, to balance, compare, and mellow, would have made it so. . . . Would your heart, could you but investigate the matter, approve such overstatement, such a crude, intemperate tirade as you have been guilty of about Mr. Alcott,—a true and noble man, a philanthropist, whom a true and noble woman, also a philanthropist, should have delighted to honor; whose disinterested and resolute efforts, for the redemption of poor humanity, all independent and faithful minds should sustain, since the "broadcloth" vulgar will be sure to assail them; a philosopher, worthy of the palmy times of ancient Greece; a man whom Carlyle and Berkely (*sic*), whom you so uphold, would delight to honor; a man whom the worldlings of Boston hold in as much horror as the worldlings of ancient Athens did Socrates. They smile to hear their verdict confirmed from the other side of the Atlantic, by their censor, Harriet Martineau.[31]

Even Alcott was shaken by the virulence of the attacks against him, but he kept his school going with a handful of students that remained. Not until 1839 would he provoke the *coup de grâce* by enrolling a little mulatto girl; but in 1837 he was almost bankrupt and, forced to auction off the school furniture and many of his own books, he could no longer pay Margaret's salary.

So she was once again uprooted. But the four short months she had spent in Boston had been a period of concentrated learning that contrasted sharply with the solitary book-learning of the Groton years. She was now back in the real world, free to effect some change in it if she could. Her first attempt at classroom teaching had been more successful than she had thought it would be, and in Alcott's school and her own adult classes she had discovered how to translate the literary ideals she had absorbed from her reading into an educational method which held, she thought, particular promise for the teaching of young women. She had Alcott to thank for this, and for the new sense of independence she had gained from earning her own income. Through Dr. Channing, too, she had met a number of people who would later be important in her life. She had listened a great deal, and in fact had been more silent in company than she ever was likely to be again. "I have learned much and thought little, an operation which seems paradoxical and *is* true," she wrote Hedge. "I faint with desire to think and surely shall, the first opportunity, but some outward requisition is ever knocking at the door of my mind and I am as ill placed as regards a chance to think as a haberdasher's prentice or the President of Harvard University."[32]

In April she prepared to leave Boston. She had two alternatives for the future. The first, and by far the most appealing, was an offer from George Ripley, who was planning to publish a series titled "Specimens of Foreign Literature." He asked Margaret to complete her book on Goethe for the series, promising her generous terms on publication. But neither she nor her family could do without the income she could earn by teaching, and she hesitated to tie her hopes for a future income to the vagaries of publishing. If Ripley had been able to pay her in advance, she would have accepted, but Ripley was just setting out on the venture himself and had nothing to spare. She reluctantly turned down the offer, but did in fact accept a less demanding invitation to translate, for the same series, Goethe's conversations with his secretary Eckermann. This much she believed she could do no matter what her teaching load was, and she hoped she would be able to work on the Goethe book at her own pace as well.

For bread labor she accepted an offer from a Mr. Hiram Fuller (no relation), who ran the Greene Street School in Providence and who claimed to be a disciple of Alcott. He was willing to pay her an unusually generous $1,000 a year, more than enough for her to support herself and contribute to her family's needs. She was to teach languages, only in the mornings, and she was promised a free hand with her classes. She could not refuse, much as she hated to leave Boston. She promised to begin teaching in Providence in June, made her farewell calls in Boston, and set off in the stage to Concord, which some early settlers, with remarkable foresight, had kindly placed midway between Boston and Groton.

VII

Providence

Margaret's Concord visit did not turn out to be the undisturbed idyl she had expected. She found her friend in rare conversational form, and their long discussions left her mind so stimulated that, always more or less insomnious, she had to give up hope of sleeping altogether. In a moment of weariness she thought of going home to Groton immediately, but to leave behind so rare and heady a mixture of ideas was unthinkable. Perhaps as a soporific, they read aloud to one another in the evening. Margaret read from Disraeli's *Vivian Gray* and again made Waldo laugh more than he liked. ("Beckendorf is a fine teaching that he who can once conquer his own face can have no further difficulty," he wrote in his journal.)[1] He in turn read to her in German, rather badly, and she ventured to criticize his pronunciation and more or less against his will gave him several lessons in improving it. When she went home on the fourth of May, she left several of her own German books behind.

A fortnight later she sent him, by way of introduction to some of her friends, a folder containing letters written by Sarah Clarke,

Anna Barker, and the Rev. William Eliot. It was the beginning of her effort not only to widen Emerson's circle of friends, in which she succeeded, but to change his view of friendship itself, in which she failed. They debated the subject vigorously over the years, for the most part with high good humor. It is not an exaggeration to say that for Margaret, especially after she had renounced hope of marriage, friendship was the *sine qua non* of life. She was blessed with a talent for it, and it was her only solid source of emotional support. She acknowledged happily her dependence on other people and theirs on her. Emerson, on the other hand, though affectionate toward his friends and family and always ready to demonstrate that affection by some generous act, valued self-sufficiency above all things and believed that each human soul was, of necessity, isolated. He believed that people, despite themselves, were "armed all over" with "subtle antagonisms," [2] and that "every man is an infinitely repellent orb, and holds his individual being on that condition." [3] At his most transcendental he saw friendships as mere steps in the progress of the soul, which are withdrawn when it has no further use for them. "Can I doubt that the facts and events and persons and personal relationships that now appertain to me will perish . . . utterly when the soul shall have exhausted their meaning and use?" [4] He wrote this a little more than a year after his second marriage, and six days before the birth of his son.

The debate gives us another insight into Emerson's rather complicated attitude toward women. *women* Once again it should be emphasized that this attitude (i.e., that women as *human beings* were entitled to full intellectual development, but as *women* should express that development in passive, noncompetitive ways) was representative of the thinking of most liberals. But in Emerson's view of friendship vs. isolation, or dependence vs. independence, the concept of manliness was very much bound up with the concept of self-reliance. He believed that women committed themselves too easily to relationships, that they gave themselves to them entirely but without "depth"—a distinction which is apparently clear in his own mind and which he does not explain. [5] He thought that if one involved oneself deeply with other people it reduced one's creativity (a quaint belief reminiscent of the warnings to Oriental men about "vital fluids"). It was manly to withhold oneself from such emotional extravagances; it was womanish and weak to indulge in them as Margaret did. He believed that women lived too much at the mercy of their emotions, and consequently were bound to be passive and lack the vitality necessary for creative work. With the complacency of a man who is having his prejudices confirmed before his very eyes, he watched Margaret repeatedly try to give her full attention and energy to "the children of the muse," only to rush "back again to persons, with a woman's devotion." [6] He saw the difficulty Margaret had with writing as the inescapable result of her having been born female, and she herself (as we shall see later) partially accepted this view. But that did not prevent her from accusing Emerson of being "commercial" in his friendships, and of valuing people only for the ideas they brought him, not for themselves.

By the time Emerson returned the folders of letters, with polite compliments, Margaret had left Groton for Providence. There she found sixty pupils, two other women teachers, and Mr. Fuller waiting to meet her, and the new building which was to house the school ready for dedication. Physically, at least, the Greene Street School conformed to Alcott's theory. The exterior design was of the neoclassical, one-story, becolumned and beporticoed type often imitated in this century by suburban banks. The inside was reminiscent of the Temple School, with a thickly carpeted floor and white walls finished in pink. Between the two main doors (one for boys, one for girls) stood a piano covered with a French shawl, and on either side of the master's desk was a tall vase which the students daily filled with fresh flowers.

Hiram Fuller had invited Alcott to speak at the dedication of the building, but Alcott, with characteristic altruism, had declined on the grounds that his participation might damage the school's reputation. Fuller then appealed to Emerson, who for Alcott's sake felt bound to accept, and accordingly the ceremony was performed with Emerson's reluctant help on the tenth of June. But as they talked with Fuller afterward it became apparent to both Emerson and Margaret that his adoption of Alcott's views was superficial.

Indeed, he naively confessed to Emerson that he was only planning to keep the school going until he could earn enough money to go abroad—which made Emerson, thinking of the deprivations Alcott and his family endured for the sake of the Temple School, even more sorry than before that he had come. When Margaret had a chance to talk to her pupils, she found that their minds were "absolutely torpid," although those who had previously been with Mr. Fuller were better off than those who had come from conventional schools. Somewhat disheartened (for she had twice as many pupils as she had had before), she tried to rise to the challenge. "There is room here, if I mistake not, for a great move in the cause of education, but whether it is I who am to help move, I cannot yet tell," she wrote early in July. "I sometimes think *yes,* because the plan is becoming so complete in my mind, ways and means are continually occurring to me, and so far as I have tried them, they seem to succeed." [7]

Some idea of the impression Margaret made on her students can be gained from several letters written by one of her older girls, who was about eighteen or nineteen. Arriving in December, she writes,

> . . . I love Miss Fuller already, but I fear her. I would not for a great deal offend her in any way. She is very strict, and I should think might be *very severe.*
> . . . She said it must not be our object to come and hear her talk. We might think it a delightful thing to her to talk to so many interesting auditors, but that was not the thing; she could not teach us so, *we* must talk and let her understand our minds.

A month later the same girl writes,

> Miss Fuller is as different from the other teachers as you can imagine. I love her, but in a different way. I consider it a very great privilege to be under her instruction. She is very critical, and sometimes cuts us into bits. When she cuts us all in a lump, it is quite pleasant, for she is quite witty; but woe to the one whom she cuts by herself! I do not know what she would say to this letter. I would not have her see it for five dollars! [8]

Clearly the love Margaret inspired in her pupils, which seems to have been universal, had nothing to do with any feeling of *bonhomie*. She was not much older than they were, but she had a clear idea of her own place and theirs. The conversational method was not particularly democratic, and the standards it set were higher, not lower, than the ones they were used to.

Margaret's day usually began at 4:30 or 5:00, when she rose, washed, and dressed, which took until 6:00. (We should remember the cold sponge baths, the elaborate coiffure and the jars of hairpins, the layers of petticoats and various rows of hooks and buttons this procedure involved.) Then she studied until breakfast at 6:30. A short walk from her lodgings brought her to school at 8:30, where she taught not only languages but composition, elocution, history, ethics, poetry, and "natural philosophy." Home for dinner at 1:30, she lay down afterward until 3:00, and the hours until tea were used for studying and writing. She spent the evening walking or in social activities. Into the three or four hours in the afternoon she fitted lesson preparation, reading, her Eckermann translation, her work on Goethe, and a voluminous correspondence.

She found Providence oppressive. It was already a substantial commercial center, and she had to walk through many blocks of paved streets before she could find any expanse of green grass and trees. "Here," she lamented in a letter to Alcott, "is the hostile element of money-getting, with but little counterpoise." [9] She escaped north whenever she could. In August there was a three-week recess, part of which she hoped to spend in Concord. She had been "in an irreligious state of mind," she wrote Emerson, "a little misanthropic and sceptical [*sic*] about the existence of any real communication between human beings. I hear constantly in my heart that text of yours 'O *my friends,* there are no friends' but to me it is a paralyzing conviction. Surely, we are very unlike the Gods in 'their seats of eternal tranquillity'—that we need illusions so much to keep us in action." [10]

On her way to visit her "dear *no friends,*" the Emersons, she was in the audience at Harvard when Waldo delivered to the Phi Beta Kappa society his address on "The American Scholar," which confirmed his reputation as an intransigent radical among the Old Guard, if any of them had had any doubts after the publication of *Nature*. He began tamely enough by saying that it was time America freed herself from a slavish imitation of European culture; this was indisputable, and it was comfortable for each of the assembled scholars to believe that it was everyone else who was slavish, and not himself. But then Emerson went on to challenge the most sacred assumptions of scholarship itself, placing the individual's own experience above books, which he said were only records of the experience of *other* individuals. Books were for a scholar's idle times; it was only when he had the courage to leave them behind and trust his own vision of the world that he could grow from a mere thinker into "Man Thinking." The scholar should learn from nature, "whose laws are the laws of his own mind." He should learn from his own experience: "So much only of life as I know by experience, so much of the wilderness have I vanquished and planted, or so far have I extended my being, my dominion." [11]

It was at once a declaration of national literary independence and an assertion, like Channing's and Alcott's, of the worth and dignity of the individual as opposed to the heavy, mechanical structure of tradition. While by no means denying the importance of history, Emerson insisted that it was a living, organic process, being formed at that moment by everyone present. Not many of the distinguished gentlemen who heard him were willing to accept such a responsibility. Emerson was politely fêted afterward, but he left not a few scholars perplexed and angry, fairly certain that they had had their beards tweaked in their own house. His friends, on the other hand, thought they had never heard him present his ideas more forcefully. The speech was a perfect rallying point for a meeting in Concord, the following day, of the group which would soon be popularly known as "the Transcendentalists."

The group had been formed the year before at the suggestion of Henry Hedge, and because it only met when Hedge came down from Bangor it was called "Hedge's Club," or sometimes "The Symposium" (after Plato) by its members. Originally a casual gathering of liberal Unitarian clergymen, it had been widened to include Alcott, who Emerson said was a "God-made priest." And really there seemed to be no reason to confine it to clergymen, or even to men, and on this occasion it was further enlarged to include four women: Margaret Fuller, Sarah Alden Ripley, Elizabeth Hoar, and Lidian Emerson.

As early as 1836, in the *Christian Examiner,* Ripley had hailed the coming of a "class of persons, who desire a reform in the prevailing philosophy of the day. These are called the Transcendentalists—because they believe in an order of truths which transcends the sphere of the external senses." [12] This was certainly the philosophical bond which united the otherwise diverse members of Hedge's Club, but at first they hesitated to apply the term Transcendentalists to themselves. It had come to be used by outsiders in a derisive sense, as indicating both metaphysical abstruseness and intellectual elitism, and some of that connotation lingers even today, in spite of the fact that few of the American Transcendentalists were particularly learned in metaphysics: the term was borrowed from Kant's *Critique of Pure Reason,* which many of them had never read. But through the mediation of Coleridge, whose distinction between "Reason" and "Understanding" was based on Kant's *Vernunft* and *Verstandt,* the term "transcendental" had been introduced into the English language as pertaining to the intuitive part of human consciousness, which to Coleridge was the root of poetic imagination and moral sensitivity and imitated, on a finite scale, the creative power of God. From Coleridge's celebration of this divine element in human consciousness, from such German philosophy as they had read, and from Channing's refutations of Calvin, each of the American Transcendentalists derived a philosophical and religious stance that seemed, superficially, quite distinct from those of the others. F. Henry Hedge, James Freeman Clarke, Convers Francis, and several of the other Unitarians remained within the Channingite wing of the church. Emerson abandoned the church as anachronistic and envisioned man and nature as a single, glorious, outward expression of an all-pervasive Deity. Alcott basically shared this view, but emphasized man at the expense of nature and accepted the Judeo-Christian concept of a personal God. George Ripley, like Emerson

Brook Farm

rejecting traditional church doctrine, retained a Christian belief in community which would soon be translated into practice at Brook Farm.

What united them was the value they placed on the suprarational and imaginative element in consciousness and a belief that through this element the human mind could realize its highest spiritual potential and could indeed become godlike. Their individual beliefs about how this could be attained varied from the humanistic (Ripley, W. H. Channing, Orestes Brownson) to the mystical (Emerson, Thoreau). But they shared a disenchantment with nineteenth-century Western man, who they thought had become spiritually cramped by an obsession with getting and spending and by a set of outmoded social and religious conventions. They felt keenly the growing alienation of human beings from nature and each other, and they thought that in America, of all places, this alienation could be reversed.

The membership of the Transcendental Club was fluid; there were fourteen present at that September meeting at Emerson's, some of whom would not attend future meetings. Emerson, Alcott, Hedge, and Ripley formed a continuing nucleus; others who came more or less regularly included James Freeman Clarke, when he was in Boston; Elizabeth Peabody; Convers Francis, professor at the Harvard Divinity School and brother of Lydia Maria Child; Cyrus Bartol and John Sullivan Dwight, both recent Divinity School graduates; and the socialist publisher of the *Boston Quarterly Review*, Orestes Brownson—a volatile Unitarian who had already traveled in the front door and out the back door of Presbyterianism and Universalism, and who would presently forsake Unitarianism in its turn to rest in the bosom of Rome. A valuable addition to the group when he came was Theodore Parker, an impressively learned, uncompromising radical who, unlike Ripley, chose to remain within the church and shake it vigorously now and then.

Margaret Fuller belonged to this group by virtue of her rebellion against the past and her belief in the possibility of change. By the very fact that she dared to break out of the role assigned to women—dared, moreover, with flags flying, in an open defiance that made few concessions to decorum—she affirmed the new belief in the spiritual worth of the individual. Hers was ostensibly a social rather than a religious rebellion, but underlying it was the religious statement of her equality in the sight of God. That she, as a woman, and Alcott, as an educator, were included in the club can be taken as an indication of the ways in which what had begun as religious speculation was now affecting people's lives on all levels.

Margaret's own religious beliefs were neither complicated nor radical; she was probably closer to James Freeman Clarke in this respect than to any of the others. She believed in a loving, anthropomorphic God, although at this point in her life she did not believe He intervened in individual lives. Like her mother, she believed in a real heaven with real souls in it, and she thought that she and everyone else except a few of the very wicked were going there. She believed in the improvement of society based on the spiritual renewal of the individual, but she did not think society was perfectible. She believed that her own country, because of its vitality and idealism and its very youth and formlessness, held the best promise for such improvement. She admired and sometimes caught a transitory glow from Emerson's mysticism, but ultimately she found his idea of the Deity too cold and his idea of immortality too vague. She loved nature, but was essentially alienated from it and could function at her best only among people. To accuse her of being unworldly and impractical, as many have (beginning with Harriet Martineau), is to speak of her almost as if she were her own exact opposite, but this accusation was leveled indiscriminately at the group en masse, not excluding the most active social reformers.

Another popular notion (strongest, perhaps, among those whose acquaintance with Transcendentalism was limited to Alcott) was that the Transcendentalists scorned creature comforts, and in any case were too busy discussing metaphysics ever to bother themselves with the ordinary, humble pleasures of daily living. Nothing could be further from the truth; these were, after all, among the first Americans to be liberated from the belief that anything pleasant must be sinful. Lidian Emerson, although she enjoyed a good

discussion, deserved her reputation as a skillful manager and boun-
tiful hostess, and when her guests gathered for the midday meal at
the September meeting they found the table loaded down with
beef, boiled mutton with caper sauce, ham, tongue, corn, beans,
tomatoes, macaroni, cucumbers, lettuce, applesauce, puddings,
custards, fruit, and nuts. Whatever twinges they suffered afterward
had nothing to do with guilt.

It was a Margaret rested and invigorated by such company, and
well fortified with Lidian's food, who wrote to her mother from
Concord urging her to resist the increasingly dictatorial control
Abraham Fuller exerted over the family's income. Insisting that
further education of the children was extravagant, he had flatly
refused to allow them money for that purpose for the coming year.
Margaret urged her mother to go ahead and prepare all the children
for school, selling livestock if necessary to pay the bills, but it was
for her sixteen-year-old sister that she was most concerned. Ellen
had had no schooling except what Margaret had given her, and
now Abraham wanted to send her off as a governess. Rather than
allow this, Margaret said, she would take Ellen to Providence with
her and find some way to pay her tuition out of her own pocket,
giving up her own portion of the family income, moving to
cheaper lodgings, and taking in private pupils if necessary. "She
shall not be treated in this shameful way, bereft of proper advan-
tages and plagued and cramped in the May of life," [13] she fumed,
and for once her mother's spirit matched her own: Mrs. Fuller had
already written a crisp letter of defiance to her brother-in-law.
Ellen did spend a short period with Margaret that winter, though it
is not clear whether she attended the Greene Street School.

Soon after Margaret returned to Providence, James Freeman
Clarke stopped there for a day or two on his way back to Louisville from Boston. Together they visited a "somnambulist," who
claimed to have second sight and who did tell Clarke some
things about a friend in the West which later proved to be true.
American cities were full of practitioners of this sort around the
middle of the century, and interest in "animal magnetism" (hypnosis), phrenology, astrology, and various other kinds of occult or
psychic powers was high. Hypnosis was a demonstrated fact, un-

accounted for by science, and it lent credibility to other inexplicable powers, with which it was often confused: the woman whom Margaret and Clarke visited, for example, also claimed to be a hypnotist, and Clarke urged Margaret to have herself hypnotized against headache, but she for some reason refused.

Believing in a universe in which everything, beginning with their own souls, was intimately touched by a divine animating spirit, and uninhibited by any great reverence for science and logic—although they respected them—some members of the Transcendentalist circle were keenly interested in various exotic forms of the supernatural. A few of them, like Orestes Brownson, Charles Newcomb, Sophia Ripley, and Margaret's friend Anna Barker, were strongly attracted by the supernatural within the established church and eventually converted to Roman Catholicism. A notable exception to all this was the most mystical of them all, Emerson, who sternly held back from all such stuff, regarding any phenomena outside the ordinary laws of nature with great suspicion.

Margaret's interest in the occult had begun with her childhood interest in mythology and the forbidden realm of the imaginative and the mysterious, and it remained with her all her life. The names of Greek gods and goddesses, as learned very early from the chaste pages of Homer, occurred in her conversation and writings as naturally as the names of her living friends, and represented to her that richness and freedom of life which was so lacking in her own society. There was something pagan about Margaret, something of Juno or Ceres. W. H. Channing calls her a bacchante, New England virgin though she was.[14] She believed in astrology, in mesmerism and extrasensory communication of various kinds, and in the special properties of certain gems and flowers. (Her "own" gem was the carbuncle or round-cut garnet, of which she believed there were two sexes: the male, which has its own light, and the female, which reflects light. "Mine," she said, "is the male.")[15] She adopted Goethe's belief in demonology, which in turn was related to the ancient Greek belief in *daemons,* or indwelling spirits. She thought she herself possessed, or was possessed by, a demonic power which accounted for those periods of depression and inactivity when nothing seemed to go well with her, and no doubt she also attributed to it, in its more benevolent aspect, her ability to attract people in spite of themselves and to speak before a group as if she were, literally, inspired. Emerson associated Margaret's belief in the occult with the "nocturnal" side of her character, with something morbidly unhealthy and, he seems to have suspected, vaguely sexual.[16] The Yankee clergyman in him was distinctly uncomfortable with the Ceres in Margaret. He says that when he first met her he "felt her to be a foreigner,—that, with her, one would always be sensible of some barrier, as if in making up a friendship with a cultivated Spaniard or Turk."[17] He accounts for what she might call the demonic in his own way: "I think most of her friends will remember to have felt, at one time or another, some uneasiness, as if this athletic soul craved a larger atmosphere than it found; as if she were ill-timed and mis-mated, and felt in herself a tide of life, which compared with the slow circulation of others as a torrent with a rill."[18]

Whatever the quality was that made her a foreigner in Boston, and more like the foundling she once pretended to be than any natural daughter of Timothy Fuller, there was no scope for it in the life she was leading at Providence. But as the fall and winter progressed she resolutely kept her mind on her teaching, grew fond of her pupils and had some satisfaction in watching them progress and become more responsive. In the afternoons she worked on her Eckermann, and in response to Clarke's urgent pleas that she send him something for the *Western Messenger,* she wrote a review of William Ware's *Letters from Palmyra* which was published in the spring of 1838. She found time to give outside lessons in German to a group of ten adults. But her time for writing was short, and not of the best. She made little progress on her Goethe book, which demanded single-minded concentration and the mental alertness of early morning. By midafternoon, too, she was often contending with headache.

In spite of her reservations about the mercenary tone of Providence life she managed to involve herself in a web of social obligations. Within a few months her life was too fragmented and she was besieged by detail. She did not want to lead a life like

Emerson's—a secluded, lotus-eating existence she thought it—and told him so often enough. But she envied Emerson, and the other men she knew, those great, uninterrupted chunks of time they could command; she saw them emerging from their libraries at mealtime with armor buckled on, so to speak, for whatever rough encounters with the world they chose to seek. They were protected by wives, mothers, and sisters, not only from the ordinary physical tasks of daily life but from the myriad little temptations to which women themselves were subjected. Margaret's self-discipline was admirable in terms of the amount of study and writing she was able to accomplish once she made time for them. But she did not make enough time; in order to do so she would have had to withdraw from society, emerging only at rare intervals and giving up almost all her nonteaching hours to work. She never succeeded in doing this, in part because she was so dependent on others for her emotional and intellectual well-being, and in part because to continue to attend lectures and concerts, to pay calls, and to visit the milliner and the seamstress was to continue to be womanly. She "love[d] best to be a woman," she said, even though "womanhood is at present too straitly-bounded to give me scope."[19]

As a bluestocking she faced a double challenge, of usurping a man's role in the face of strong opposition, and of doing so without actually becoming that asexual being which the very term bluestocking suggests. Emerson, her conscience and alter ego in this as in many things, thought her social life was frivolous and warned her against becoming "the servant of a visiting-card-box."[20] But Emerson, in addition to being the uniquely self-sufficient being he was, had the advantage of simply being a man doing a man's job. And he had his Lidian to help him keep his life in order, as Alcott had his Abby, Hawthorne his Sophia, and Carlyle his Jane. Many of the literary women of that last century—the Brontës, Emily Dickinson, George Eliot, and Elizabeth Barrett Browning, to name a few—did not work alone in the midst of society, but succeeded either by withdrawing from it altogether and living virtually as hermits, or by being fortunate enough to find men who would fulfill for them the protective and supportive role usually assigned to literary men's wives.

Insisting as she did on living the intellectual life of a man and the social life of a woman, Margaret set herself a pace which literally brought retribution on her head. Slowed down only momentarily, she would pick herself up again as soon as she was able and set out to begin the whole cycle again. She went to lectures, concerts, galleries, and parties, and on one occasion (to the consternation of her employer) attended a Whig caucus. She heard with distaste the celebrated English Quaker Joseph John Gurney, whose "well-to-do-in-the-world air of pious stolidity" offended her in proportion to her high expectations of Quakerism. "One could not but pity his notions of the Holy Ghost, and his bat-like fear of light," she wrote. "His Man-God seemed to be the keeper of a mad-house, rather than the informing Spirit of all spirits." Similar echoes of Transcendentalism are heard in her praise of Mr. Hague, a Baptist whom she admires for his freedom from dogma, his individuality, and his ability to speak "direct from the conviction of his spirit, without temporizing, or artificial method."[21] On the other hand, her classical sense of restraint helped her perceive the intellectual fuzziness to which the new thinking could lead. She heard the Shakespeare lectures given by Richard Henry Dana, whom she had met the previous winter, and her criticism of him was trenchant (and, incidentally, sets up some ironic echoes of the kind of criticism that was directed at Margaret herself). She says she has never met a person with finer perceptions; he "freshens the souls of his hearers with ever new beauty." But his views are based on prejudice, not reason, and "when he has told you what *he* likes, the pleasure of intercourse is over. . . . In a word, Mr. Dana has the charms and the defects of one whose object in life has been to preserve his individuality unprofaned."[22]

She visited the French frigate *Hercules,* anchored in Narragansett Bay, and sent her younger brothers a detailed description. In a spirit of remarkable hospitality, or perhaps in honor of the son of Louis Philippe, who was one of the crew, the *Hercules* carried a dancing master, a fencing master, a lion, a bear, a fawn, and assorted "parroquets." Nevertheless, she was primarily a warship, huge for her time, pierced for 112 guns and equipped with 80, and manned by a crew of 1,000. "I thought," Margaret wrote the boys, "I should much like to command such a vessel, despite all the hardships and privations of such a situation."[23]

As a step toward the day when such a choice would be possible for women, she asked John Neal, rough-and-ready Yankee novelist and early exponent of women's rights, to address her girls on "the destiny and vocation of Woman in this country." It is not likely he told them they could be sea-captains; it would be up to Margaret herself to do that, several years hence. But he probably told them they should have the vote, which was a step Margaret was not prepared to advocate. She centered her hopes on equal education, believing that political rights were secondary; Neal, very much in advance of his time, maintained that without the vote equal education would only bring women increased frustration with their lot—as of course was true in the case of the few slaves in the south who managed to gain an education. He tried valiantly to bring Margaret over to his point of view at a gathering that evening, but in the course of a long discussion which began with women's rights and ended with Shakespeare's *Richard III*, he succeeded only in rousing her admiration for his "fervid eloquence," "infinite brilliancy," and "lion heart."[24] He left for Portland shortly afterward, to her keen regret.

Spring brought renewed opportunities to visit Boston as well as a renewed feeling of restlessness. It was in a "sombre and sullen mood" that she wrote Emerson regretting that she had missed his winter lectures in Boston:

> I have shut the door for a few days, and tried to do something; you have *really* been doing something. And that is why I write. I want to see you, and still more to hear you. I must kindle my torch again. Why have I not heard you this winter? I feel very humble just now, yet I have to say that being lives not who would have received from your lectures as much as I should. There are noble books, but one wants the breath of life sometimes. And I see no divine person. I myself am more divine than any I see. I think that is enough to say about them. I know Dr. Wayland [president of Brown University] now, but I shall not care for him. He would never understand me, and, if I met him, it must be by those means of suppression and accommodation which I at present hate to my heart's core. I hate ev-

erything that is reasonable just now, "wise limitations" and all. I have behaved much too well for some time past; it has spoiled my peace. What grieves me, too, is to find or fear that my theory is a cheat. I cannot serve two masters, and I fear all the hope of being a worldling and a literary existence also must be resigned. Isolation is necessary to me, as to others.[25]

The sentence "I myself am more divine than any I see," quoted often as evidence of Margaret's arrogance, speaks for itself in context. Beyond that, the letter expresses her realization that her twenty-eighth birthday was approaching and her life's goal was receding. She could, by means of that "suppression and accommodation" practiced by many other women besides herself, go on indefinitely in her present way of life. That was precisely why she had to break away from it. She had grown to love her pupils, and they her, and living in Providence had broadened her experience. But she would gain absolutely nothing by remaining where she was, and she resolved to leave Providence as soon as she could afford to.

In June she went to Concord to "kindle her torch," bringing along her friend Caroline Sturgis. Several years younger than Margaret, Caroline belonged to a wealthy and highly respectable Boston family. Like Margaret she gave the impression of having been transplanted from her proper time and place: G. W. Cooke describes her as "picturesque" and "gypsy-like."[26] Her letters to Margaret reveal a sensitive, intelligent personality, keenly aware of the richness of experience beyond her reach, subject to moods of largely unfocused depression and rebelliousness, and characterized by a fitful exuberance of imagination. She was the first of the "diamonds" Margaret brought Emerson, who formed an enduring friendship with her. "For a hermit," he wrote to Margaret, "I begin to think I know several very fine people."[27]

Returning to Providence, Margaret left with Emerson a portfolio of engravings borrowed from her friend of the Trenton Falls excursion, Samuel Gray Ward. Soon after their meeting in 1835, Ward had gone off to Europe to study art and literature. Recently he had returned, bringing with him several hundred engravings after the

Renaissance masters. He was eager to share his newly acquired knowledge of art history, and he found in Margaret an interest that nearly matched his own. Margaret shared the abysmal ignorance of her countrymen in this subject; her knowledge of art, like that of most Bostonians, having been formed almost entirely from engravings and plaster casts. Her reaction to a painting depended mostly on whether she liked the face of its subject, and of course she had no idea whatever of color. With Ward's advice she now began to read every book she could find on the Italian masters, particularly Raphael and Michelangelo, and she fell into the custom of meeting her new friend in the sculpture room of the Atheneum whenever she came to Boston. The art criticism she later had the temerity to write for the *Dial* shows how little she gained from Ward's instruction, but their friendship rapidly outgrew the tutorial stage, in any case.

With Margaret's encouragement Emerson met Ward, the second diamond in her chain of friends, late in the summer of 1838. They forthwith became close friends, and years afterward Ward would be one of the small group who gathered Margaret's papers for the *Memoirs*. This may help explain why her correspondence with Ward was suppressed. Only three letters survived, two with the superscriptions deleted, but luckily these are more revealing than Emerson and his coeditors probably realized. There are also one or two journal entries which apparently were thought sufficiently oblique to be safe. One was written in August 1838:

> I left [Providence] for Boston—August. How wearied I was, how tossed to and fro, what an agonizing conflict between my duty and my nature. At such times my only way is to seek some influence which might draw me from myself—I am in a state of sickly unresisting sensitiveness such as I do not remember in myself ever before—I despise but cannot conquer it. I want to lean my head on some friendly bosom
>> "And weep away this world of care."
> I am, indeed, a "tired child" and the grasshopper is a burden.
> I went to the Atheneum to meet Rafaello [Ward]—He had not yet come—I sat down in the gallery, looked at the Judith, a Madonna (called a Carlo Monotti) beautiful, but not to my taste, though

brightly tender beyond compare. But its beauty may all be seen at a glance. I did not, however, feel in the critical mood. I sank into a soothing reverie. I felt the blessed influence of the ideal world. Once more I am surrounded with records of those lives which have passed in embodying thought, not in laboring for clothes, furniture, and houses. I breathed my proper atmosphere, and pruned my ruffled pinions. Rafaello when he came did not seem to be more disposed to observe than myself. So I had not the benefit of his exquisite taste. But perhaps there was nothing worthy its exercise.

What a drive we had that afternoon! It was one of those soft gloomy times [when] the sun is wearied out, he is asleep; and you feel a right to rest also. Gleams of brassy light succeeded a gently pattering shower and we sped homewards by the palest starlight. Nature seemed to sympathize with me today; she was not too bright, she was not too wild and I was with the only person who ever understood me at once in such moods.[28]

If she was not yet in love—and she may not have been, though to be the "only" person among so many who ever understood her in such moods was to be singled out for a unique kind of praise—she was clearly in a very lonely, discouraged, dependent, and altogether susceptible state of mind. As early as 1832, when she had suffered a sharp disappointment over Davis, she had made a firm commitment to a single life which she thought nothing could change. She was aware of the depth of her own emotional needs, but she had never met a man who was strong enough to allow her to be herself within the framework of marriage, and she had decided that such a man was never to be met outside of fantasy. She assumed the mask of the brisk, self-reliant, neutered being an aggressively intellectual woman was expected to be, and continued to dispense sisterly advice to her lovelorn friends throughout the years as she once had to James Freeman Clarke. The chaste virgin, the cool, pure queen who is above all the "fury and the mire of human veins," has been a strong image in our literary tradition, and as everyone knows she enjoyed a renaissance during the last century. Margaret outwardly adopted her as her own model; in her discussions of Goethe's heroines it is the virginal Iphigenia and Ottilia who are the highest examples of womanhood, and in

Woman in the Nineteenth Century she sings the praises of several virginal heroines and celebrates their "purity" a bit too much for the modern taste. But her journals poignantly reflect her inner wish to lead the life of a normal woman and the frequent moods of all-but-paralyzing dependence and "languor" which were closely related to that conflict. It was not the Goethe who praised virginity, but the Goethe who advocated the development of the whole being that she most admired. "With the intellect," she wrote, "I always have, always shall, overcome . . . [But] the life! the life! My God, shall the life never be sweet?"[29] And in spring, a time of year she never entirely learned to welcome: "When all things are blossoming, it seems so strange not to blossom too; that the quick thought within cannot remould its tenement. Man is the slowest aloes, and I such a shabby plant, of such coarse tissue. I hate not to be beautiful, when all around is so."[30]

Seven years younger than Margaret, Sam Ward at first seemed to be only a promising youngster. She adopted a maternal attitude toward him and called him "Rafaello" after the artist he most admired. He seemed in need of protection and sympathy. For several years he had been vacillating painfully between a career in art and a career in his father's New York banking firm. Now, decked with imaginary garlands by his friends like some bright youth about to be sacrificed to Baal, he was about to commit himself to the more worldly course. In the summer of 1838 he returned to Boston, very downcast over his choice, and Margaret did her best to comfort him even though she thought he was wrong. In turn, she went to him with her own rebellious moods and found she did not have to explain them. Imperceptibly their friendship became deeper than either wished. In spite of her efforts to limit it to the kind of passionately platonic intimacy she had achieved with other friends, it seems clear that by the end of 1838 Margaret was falling in love with Ward, and that he felt in return, if not love, at least a confusingly warm affection.

There was no conscious thought of marriage on either side, and Margaret, having successfully defined the boundaries of several such friendships before, apparently thought she could do so again. She may even have thought she *was* doing so until the end of the relationship, which will be discussed in a later chapter. What should be remembered now is that such a profound conflict, half-buried and half-recognized, carried on over several years and now made acute at a time when renewed initiative and resourcefulness were demanded by other circumstances in her life, was like living with an emotional millstone around her neck. She may indeed have been a "shabby plant," yet Massachusetts was full of plain women who were happy wives and mothers. The price demanded for a female intellect as flamboyant as Margaret's was the denial of marriage and motherhood, and with them the denial of any defined place in society as a whole. The entire pattern of her life was disrupted by her celibacy, while at the same time she had no access to those vocational compensations available to unmarried men.

It is little wonder that Margaret, as the bluestocking par excellence of her time, was afflicted—for lack of a better word—with a variety of "neurotic" characteristics: the supercharged feelings which found expression in hyperbole; the vehement, occasionally strident assertions of self-confidence; the moods of lassitude, like the one described above, which could suddenly flare into restless high spirits; the quasi-erotic intensity of her friendships with both sexes; and the hysterical illnesses (to the degree that they *were* hysterical). It is one of the ironies of her life that society, having required the denial of an important and powerful force in her nature, should have found cause for ridicule in the traits which probably resulted from that denial.

But such pronouncements, made in hindsight, are the privilege of biographers and not of their subjects. Margaret herself, though not unaware of the narrowness of the line she was walking, continued for a long time to believe she could walk it with impunity. She saw Ward often, wrote when she could not see him, borrowed his books and engravings, sought his sympathetic words and his even more sympathetic silences and offered her own in return.

So the summer passed. In August she again visited Concord for a few days, carrying a second portfolio to share with Emerson, and from there she probably went on to Caroline's secluded summer house on the Merrimac River. By September she had definitely made her decision to leave the Greene Street School, and she told Hiram Fuller she would stay in Providence only through December. By then she would have earned $1500, enough to keep the wolf from the door for several months while she tried to determine her future course.

On December 22 she took leave of each of her classes. She called the older girls together last of all and sat for a long time with them, talking of what she had tried to accomplish by her method of teaching, and of her own hopes and disappointments. She said she thought she might have been unintentionally too harsh with some of them and asked their pardon. They all sat in tearful silence for some time, and then she kissed each of them and left.

William Henry Channing, who was living in Cincinnati, had revived the old suggestion of her teaching in that city and wrote to offer his help in establishing a school. The prospect of teaching in her own school, and of trying in perfect freedom to develop her ideas on the education of women, was not unattractive. But she wanted more than anything else to stop teaching altogether. "I am wearied out," she wrote Almira Barlow. "I have gabbled and simpered and given my mind to the public view these two years back, till there seems to be no good left in me." [31] Emerson, still hopeful of luring all his friends into living within sight of his own dooryard, tried to persuade her to look for a house in Concord and offered her his guest room until she found one. But she decided to go home to Groton. Her mother had found a buyer for the farm, and now that its solitude was no longer forced upon her and the family had only a few more months to live there, Margaret found it a welcome refuge. She could not entirely escape teaching even there, for Ellen and Richard coaxed her into giving them lessons once a week. But at snowbound Groton she found the quiet she craved. Arthur was at the Ripleys' school in Waltham, William Henry was in New Orleans, and Lloyd, at Margaret's request, had been sent to live with a tutor at Stoughton. Only her mother, Eugene, Ellen, and Richard were home with her, and they were all the company she wanted.

VIII

*Conversations
and the* Dial

By the time the redwinged blackbirds had returned to the Groton marshes that spring, the Fullers were preparing for their own migration. Eugene had found and rented a house in Jamaica Plain, which was part of the rural suburb of Roxbury, an hour's walk south of Boston. "Willow Brook," named for its two most distinguishing features, was set on a hill, as the Groton house was. Behind it rose a formation of those layered, granite ledges peculiar to New England, with broad tables worn smooth by glaciers and covered with moss in shaded corners; this was to be Margaret's study. The house itself was sunny and comfortable, large enough to accommodate what was now a considerable ménage: Mrs. Fuller and her daughters, as many sons as were likely to be home at once, a servant or two, two boarding pupils who had followed Margaret from Providence, and frequent guests. The cultivated land included vegetable and flower gardens, and the outbuildings were adequate to house a cow, a horse, some hens, the old black pig which remained after the others were sold that spring, and

Arthur's pet ducks and doves. All this was to cost $200 a year, which they could manage to pay among them without hardship.

Finding a house was a task which would have fallen to Margaret if Eugene had not come home from Virginia, and she was grateful for his help. She was relieved of the majority of the packing and moving chores by Ellen and Richard, so that for the first time since her father's death she had little to do at home beyond her own teaching and studies. She was fit for little else, for although the winter had brought rest it had not brought relief from the headaches which now lasted for weeks at a time—a condition which was not improved by her deciding to put her father's papers in order during the last few weeks in Groton. She spent most of the winter in her own room. In March, when almost all the furniture had been auctioned off or sent back down the same muddy roads it had traveled six years before, she was persuaded to leave early and visit the Emersons, since for the time being, as she wrote Waldo, she seemed to have become "that extremely common character, a confirmed invalid." [1]

In Concord she managed to forget, if not cure, her headache by walking for hours in the pale March sunlight with her friend. She had half-expected to find him changed. She had not seen him over the winter, and in the interim he had been undergoing the sharpest censure of his career. In August 1838 he had delivered an address at the Harvard Divinity School to which "The American Scholar" now seemed a mild prelude. This time he had challenged religious rather than scholarly tradition, calling into question the primary importance of the Scriptures as a source of revelation and scolding Christians for worshiping the person of Jesus rather than following his teachings. He had urged young ministers, as before he had urged young scholars, to seek a firsthand revelation in nature and their own experience. In the mildest possible way, he had picked up the neglected gauntlet of Protestantism and flung it at the feet of the assembled clergy: "Let me admonish you, first of all, to go alone; to refuse the good models, even those which are sacred in the imagination of men, and dare to love God without mediator or veil." [2]

By the time the venerable Andrews Norton had come galloping

out of retirement to do battle, Emerson had retreated to Concord, where he listened with pained surprise to the din he had left behind him. The controversy still continued and, like Alcott before him, Emerson heard himself compared with the convicted blasphemer Abner Kneeland. For the first time his future ability to support himself and his family was in serious question. Nevertheless Margaret found him secure in his old inner fortress, the only sign of strain being a barely noticeable tendency to disregard the outer world even more than before. The Emerson family, however, had changed very much, thanks to the birth of a new baby, Ellen, the month before. Little Waldo, too, had suddenly matured from a round toddler to an articulate child whose refusal to take for granted even the most obvious facts of the universe was a source of endless delight to his father.

The conversation during this visit was much taken up with the youngsters in the Transcendental movement, in whom Emerson and Margaret took a parental interest. It was strange that these two, at the ages of thirty-five and twenty-eight respectively, should find themselves in the position of an older, more cautious generation of rebels, but in fact this is what was happening. Some of the young men now emerging from college took up the Emersonian theme of self-realization with uncompromising zeal, refusing to entangle themselves in any way with a society they believed was grossly materialistic.

It was a dangerous course for any but the very strong; the hypersensitive, the irresolute, and the unstable could—and did—permanently lose their bearings. One of these was a new protégé of Emerson's, Jones Very, who had been a Greek tutor at Harvard until he was seized by a religious mania which made him believe he was a resurrected spirit, sent back to earth as a messenger of God. Under this delusion he had written some poetry, which Emerson later undertook to have published, and some Shakespearean criticism, which Margaret now read at her friend's request. But much as she would have liked to, she could not find in Very the holy lunatic, the "profoundly sane" prophet that Emerson did. She had to confess that all she saw was a subjectivism as wrong-headed as R. H. Dana's, lit here and there with flashes of real insight. If God had inspired Jones Very's interpretation of *Hamlet,* then there was not much hope for the future of Shakespearean criticism.

Margaret had a protégé of her own, who walked out from Boston to visit her while she was in Concord. Unlike Jones Very, Charles King Newcomb could not be called mad, but his preoccupation with religion excluded almost everything else from his mind, and, doubly handicapped by a shy, vacillating nature and a domineering mother, he would never be able to cope with the world on its own terms. Margaret had met him in Providence in 1837, when, drawn out by her sympathy and the example of her stronger sense of purpose, he had confided to her his overwhelming wish to enter the ministry together with his dissatisfaction with all existing religions except Catholicism. But even Catholicism he could not totally accept, and so he hovered around the edges, fascinated by its esthetic richness and its mysticism. He had tried to compromise by studying for a year at an Episcopal seminary, but had given it up. His dilemma was not unusual, as has been noted. One could sail away from the dry deserts of rationalism in any number of vessels, some of them antique in design; even Henry Hedge was known as a "high church" Unitarian, the only one in New England to wear a gown in the pulpit.

A third young man, Henry David Thoreau, was one of the strong ones, though this was not yet evident. He lived in Concord and Emerson had high hopes for him, but he was uncomfortable in the presence of women and Margaret found him difficult to know. Once or twice in talking to him she thought she saw glimpses of that purely original spirit which Emerson insisted was there and which she could not see in the rather stilted, academic poetry he showed her. Thoreau had graduated from Harvard two years earlier and had since taught school and worked in his father's pencil factory, but it did not seem likely that this shy, smoldering young man would stay so tamely confined much longer.

Leaving Concord after a few days, Margaret went to Boston to spend a week with Dr. Channing and his family, where she and the doctor resumed their old custom of reading and talking in the evening, and where she was accorded the rare courtesy of being left alone as much as she liked. Arriving in Jamaica Plain much refreshed, she set about the hanging of curtains and the arranging of shelves with rejuvenated spirits, pleased no less with the house than with its proximity to her friends. She looked forward to the luxury of seeing Sam Ward almost as often as she liked, and her other friends were not slow to visit her. Anna Barker, recently home from Europe, came to spend several days at a time, as did Sarah Clarke and Elizabeth Hoar. Caroline Sturgis's Brookline home was now only a few miles away. Charles Newcomb trudged out regularly from Cambridge, faithfully bringing her bouquets until she had to remind him that the house was already overflowing with flowers from her mother's garden. She began to know George and Sophia Ripley better, and Theodore Parker's Roxbury church was not far away. Bronson Alcott came to see her once or twice, still seeking that meeting of minds that he and Margaret had never quite achieved. It eluded them still, but she found her admiration for him, as for Emerson, increased by new evidence of his courage in adversity. Having expressed his ultimate defiance of Boston by accepting a Negro pupil, Alcott was forced to close his school in June. He would soon take Emerson's advice and move to Concord, but from now on his passion for teaching would find its sole outlet in the education of his own daughters.

Invigorated by her new freedom, Margaret found spring more in harmony with her own spirits than she had in other years. She spent long afternoons with her books on Goethe writing a detailed outline of her biography, sitting next to the brook or up on the sun-warmed ledges, surrounded by masses of wild columbine. Whatever unpleasantness the future held—and she knew there was bound to be unpleasantness—she would allow it to remain suspended until fall. In no small measure her tranquil mood was due to the June publication of her translation of Goethe's *Conversations with Eckermann*. It not only was her first book, it represented a step toward the completion of her biography. In spite of the fact that she and Ripley had reached no formal agreement, he had gone so far as to promise the public a *Life of Goethe* in his introduction to the series, and she now felt she had accumulated enough material to write an experimental chapter.

I find daily new materials and am at present almost burthened by my riches. I have found for instance all the Frankfort particulars in letters to Meyer. And Goethe's Darstellunggabe lends such beauty to the theme that I shall often translate, and string rather than melt my pearls. I do not write steadily for the subject keeps fermenting and I feel that the hour of precipitation is not arrived. Often a study is suggested and I pass several days in the woods with it before I resume the pen. It would make quite a cultivated person of me, if I had four or five years to give to my task. But I intend to content myself with doing it inadequately rather than risk living so long in the shadow of one mind.[3]

She was not free from domestic interruptions, for her mother continued to look to her to manage the family's money and to make even small, day-to-day decisions, and Lloyd, who was moved from tutor to tutor and was miserable when he was away from home and fractious when he returned, was a constant source of guilt and anxiety to them all. But apparently Margaret worked fairly steadily at her book, reserving time for it each day after she had finished teaching the three pupils who boarded with them.

In Boston she continued to meet Ward at the Atheneum and at the new Allston gallery, but she discovered that the other members of the Transcendentalist group had found a more comfortable meeting place, and that if she went there on the spur of the moment she was almost certain to find several people she knew. Elizabeth Peabody had interrupted her teaching career to open a bookstore on West Street, offering for sale those German and French publications which could not be found anywhere else in Boston. Most of the people who read German and French publications were the members of Hedge's Club and their friends, and so the bookstore became their meeting place. Miss Peabody found them chairs and made them welcome, and the resulting conversation was something like a country soup pot, simmering all the time although the ingredients kept changing. Elizabeth herself was a constant active ingredient. Two other people who were often present but who rarely said anything were Horace Mann and Nathaniel Hawthorne, both courting Elizabeth's younger sisters. Mann was an educational reformer who had recently been instrumental in founding a State Board of Education in Massachusetts. Hawthorne was a handsome, intense young writer from Salem for whom the goodhearted Elizabeth had found a job in the Boston Custom House—the chief merit of this occupation being that it interfered very little with the composition of a novel. He was not unfriendly behind his watchful reserve, but oddly detached from the warm currents of optimism that flowed about him.

Margaret's conversational powers had never been better, and she became the natural center of the bookstore conversation whenever she was present. W. H. Channing describes her entering a conversation at this time, not in the bookstore but at a Transcendental Club meeting, where of course the same people would be gathered:

> When her turn came, by a graceful transition she resumed the subject where preceding speakers had left it, and, briefly summing up their results, proceeded to unfold her own view. Her opening was deliberate, like the progress of some massive force gaining its momentum; but as she felt her way, and moving in a congenial element, the sweep of her speech became grand. The style of her eloquence was sententious, free from prettiness, direct, vigorous, charged with vitality. Articulateness, just emphasis and varied accent, brought out most delicate shades and brilliant points of meaning, while a rhythmical collocation of words gave a finished form to every thought. She was affluent in historic illustration and literary allusion, as well as in novel hints. She knew how to concentrate into racy phrases the essential truth gathered from wide research, and distilled with patient toil; and by skilful treatment she could make green again the wastes of commonplace. Her statements, however rapid, showed breadth of comprehension, ready memory, impartial judgment, nice analysis of differences, power of penetrating through surfaces to realities, fixed regard to central laws and habitual communion with the Life of life. Critics, indeed, might have been tempted to sneer at a certain oracular grandiloquence, that bore away her soberness in moments of elation; though even the most captious must presently have smiled at the humor of her descriptive touches, her dextrous exposure of folly and pretension, the swift stroke of her bright wit, her shrewd discernment, promptitude, and presence of mind. The reverential, too, might have been pained at the sternness

wherewith popular men, measures, and established customs, were tried and found guilty, at her tribunal; but even while blaming her aspirations as rash, revolutionary and impractical, no honest conservative could fail to recognize the sincerity of her aim. And every deep observer of character would have found the explanation of what seemed vehement or too high-strung, in the longing of a spirited woman to break every trammel that checked her growth or fettered her movement.

In conversations like these, one saw that the richness of Margaret's genius resulted from a rare combination of opposite qualities. To her might have been well applied the words first used as describing George Sand: "Thou large-brained Woman, and large-hearted Man." She blended in closest union and swift interplay feminine receptiveness with masculine energy.[4]

Her conversation, Emerson said simply, was the most entertaining in America. And it may very well have been during one of the bookstore discussions that someone suggested that the most entertaining conversation in America might be worth paying for. In an era earnestly bent on self-culture, when almost anyone who wanted to give a speech on free will, cold baths, or the bumps on the human head could fill a lecture hall, the idea was not far-fetched. In fact, Alcott had already begun to augment his income by holding conversations in private homes in the suburbs. (Being Alcott's, they were not so much conversations as monologues on a single, never-exhausted subject, punctuated occasionally by approving noises from his audience.) Elizabeth Peabody too had held conversational teaching sessions in the homes of friends. To be paid for doing what she liked best to do while living where she liked best to live seemed far too easy to Margaret, whose Fuller ancestry led her to regard this life as a series of ordeals set by the Lord to purify the soul. But several of her woman friends promised among them to form the solid core of a group: the Peabody sisters, Anna Barker, Eliza Farrar, Sophia Ripley, Sarah Clarke, Caroline Sturgis, and her sister Ellen Hooper. It would not be difficult to find eleven more to make up a group of twenty, and if each paid $20 for a series of ten conversations (a high fee for those days) she could support herself this way for several months. Elizabeth generously offered the use of the bookstore as a meeting place.

Men were excluded not out of any lack of interest on their part or false sense of propriety on Margaret's, but because her purpose in the Conversations had to do with changing the status of women. She did not want primarily to entertain or instruct (though she hoped to do both), but to alter the image women had of themselves. This was the purpose she had half-realized in her evening classes and in her classes in Providence, and it was this that had made the idea of opening a school in Cincinnati briefly attractive. In spite of the liberal rhetoric about universal equality, and in spite of scattered gestures that were being made toward higher education for women, individual women found it difficult to believe that their minds were equal to men's. She herself was not free from self-doubt, in spite of the brave show she made. Her own education had been reversed in the middle, and her intellectual self-assurance drew heavily on her experience as a young child; her social experience whenever she stepped out of her own circle, and sometimes even within it, demonstrated to her in a thousand little ways that insofar as she was bright she was not quite a whole woman. She wanted to help women overcome the double educational and social handicap by forcing them to fully engage their minds in an atmosphere that was as free as possible from censure. Women were taught a great many subjects in school, but they were not really expected to remember them. Except in a few academies, they were not required to reproduce what they had learned in examinations as men were; nor, except for teachers, were they required to do so in vocational life. Margaret hoped to induce them to systemize their thought and express themselves boldly as they had never been asked to before. She hoped to sharpen their thinking habits, but beyond that, and more important, she hoped to bring them to an understanding that their inadequacies were not innate, but were the result of superficial education and the attitude of self-deprecation instilled by social custom. If she could do this much, a small revolution might begin in Boston. And if such a plan failed in Boston, she told Sophia Ripley, it could not succeed anywhere in America.

The Conversations were very popular and continued for four years, with two series a year, one beginning in November and the other in March. Twenty-five women joined the first series, and in subsequent series the number rose to thirty-five or more, although all the members were never there at one time. The *Memoirs* list about forty women who participated at one time or another. Some, like Jane Tuckerman, were former students. Others were friends who had to travel some distance: Lidian Emerson, Sarah Alden Ripley, Almira Barlow, and Elizabeth Hoar. Lydia Maria Child came, and her fellow abolitionist Louisa Loring. But the list itself as given in the *Memoirs,* with its frequent omission of the women's Christian names and its allusions to their male relations, suggests how strongly these women were overshadowed by fathers, husbands, and fiancés. There are Shaws, Russells, Higginsons, Lees—all daughters and wives of the mercantile Boston aristocracy. Mrs. George Bancroft attended; Mrs. Theodore Parker; Maria White (the fiancée of James Russell Lowell); Mrs. Josiah Quincy; Mrs. Charles Newcomb (his mother, not his wife); Marianne Jackson (sister-in-law of Oliver Wendell Holmes); and Mary Channing, who, as Higginson explains, was Dr. Channing's only daughter. Most of those who were married or engaged had been singled out by their men because, among other reasons, their intelligence made them very satisfactory attendant spirits. Having the money and leisure to attend the Conversations, they also had very good cause.

The topics were deliberately broad, so as to allow everyone to participate without special preparation. One series was devoted to "Education," under which they discussed "Culture," "Ignorance," "Vanity," "Prudence," "Patience," and "Health." Another was on the Fine Arts. But Margaret's favorite topic, often repeated, was Greek Mythology, or rather the universal themes of will, reason, understanding, love, beauty, and so on, as objectified by the Greeks and other cultures. This may seem to be a more specialized subject than the others, but even women customarily received the rudiments of a "classical" education, and Margaret told them they need know only what they had learned from Homer and the fine arts.

The Conversations were usually held on Saturdays at 11:00 A.M.

MARCHESE GIOVANNI ANGELO OSSOLI
(By permission of Houghton Library, Harvard University)

Margaret Fuller during the siege of Rome; portrait by Thomas Hicks
(By permission of Houghton Library, Harvard University)

MARCHESA COSTANZA ARCONATI VISCONTI
(By permission of the Museo di Risorgimento, Milan)

Bombardment of the Porta San Pancrazio viewed from the French battery at the Villa Corsini *(By permission of the Museo di Risorgimento, Rome)*

GIUSEPPE MAZZINI
(By permission of the Museo di Risorgimento, Rome)

RALPH WALDO EMERSON
*(By permission of the
Concord Free Public Library)*

BRONSON ALCOTT
*(By permission of the
Louisa May Alcott Memorial Assn.)*

HORACE GREELEY
(By permission of the Library of Congress)

ADAM MICKIEWICZ
(By permission of the Library of Congress)

MARGARET FULLER;
engraving from Chappel
(By permission of Willard P. Fuller, Jr.)

Members of the Fuller family. Seated, l. to r.: Arthur, Ellen, Richard;
standing: Eugene, Margaret Crane Fuller
(By permission of Willard P. Fuller, Jr.)

The Fuller house in Groton as it appears today

The members would sit in a semircircle and Margaret would stand in front of them, dressed in one of the full-sleeved, long-waisted gowns of the period, sometimes with a bowl of yellow chrysanthemums on the table beside her. Around her neck she wore a lorgnette, which she raised from time to time in order to see the people in the back of the room. At the beginning of the session she would give an introductory statement on the subject of the day, and then she would ask for comments. If none were forthcoming, she would ask for written statements to be read at the beginning of the next session. But apparently this seldom happened; the response of the group was enthusiastic, and she usually had no more to do than guide the conversation once it was under way. Even among this group she did not entirely escape the old criticism that she was too domineering, but it was limited to a few. The majority would have agreed with the description of one of the sessions written by a member to a friend:

Christmas made a holiday for Miss Fuller's class, but it met on Saturday, at noon. As I sat there, my heart overflowed with joy at the sight of the bright circle, and I longed to have you by my side, for I know not where to look for so much character, culture, and so much love of truth and beauty, in any other circle of women and girls. The names and faces would not mean so much to you as to me, who have seen more of the lives, of which they are a sign. Margaret, beautifully dressed (don't despise that, for it made a fine picture,) presided with more dignity and grace than I had thought possible. The subject was Beauty. Each had written her definition, and Margaret began with reading her own. This called forth questions, comments, and illustrations, on all sides. The style and manner, of course, in this age, are different, but the question, the high point from which it was considered, and the earnestness and simplicity of the discussion, as well as the gifts and graces of the speakers, gave it the charm of a Platonic dialogue. There was no pretension or pedantry in a word that was said. The tone of remark and question was simple as that of children in a school class; and, I believe, every one was gratified.[5]

The main defect of the plan seems to have been that since the subjects were so general (general enough to be thought grandiose by the critical), the women were not in fact called upon to reproduce what they had learned, or at least not what they had formally studied. But they were obliged to formulate opinions on subjects which they had been led to believe they could have no opinions about. Margaret demanded that they "lay aside the shelter of vague generalities, the art of coterie criticism, and the 'delicate disdains' of *good society,*" and be "willing that others should think their sayings crude, shallow, or tasteless." It was only by acquiring the courage to do so, she told them, that they could "attain the real health and vigor, which need no aid from rouge or candlelight, to brave the light of the world." [6]

There are no accurate records of any of the sessions, although Elizabeth Peabody wrote some general summaries from memory. The one attempt made to record the Conversations on the spot was a failure, [7] although in justice to the writer, Caroline Dall, it must be said that the series itself was a failure. In 1841 Margaret decided to include men in the discussion and she gave a Monday evening series open to all. The men present included Emerson, Alcott, Ripley, Hedge, Clarke, Jones Very, William Wetmore Story, Messrs. Mack of Belmont and Shaw of Boston, and Charles Stearns Wheeler, the only one of the group who could claim to be a Greek scholar. But the spontaneity of the other series was missing. The women were intimidated by the very presence of men and lapsed into deferential silence, except for a few brave spirits like Elizabeth Peabody and Caroline Sturgis. The men picked up the abandoned discussion and made off with it wherever they chose, the worst offender probably being Bronson Alcott. Margaret's attempts to round them all up again were only momentarily successful. Emerson seems to have made himself deliberately obtuse, as he sometimes did, making his idealism seem more rigid than it actually was and pronouncing his opinions with a finality that left no room for compromise. Afterward, trying to be contrite in a letter to Margaret, he succeeded only in being petulant:

> The young people wished to know what possessed me to tease you with so much prose, and becloud the fine conversation? I could only answer that it was not an acute fit of Monday evening, but was

chronic and constitutional with me, and I asked them in my turn when they had heard me talk anything else? . . . You, instead of wondering at my cloistered and unfriendly manners, should defend me if possible from friendship, from ambition, from my own weakness which would lead me to variety, which is the dissipation of thought. You and those others who are dear to me should be so rightly my friends as never to suffer me for a moment to attempt the game of wits and fashionists, no nor even that of those you call Friends. . . .[8]

The following year the Conversations reverted to the original plan and were as successful as ever, in the way Margaret had intended. To discover that they actually were able to think and speak for themselves on subjects outside their "sphere" had an intoxicating effect on many of the women, unlike anything they had ever experienced. Much of this overflowed into a feeling for Margaret herself which was close to adulation, especially among the young. Mrs. Dall herself, then in her teens, was an example:

Our last talk, and we were all dull. For my part, Bacchus does not inspire me, and I was sad because it was the last time that I should see Margaret. She does not love me; I could not venture to follow her into her own home, and I love her so much! Her life hangs on a thread. Her face is full of the marks of pain. Young as I am, I feel old when I look at her.[9]

This kind of uncritical devotion was widespread, not only among the girls in the Conversations but among Margaret's other students. "Had she been a man," Elizabeth Hoar once told Emerson, "any one of those fine girls of sixteen, who surrounded her here, would have married her; they were all in love with her, she understood them so well."[10] Emerson says some of the girls complained that "she quite reduced them to satellites" with her "burly masculine existence"; yet women all over Boston "were eager to lay their beauty, their grace, the hospitalities of sumptuous homes, and their costly gifts, at her feet."[11] She was all the more idolized by her teen-age students because they had convinced themselves that she was doomed to an early grave. (This is not as preposterous as it seems. People died all the time of ailments that seemed no worse than migraine headache, and Margaret herself did not believe she would reach old age.) Nor was the feeling Margaret inspired limited to the very young. Elizabeth Peabody, herself no melting sixteen-year-old, wrote of the Conversations: "It is sometimes said, that women never are so lovely and enchanting in the company of their own sex, merely, but it requires the other to draw them out. Certain it is that Margaret never appears, when I see her, either so brilliant and deep in thought, or so desirous to please, or so modest, or so heart-touching, as in this very party."[12] She was brilliant in any group, but when she was with other women she discarded the mask she more or less consciously assumed in everyday life and actually became that warmer, less cerebral person she would have liked to be all the time.

The object of such adulation was bound to provoke criticism, even if she were not engaged in a radical enterprise. But the most memorable shot against Margaret, as against Bronson Alcott, came from England. Harriet Martineau had not said all she had to say about America in her earlier book. Miss Martineau's *Autobiography,* published long after Margaret's death, added to the distortions and half-truths clustered about her memory:

> The difference between us was that while she was living and moving in an ideal world, talking in private and discoursing in public about the most fanciful and shallow conceits which the transcendentalists of Boston took for philosophy, she looked down upon persons who acted instead of talking finely, and devoted their fortunes, their peace, their repose, and their very lives to the preservation of the principles of the republic. While Margaret Fuller and her adult pupils sat "gorgeously dressed," talking about Mars and Venus, Plato and Göthe, and fancying themselves the elect of the earth in intellect and refinement, the liberties of the republic were running out as fast as they could go, at a breach which another sort of elect persons were devoting themselves to repair; and my complaint against the "gorgeous" pedants was that they regarded their preservers as hewers of wood and drawers of water, and their work as a less vital one than the pedantic orations which were spoiling a set of well-meaning women in a pitiable way.[13]

Miss Martineau had no firsthand knowledge of the Conversations, having left the country four years before they were begun; but clearly Margaret's letter about Alcott had rankled, although the two women were still corresponding affectionately during the 1840s. The remark about "gorgeousness" is traced by Higginson to a comment by one of Margaret's admirers that she "used to come to the conversations very well dressed, and altogether looked sumptuously." [14] Since Margaret's income hardly allowed her to buy anything more sumptuous than calico and bombazine,* her reputation for dressing well rested entirely on her knowing what to do with them. As for her "looking down" on activists, more than half the members of the Conversations were abolitionists, and Mrs. Child and Mrs. Loring were leaders of the movement. Margaret herself, though put off by the shrill rhetoric of the abolitionists and the violence many of them advocated, sympathized with the cause and in later years wrote effectively in its support. Miss Martineau was still unable to see the close relationship between Transcendentalism and abolitionism, and ironically, she was also blind to the contribution these discussions were making to the emancipation of her own sex. Beyond that, her comments are a typical illustration of the vituperative tone Margaret's critics assumed, and of the way her eccentricities could easily be fashioned into a one-dimensional, larger-than-life symbol of whatever bugaboo it was her detractors most hated and feared.

During the four years of the Conversations, Margaret supplemented her income by teaching private pupils, occasionally having one or two boarding with her. The remainder of her time she had intended to devote to her Goethe biography, but during the summer of 1839 another project took shape which was to shoulder her book aside and prevent her completing it. At a September meeting of the Transcendentalist Club the idea of a journal, which had first been proposed in 1835 by Henry Hedge, was revived. Since the "Divinity School Address" it had been almost impossible for members of the circle to publish except at their own expense, and Alcott pointed out to them the modest success a similar journal,

---

* A twill blend of cotton or silk mixed with wool.

The London Monthly Review, was enjoying in Britain. Why, Alcott wanted to know, could not New England have such a review? In fact Emerson had been trying to persuade Carlyle to edit a journal in America for some time, but Carlyle's evasiveness had at length crystallized into refusal. Unless one counted the Unitarian *Christian Register,* or Orestes Brownson's erratic *Quarterly Review,* the only literary journal in New England was the stolidly conservative *North American Review* ("the snore of the Muses," Emerson called it). The *North American*'s editors, George Bancroft and Edward Everett, may well have lain awake nights ruing the day they had helped introduce German literature to America.

Everyone agreed that the journal was a fine idea, but of course no one wanted to edit it, Emerson—the obvious choice—least of all. Henry Hedge, who had suggested it five years before, then had no inkling of the distance some of his friends would put between themselves and the liberal church. Now among the most conservative of the group, he could not be considered as editor of a review which would espouse George Ripley's associationism, William Henry Channing's socialism, and what many believed to be Waldo Emerson's pantheism. The person chosen would have to be one whose sympathies were broad enough to include all these, whose convictions were strong without being narrow, and whose literary background was firm. None seemed better qualified than Margaret, and after careful thought she accepted on the condition that George Ripley take care of the business arrangements. It was hoped that enough subscriptions could be obtained to pay her $200 a year after the publisher received his share. They decided to call the journal the *Dial,* after a portion of Alcott's diaries.

Margaret's expectations of the *Dial* were realistic. She did not propose to establish a new standard of literary quality, but rather to bring a freshness of thought and style to the stale atmosphere of literary convention. It was important to shake off the Nay-saying strictures of the past, whether they were represented by the division between the elect and the damned, the lines between social classes, the hard rows of benches in the schoolroom, or the neat little enclosure of the heroic couplet. She realized that much of the writing would be rough, but all pioneering was rough; it would be up to those who came later to smooth the edges. A beginning had to be made if American literature, like American women, was to find its own identity. She expressed her limited hopes for the journal to W. H. Channing while she was preparing the first issue:

> A perfectly free organ is to be offered for the expression of individual thought and character. There are no party measures to be curried, no particular standard to be set up. A fair calm tone, a recognition of universal principals will, I hope pervade the essays in every form. I hope there will neither be a spirit of dogmatism nor of compromise. That this periodical will not aim at leading public opinion, but at stimulating each man to think for himself, to think more deeply and more nobly by letting them [sic] see how some minds are kept alive by a wise self-trust. . . . I am sure we cannot show high culture. and I doubt about vigorous thought. But I hope we shall show free action as far as it goes and a high aim. It were much if a periodical could be kept open to accomplish no outward object, but merely to afford an avenue for what of free and calm thought might be originated among us by the wants of individual minds.[15]

As for her own part in it, she expected mainly to "urge on the laggards and scold the lukewarm, and act Helen MacGregor to those who love compromise, by doing my little best to sink them in the waters of oblivion!!"[16] The date for the first issue was tentatively set for April 1840. Emerson, Ripley, and Alcott could be depended on to write, and she asked Hedge, W. H. Channing, and James Freeman Clarke for contributions. Thoreau promised to send something and Emerson wrote to another of his protégés, William Ellery Channing (who had left Harvard and was living by himself in a hut in Illinois) asking for permission to publish some of his verses. Theodore Parker promised some of his workmanlike prose. Caroline Sturgis and her sister Ellen Hooper put the poems they had written in their journals at Margaret's disposal, with the prim condition that not even the other Transcendentalists be told who had written them. (Public anonymity was not an issue, since periodical articles usually were left unsigned.) Emerson selected passages from the journals of his dead brothers and verses written by his first wife, Ellen Tucker Emerson.

But by spring there was not nearly enough material for the 136 pages agreed on with the publisher. Margaret set about writing as much as she could herself, and her attempts to coax the more shy Transcendentalists out of their winter dens became a little desperate. Shyest of all was Henry Hedge:

> Henry, I adjure you, in the name of all the Genii, Muses, Pegasus, Apollo, Pollio, Apollyon, ("and must I mention"————) to send me something good for this journal before the 1st May. All mortals, my friend, are slack and bare; they wait to see whether Hotspur wins, before they levy aid for as good a plan as ever was laid. I know you are plagued and it is hard to write, just so it is with me, for I also am a father. But you can help, and become a godfather! if you like, and let it be nobly, for if the first number justify not the magazine, it will not find justification; so write, my friend, write, and paint not for me fine plans on the clouds to be achieved at some future time, as others do who have had many years to be thinking of immortality.
>
> I could make a number myself with the help Mr. E[merson] will give, but the Public, I trow, is too astute a donkey not to look sad at *that*.[17]

Hedge, however, was appalled at the guise in which his own suggestion had returned to haunt him, and now flatly refused to have anything to do with the *Dial,* though he later relented enough to contribute to the second issue and one or two after that. James Freeman Clarke, newly married and living in Pennsylvania, also disappointed her for the first issue. Emerson sent two poems and the family selections he had promised, and wrote most of the introduction. Otherwise he kept aloof, content to let the *Dial* be stillborn rather than divert his attention from the preparation of his first book of *Essays.* He urged Margaret to take the same view of it, and not to run down her health, which was worse as it always was in winter. But she developed a stubborn affection for the *Dial,* or at least for the idea of the *Dial,* and she kept scribbling away, the old distaste for writing dragging at her pen. She told Channing,

> I have myself a great deal written, but as I read it over scarce a word seems pertinent to the place or time. When I meet people I can adapt

myself to them, but when I write it is into another world, not a better one perhaps, but one with very dissimilar habits of thought to this where I am domesticated. . . . What others can do, whether all that has been said is the mere restlessness of discontent, or there are thoughts really struggling for utterance will I think be tested now.[18]

When the first issue at last appeared, Margaret was by far the largest contributor. Others, besides the Emerson family, were Parker, Ripley, John Sullivan Dwight, Christopher Cranch, H. D. Wilson, Alcott, Ward, Ellen Hooper, Sarah Clarke, and Thoreau, who sent the poem "Sympathy." The literary quality in this as in later issues was uneven, the most solid pieces being Parker's on "The Divine Presence in Nature and the Soul," Ripley's discussion of the writings of Brownson, and Margaret's own "Essay on Critics." The verse in the *Dial,* notwithstanding poems by Thoreau and Emerson, was always its weakest feature: American Transcendentalism, which had seemed to offer a fertile field for poetry, proved a veritable quagmire. But the prose was often good, sometimes memorable, and in its primary purpose of giving expression to the spirit of democratic idealism at its best, the *Dial* was a success. It was a rallying point for the young, as Emerson pointed out in defending it to Carlyle:

If the direction of these speculations is to be deplored, it is yet a fact for literary history, that all the bright boys and girls in New England, quite ignorant of each other, take the world so, and come and make confessions to fathers and mothers,—the boys that they do not wish to go into trade, the girls that they do not like morning calls and evening parties. They are all religious, but hate the churches: they reject all the ways of living of other men, but have none to offer in their stead. Perhaps, one of these days, a great Yankee shall come, who will easily do the unknown deed.[19]

The *Dial* was greeted with whoops and chortles by those already disposed to be its natural enemies. "It is, to us, humble uninitiated sinners, yet ignorant of the sublime 'mysteries,' one of the most transcendentically (we like big words) ridiculous publications," sneered the editor of the *Boston Times.*[20] None of those who had worked to bring it about were satisfied with it, although their reasons were sometimes poles apart. The most frequent criticism was the most justified: it was ethereal, abstract, and precious. "Too much of a soul,"[21] growled Carlyle, while Alcott thought it did not have soul enough: "It is but a twilight 'Dial'," he wrote sadly to an English friend.[22] Ripley thought it was "not *prononcé* enough"; instead of sporting "hoofs and horns," it was "gentle as any sucking dove." All the same, he noted happily, "the Philistines, who dare show out, are wrathy as fighting-cocks."[23] Not surprisingly, its shortcomings were occasionally blamed on the fact that it had a woman editor. Carlyle's objections seem to have been at least partly on this score: "[The *Dial*] is all spirit-like, aeriform, aurora-borealis like. Will no *angel* body himself out of that; no stalwart Yankee *man,* with colour in the cheeks of him, and a coat on his back!"[24] Theodore Parker, whose personal distrust of aggressively intellectual women did not interfere with his being Boston's most eloquent preacher on behalf of human equality, remarked that the chief thing wrong with the *Dial* was that it needed a beard. But the new journal was generally well received by the readers for whom it was meant.

Margaret was editor of the *Dial* for two years. Her editorial policy was set forth in her "Essay on Critics," in the first issue. She did not believe that a work of art should be measured against some ideal, inflexible standard, but thought that the critic should encourage talent as well as genius, while clearly distinguishing between them. She encouraged freshness and vitality in the *Dial,* even though the writing might be technically flawed. In this she differed from Emerson, who would have tightened up the literary quality even though it meant excluding more writers. The difference was probably more theoretical than actual, for the *Dial* changed little after Emerson took it over in 1842, and Margaret was firm in trying to bring her writers (including Emerson himself) up to the mark. She offended Alcott by discontinuing his "Orphic Sayings"—apothegms taken from his diaries which were much parodied in the establishment press. And she wounded Thoreau's pride by returning several of his pieces for revision.

Emerson and Parker continued to be the heaviest contributors after Margaret herself, Emerson assuming a large share of the writing after the first issue. Parker was very popular with the readers, and it is doubtful that the journal could have survived without him. Besides Margaret and the Sturgis sisters, women who ventured into print in the *Dial* included Elizabeth Peabody, Sarah Clarke, Lydia Maria Child, and a follower of Emerson's from Dorchester named Eliza Thayer Clapp.

The *Dial* soon absorbed nearly all of Margaret's working hours, and she was forced to set aside her Goethe biography, promising herself she would return to it when she had time. But the succeeding years offered no such opportunity, and all that remains of the book is a detailed outline of the early chapters and a collection of notes. For her *Dial* editing she never received a salary, since the journal barely supported itself. In 1841 its printers went bankrupt and refused to return the subscription list without payment for it. An arrangement was reached, and Elizabeth Peabody printed the *Dial* on her own press until it was placed with the company of James Munroe. But its financial position went from bad to worse, and in 1843 Emerson paid for the last few issues out of his own pocket.

As editor Margaret was largely spared the financial haggling over the journal, but she shouldered the responsibility for its contents. Contributors continued dilatory, and she made up the missing copy herself. She wrote more than half the October 1841 issue, her essays on "Lives of the Great Composers" and Bailey's "Festus" numbering eighty-five pages. Christmas of the same year found her racing the printer in order to finish the January issue: "I am in a state of extreme fatigue," she wrote her mother, who was in Canton. "This is the last week of the Dial, and as often happens, the copy did not hold out, and I have had to write in every gap of time. Marianne J., and Jane [two of her pupils] have been writing for me extracts etc., but I have barely scrambled through, and am now quite unfit to hold a pen." [25] In July 1842, anxieties over her income, her family, and her health forced her to resign the editorship; Emerson carried it on for two more years.

Margaret's writing for the *Dial* varies widely in quality. This reflects partly the conditions of haste, fatigue, and pain under which it was produced, and partly her reluctance to write instead of talk. But these years were a valuable apprenticeship for her, and some of her *Dial* writing is as good as anything she did. She still lapses into sentimentality and digression, and she is clearly out of her depth in her discussions of art and music: her article on "The Great Composers," for example, suffers from the common Romantic fallacy of equating esthetic and moral excellence. Passionately loving the music of Beethoven, she concluded that he must have been an altogether admirable human being and elevated him to chief position in her own private pantheon. No more enlightened, for similar reasons, are her discussions of sculpture and painting, which are almost entirely concerned with the physiognomy of the models (noble brows and pure eyes lifted heavenward, etc.). Having very little technical knowledge of these subjects and a great deal about literature, she is at her best in the latter field. Her *Dial* essay on Goethe contributed significantly to an acceptance of the great German poet in this country, and her "Essay on Critics" signals the beginning of her development as one of America's first two literary critics worthy of the name, the other being Poe.

But Margaret's most important contribution to the *Dial* was published in the July 1843 issue under the ponderous title, "The Great Lawsuit: Man vs. Men. Woman vs. Women." This article, the most radical feminist document yet produced in America, brings together the liberal thought she had distilled from years of study and the bitter contradictions and disillusionment she had experienced, not only in her own life but in the lives of literally dozens of other women who had confided in her as in no one else. She wrote it while she was still conducting the Conversations, having constantly before her the contrast between the heady sense of freedom a few women could achieve for two hours once a week, and the carefully limited reality to which they went home afterward. Among the various benevolences to which the Unitarian and Transcendentalist movements had contributed—abolitionism, educational reform, the amelioration of conditions for the poor, the insane, and the criminal—feminism was the last to be recognized because it was the most fundamental of all. To radically change the status of their wives and daughters (especially their wives) was a challenge from which even the most dedicated Transcendentalists inwardly shrank, no matter how generously they maintained the justice of it on an intellectual plane. To face squarely the changes in domestic life which were implied by that equal education they so cheerfully promulgated was so difficult that they closed their eyes to it, as had Timothy Fuller when he set out to educate his small daughter. The male liberal would lend his books to the intellectual woman and invite her to his discussions; he would congratulate her on how accomplished she was, "for a woman." He would even accept her as editor of a journal for which he wrote. But she remained apart from the mainstream of society; she was seen as an anomaly. With rare exceptions men did not marry such women, because the vocation of wife excluded all others. (No better example of liberal male doublethink can be found than the exclusion of woman delegates from the 1840 World Anti-Slavery Convention, which would not have been possible without the efforts of women.)

In three years of existence (two of them admittedly under Margaret's direction) the *Dial* had touched on the "woman question" only once before, in an 1841 article by Sophia Ripley titled simply "Woman." But Mrs. Ripley had not led her men friends any further than they were already willing to go. After expressing with some force her complaint that a woman loses her individuality in marriage and becomes "an appendage . . . the upper nurse," she goes meekly back to her corner: a woman should be educated so that she will not lean on her husband, but will "attend on him as a watchful friend." Only then can she pursue her "high vocation of creator of a happy home." [26] There was nothing here to alarm the menfolk, and at Brook Farm later that year Sophia Ripley stayed indoors, cooked, taught the children, and worked long hours in the laundry; it would not have occurred to her to go out in the fields and hoe corn.

Margaret's article, on the other hand, is deeply, basically radical. Beginning with the premise that all souls are equal before God, and its application to Negroes and American Indians, she goes on to claim the same equality for women: "We would have every arbitrary barrier thrown down. We would have every path laid open to women as freely as to man.'' She asks for educational equality, but not for the same stultifying education that is available to men; rather she asks for new institutions of higher learning specifically for women, and run by women. She goes on to appeal for that vocational equality which follows from equal education, and for legal and political equality as well, including by implication the right to vote, though she stops short of advocating it in so many words. ''The Great Lawsuit'' suffers from a digressive style, and once Margaret betrays her own inner conflict about whether women can become first-rate artists: ''More native to her is it to be the living model of the artist, than to set apart from herself any one form in objective reality, more native to inspire and receive the poem than to create it.'' But immediately she goes on to recognize the androgynous nature of the individual mind: ''There is no wholly masculine man, no purely feminine woman. . . . Man partakes of the feminine in the Apollo, woman of the masculine as Minerva.'' She defends women's right to remain unmarried, if they choose, without social penalty. Above all, she would not have them defined by relationships to men:

> A profound thinker has said ''no married woman can represent the female world, for she belongs to her husband. The idea of woman must be represented by a virgin.'' But that is the very fault of marriage, and of the present relation between the sexes, that the woman does belong to the man, instead of forming a whole with him. Were it otherwise there would be no such limitation to the thought. Woman, self-centred, would never be absorbed by any relative; it would be only an experience to her as to man. It is a vulgar error that love, *a* love to woman is her whole existence. . . .[27]

Deceptively gentle in tone, ''Lawsuit'' undermined even the most liberal assumptions of the day. It was a courageous statement, and it brought Margaret to the notice of a wider public, while it brought her Transcendentalist friends face to face with their own ideals.

IX

Vicissitudes

The American 1840s were a decade of expansion fittingly climaxed by the gold rush of 1849, and what Margaret and Emerson called the "go-ahead" spirit of America came into its own. The size of the continent and the size of the fortune one man could make—and lose—seemed limitless. The population of the country as a whole rose by 36 percent, and of the urban areas by an astonishing 90 percent, thanks partly to the first large waves of immigrants from western Europe. Philadelphia and New York, having been more foresighted in looking westward for their prosperity, outdistanced Boston in rate of growth. But Bostonians, preoccupied with spending their shipping and textile fortunes on newer and fancier mansions on Beacon Hill, scarcely seemed to notice. Local wonders abounded: water from Lake Cochituate was piped into the city and, after appropriate words had been said over it, spurted eighty feet into the air in the middle of the Frog Pond on the Common, to the accompaniment of cheers, bells, cannonade, band music, and fireworks. The first two steamships to sail between England and America docked in Boston, to the chagrin of New Yorkers, and in 1846 a Boston dentist, Thomas Green Morton, relieved the world of the medieval horrors of surgery by extracting a tooth with the help of sulphuric ether.

Nevertheless, the burgeoning expansion of Boston and the nation brought with it an assortment of injustices and hardships not unlike those which already plagued Europe. The depression of 1837 had provided a sobering reminder of the unreliability of wealth in a young nation with a devil-take-the-hindmost economy. The floods of new immigrants, chiefly from the starving villages of western Ireland, congregated in deteriorating sections of Boston and undercut local wages in their efforts to feed themselves and their families. "Anti-popish" feeling literally burst into flame with the burning of a Charlestown convent in 1834, while the Irish in turn fanned the fires of antiabolitionism in their determination to protect *their* livelihood from free Negroes.

The new prosperity brought a rise in the incidence of alcoholism. In general, although American attitudes toward alcohol had been remarkably lenient in the previous centuries and strong drink had been readily available, drunkenness had rarely been a social problem. But now alcohol became a means of escape from the increasing problems of overcrowding and unemployment. Temperance societies sprang up throughout the country, and women, having tried their strength in the abolitionist movement and having the most to suffer from the abuse of alcohol, were among the leaders.

Relatively few people were aware of the plight of the American Indians, now hard-pressed to defend their remaining lands from annexation. But sensitivity to the issue of black slavery was growing, and the abolitionists, though still outnumbered, gained followers in Boston. Many Bostonians were outraged by the 1837 mob murder of the Rev. Elijah Lovejoy, an Illinois abolitionist editor, and were fiercely opposed to the Mexican War and the passage of the Fugitive Slave Law. The year 1851 would see a Boston Negro forcibly rescued from his abductors and carried in triumph through the same city that had witnessed the 1835 mobbing of William Lloyd Garrison.

On a spiritual level, both the hope and the despair of the 1840s were reflected in a proliferation of extremist sects whose members anticipated in various ways the coming of a new order. In Illinois the Mormons were defending by force of arms their belief in the teachings of Joseph Smith, while in upstate New York the followers of William Miller confidently prepared for the world to end in 1843. Made up chiefly of unlettered, rural people, these sects shared with Transcendentalism that new reliance on faith and mysticism which also was expressed in the rising interest in psychic phenomena. And, like the Transcendentalists, these people could be said to be searching for a renewed, relatively untarnished version of the American ideal. If the Transcendentalists did not cry "Repent!" like the Evangelists, still their denunciation of present evils and their hope for their own kind of millennium were not dissimilar. Visiting a convention of Millerites, "Come-Outers," and people of other unusual persuasions in 1840, Parker, Alcott, Ripley, and Christopher Cranch found themselves at least superficially in agreement with the "Come-Outers" of Cape Cod, who refused to worship under any roof and looked on all nature as their church.

It was during this decade, with the "Divinity School Address" and the publication of the *Dial,* that Transcendentalism came of age. Two years after Emerson delivered his address the air was still thick with pamphlets, and Ripley, Parker, and Clarke (who had returned to Boston) were all enlisted in that ecclesiastical tournament from which Emerson himself had simply withdrawn. By 1840 George Ripley, having ably refuted Andrews Norton's attacks on Emerson, Carlyle, and the German school, had decided to leave the ministry altogether and found a purer, more peaceful model of Christian society at Brook Farm. Parker and Clarke continued to defend the liberal point of view from their pulpits, until by 1842 only five Unitarian ministers would exchange with Parker. Clarke was one of them, and as a result fifteen of his congregation left in protest. The whole controversy had its droll side, as the Transcendentalists themselves were the first to see. But nevertheless, to maintain as Parker did that "man was made to be religious, as much as an ox was made to eat grass," [1] was to offend some basic convictions in the descendents of the Massachusetts Bay puritans. Those who flouted the authority of the Bible, it was said, would flout all other authority. "The view taken of Transcendentalism in State Street," Emerson recorded only half-jokingly in his journal, "is that it threatens to invalidate contracts." [2]

This was the atmosphere in which Margaret undertook to edit the *Dial* and give her Conversations—an atmosphere of apparent prosperity, but also of great uncertainty and dramatic contrasts, of extraordinarily rapid change and bitter resistance to change. Both the journal and the Conversations drew immediate censure from the State Street contingent, and as editor she had to serve as diplomatist among the varied and often discontented ranks of the Transcendentalists themselves. But Margaret's ability to steer a steady course in the midst of flux was one which, as a woman having made the choice she made, she had been obliged to learn early, and it was one of her chief strengths. Personally unshaken by criticism, she was unusually well-balanced intellectually, able to examine critically the various "isms" she saw around her and extract what was best from each without being swept away by any of them or retreating into a facile skepticism. Her sympathies with opinions, as with people, were almost entirely free from prejudice.

Her intellectual poise did not extend to her emotional life. Here she was far from balanced, subject to wide fluctuations of mood which are amply revealed in her letters and journals. She had frequent periods of depression, lassitude, self-abasement and morbid religiosity, but only her closest friends were aware of this side of her personality, and the impression gained from reading her personal papers is markedly different from the impression she made on casual acquaintances. She continued to repel almost everyone she met by her air of pompous intellectual vanity. She was capable, Emerson observed, of saying "as if she were stating a scientific fact, in enumerating the merits of somebody, 'He appreciates *me*.' " [3] She reportedly once remarked, "I now know all the people worth knowing in America, and I find no intellect comparable to my own." [4] (In this instance, as Perry Miller notes in retrospect, she may have been telling no more than the simple truth.) [5]

She herself realized how much the arrogance and pedantry of which she was accused were defensive:

[Ellery] began by railing at me as artificial. "It don't strike me when you are alone with me," he says, "but it does when others are present. You don't follow out the fancy of the moment,—you *converse*." . . . I listened attentively, for what he said was excellent. . . . A path has been appointed for me; I have walked in it as steadily as I could; I am what I am; that which I am not, teach me in others. I will bear the pain of imperfection, but not of doubt. Mr. [Emerson] must not shake me in my worldliness,—nor [William Channing] in the true motion that has given me what I have of life; nor this child of genius make me lay aside the armor without which I had lain bleeding in the field long since. . . .[6]

She loved hyperbole as much as ever. Emerson winced at her sentimentalism (which he distinguished from that of women in general only in its being better expressed).[7] Taken to task by her friends for making a public spectacle of her emotions, she would maintain that strong feelings require strong expression, and that to appear colder than she was would be dishonest. Any changes, she believed, would have to come from the inside out. "I am 'too fiery,' " she replied to a rebuke from William Channing,

Even so. Ceres put her foster child in the fire because she loved him. . . . I wish to be seen as I am, and would lose all rather than soften away anything. Let my friends be patient and gentle, and teach me to be so. I never promised any one patience or gentleness, for those beautiful traits are not natural to me; but I would learn them. Can I not?[8]

If she had thought age might temper her, and that in her thirties she would be able to look back with calm detachment on the emotional turbulence of her twenties, she found she was wrong:

Once I was almost all intellect; now I am almost all feeling. Nature vindicates her rights, and I feel all Italy glowing beneath the Saxon crust. This cannot last long; I shall burn to ashes if all this smoulders here much longer. I must die if I do not burst forth in genius or heroism.[9]

In the year 1840 she underwent an emotional upheaval the extent of which only she herself knew, although Emerson guessed at it. There is strong indirect evidence that during the preceding year Margaret had fallen in love with Sam Ward. But by July 1839 he was avoiding her and she did not understand why. Her anger was characteristically regal:

> No, I do not distrust you, so lately as you have spoken the words of friendship. You would not be so irreverent as to dare to tamper with a nature like mine, you could not treat so generous a person with levity. The kernel of affection is the same, no doubt, but it lies dormant in the husk. Will ever a second Spring bid it put forth leaf and flower? I can make every allowance. The bitterness of checked affections, the sickness of hope deferred, the dreariness of aspirations broken from their anchorage. I know them all, and I have borne at the same time domestic unhappiness and mined health. I know you have many engagements. What young man of promising character and prosperous fortunes has not one waiting his every hour? But if you are like me, you can trample upon such petty impossibilities: if you love me as I deserve to be loved, you cannot dispense with seeing me. . . . We knew long ago that age, position and pursuits being so different, nothing but love bound us together, and it must not be *my* love alone that binds us. . . .[10]

September found him still evasive, and Margaret no closer to an explanation:

> . . . The sympathizing contemplation of the beautiful in Nature, in Art is over for us, that for which I loved you first, and which made that love a shrine at which I would rest upon my weary pilgrimage. —Now—moons wax and wane, suns rise and set, the summer segment of the beautiful circle is filled, and since the first flush on the cheek of June we have not once seen, felt, admired together. You come here—to go away again, and make a call upon me in the parlor while you stay! You write to me—to say you could not write before and ask me why I do not write. —You invite me to go and see Michel's work—by myself! You send me your books and pictures—to ask me what I think of them! Thus far at least we have walked no step together and my heart deceives me wildly if this be love, or if we live as friends should live![11]

On Sam's side, at least, there was no longer any doubt. By October he had confessed to Margaret that he was in love with Anna Barker, whom he had met in 1835 and again the following year while they were both abroad. Margaret's magnanimity was Roman:

My dearest S[am],

Although I do not feel able at present to return a full answer to your letter I will not do myself the injustice of preserving entire silence.

Its sincerity of tone is all I asked.   —As I told you hastily the last time I had any real conversation with you—I never should make any claim upon the heart of any person on the score of past intercourse and those expressions of affection which were the flower and fruitage of its summer day. If autumn has come, let come also chill wind and rain like those of today. But on the *minds* of those who have known me once I have always a claim. My own entire sincerity in every passage of life gives me a right to expect that I shall never be met by unmeaning phrases or attentions.

For the rest believe me I understand all perfectly. In some future step of our being you will feel that I did so. And, though I might grieve that you should put me from you in your highest hour and find yourself unable to meet me on the very ground where you had taught me most to expect it, I would not complain or feel that the past had in any way bound either of us as to the present. If I had not been able to sympathize with you, I should have felt myself free to show it, should have thought it unworthy of myself or you to do otherwise, of course I am willing you should do the same. Truth and honor noble natures owe to one another, but love and confidence are free gifts or they are nothing.—

"The world has separated us as intimates and may separate us more"—'tis true, but no more than I had expected though you, dear friend, were more hopeful as became the sweetness of your earlier age.   —I had thought, too, that in ceasing to be intimates we might cease to be friends. I think so no longer. The knowledge I have of your nature has become a part of mine, the love it has excited will accompany me through eternity. My attachment was never so deep as now, it is quite unstained by pride or passion, it is sufficiently disinterested for me to be sure of it. Time, distance, different pursuits may hide you from me, yet will I never forget to be your friend, or to visit your life with a daily benediction. Nor can you, I feel it, while true to yourself be otherwise than true to me.

For these nearest coming days—I cannot of course dictate to your spirit, yet as far as I can see I would say think of me no more at present. Give yourself up to the holy hour and live in the celestial ray which shines on you at present. O I could weep with joy that real life is lived. Do you not feel how I should grieve to be the ghost to cross the path of true communion in the Elysian grove. Live without me now. Do not bid yourself remember me, but should an hour come by and by when the curtain shall be dropped and the lights extinguished and you have any need of me, you will find me in my place and find me faithful to you. If you would wish to hear aught else of me, I may say that the day is "solemn and serene" as is its wont after a flood of noonday light and I am tranquil after the season when

> "many a feeling long, too long, repressed
> Like autumn flowers dared blossom out at last"

That I am very busy with affairs I had deferred till I could bind my mind to them, and so prayerful that I do not for the present need though I might be grateful for even your prayers. With unchangeable affection,

Margaret F.[12]

Even in this letter there are suggestions of that confusion between passion and mere affection which Sam had apparently found too baffling to cope with, for in the third paragraph she clearly reproaches him for not confiding to her his love for Anna, while the tone of the letter elsewhere is that of the injured but forgiving lover.

Margaret's friendship with Anna in these difficult months remained sublimely undisturbed. Anna was visiting Jamaica Plain in October 1839 when Emerson wrote to Margaret that he was coming to meet "your Récamier." He had been looking forward for some time to meeting Anna, in whom he probably expected to find the mental acuity and the freshness of a Caroline Sturgis or a Sarah Clarke. But the harmonious perfections of the beautiful Anna fell just short of blandness, and at first he could find no distinguishing characteristic about her. It was only on closer acquaintance that he decided "the predominating character in her nature is not thought, but emotion or sympathy. . . . She does not sit at home in her mind, as my angels are wont to do, but instantly goes abroad into the minds of others, takes possession of society and warms it with noble sentiments."[13] This is the most accurate description we have of a woman who is otherwise conventionally described as charming, cultivated, and beautiful. One can see in Anna the successor in Margaret's affections to Ellen Kilshaw, whose "proper atmosphere was dance and song." Sharing with Margaret the dominant trait of empathy, Anna was otherwise everything Margaret was not. It must have made the Ward situation particularly difficult to have lost him, not just to a close friend, but to this close friend.

Margaret apparently overcame it by once more rising into a prolonged ecstasy of nunlike self-denial much like that she had experienced at Groton. She renewed her "vows of renunciation," determined once more to lead a celibate life and blessed the union of her friends with a maternal benignity from which she rigorously exorcised all trace of jealousy. She basked, rather excessively, in the light of her own saintliness, and her journals for this period make difficult reading. Few moods are less accessible to twentieth-century readers than that expressed in Shelley's lines, "I fall upon the thorns of life! I bleed!" We can forgive arrogance, as a rule, far more easily than we can sentimentality. But it was not Margaret's fault that she, like her fellow Romantics, was mired in the sticky remains of an outworn idiom. Her journals are saved from bathos by the reality of her suffering and by the absolute honesty with which she tried to use it to achieve that "harmonization" of her character which she thought would somehow mitigate the conflict between herself and her surroundings:

> Strive, strive, my soul, to be innocent; yes! beneficent. Does any man wound thee? not only forgive, but work into thy thought intelligence of the kind of pain, that thou mayest never inflict it on another spirit. Then its work is done; it will never search thy whole nature again. O, love much, and be forgiven![14]

Not surprisingly, the fusion of God, father, and lover that recurs in the imagery used by Christian mystics and poets of both sexes is a frequent theme:

I am weary of thinking. I suffer great fatigue from living. Oh God, take me! take me wholly! Thou knowest that I love none but Thee. All this beautiful poesy of my being lies in Thee. Deeply I feel it. I ask nothing. Each desire, each passionate feeling, is on the surface only; inmostly Thou keepest me strong and pure. Yet always to be thus going out into moments, into nature, and love, and thought! Father, I am weary! Reassume me for a while, I pray Thee. Oh let me rest awhile in Thee, Thou only Love! In the depth of my prayer I suffer much. Take me only a while. No fellow-being will receive me. I cannot pause; they will not detain me by their love. Take me awhile, and again I will go forth on a renewed service. It is not that I repine, my Father, but I sink from want of rest, and none will shelter me. Thou knowest it all. Bathe me in the living waters of Thy Love.[15]

In this state of religious rapture she remained all summer, while outwardly appearing composed and working vigorously on the first few issues of the *Dial*. "I have plagues about me, but they don't touch me now," she told Emerson. "I thank nightly the benignant Spirit, for the unaccustomed serenity in which it enfolds me."[16] By the time of the Ward marriage in October 1840 she was ready to continue her friendship with both of them on a tranquil, not to say beatific, level.

Not that the generalized sense of deprivation did not return, but she was in some ways better able to deal with it than before. It appeared sometimes frankly as itself, sometimes in the old guise of an enervating mood of lethargy and dependency. "I am very sorry," she wrote Emerson three months before the Ward marriage,

. . . to be inattentive, but I have felt entirely unlike writing. I have moods of sadness unknown I suppose to those of your temperament, when it seems a mockery and mummery to write of literature and the affairs of my acquaintance. Then I plunge into occupation and this fortnight past have been no moment idle. I do hope that in the next stage of our existence whatever may be our pains and difficulties we may not have these terrible seasons of faintness and discouragement. I ought not to have them now for I will never yield to them or live in their spirit a moment.[17]

Of all the passages in her journals and letters in which she deals frankly with her own sexual and maternal longings, none is more moving than this one, which has often been quoted before:

> I have no home on earth, and I can think of one that would have a degree of beautiful harmony with my inward life. But, driven from home to home as a renouncer I get the picture and the poetry of each. Keys of gold, silver, iron, and lead are in my casket.
>
> No one loves me.
>
> But I love many a good deal, and see some way into their eventual beauty. I am myself growing better, and shall by and by be a worthy object of love, one that will not anywhere disappoint or need forbearance. Meanwhile I have no fetter on me, no engagement, and as I look on others almost every other, can I fail to feel this a great privilege? I have no way tied my hands or feet. And yet the varied calls on my sympathy have been such that I hope not to be made partial, cold or ignorant by this isolation. I have no child, and the woman in me has so craved this experience that it has seemed the want of it must paralyze me. But now as I look on these lovely children of a human birth what slow and neutralizing cares they bring with them to the mother. The children of the muse come quicker, with less pain and disgust, rest more lightly on the bosom and have [not on them the taint of earthly corruption].[18]

Unable to live fully as both woman and artist, she consciously looked to the "children of the muse" to fill the place of the children she otherwise would have had. This meant that, although she was the conversationalist par excellence of her time, she undervalued her primary talent while placing on her writing an importance it was scarcely able to bear. Like all Romantics she valued poetry above all other literary forms, and she had to admit that her own verses were best confined to private papers. Her prose writings are indeed valuable, but for their content rather than their style, which is far from polished. At its best her writing shows a generosity and balance of mind that sets it apart from local and contemporary biases, and an insight into literature, the "woman question," and American life as a whole, which adds to our understanding of the malaise of her own century and ours. But she was never able to satisfy her own critical standards:

How can I ever write with this impatience of detail? I shall never be an artist; I have no patient love of execution; I am delighted with my sketch, but if I try to finish it, I am chilled. Never was there a great sculptor who did not love to chip the marble.[19]

One is reminded first of all of her childhood, and of her father's obsessive concern with accuracy and detail, but of course it is impossible to know how much this affected the ultimate distribution of her talents. It is notable, though, that she herself was unable to shake free of the belief, which was held by everyone around her, that artistic achievement was reserved for men. That Emerson, the most important person in her life at this time, held this view must have added a heavy weight to her own self-doubt. "The Muse is feminine. But action is male,"[20] Emerson confided to his diary; woman's role in life and art was as "a docile daughter of God with her face heavenward endeavoring to hear the divine word and to convey it to me."[21] And again:

Woman should not be expected to write, or fight, or build, or compose scores; she does all by inspiring man to do all. The poet finds her eyes anticipating all his ode, the sculptor his god, the architect his house. She looks at it. She is the requiring genius.[22]

In such a climate Margaret's confidence in women and in herself was strong, but no more than mortal. The great nineteenth-century English woman novelists and her own countrywoman Emily Dickinson had not yet entered the literary scene, and Margaret doubted at times whether any woman could produce a lasting work of art. In a passage reminiscent of her earlier remarks on Dr. Channing, but with different emphasis, she writes:

A woman of tact and brilliancy, like me, has an undue advantage in conversation with men. They are astonished at our instincts. They do not see where we got our knowledge; and, while they tramp on in their clumsy way, we wheel and fly, and dart hither and thither, and seize with ready eye all the weak points, like Saladin in the desert. It is quite another thing when we come to write, and, without suggestion from another mind, to declare the positive amount of thought that is in us. Because we seemed to know all, they think we can tell all; and, finding we can tell so little, lose faith in their first opinion of us, *which, nathless was true.* [23]

One scarcely knows whether there is more praise or blame in this passage, but there certainly is a good deal of generalization. The exhilarating success of the Conversations did much to reinforce her basically strong faith in the intellectual equality of women, but did not help answer the question of woman-as-creator. Here she suggests that her impatience with detail and systematic thought, and her need for "suggestion from another mind," are unavoidable consequences of her sex, and that in fact anatomy is destiny. Her difficulties with writing become representative of all women, and she momentarily slips into the old stereotype and seems to abandon her belief in the essentially androgynous nature of the individual mind. She celebrates womanly "instinct" but implies that no woman is really capable of creative thought. Herself weary of independence, weary of celibacy, she occasionally wondered if women were not merely satellites after all. But she did not accept such a conclusion all the time, or with an easy grace: "Who would be a goody that could be a genius?" [24] she asked Emerson. And, more bitterly in her own journal: "There is no need of an Inferno. It will be punishment enough for every fault, if we never become creators." [25]

How much these doubts became self-fulfilling can only be guessed at, but they do remind us that not even the strongest women of the time could escape the feminine tradition of self-deprecation. Nevertheless Margaret never appeared more outwardly confident, and was never more active and productive, than during these years. She simultaneously edited the *Dial,* conducted her Conversations, taught privately up to ten hours a week, sustained her role as paterfamilias, and continued to cut her accustomed swathe through the Boston social scene. During the spring of 1842 she also found time to translate part of Bettina Brentano's correspondence with Caroline von Günderode, which was published by Elizabeth Peabody.*

---

* The original German version was, alas, largely spurious, but neither Margaret nor anyone else was aware of this at the time.

In order to manage all this she allowed her life to assume a cyclical pattern, in which winters of heroic effort were succeeded by summers of visiting and "dissipation." January of 1840 or 1841 would find her racing deadlines for the *Dial,* with the printer all but camped on her doorstep, racking her brains to fill in missing copy, peering nearsightedly at galley proofs by lamplight, breathing the fumes from the oil burned in those lamps and from the wood and coal used as fuel in the closed rooms in which she worked, and complaining bitterly of headache. No doubt more outdoor exercise would have relieved her winter illnesses somewhat, but she seldom walked outdoors in the winter, probably because the discomfort of having several layers of soggy, cold petticoats dragging in the snow and flapping about one's ankles was enough to discourage even an Englishwoman, let alone an American.

After such a winter she would be close to exhaustion by March, and in April or May she would begin her summer rounds of visiting. The homes or rented summer retreats of Emerson, the Farrars, Caroline Sturgis, Dr. Channing, her Quaker friend Mary Rotch, Sarah Clarke, and several others were open to her; she made frequent trips to Newport, Rhode Island, and one or two to the "White Hills" of New Hampshire. She never stayed very long at one place, but toured like visiting royalty, bringing with her the inevitable battered camp chest containing manuscripts and proofs for whatever issue of the *Dial* she was working on at the moment. "She was everywhere a welcome guest," says Emerson:

> The houses of her friends in town and country were open to her, and every hospitable attention eagerly offered. Her arrival was a holiday, and so was her abode. She stayed a few days, often a week, more seldom a month, and all tasks that could be suspended were put aside to catch the favorable hour, in walking, riding, or boating, to talk with this joyful guest, who brought wit, anecdotes, love-stories, tragedies, oracles with her, and, with her broad web of relations to so many fine friends, seemed like the queen of some parliament of love, who carried the key to all confidences, and to whom every question had been finally referred.[26]

The early 1840s were particularly difficult years for the Fuller family, for whom Margaret always provided a center of stability.

"Go-ahead" America was a hazardous place for young people to begin life in, and Margaret had five younger brothers and a sister all to be launched more or less at once. None of them had an easy time of it, and Margaret's mother, herself fluttering nervously from one to another and succumbing to attacks of her stomach complaint, was more hindrance than help. The two older brothers, Eugene and William Henry, went to New Orleans, where William Henry married and where they both became involved in a succession of unfortunate business ventures. The third brother, Arthur, had the smoothest road but did not escape his share of trouble: he entered Harvard in 1839, teaching school between terms as his father had, and after graduation in 1843 went to Illinois and opened a school of his own, which promptly slid into financial difficulty. Margaret did her best to raise assistance for him in Boston, and the school lasted a year, after which he returned and entered Divinity School. Her fourth and favorite brother, Richard, at first elected not to go to college and worked for several months for a Boston merchant. This disenchanted him so violently with mercantile life that he determined to go to Harvard after all, and to make up the time he had lost he went to Concord and put himself under the tutelage of Henry Thoreau. There he spent the winter of 1840–41, living in the most monastic frugality on bread, milk, crackers, applesauce, and now and then a pie baked by Mrs. Emerson or Mrs. Thoreau. At the end of that time, having survived a preparation which also seems to have been a kind of penance and which caused his family some anxiety about his health, he entered Harvard as a sophomore.

The fifth brother, Lloyd, was both mentally deranged and mildly retarded, and as he neared manhood Margaret attempted to help him learn to be marginally self-sufficient. During the winter of 1840–41 she lived alone with him in Jamaica Plain (her mother having followed her sons to New Orleans) and tutored him as well as she could, but he was unable to concentrate or bear even the slightest restraint, and she had to give it up. In the spring she sent him to live at Brook Farm, where the Ripleys boarded him without charge as a kindness to Margaret. In the summer of 1842 she arranged for him to be apprenticed to a Cambridge printer for six months, but the choice of trade was a poor one and he was miserable in the confinement of the dark office. She sent him back to Brook Farm, but he was a disruptive influence there and the following year found him at Andover Academy, set to do the book-learning he loathed in the only institution available to one so mildly afflicted, an ordinary boarding school.

Margaret's sister Ellen had her own part in the ill-luck that seemed to follow the whole family. At the age of twenty Ellen had matured into a pretty young woman who had inherited her mother's oval face and delicate coloring, but lacked her gentle disposition and was inclined to be quick-tempered and impulsive. In 1840 Ellen went west with William Channing to find work as a teacher or governess, since this fate could be postponed no longer. She found it in Louisville, in the family of Margaret's former pupil Emma Keats, whose father was the poet's brother. While she was there she contracted rheumatic fever, and although she recovered she was left with rheumatic pains that proved to be permanent. Of all her visitors during her illness, none was more solicitous than the young poet Ellery Channing, who was now living in Cincinnati. In the fall of 1841, to the dismay of their families and friends, the couple announced that they were about to be married. Margaret in particular was upset, foreseeing nothing but unhappiness from the alliance of two people so unprepared for adult life. Ellery was a charming, totally irresponsible waif whose disdain for money-making was so extreme that he looked on all work save the writing of poetry as demeaning, and his poetry he would not revise for fear of spoiling its freshness. (The Emersonian theme of joyful self-confidence tinged with mysticism was an equivocal influence in literature. It would encourage the development of that quintessentially American poet, Walt Whitman; but it could easily foster a certain cockiness in lesser poets who, like Ellery, believed that all their first drafts were written on tablets of stone.)

After the couple's marriage Mrs. Fuller spent several months with them in Cincinnati, where Ellery worked for a while as a subeditor for the *Cincinnati Gazette*. But his small salary was paid sporadically, if at all, and their financial plight became nearly desperate. In 1842 they all returned to Cambridge, and Ellen and her mother spent the winter with Margaret while Ellery went to Con-

cord to look for a farm. Eventually he found one with the help of
Henry Thoreau, whose close friend he became. He and Ellen settled there and were very poor; children arrived with some regular-
ity; Ellen taught school to help keep the family together; Ellery's
black moods became blacker and he periodically disappeared on
long junkets by himself or with male friends.

The threads of this tangled skein wove in and out of Margaret's
history from 1839 to 1844. She was kept busy making arrangements for Richard and Lloyd; she sent money of her own to William Henry and arranged for various jugglings of the estate on
behalf of Eugene and Richard, enduring more than one unpleasant
interview with Abraham Fuller. She visited and offered moral support to William Henry's wife when she came north to have her
baby; she did what she could to rescue Arthur's school; in 1841
she considered, but rejected, the idea of moving to Cincinnati and
living with Ellen and Ellery, instead soliciting help from her Concord friends to get the couple settled there. In 1842, having given
up Willow Brook while their mother was away, Margaret and
Richard found her a house in Cambridge at 8 Ellery Street, and
saw to it that her furniture and plants were installed there before
she arrived home. The number of disruptions the family underwent
in this period is amazing; their physical restlessness alone makes
the modern "revolving executive" look the very model of stability.

During the winter of 1840–41, while several of these domestic
worries were very much on her mind, Margaret's old incubus of
headache assailed her with particular force. She wrote William
Henry Channing that she had had "one of her nervous attacks"
and had lost "too much blood"[27]—probably a reference to one of
her nosebleeds. She was feeling better in a month or two, but the
following winter the malady recurred, and under the triple weight
of sickness, financial worries, and anxiety over her family, she felt
compelled to give up the *Dial*. It was money that finally forced her
to act. The *Dial* had never paid her the promised salary of $200 a
year, and now Elizabeth Peabody, who had taken over publication
from Weeks and Jordan, said that in the future it would do no
more than pay for itself. Margaret's income from the Conversa-

tions was not enough to allow her to continue to donate most of her working hours to the *Dial,* and she felt she had no choice but to shift it onto Emerson's unwilling shoulders, though she intended to keep on contributing as many articles as possible.

It was a difficult time for Emerson and his wife as well as for Margaret, and for a while it seemed as though the *Dial* might slip into oblivion after all. In January the Emersons had suffered the loss of their five-year-old son Waldo, who died suddenly of scarlet fever. Numbed by this latest and most severe blow, Emerson once more grieved that he could not grieve, and with a stoicism that must have seemed indifference to those who did not know him well, went to New York to fulfill a series of lecture engagements barely a month later. "I comprehend nothing of this fact but its bitterness," he wrote in his journal. "Explanation I have none, consolation none that rises out of the fact itself; only diversion; only oblivion of this, and pursuit of new objects." [28] The *Dial* at least offered him this much, and after some hesitation he decided to take it on rather than let it die or pass into "hands that know not Joseph" [29]—probably meaning Theodore Parker's. Margaret, relieved of the primary responsibility, wrote reviews of Hawthorne's *Twice Told Tales* and *Stories for Children* for the next issue, and a forty-three-page article on "Romaic and Rhine Ballads" for the following one.

It was primarily with the writing of this article in mind that she wrote Emerson from the Farrars' home in Cambridge in the summer of 1842:

Dear Waldo,

I have been waiting to write to you till Mr and Mrs Farrar should decide whether to go a journey they had in view. If they had gone, I was to have staid here during their absence for this would have ensured me several weeks of stillness and solitude, so that I could have fixed my mind on writing. But they have given up this journey, and I should like to come to you next week, if you please. Now I want you to be perfectly frank in answering what I shall say. I am tired to death of dissipation; I do not enjoy it, nor find any repose in mere observation now I long to employ myself steadily. I have no inspiration now, but hope it might come, if I were once fixed in some congenial situation. Should you like it should be with you, that I should come and really *live* in your house a month, instead of making a visit, as I should here. Would it entirely suit Lidian's convenience? Do not regard hospitality in your answer for if I am to feel quite happy and at my ease it must be perfectly pleasant for you. I must feel that I shall not be in any one's way. I am always sensitive about encamping on your territories, for I think so many tax your hospitality without mercy. . . . Now, dear friend, be entirely frank, and induce Lidian to be so. I should be with you.

Emerson replied,

Dear Margaret,

Well now, please to come, for this I have always desired that you will make my house in some way useful to your occasions and not a mere hotel for a sleighing or summering party. I admire the conditions of the treaty, that you shall put on sulkiness as a morning gown, and I shall put on sulkiness as a surtout, and speech shall be contraband and the exception not the rule. . . .[30]

She arrived on August 17, a foggy evening, and found there Henry Thoreau, who was living with the Emersons, and Ellery Channing, who had come East to look for winter quarters for himself and Ellen. The conditions of the "surtout" agreement were met. Emerson presented Margaret with a pen and inkhorn the following day, and she set to work on her article for the *Dial,* spending her mornings and sometimes the whole day in the red room that was hers when she came to visit.

This visit marks the period of their closest friendship, and also the end of that prolonged analysis of friendship in general which overflowed into Emerson's letters to Caroline Sturgis and the Wards and finally found its way into his essay on the subject. The tension in their relationship was an enigma they never solved, but during this visit they simply wore it out. They were both sovereigns, in their way, and if Margaret would brook no reserve, Waldo would brook no trespass. Consequently, as Emerson said, they would "meet and treat like foreign states, one maritime, one inland, whose trade and laws are essentially unlike."[31]

To this Margaret replied,

> I have felt the impossibility of meeting far more than you; so much,
> that, if you ever know me well, you will feel that the fact of my abid-
> ing with you thus far, affords a strong proof that we are to be much
> to one another. How often have I left you despairing and forlorn.
> How often have I said, This light will never understand my fire; this
> clear eye will never discern the law by which I am filling my circle;
> this simple force will never interpret my need of manifold being.[32]

Her admiration for this "simple force," which was what she
most appreciated in him, is shown in a letter she wrote from room
to room, while both preserved their working-day isolation:

> I like to be in your library when you are out of it. It seems a sacred
> place. I came here to find a book, that I might feel more life and be
> worthy to sleep, but there is so much soul here I do not need a book.
> When I come to yourself, I cannot receive you, and you cannot give
> yourself; it does not profit. But when I cannot find you the beauty
> and permanence of your life come to me.[33]

Sometimes taken to be a love letter, this is put in its proper context in a recent article by Joel Myerson, in which he publishes for
the first time the journal Margaret kept during these weeks.[34] It
sheds new light on the sometimes clouded picture scholars have
had of the Emerson marriage, and it lays to rest any speculations
that the Emerson-Fuller friendship was more than just that.

Lidian, still grieving for her son and dressed in mourning, suffering from toothache and a "slow fever" while Margaret was
there, was in an altogether wretched state and usually kept to her
chamber, while her husband went about his affairs in his usual ab-
stracted way. Such were the independent habits of everyone in the
household that it was two weeks before Margaret fully realized
how little she was seeing of Lidian, and thereupon paid her a visit.
To her confusion, Lidian burst into tears on seeing her:

> Presently she said something which made me suppose she thought
> W. passed the evenings in talking with me, & a painful feeling

flashed across me, such as I have not had, all has seemed so perfectly understood between us. I said that I was with Ellery or H[enry]. T[horeau]. both of the eve gs [*sic*] & that W. was writing in the study.

I thought it all over a little, whether I was considerate enough. As to W. I never keep him from any such duties, any more than a book would. —He lives in his own way, & he dont soothe the illness, or morbid feelings of a friend, because he would not wish any one to do it *for him*. It is useless to expect it; what does it signify whether he is with me or at his writing. L. knows perfectly well, that he has no regard for me or any one that would make him wish to be with me, a minute longer than I could fill up the time with thoughts.[35]

This incident led to a long talk the following day, in which Lidian complained bitterly to Margaret of Waldo's neglect of her. After that Margaret tried to be more attentive to Lidian, who hitherto had always seemed as content to go her own way as Emerson himself. But though she sympathized with Lidian's distress and came back to the subject several times in her own mind, Margaret always returned to the same conviction, that as long as Lidian hoped for her husband to change she would continue to be miserable. ". . . The influence of any one with him would be just in proportion to independence of him, combined with pure love of him for his own sake."[36] She herself was not sure she would have "fortitude" enough for such forbearance, were she in Lidian's shoes.

It all came back to the same closed quality in Emerson which was at the root of their continuing debate about friendship. In these discussions Margaret now found herself in the middle, intellectually defending Lidian's position as well as her own, while daily growing impatient with Lidian's possessiveness. She was irritated, too, by Emerson's insensitivity, but at the same time she admired him for being "true to himself." Her customary view of him was esthetic, as if he were a self-contained universe whose fixed laws were beyond anyone's power to change, including his own. Ultimately it seems probable that Lidian's revelations were one reason why Margaret and Emerson, after this visit, agreed to let the long debate on dependence and independence subside.

Meanwhile, whenever they both emerged from their studies there was conversation on "God and the world" and other familiar topics. But with four other adults and two children in the house, and Elizabeth Hoar and the Hawthornes as neighbors, she by no means spent all her free time with Emerson. Her brother Richard came to spend a day, as did Sam Ward and Henry Hedge. She had long walks and talks with Ellery, whom she loved as a gifted, whimsical child whenever she could manage to forget that he was all that stood between her sister and destitution. She saw the Hawthornes several times, and this journal (along with one written during an 1844 visit to Concord) amply demonstrates the easy cordiality of her relations with them. It was during this visit, at Ellery's request and probably against her better judgment, that she asked the newlyweds if Ellery and Ellen could board with them and received separate, equally tactful refusals. She spent August 21 in Sleepy Hollow with Hawthorne and Emerson, but left it to Hawthorne to describe that meeting in his own journal.[37] All she could say in hers was "What a happy, happy day, all clear light. I cannot write about it."[38]

Toward the end of the visit Ellen arrived from Cincinnati, which gave rise to a situation painfully resembling that between Waldo and Lidian. Before Ellen's arrival Ellery abruptly left to pay one more visit to Caroline Sturgis, with whom he had had a closer friendship than his bride realized. He did not return before Ellen arrived, and Margaret was put in the awkward position of having to cover up for him. The next day he did return and "told Ellen at once how it was, and she took it just as she ought." Margaret saw the whole incident as one more example of the dependence-independence conflict, and again she decided in favor of independence: "If I were Waldo's wife, or Ellery's wife, I should acquiesce in all these relations, since they needed them. I should expect the same feeling from my husband, & I should think it little in him not to have it."[39]

Her own independence asserted itself when, during this visit, Emerson revived the old suggestion that she move to Concord and join the long-hoped-for little colony of his friends that were beginning to gather there. But Margaret retreated, as she always had before: "It is not yet time for me to have my dwelling near you," she wrote from Cambridge after she had left. "I get, after a while, even *intoxicated* with your mind, and do not live enough in myself." [40] She was careful of her intellectual integrity, and for all the worshipful tone in this letter she was in fact beginning to diverge more widely from Emerson in her thinking. She would shortly write "The Great Lawsuit," which he would praise generously but could not wholeheartedly endorse. Soon after that she would leave Cambridge and Concord behind in every sense, and begin a phase of her life which brought out that side of her personality most unlike Emerson's.

By the fall of 1842 Margaret was newly established in the Ellery Street house and her life had become, if not calm, at least less complicated than it had been for the past year and a half. As always when she lived with her family, she found it very difficult to protect her working time. Moreover, between Richard and Arthur, now both at Harvard, and their ever-anxious, hovering mother there was a less than perfect meeting of minds. But her new series of Conversations and lessons at home began well, and from the upper windows of the house she could look out on the blue line of hills she remembered from her childhood.

On October 2 Dr. Channing died at the age of sixty-two. The Boston community mourned the loss of its strongest link with an earlier, more orderly time. Channing in his last years had become a sort of monument, whom all loved at a distance but few knew, but as a man he had been perplexed and saddened by the new set of heresies which his own heresies had helped to bring about. Struggling to write a eulogy for the *Dial,* Margaret had to give it up, finding there was nothing she could say about this man to whom they all owed so much without sounding cold and ungrateful. "He could not have died at a better time," she wrote in her journal. "It was indeed for him the fullness of time; but it is sad that we shall see him no more,—meet no more the pale benignant countenance,—be greeted no more by the gentle, formal courtesy; nay, it is even sad that we shall be catechized no more for great truths to feed his earnest mind." She went to the funeral the following Friday, but felt the elaborate public obsequies to be even more irrelevant than such things usually were. "The sun shone in at the windows, and I smiled at all they said. Yet it was well they should say it; every inner must have an outer." [41]

The death of Channing marked a transition in Margaret's own history as well as that of Boston, though she did not yet realize it. With Emerson, Thoreau, Parker, Ripley, and Alcott, she was one of the most active leaders of the Transcendentalist movement, though like them she would have disliked being identified with any kind of "movement" and would have insisted that she was merely living and thinking as honestly as she could, without betraying what she knew to be the best in herself. This, of course, was and remains an extremely difficult thing to do; for a woman it was doubly difficult, since her own rebellion involved overturning even those few landmarks that remained to her male friends, and sometimes required her to resist the prejudices of those friends themselves. In the Conversations and in her very life style Margaret had permanently altered the image women had of themselves and passed on to their daughters, and it is in this influence, no less real for being impossible to measure, that her strongest contribution lay. This much she had achieved in Boston, and by the spring of 1843 she was giving it written expression in "The Great Lawsuit," to be published in July. Shortly thereafter she left for a tour of the West with James and Sarah Clarke, and although she returned briefly afterward to live in Boston, it would never again be a permanent home for her.

X

Hawthorne
and Margaret Fuller

No book on Margaret Fuller would be complete without a discussion of Brook Farm and of the controversy over her relationship with Nathaniel Hawthorne. The two are related, since Hawthorne was a member of Brook Farm and later drew heavily on his recollections of the community for his novel *The Blithedale Romance.* Zenobia, one of the two leading female characters in the novel, is generally acknowledged to be partially based on Margaret Fuller.

Margaret never actually joined Brook Farm, but she sympathized with its high purpose and often stayed there for a week or more at a time. She seems to have made a habit of spending New Year's Eve there, and in autumn 1842 she gave a series of Conversations there, on alternate evenings with husking parties. Her brother Lloyd was there, and several of the members were good friends, among them George and Sophia Ripley, Charles King Newcomb, John Sullivan Dwight, Christopher Cranch, Nathaniel Hawthorne, and Almira Barlow, now separated from her husband and living at the farm with her son.

Brook Farm was one of many planned communities that sprang

up in the middle of the century in response to the increasing complexities of society at large. Shaker communities were already thriving in the United States, and in Europe the theories of Robert Owen and Charles Fourier were attracting widespread attention. In 1840 George Ripley decided to form a model community that was less rigidly structured than any of these, and that would depend for its success on the voluntary goodwill and cooperation of its members rather than on any complicated set of rules. It thus was based on the ideals of Christianity and Transcendentalism, and to it flocked the young men and women Emerson had described to Carlyle, as well as older people who wanted to lead a simpler, more honest life. A disproportionate number of Brook Farmers, like Ripley, Cranch, and Dwight, were ministers who had left the pulpit.

Margaret and Emerson were among the first people Ripley approached with his plan, but they both declined, for different reasons. To Emerson there was a large difference between living in such a community and having his own friends come to Concord to live, each under his own fig tree. "At the name of a society all my repulsions play, all my quills rise and sharpen," he told Margaret.[1] Margaret's objections were on both personal and philosophical grounds. In many ways life at Brook Farm would be preferable to living with her own family. There would be no interruptions, since the members were willing that she should be exempt from physical work and devote all her time to writing. Her financial worries would be eased, at least regarding her own support. Naturally gregarious as Emerson was not, she would not find communal living irksome.

But she was afraid that the exemption from work would be a source of strain, since she would be under constant pressure to prove she was worth it. Moreover, though the Brook Farmers saw their community as an experiment in a more humane social order, Margaret could not help but feel that they were burying their heads in the sand. She did not believe that utopia could be built, either on a small scale or a large; and given the fact that human frailty was everywhere, it might as well be dealt with in its grosser forms. She was neither sanguine nor despairing about American society. She thought it could be improved, though only slowly, and that on the whole it was better than any other.

Then too, she and Emerson shared a distrust of what they called the *sans-cullotism* of Brook Farm. Margaret was mildly offended when she led a conversation there and the audience sprawled all over the floor, yawned and stretched, and wandered in and out. It was not that she cared about formal manners, but she was enough of a classicist to suspect that "natural man," Rousseau notwithstanding, was a slushy sort of creature at best. *Sans-cullotism* implied a simplistic glorification of impulse, and an overzealous admiration for the primitive and the picturesque. There was something a little ridiculous, after all, in the affectation of smocks and broad-brimmed hats, the idealization of manual labor, and the elaborately monastic surroundings: there was, for example, only one china cup and saucer, in which Georgianna Bruce, one of Margaret's young admirers, served her morning coffee as a tribute. But china cups were not an adequate symbol of evil, nor dirty fingernails an adequate symbol of good. It all savored of an earnestly played pretend-game, as Emerson said, "a perpetual picnic, a French Revolution in small, an Age of Reason in a patty-pan."[2] Margaret was never willing to settle for easy answers, and Brook Farm was too easy an answer; it excluded too much.

Nathaniel Hawthorne was one of the original members of Brook Farm, and the question of whether the character of Zenobia is modeled on Margaret Fuller has intrigued a long succession of biographers. On the whole, the consensus seems to be that Zenobia is chiefly, though not entirely, modeled on Margaret. This leads to the further question of what Margaret represented to Hawthorne, since his feelings about her were evidently complicated.

On the whole, Hawthorne was a gentle, scrupulously fair-minded man. In a time that was rife with ideologies of all kinds, he kept apart from them. He did not even "believe" in Brook Farm, but simply lived there because it was convenient to do so. In his best writing he sets the imaginative depiction of character above any overtly moral theme. But he had his crochets, among which was a dislike of strong women. His shyness (or reserve, as some of his biographers prefer to call it) made him averse to company and silent in the presence of others. Talkative, spirited people annoyed him, and talkative, spirited women most of all.

In his relationships with women generally, Hawthorne is an extreme example of the prevailing attitudes of his time, attitudes which he shared with Timothy Fuller, James Freeman Clarke, Theodore Parker, and sometimes (though he would deny it) Ralph Waldo Emerson. He would not gainsay, in theory, a woman's right to be all she could be. But personally he expected women to be pretty, sensitive, silent, passive, and spiritually "higher" than men because altogether sexless. In Hawthorne's case this image was realized in his choice of a wife. Sophia Hawthorne, the artistic, semi-invalid, youngest sister of Elizabeth Peabody, expected of herself exactly what her husband expected of her. Theirs was an idyllic marriage, characterized by unflagging tenderness, but based on Hawthorne's assuming absolute sovereignty over his wife, whom he treated as half-angel, half-idiot, and whom he undertook to lead through the wilderness by the hand:

> Dearest, I never think you to blame; for you positively have no faults. Not that you always act wisely, or judge wisely, or feel precisely what it would be wise to feel, in relation to this present world and state of being; but it is because you are too delicately and exquisitely wrought in heart, mind, and frame, to dwell in such a world—because, in short, you are fitter to be in Paradise than here. . . . Were an angel, however holy and wise, to come and dwell with mortals, he would need the guidance and instruction of some mortal; and so will you, my Dove, need mine—and precisely the same sort of guidance that the angel would.[3]

He disapproved of her attending Margaret Fuller's Conversations, but he need not have worried. No woman there could have avoided their influence more successfully.

As for Margaret's effect on Hawthorne, it would be hard to improve on Henry James:

> It is safe to assume that Hawthorne could not on the whole have had a high relish for the very positive personality of this accomplished and argumentative woman, in whose intellect high noon

seemed ever to reign, as twilight did in his own. He must have been
struck by the glare of her understanding, and, mentally speaking,
have scowled and blinked a good deal in conversation with her. But
it is tolerably manifest, nevertheless, that she was, in his imagination,
the starting point of the figure of Zenobia. . . .[4]

As has been noted, to all appearances Margaret's relationship
with Hawthorne was cordial. In his journal there is a pleasant
description of that afternoon in the Concord woods which
Margaret found too perfect to write about, and on hearing of his
engagement to Sophia, Margaret had written: "I think there will
be great happiness; for if ever I saw a man who combined
delicate tenderness to understand the heart of a woman, with quiet
depth and manliness enough to satisfy her, it is Mr. Hawthorne."[5]
When she learned that the Hawthornes were moving to Concord,
she wrote to Emerson (who knew Hawthorne only slightly), "I
think you must take pleasure in Hawthorne when you know him;
you will find him more *mellow* than most fruits at your board, and
of distinct flavor too."[6]

In July 1844 Margaret visited Concord for almost a month, staying alternately at the Hawthornes' house and her sister Ellen's.
The journal she kept then, which fortunately has been preserved
almost intact, proves beyond doubt her growing affection for
Hawthorne:

> [July 17] . . . We went out on the river. . . . He talked a great
> deal this time. I love him much, and love to be with him in this
> sweet tender homely scene. But I should like too, to be with him on
> the bold ocean shore.[7]

On the first or second night in August, Margaret and Hawthorne
went for a long, moonlit row on the river:

> . . . The wind being against us made it too hard for the boatman
> and soft clouds overspreading the whole sky, it seemed that we
> should have no moon back, so we did not go quite to Fairhaven
> [Bay], but stopped about half a mile this side and went on shore to
> walk. But soon the moon rose in great beauty, above a wood and we

went to the boat again. We floated carelessly, running ashore every now and then, and reached home a little after ten. O it is a sweet dream in memory! Yet I regretted afterward that I had been led to talk so much. . . .[8]

In fantasy she made what seems to be a composite ideal man of Hawthorne, Emerson, and William Channing, wistfully setting them all against the background of her own reluctant celibacy:

Last night in the boat I could not help thinking each has something—more all. With Waldo how impossible to enjoy this still companionship, this mutual visionary life. With William even! . . . But then H. has not the deep polished intellect of the one or the pure and passionate beauty of the other. He has his own powers: I seem to want them all. . . .[9]

She was enchanted with the Hawthornes' daughter Una, frankly preferring her to her own niece and namesake. And perhaps no more telling evidence exists of the Hawthornes' friendship to the Fullers as a family than the fact that Sophia Hawthorne nursed Ellen Channing's baby once a day to supplement the frail Ellen's inadequate supply of milk.

Yet there were several equivocal incidents, innocent in themselves, which taken together suggest that Hawthorne's feelings toward Margaret were mixed. Invited to dine at George Bancroft's with Margaret, Hawthorne wrote in his journal that he was thankful to have business elsewhere: but this may have indicated an aversion to Bancroft, who was something of a dandy, or to dinner parties in general. There are also in his Brook Farm journal some remarks about a "Transcendental heifer" which Margaret's friends had teasingly named after her. (It was probably Margaret's own cow, sent to help pay Lloyd's expenses.) Hawthorne writes that the animal is "fractious," "hooks other cows, and has made herself ruler of the herd, and behaves in a very tyrannical manner." Two days later:

The herd has rebelled against the usurpation of Miss Fuller's heifer; and whenever they are turned out of the barn, she is compelled to take refuge under our protection. So much did she impede my labors by keeping close to me, that I found it necessary to give her two or three gentle pats with a shovel. She is not an amiable cow; but she has a very intelligent face, and seems to be of a reflective cast of character.[10]

Mischievous remarks, surely, and it is interesting to see how Hawthorne mellows after the cow is compelled to ask for his "protection." But it is hard to see in this evidence of any real malice, and during this period Hawthorne knew Margaret only slightly.

The third incident sometimes mentioned is the tactless blunder Margaret made in 1842 when she asked the newlywed Hawthornes, at Ellery's insistence, whether her sister and brother-in-law could live with them when they came to Concord. Hawthorne declined gracefully, without any show of rancor, but privately doubtless resented even the suggestion of intruders.

The woman called Zenobia in *The Blithedale Romance* is tactless, willful, passionate, and egotistic. She is also a brilliant conversationalist and an advocate of women's rights, and she dies by water. But in some respects she is different from Margaret. She is dark and beautiful, as Margaret certainly was not, and it is generally supposed that Hawthorne derived her physical characteristics from Almira Barlow. Moreover, Zenobia's mind is "full of weeds." She is all instinct and passion. Whatever Hawthorne thought of Margaret Fuller, he must have been aware that she had a disciplined mind. At one point in the book he mentions Margaret by name, as if trying to prevent the reader from identifying her with Zenobia. No other nonfictional person is thus singled out.

In *The Anatomy of Criticism,* Northrop Frye refers to the nineteenth-century literary convention of two heroines, one dark, erotic, and disruptive or evil; the other pure and fair.[11] These two archetypal characters are in fact to be found throughout English literature, appearing in the Arthurian cycle as Guinevere and Elaine, in the "Dark Lady" sonnets of Shakespeare and several of the plays, in Spenser's *Faerie Queene,* in Thackeray's *Vanity Fair,* in Hardy's *Return of the Native,* in *Hedda Gabler,* in *Gone with the Wind,** and most strikingly in Coleridge's "Christabel." Randall

---

* Margaret Mitchell is an interesting example of how women authors have themselves followed this tradition, as is Emily Brontë.

Stewart has pointed out that in Hawthorne's woman characters intellectual ability is invariably linked with sin and a dark, voluptuous kind of beauty which suggests something demonic.[12] In the novels the dark woman shows up as Zenobia, Meriam, and Hester Prynne, the fair one as Hilda and Priscilla.

It is not intellect alone that makes the dark woman evil, but intellect plus erotic passion and will. She is the temptress, the personification of sin, and if she is not kept in her place, where will the world be? In this respect Hawthorne is a puritan, as he sometimes is accused of being, but no more so than Shakespeare, Coleridge, et al. The "safe" woman is pallid, pure, and a little stupid; the dark woman is dangerous because she is strong and because she represents what the author would like to suppress in himself. In Zenobia, Hawthorne begins with Margaret's passionate nature and strong will, adds the physical qualities she lacked to make her an acceptable antiheroine, and then shows how the combination leads the dark woman to destruction.

Hawthorne's denial that Zenobia was based on Margaret would have been more convincing if he had not written a startlingly venomous passage about her in his journals after her death. Because Hawthorne was nearing the end of his own life by this time and his mind was beginning to fail, it has been suggested that the passage does not fairly reflect his feelings toward Margaret. That may be true, but it also may be true that the irrational hatred which was present all along was now no longer controlled by his kinder, younger self. The passage reads, in part:

> It was such an awful joke, that she should have resolved . . . to make herself the greatest, wisest, best woman of the age. And to that end, she set to work on her strange, heavy, unpliable, and, in many respects, defective and evil nature, and adorned it with a mosaic of admirable qualities, such as she chose to possess; putting in here a splendid talent and there a moral excellence, and polishing each separate piece, and the whole together, till it seemed to shine afar and dazzle all who saw it. She took credit to herself for having been her own Redeemer, if not her own Creator . . .[13]

To this woman whose humility before God was profound, even if her humility before her fellow mortals was not, he attributes the primary sin of hubris, the sin of Satan. God could not possibly have endowed her with so many "admirable qualities," so with the power she derives from the devil she has given them to herself. To say that Margaret's nature was "strange, heavy, and unpliable" is a (barely) recognizable perversion of the truth; to say that it was "defective and evil" is to go utterly beyond the pale, into the realm of the writer's own neurotic fantasies. There is no possible way that anyone can accuse Margaret of being evil—if he is thinking of Margaret herself. But Hawthorne was not; he was thinking of what she represented to him.

Hawthorne's antagonism did not affect Margaret directly, first because she was unconscious of it, and second because she and Hawthorne never became close friends, despite the promise of the 1844 visit. It did very much affect her posthumous reputation, however, and that in turn has contributed to the general image of feminists in the popular mind. Hawthorne's prejudices, when considered in the context of the prejudices of other people in her life, must be seen as part of that pervasive, half-acknowledged atmosphere of hostility which all early feminists had to breathe.

XI

The West

In the summer of 1843 Margaret and her friend Sarah Clarke set off on a tour of what was still known as the American Northwest: Chicago and Milwaukee and the countryside around them. James Clarke escorted them to Niagara Falls, where they all spent a week, and thence to Buffalo, where he saw them safely aboard a steamboat before leaving to return to his family. A five-and-a-half-day voyage brought them to Chicago, where they were met by the Clarkes' brother William, who had settled there some time earlier. Under his guidance they were able to explore the Illinois prairie, and later they made a side trip on their own, intrepid ladies that they were, to Milwaukee and the burgeoning territory of Wisconsin.

Margaret kept a detailed journal, and after she returned in September she began organizing it into a book which she called *Summer on the Lakes*. This took her several months, not only because she had to sandwich it in between her teaching and Conversations but because she decided that she needed to read more extensively on the history of the Great Lakes region. This led to the breaking of another Cambridge taboo. The libraries of her friends, well stocked as they were, were of no use at all in this case, and the only local library adequate to her purpose was at Harvard. Somehow she talked the college authorities into allowing her to work there, and the effect of this intrusion, particularly on those older members of the faculty who were accustomed to think of the library as a kind of private club to which a gentleman could retreat after dinner, can well be imagined. But by now Margaret had become one of those Cambridge oddities, like Memorial Day snowstorms, which one put up with in the faith that the laws of a well-governed universe allowed such phenomena to occur only rarely.

Though designed for light reading and marred by Margaret's usual digressiveness, *Summer* has value to both historian and biographer. It preserves a casual but fascinating picture of the Great Lakes region as it was during an ephemeral period in its history which lasted only a few years. With the opening up of California and Oregon, which was already beginning, the region would lose its frontier status and become, as others had before it, the last way-station of comfort and safety for those heading into dangerous territory farther west. The nation would soon cease to depend on the canal system for transportation between east and west; soon the railroad would supersede the ubiquitous steamers, bringing eastern culture and amenities to the settlers in the Lakes region with more speed and efficiency than had been possible before. The diversity which was so striking to Margaret as she met English, Irish, American, German, and Scandinavian settlers, each living on a little cultural oasis of his own, would become blurred. The people she describes—the doomed, lingering Indians determined to live, if only as beggars, in their old lands; the newly arrived British country gentry who tried to live like Herefordshire squires and who saw in the gentle Illinois landscape one vast, inviting deer park; the boisterous Irish, the weary, travel-stained Norwegians and Swedes, the New Englanders with their spare, careful houses and their spare, careful ways—would gradually lose their separate characteristics or (in the case of the Indian) vanish altogether. In another generation the granddaughters of an English country gentleman Margaret visited probably would neither speak fluent French, as their mothers did, nor kill rattlesnakes in the chicken-house, as their mothers also did. And a later visitor would not be likely to stay in a boardinghouse kept by the daughter of a famous "Indian-fighter" (i.e., fighter against the Indians) where little Indian boys brought raspberries for sale every day.

To a biographer *Summer on the Lakes* is a personal book, retaining the tone of a diary even though the most intimate (and often the most lively) passages have been excised. Margaret does not spend much time describing the scenery, observing that others have done so before her. But the countryside moved her greatly, and she saw it, as she saw the people she met, with a Transcendentalist's eye. Once she had overcome her New England habit of looking for hills on the prairie, she said she had never seen lovelier country. The generous, elemental western landscape, with its subtle patterns of waving grasses, flowers, and moving cloud shadows, its isolated herds of grazing cattle and its groves of "cathedral-like trees," became for her an appropriate stage for the rise of that still-hoped-for native American culture. The contrast between the prodigality of nature and the squalid ugliness and petty greed she found in the cities repelled her, as did the ruthless displacement of the Indian. But like Emerson welcoming the railroad to Concord as the herald of a new age, she saw present evils as a phase in the development of a sane, healthy society in which the material wants of all would be satisfied and economic growth would be balanced by cultural and moral maturity:

> I come to the West prepared for the distaste I must experience at its mushroom growth. I know that, where "go ahead" is the only motto, the village cannot grow into the gentle proportions that successive lives and the gradations of experience involuntarily give. In older countries the house of the son grew from that of the father, as naturally as new joints on a bough, and the cathedral crowned the whole as naturally as the leafy summit the tree. This cannot be here. The march of peaceful is scarce less wanton than that of warlike invasion. The old landmarks are broken down, and the land, for a season, bears none, except of the rudeness of conquest and the needs of the day, whose bivouac-fires blacken the sweetest forest glades. I

have come prepared to see all this, to dislike it, but not with stupid narrowness to distrust or defame. . . . I trust by reverent faith to woo the mighty meaning of the scene, perhaps to foresee the law by which a new order, a new poetry, is to be evoked from this chaos. . . .[1]

In Chicago, where she and Sarah stayed at a boardinghouse, she found herself more alone than she had been even in Groton or Providence. People were all around her, but she could find no ground on which to meet them. The old sense of isolation and depression crept into letters which, needless to say, did not find their way into her book. In the countryside, she writes William Channing, she has been rapturously happy,

. . . but among *men* oh, how lonely! If it is my fault that I have met with so little congenial, it has not been for want of good will. . . . Always it has been that I should hear from them accounts of the state of the country, in politics or agriculture, or their domestic affairs, or hunting stories. Of me, none asked a question. Like Mr. E's lonely poet
What she has, nobody wants
I have not been led to express one thought of my mind with warmth and freedom since I have been here. . . .[2]

She is deeply homesick, "yet where is that home? —If not on earth, why should we look to heaven. I would fain truly live wherever I must abide. . . ."

To Emerson, on the night of her departure from Chicago, she wrote,

I shall scarce leave friends behind me though, perhaps, no foes. I have not reached forth the hand, neither has it been offered to me. I am silenced by these people, they are so all life and no thought, any thing that might fall from my lips would seem an impertinence. I move about silently and look at them unnoticed.

Truly there is no place for me to live, I mean as regards being with men. I like not the petty intellectualities, cant, and bloodless theory there at home, but this merely instinctive existence, to those who live it so "first rate" "off hand" and "go ahead," pleases me no better.[3]

But even in Chicago, and especially out in the country, she found the forthrightness of westerners refreshing:

> The dissipation of thought and feeling is less painful than in the eastern cities in this that it is at least for *material* realities. The men are all at work for money and to develope the resources of the soil, the women belong to the men. They do not ape fashions, talk jargon or burn out life as a tallow candle for a tawdry show. Their energy is real, though its objects are not invested with a poetic dignity.[4]

Listening to the talk of settlers in solitary cabins or of illiterate trappers and traders on board the boat to Mackinaw and Sault Ste. Marie, she felt that she was among people who, like the Romans of her childhood, lived their lives "in the day." If she felt the incompleteness of a life so absorbed in the present, she also felt its appeal, and she could look back at the equally incomplete, inbred intellectualism of Boston with the dispassion of an outsider. She thought "how pleasant it was to sit and hear rough men tell pieces of their own common lives, in place of the frippery talk of some fine circle with its conventional sentiment, and timid, second-hand criticism." Americans were strange creatures, either all head or all hands. What the country needed, she thought, was a man like Taylor's Philip Van Artevelde, "no thin Idealist, no coarse Realist, but a man whose eye reads the heavens, while his feet step firmly on the ground, and his hands are strong and dexterous for the use of human implements." In the West the gap between material and cultural growth was even wider than in the East, but at least here there seemed to be a chance for a truly indigenous culture to grow out of the strenuous daily confrontation between man and nature.

After spending two weeks in Chicago, Margaret, Sarah, and William Clarke struck out across country in a covered wagon which was loaded down with provisions in case the settlers they stayed with could give them none. Drawn by two sturdy, prairie-wise horses who were equally at ease on the road or off it, they set a course straight across the untracked grasslands toward the Rock River country, where Margaret's Uncle William Williams Fuller had settled years earlier. From there they traveled northeast to Belvidere, where her brother Arthur planned to open a school, and then back to Chicago. On this excursion, which lasted approximately a fortnight, and on a subsequent shorter one in Wisconsin, Margaret came to fully appreciate the limitless freedom of a landscape where there were no roads or fences or cultivated fields and where "Nature seems to have poured forth her riches so without calculation, merely to mark the fullness of her joy."[5] Here too she came to realize the diversity of the people who were attracted to the West. In the city she saw a great many northern Europeans and New Englanders; here on the prairie she met those too, but also English, Irish, and Welsh settlers, who brought the customs not only of the country but of the class to which they happened to belong. She visited the estate of an Irish gentleman who had built a mansion on spacious, manicured grounds overlooking the Rock River, leaving next to it as an "ornamental accessory" the log cabin in which he had lived while he was building it. She heard of, but did not meet, a Hungarian count who had transported a number of serfs from his homeland to work his estate in Illinois. In Oregon, Illinois, she stayed in a double log cabin and heard a Fourth of July oration that "smacked loudly of Boston." A few days earlier she had stayed with a well-to-do Englishman with a vaguely maritime air, who had retired with his books and his two convent-educated daughters to enjoy "the quiet influences of country life." Margaret suspected that his choice of Illinois quiet influences rather than English ones might have something to do with a career in smuggling, since it was hard to explain otherwise why he had gone to all the trouble of crossing the Atlantic:

> He rises at dawn, rides out to see to his farm for an hour or two,—then comes back and sleeps often till his breakfast hour of nine or ten. They dine at five, awhile after have tea or coffee served, and then the old gentleman has out the decanters, of which there are no lack at dinner table, sits down to drink his brandy and water, and hear his daughters play duets on the piano, which they do in a style equally correct and monotonous.[6]

It was these same daughters, however, who had learned to deal so efficiently with rattlesnakes.

Another example of incorrigible anglitude was an Englishwoman who arrived, like Margaret and her party, at an isolated tavern which was already full of guests. There was no place to sleep except the barroom, and the landlord chivalrously evicted his customers so that the ladies could have the room to themselves. Sarah and Margaret made themselves as comfortable as possible on the barroom tables, but their companion was so anxious over her virtue that she sat up all night in a chair, wrapped in a shawl and wearing a lace cap, in case anybody should come in.

Inflexibility as blind as this was easy to laugh at, but it was after all based on fear, and in an altered, less ludicrous form it was the cause of a great deal of misery in the West. Margaret soon found, like other observers, that the country was much harder on women than on men:

> The great drawback upon the lives of these settlers, at present, is the unfitness of the women for their new lot. It has generally been the choice of the men, and the women follow, as women will, doing their best for affection's sake, but too often in heartsickness and weariness. Besides, it frequently not being a choice or conviction of their own minds that it is best to be here, their part is the hardest and they are least fitted for it. The men can find assistance in field labor, and recreation with the gun and fishing-rod. Their bodily strength is greater, and enables them to bear and enjoy both these forms of life.
>
> The women can rarely find any aid in domestic labor. All its various and careful tasks must often be performed, sick, or well, by the mother and daughters, to whom a city education has imparted neither the strength nor skill now demanded. The wives of the poorer settlers, having more hard work to do than before, very frequently become slatterns; but the ladies, accustomed to a refined neatness, feel that they cannot degrade themselves by its absence, and struggle under every disadvantage to keep up the necessary routine of small arrangements.

The women Margaret saw obviously were not the "sturdy pioneer women" of popular legend, but city-bred women whose personal identity was inseparable from their sexual identity, which in turn depended heavily on external things. They were not only physically unequal to the demands of western life, they found—as the men did not—that to adapt to it was to go against everything they had been taught to value in themselves. Many, for example, had insisted on bringing pianos to the prairie, and the instruments sat neglected in the rough parlors because no one knew how to tune them. Margaret saw this as symbolic of the artificial standards by which "femininity" had always been defined, and by which these women continued to judge themselves:

> When they can leave the housework, they have not learnt to ride, to drive, to row, alone. Their culture has too generally been that given to women to make them "the ornaments of society." They can dance, but not draw; talk French, but know nothing of the language of flowers; neither in childhood were allowed to cultivate them, lest they should tan their complexions. Accustomed to the pavement of Broadway, they dare not tread the wild-wood paths for fear of rattle-snakes!

The Scandinavian and German women, though hardly better off in other ways, had at least the advantage of being accustomed to farm work before they came. But the urban American and British women wilted under the combined burdens of physical drudgery, childbearing, loneliness, and lack of recreation. Margaret saw only one contented woman, an Englishwoman in Wisconsin who "said she had seen so much suffering in her own country that the hardships of this seemed as nothing to her." It was especially disheartening to see these women, not comprehending the cause of their own unhappiness, stubbornly set upon perpetuating the sins of the past in the lives of their own daughters:

> Everywhere the fatal spirit of imitation, of reference to European standards, penetrates, and threatens to blight whatever of original growth might adorn the soil. If the little girls grow up strong, reso-lute, able to exert their faculties, their mothers mourn over their want of fashionable delicacy. . . . Their grand ambition for their children is to send them to school in some Eastern city, the measure most likely to make them useless and unhappy at home.

The only Americans entirely free of European standards were, of course, the Indians (although Indian women, she would discover, might have been thankful to have themselves defined as the "ornaments of society.") The absence of the true natives of the prairie, which was only emphasized by their occasional fleeting presence, haunted the countryside like a dispossessed ghost. At the beginning of the trip, Margaret, Sarah, and James had spent a week at Niagara Falls. There they had spent several hours a day under sodden, chill skies, viewing the falls from all angles and hoping, like true Romantics, to see a lunar rainbow. In fact they did not even get to see a workaday solar one, and Margaret could express only a "quiet satisfaction" that the falls, in their somewhat dampened sublimity, looked just as she had expected them to. But after a few days she noticed a curious effect of spending so much time near them. The incessant roar, excluding other sounds, gave the effect of deafness, and she began to imagine that there was a stealthy figure creeping up behind her with tomahawk upraised. She could not help constantly glancing over her shoulder; not for the first time during this trip, she felt like a trespasser.

On the voyage from Buffalo to Chicago she caught glimpses of Indians, camped along the shore of the St. Clair River and again on Mackinaw Island, where the boat was greeted by a band of braves richly dressed in blue, wearing "splendid leggings with knee-ties" and crimson, beaded scarves around their heads. On the once-sacred Manitou Islands she found the ancient trees rapidly being felled to feed the steamboats, and the irony was not lost on her, though she pushed it away in her determination to be tough-minded and progressive. What she subsequently saw of the remnants of Indian life in the Midwest did not change her conviction that nothing could be done to restore what the Indian had lost, and that Indian culture could not survive; the best that could be hoped would be that it would be recorded before it was utterly lost. But her sense of the tragedy of the Indian grew the longer she stayed in the West:

> Seeing the traces of the Indians, who chose the most beautiful sites for their dwellings, and whose habits do not break in on that aspect of Nature under which they were born, we feel as if they were the rightful lords of a beauty they forbore to deform. But most of these settlers do not see it at all; it breathes, it speaks in vain to those who

are rushing into its sphere. Their progress is Gothic, not Roman, and their mode of cultivation will, in the course of twenty, perhaps ten years, obliterate the natural expression of the country.

This is inevitable, fatal; we must not complain, but look forward to a good result. Still, in traveling through this country, I could not but be struck with the force of a symbol. Wherever the hog comes, the rattlesnake disappears; the omnivorous traveller, safe in its stupidity, willingly and easily makes a meal of the most dangerous of reptiles, and one which the Indian looks on with a mystic awe. Even so the white settler pursues the Indian, and is victor in the chase.

During that dull fortnight in the Chicago boardinghouse she read all the books she could find on Indians: Catlin's *North American Indians,* which she thought the best, though sentimentalized and occasionally unreliable as to facts; Mrs. Jameson's account of her captivity among the Mohawks; and several others, among them some by Washington Irving, which she thought had a "stereotype, second-hand air." On the excursions into the Illinois and Wisconsin interior she was conscious of the increasing evidence of recent Indian habitation as they moved farther west, until they reached the Rock River, scene of Black Hawk's desperate last stand only thirteen years earlier. Black Hawk and his band had been killed some distance south of Oregon, where Margaret stayed, but in this more remote region of the river stragglers had remained several more years, and everywhere underfoot were reminders that this was the country of the Foxes and the Sauks. Here the lush countryside was like a cultivated park, through which the river had carved tree-crowned bluffs 300 feet high. On an island in the river almost opposite the house where she stayed, she found caches for food, wooden troughs for pounding corn, tomahawk marks on the trees, and the body of an Indian woman, lying in a canoe elevated on poles.

In Wisconsin she stayed near the site of a particularly fine Indian village, with a man whose attitude toward the Indians was typical of the white settlers she encountered:

Our host said, that once, as he was lying there beneath the bank, he saw a tall Indian standing at gaze on the knoll. He lay a long time, curious to see how long the figure would maintain its statue-like absorption. But at last his patience yielded, and, in moving, he made a slight noise. The Indian saw him, gave a wild, snorting sound of indignation and pain, and strode away.

What feelings must consume their hearts at such moments! I scarcely see how they can forbear to shoot the white man where he stands.

The man, Margaret continues,

> . . . in other respects of most kindly and liberal heart . . . observed: "They cannot be prevented from straggling back here to their old haunts. I wish they could. They ought not to be permitted to drive away *our* game." OUR game,—just heavens!

A day or two later Margaret and her party, driving back toward Milwaukee, saw the lodges of a band of wandering Potawatomis, and could not resist stopping and walking across the intervening field for a closer look. Halfway across they were overtaken by a sharp thunderstorm, and they were obliged to ask the Indians to shelter them:

> They showed all the gentle courtesy which marks their demeanor towards the stranger, who stands in any need; though it was obvious that the visit, which inconvenienced them, could only have been caused by the most impertinent curiosity, they made us as comfortable as their extreme poverty permitted. They seemed to think we would not like to touch them; a sick girl in the lodge where I was, persisted in moving so as to give me the dry place; a woman, with the sweet melancholy eye of the race, kept off the children and wet dogs from even the hem of my garment.

At a nearby settler's house they were told that the band, who had only recently returned to their old lands, were destitute:

> The women had been there to see if they could barter for food their head-bands, with which they club their hair behind into a form not unlike a Grecian knot. They seemed, indeed, to have neither food, utensils, clothes, nor bedding; nothing but the ground, the sky, and their own strength. Little wonder if they drove off the game!

On the way back east Margaret spent nine days by herself in a
hotel on Mackinaw Island, in the straits between Lakes Michigan
and Huron. Here thousands of Ottawas and Chippewas came every
August to collect annual payments from the government, and they
were camped by the thousands on the beach before the hotel. She
had a rare opportunity of mingling freely with Indians who were
living much as they had for centuries. She spent a large part of
each day sitting or walking among them, learning to pound corn,
communicating by signs, listening to the young men playing their
courting flutes. They were no less curious about her than she about
them and crowded around her to inspect her parasol, her locket,
and whatever else she was wearing or carrying, though always
with scrupulous courtesy.

Not surprisingly, she concerned herself with the status of Indian
women, wondering if it was as low as popular anecdote claimed.
From what she could observe she suspected it was. The women
did almost all the hard physical work, and as a result their forms
were bent and they walked with a shuffling, awkward gait entirely
different from the free stride of the men. But it was their expression, the timidity and utter resignation of their looks and gestures,
which conveyed most clearly to Margaret a condition of servitude
so abject that it had become in large measure self-imposed. In this
respect they resembled white pioneer women, though their plight
was incomparably worse:

> More weariness than anguish, no doubt, falls to the lot of most of
> these women. They inherit submission, and the minds of the gener-
> ality accomodate themselves more or less to any posture. Perhaps
> they suffer less than their white sisters, who have more aspiration
> and refinement, with little power of self-sustenance. But their place
> is certainly lower, and their share of the human inheritance less.

At the end of the week she watched the Indians strike camp,
each family taking no more than twenty minutes to do so. The
flocks of canoes gliding away were a picturesque sight, but the
abandoned beach, littered with every kind of refuse, was a compelling reminder that the red man's much-vaunted rapport with nature was far from perfect. A day or two later Margaret, accom-

panied by Sarah, left the island as well and headed east. Perhaps in order to ease herself gradually back into the narrowing confines of Boston, she returned by way of New York, where she saw Emerson's brother William, Thoreau (now tutoring William's children), Lydia Maria Child, and William Henry Channing.

She also renewed her acquaintance with Horace Greeley, the editor of the crusading *New York Tribune,* who as a dedicated Fourierist was a familiar visitor at Brook Farm. His wife too stayed there frequently and had attended some of Margaret's Conversations. A year younger than Margaret, Greeley was a self-educated man from the backwoods of New Hampshire and Vermont, who had worked his way up through a series of apprenticeships in printers' shops and small newspapers to found the *Tribune* in 1841. He was a conspicuous champion of lost and endangered causes from abolitionism to vegetarianism, and having gained so much himself by dogged perseverance, was quick to recognize it in others. Soon after "The Great Lawsuit" had been published in the July *Dial* he had printed a generous extract in the *Tribune*. His meeting now with Margaret did nothing to diminish his high opinion of her, while she saw in his vitality and moral courage that combination of qualities she had so often missed in easterners and westerners alike.

Back in Cambridge she quietly commenced her one-woman invasion of Harvard Library and resumed her routine of teaching and writing. The group that assembled for her November series of Conversations was small. This was inevitable, given the size of the community and the fact that some of the most loyal women had already attended two or more series. "There is no persuading people to be interested in one always or long even,"[7] she wrote philosophically to Emerson, but the diminishing size of her income worried her. The *Dial,* too, was on the wane: Emerson, under pressure to finish his second book of *Essays,* had decided to let the journal die a quiet and dignified death, and after the January issue it simply stopped. Margaret took time out from writing *Summer on the Lakes* to contribute a piece on "The Modern Drama" and a short review of Mrs. Child's *Letters from New York* to this last issue, and Emerson returned the favor by helping her negotiate with publishers—a process which in those days was not unlike buying a pot in a Turkish bazaar. In June *Summer on the Lakes* was brought out by Little & Brown, receiving a subdued but cordial welcome in the press.

It was probably during a second visit to New York, in April, that Horace Greeley urged Margaret to expand "The Great Lawsuit" into a book, offering to publish it for her. She needed little persuading to undertake this, but it did nothing to banish her fear that she would once again have to turn to full-time schoolteaching to remain free from debt. For this, too, the benevolent Greeley had an answer. Prompted by his wife, he offered Margaret a job writing for the *Tribune* and a room in his house for as long as she chose to stay. The luxury of earning a living with her pen was finally within reach, but Margaret hesitated, doubting whether a journalistic career and so drastic a separation from family and friends was the best course.

Still wrestling with her decision, she began working on the "pamphlet" that would become *Woman in the Nineteenth Century*. July found her in Concord, staying first with the Hawthornes and later at her sister's house while Ellen visited Cambridge. The Channings' troubled marriage, now further strained by the birth of a child,* was a strong argument in favor of not leaving Massachusetts. Margaret foresaw that the whole burden of helping Ellen cope would fall on her mother. (At the moment Ellery, finding a new baby and an ailing wife rather too much for his nerves, was off on a walking trip to the Catskills with Thoreau.) But on the whole the month in Concord was soothing, and the obvious domestic bliss of the Hawthornes was a reminder that such couples did exist in the world.

She saw Emerson only occasionally, since his attention and Lidian's were centered on a baby son, born July 10. When she did see him he was as elusive as ever, and her journal shows that even now she had much ado to resist trying to melt his reserve: ". . . It is deeply tragic on the one side, any relation to him, but on the other, how noble how dear! . . . Let me once know him and I

---

* Born on Margaret's birthday and named after her.

shall not be disappointed. But he is hard to know, the subtle Greek!'' [8]

In September she accepted Greeley's offer, still wondering whether it was the wise thing to do. She went off to Nantasket Beach for a few days with Caroline, but was cheated of rest by headache and nightmares. She dreamed of falling off the rocks at Nantasket into the ocean, and of ''great spiders running over me.'' On the way home she dreamed that Caroline was drowning in the ocean and that she was unable to save her: ''My feet seemed rooted to one spot: and my cloak of *red silk* kept falling off when I tried to go. At last the waves had washed up her dead body on the hard sand and then drew it back again. It was a terrible dream.'' And the next night she had the recurrent nightmare she had had since childhood, of the death of her mother. ''I seemed left to think of it alone and the pathos almost overpowered me. I lay sobbing and could not waken. This morning letter from N.Y. about going.'' [9] But in the light of day her plans had much in their favor. Her younger brothers were more than willing to take over the responsibility of looking after her mother, and her worry over Ellen was lessened when Greeley extended an offer to Ellery to work on the *Tribune* as well. It was agreed that he would go to New York in November, and Margaret would follow later.

In October, after taking Lloyd to Andover and settling her mother in yet another house in Cambridge, she said her goodbyes and went with Cary to the small resort community of Fishkill Landing, on the Hudson, to rest and finish *Woman in the Nineteenth Century*. There she spent seven idyllic weeks, writing in the evenings or in rainy weather and spending her days in walking, boating, and bathing. For a while she and Cary were joined by Christopher Cranch and William Henry Channing, making up a tiny circle of transplanted Transcendentalists.

Her holiday mood was clouded temporarily by the arrival of Ellery, who had left the *Tribune* in a burst of temper against his new employer. The relationship in any case would have been precarious, made up as it was of two excitable men, one of whom made a religion of work while the other made a religion out of what might best be called creative contemplation. Ellery's arrival at the

Tribune had been ill-timed. Greeley, exhausted from the summer's futile presidential campaign for Henry Clay, was to leave town for a rest, and he was even less disposed than usual to coddle his journalists. He threw Ellery some vague instructions, which Ellery took to mean he was expected to write "Whig editorials," and left. After staring helplessly at his desk in the noisy, hectic *Tribune* office for a few days Ellery had left too, and it seemed that no amount of persuasion could make him return. He stayed long enough with Margaret to soak up some sisterly comfort and then went home.

Margaret had already decided to begin her career in New York with a series of articles on the various city institutions that needed reform. One of these was Sing Sing, where a more humane atmosphere for women prisoners was being established, and where her young English friend Georgianna Bruce was working as a matron. Intending to visit the prison, Margaret and Caroline took a river boat to the city, where they were joined by William Channing. They arrived at the island on a Saturday and spent the night there. Sunday morning Channing preached in the prison chapel while Margaret spoke with the woman inmates, almost all of whom were prostitutes. Margaret was by no means innocent, but this was probably the first time she had ever knowingly seen a prostitute, let alone talked with one. All the Victorian fascination and revulsion about sex was united in the public's condemnation of these women, whose crime ultimately consisted more in what they knew than in what they did. After such knowledge there was indeed no forgiveness, and the stock literary figure of the seduced woman forced into a life of prostitution was based on reality. Talking to them, and seeing the contrast between their gentle, ordinary manners and the irredeemable wickedness of which they were accused, Margaret was freshly struck by the arbitrariness of the line between the behavior of "good" women and prostitutes; between the flirtatiousness of the society belle, who used sex for economic gain without quite knowing what she was doing, and the prostitute, who also used sex for economic gain but knew exactly what she was doing. She left Sing Sing determined to try to make the public think about the unthinkable, and went back to Fishkill to write the last pages of *Woman in the Nineteenth Century,* dealing with prostitution as the ultimate example of the hypocrisy upon which the oppression of all women was based. The following week she and her book arrived in New York together.

XII

Woman in
the Nineteenth Century

Like its predecessor "The Great Lawsuit," *Woman in the Nine-teenth Century* is based on the belief that all souls are equal, not only in heaven but here on earth. For a full thirteen pages Margaret reviews in wearying detail mankind's uncertain progress toward this ideal, circling around her main subject but touching it directly only when apropos of the French Revolution, she remarks that it conferred to woman the dubious privilege of being executed as a *citoyenne* rather than as a subject. Finally she narrows her discussion down to the destiny of her own country, which despite its "monstrous display of slave-dealing and slave-keeping," is still "destined to elucidate a great moral law, as Europe was to promote the mental culture of Man."[1] Here the statement "all men are born free and equal," if not yet a reality, remains "a golden certainty wherewith to encourage the good, to shame the bad. . . . It is inevitable that an external freedom, an independence of the encroachments of other men, such as has been achieved for the nation, should be so also for every member of it." She points to the prominence of women in the abolitionist movement, and says it is not surprising that the warmest appeal on behalf of women comes from the "champions of the enslaved African." She goes on to cite specific injustices which these women have come to realize they share with slaves: the inability of married women in most states to own property, to inherit more than one-third of their husband's property unless a will specifically provided otherwise, to keep their own earnings, or to prevent their husbands, no matter how shiftless and abusive, from forcibly taking their children from them if they leave home.

To remedy these particular evils, she says, legal protection must be established for women. And, "knowing that there exists in the minds of men a tone of feeling toward women as toward slaves . . . can we wonder that many reformers think that measures are not likely to be taken in behalf of women, unless their wishes could be publicly represented by women?" As for the old quibble that every man is influenced by a woman anyway, she doubts the truth of this, given that "not one man, in the million, shall I say? no, not in the hundred million, can rise above the belief that Woman was made *for Man*." Nor would women's participation in political life unduly tax their strength: "Those who think the physical circumstances of Woman would make a part in the affairs of national government unsuitable, are by no means those who think it impossible for negresses to endure field-work, even during pregnancy, or for sempstresses to go through their killing labors." Thus Margaret implies strongly that she has finally come to support the vote for women and share the views of John Neal. But she does not come out and say so flatly, and Neal wrote to reproach her for her timidity in this. If she did have lingering reservations (and her subsequent silence on the subject suggests she did), they are belied by her ringing statement that "we would have every arbitrary barrier thrown down. We would have every path laid open to Woman as freely as to Man."

For the prejudice that women's inferior judgment bars them from the full exercise of power, Margaret blames women themselves no less than men. Such real but indirect power as women have historically wielded they have used badly, behaving like the mindless playthings men believe they are. Thus both sexes are deluded:

Woman has always power enough, if she choose to exert it, and is usually disposed to do so, in proportion to her ignorance and childish vanity. Unacquainted with the importance of life and its purposes, trained to a selfish coquetry and love of petty power, she does not look beyond the pleasure of making herself felt at the moment, and governments are shaken and commerce broken up to gratify the pique of a female favorite.

So the age-old cycle is perpetuated, whereby a woman derives her self-image from men, whose image of her is partially distorted by their own need to dominate. In order to break free of it Margaret believes each woman must form her own idea of herself on the basis of inner standards, and "lay aside all thought, such as she habitually cherishes, of being taught and led by men." Here she arrives at the unifying theme which flows through *Woman in the Nineteenth Century* (though sometimes at subterranean depths), the familiar Transcendentalist theme of self-reliance. In no other work does Margaret so clearly show her debt to Emerson, although it must be remembered that the debt extends only as far as strengthening and focusing a native independence that was Margaret's by virtue of temperament and circumstance. It is this theme that makes the essay still relevant today, long after the skirmishes over property rights, divorce, political rights, and education have been all but won.

Such self-reliance must be achieved, she says, without the expectation of help from even the most liberal-minded men. Speaking through the persona of an invented but largely autobiographical character, "Miranda," Margaret discusses the ambivalence of well-intentioned males who, though they "seemed so glad to esteem women whenever they could," would "never, in any extreme of despair," wish they were women, so deeply ingrained is their belief in the superiority of "manly" qualities. Throughout literature, heroic qualities when displayed by a woman have been praised as "manly." (This was, revealingly enough, one of Margaret's own favorite words of praise.) When a woman displays energy or creative genius, she is told that she has a "masculine mind" or that she "surpasses her sex." Yet, she says, "this by no means argues a willing want of generosity toward Woman. Man is as generous toward her as he knows how to be." Men simply cannot resist their own need for power: "Each wishes to be lord in a little world, to be superior at least over one." At the same time, "he does not feel strong enough to retain a life-long ascendency over a strong nature." Therefore, although a woman cannot expect men to support her struggle for independence, once it is a *fait accompli* she will find that they offer her "not merely approval, but homage."

Women must decide for themselves what their lives will be, and the range of their choices must be as broad as men's. There needs first of all to be an educational system that will give girls "as fair a field as boys," though not by "giving them young men as teachers, who only teach what has been taught themselves at college, while methods and topics need revision for these new subjects, which could better be made by those who had experienced the same wants." She is vague about which "new subjects" should be included in women's education, but it is clear that she is *not* advocating the kind of home-economics-cum-classics education proposed by conservative woman educators like Catherine Ward Beecher: "Too much is said of women being better educated, that they may become better companions and mothers *for men.*" Although motherhood is all very fine (and she goes on to pay the obligatory tribute), it should be postponed, like marriage, until a woman has become a fully integrated person in her own right: "Give the soul free course, let the organization, both of body and mind, be freely developed, and the being will be fit for any and every relation to which it may be called."

To illustrate the theme of self-reliance Margaret describes an imaginary interview with Miranda, "a woman who, if any in the world could, might speak without heat and bitterness of the position of her sex":

> Her father was a man who cherished no sentimental reverence for Woman, but a firm belief in the equality of the sexes. She was his eldest child, and came to him at an age when he needed a companion. From the time she could speak and go alone, he addressed her not as a plaything, but as a living mind. . . . He called on her for clear judgment, for courage, for honor and fidelity; in short, for such virtues as he knew. . . .

A dignified sense of self-dependence was given as all her portion, and she found it a sure anchor. Herself securely anchored, her relations with others were established with equal security. She was fortunate in a total absence of those charms which might have drawn to her bewildering flatteries, and in a strong electric nature, which repelled those who did not belong to her, and attracted those who did. With men and women her relations were noble,—affectionate without passion, intellectual without coldness. . . .

Of Miranda I had always thought as an example, that the restraints upon the sex were insuperable only to those who think them so, or who noisily strive to break them. She had taken a course of her own, and no man stood in her way. Many of her acts had been unusual, but excited no uproar. Few helped, but none checked her; and the many men who knew her mind and her life, showed to her confidence as to a brother, gentleness as to a sister. . . .

When I talked with her upon these matters, and had said very much what I have written, she smilingly replied: ''And yet we must admit that I have been fortunate, and this should not be. My good father's early trust gave the first bias, and the rest followed, of course. It is true that I have had less outward aid, in after years, than most women; but that is of little consequence. Religion was early awakened in my soul,—a sense that what the soul is capable to ask it must attain, and that, though I might be aided and instructed by others, I must depend on myself as the only constant friend. This self-dependence, which was honored in me, is deprecated as a fault in most women. They are taught to learn their rule from without, not to unfold it from within. This is the fault of Man, who is still vain, and wishes to be more important to Woman than, by right, he should be.''

''Men have not shown this disposition toward you,'' I said.

''No; because the position I early was enabled to take was one of self-reliance. And were all women as sure of their wants as I was, the result would be the same. . . . The difficulty is to get them to the point from which they shall naturally develop self-respect, and learn self-help.''

After *Woman* was published, an acute public persisted in seeing Margaret's self-portrait in Miranda, as they had in the Mariana of *Summer on the Lakes*. Margaret was a little put out, although she should have expected this. ''People seem to think that not more than one phase of character can be shown in one life," she complained to Channing.[2] In fact, the two are reasonably accurate personifications of those two sides of Margaret's personality that she found it hardest to reconcile. Miranda is totally lacking in the exuberance, the rebelliousness, the vulnerability of Mariana, and because of this Margaret is being less than fair to the women she is writing for as well as to herself. In giving them a model to follow who is without passion and without sex, she is evading the full difficulty of the course she is urging on other women. She might more honestly have urged it by warning them of the emotional turmoil and the social pressures it involved, and then persuading them that becoming a whole person is worth it all. But Miranda, that wise virgin, is only a paper Margaret, a Margaret purged both of pain and humanity, a Margaret whose education has not been fraught with contradictions, whose father never worried over her posture or her dowry, whose emotional life has never been stifled because it never existed, and whose "total absence" of personal charm is an unalloyed blessing.

Elsewhere in the essay she celebrates virginity with an emphasis that can be easily misunderstood by the casual reader. In order to achieve self-reliance, Margaret says, a woman must withdraw from the deceptive influence of relationships and "meditate in virgin loneliness":

> If any individual live too much in relations, so that he becomes a stranger to the resources of his own nature, he falls, after a while, into a distraction, or imbecility, from which he can only be cured by a time of isolation, which gives the renovating fountains time to rise up. With a society it is the same. Many minds, deprived of the traditionary or instinctive means of passing a cheerful existence, must find help in self-impulse, or perish. It is therefore that, while any elevation, in the view of union, is to be hailed with joy, we shall not decline celibacy as the great fact of the time. It is one from which no vow, no arrangement, can at present save a thinking mind. For now the rowers are pausing on their oars; they wait a change before they can pull together. All tends to illustrate the thought of a wise contemporary. Union is only possible to those who are units. To be fit for relations in time, souls, whether of Man or Woman, must be able to do without them in the spirit.

The "wise contemporary" is of course Emerson, and here Margaret relates the plight of women to the larger difficulty of achieving individual identity in a conformist, materialistic society. But in hailing "celibacy as the great fact of the time," she recognizes that for most people it will not be a permanent fact. She herself had achieved self-reliance at the cost of outwardly renouncing her own sexuality, as had a handful of other women she knew: Sarah Clarke, Elizabeth Peabody, and (as a result of circumstance) Elizabeth Hoar. She expects that, if women were economically self-sufficient and were not subjected to such strong social pressure to "get married" (and she particularly notes the aptness of that phrase), many of them would choose to remain single and devote themselves to a wider human circle than that of the family. But she is not advising women en masse to remain celibate all their lives, only until they are strong enough to choose freely whether to marry or not. Given the economic status of women and the fact that, for most of them, to postpone the subservience of wifehood meant simply to prolong that of daughterhood, even this realistic advice was hard to follow. But a beginning had to be made.

She discusses marriage at some length, beginning with the degradation of women in marriages of convenience, which were still not uncommon in Europe a quarter-century after Ellen Kilshaw had so narrowly escaped one. She goes on to define four other kinds: "mutual idolatry" (bad, needless to say); "household partnership" (better); "intellectual companionship" (better still); and the "religious" marriage, which is best of all and which includes the previous two. In this kind of marriage the woman is a full partner. Margaret quotes an observer of one such wife, the Countess Zinzendorf: "She was not made to be a copy; she was an original; and, while she loved and honored him, she thought for herself, on all subjects, with so much intelligence, that he could and did look on her as a sister and friend also." In the "religious" marriage the wife may have her own work, or collaborate on her husband's; she may choose the traditional housewifely employment, which does not in itself mean that she is less emancipated. But Margaret's argument for the success of this kind of marriage would have been strengthened if she had been able to point to a woman whose relationship with her husband had remained firm even though she worked at something that was both untraditional and distinctly her own. The only example of this she could find was Mary Wollstonecraft, whose name had to be whispered in respectable circles.

This points to the chief weaknesses of *Woman in the Nineteenth Century,* which are stylistic. Several times longer than "The Great Lawsuit," it is even more casually organized and is padded heavily with examples drawn from Margaret's exhaustive knowledge of history and literature. Many of them are obscure, and obscure or not they dissipate the force of her argument. These women are certainly strong, but their strength is that of sublime passivity. Their courage too often takes the form of volunteering to accept death for the sake of husband, lover, or god, as do Panthea and Iphigenia; or taking religious vows, like Héloïse. Margaret makes a praiseworthy but ultimately unconvincing effort, as modern Christian women continue to do,* to find in the Virgin Mary an illustration of active, creative womanhood. But none of her examples comes up to the mark she sets for them, and her Romantic bias toward Mary Stuart leads her to grant only a grudging recognition to the statecraft of Elizabeth I, whom she accuses of being "without magnanimity of any kind." The women she does ask us to admire, instead of actively confronting the world usually stand and wait, albeit with exemplary fortitude.

But in fact there were few models to choose from in a world in which women had been so effectively subjugated. She praises those she can find, all more or less her contemporaries, who are indeed true rebels: Mme de Staël, George Sand, and Mary Wollstonecraft. They had all misbehaved sexually, of course, and her praise of them would prompt some of her readers to abandon her book then and there. She criticizes them sensibly, de Staël for her sentimentality and manipulativeness, Sand for the melodrama in both her life and work. Of the unconventionality of their sex lives, she says simply, "Such beings as these, rich in genius, of most tender sympathies, capable of high virtue and a chastened harmony, ought not to find themselves, by birth, in a place so narrow, that, in breaking bonds, they become outlaws." But by and large

* Notably Mary Daly in *Beyond God the Father.*

the book would be better without the examples she so laboriously parades before us, because in fact what she and the other early feminists were advocating was without precedent.

In coming to grips with the still-unresolved problem of defining "the feminine principle," Margaret clearly shows the traces of her personal struggle to unify thought and feeling. Ostensibly she divides "Woman's nature" into two aspects, "the Muse" and "Minerva." But it is the "Muse" aspect on which she concentrates, or what she calls variously the "electrical," the "intuitive," or the "magnetic":

> The especial genius of Woman I believe to be electrical in movement, intuitive in function, spiritual in tendency. She excels not so easily in classification, or recreation, as in an instinctive seizure of causes, and a simple breathing out of what she receives, that has the singleness of life, rather than the selecting and energizing of art.

There follows the statement, quoted earlier, that it is more "native" to her to "inspire and receive" the poem than to create it. The examples of "electrical" women she cites, with the exception of the great actress Mlle Rachel, are passive: she finds the "electrical" element at its purest in the prophesying of Cassandra and the occult powers of the Seeress of Prevorst, "the best observed subject of magnetism in our present times, . . . who, like her ancestresses of Delphos, was roused to ecstasy or phrensy by the touch of the laurel." This intuitive apprehensiveness, the perception of "the fine invisible links which connect the forms of life around them," this "sight of the world of causes," she links to poetry as well as to prophecy, but only in passing. It bears a strong resemblance to the Coleridgean poetic vision, which sees the divine unity behind the fragmentary visible world. But she does not follow this up, nor does she cite us a Sappho to balance the Trojan prophetess and the German seeress, both of whom were instruments of powers outside themselves. In the face of her statement about what is "native" and "not native" to women, we are left once again wondering if Margaret herself believed that woman was only the Abyssinian maid, while to man alone was reserved the right to drink the milk of Paradise.

The whole question, of course, hinged on what proportions of "feminine" to "masculine" qualities were found in the individual psyche, and the ambiguity comes in when Margaret becomes so absorbed in her definition of the "feminine principle" that she neglects to keep it distinct from the complex individual, woman herself. As if to retrench, she now states firmly that the "feminine principle" is balanced by its opposite in every living being:

> It is no more the order of nature that it should be incarnated pure in any form, than that the masculine energy should exist unmingled with it in any form. Male and female represent the two sides of the great radical dualism. But, in fact, they are perpetually passing into one another. Fluid hardens to solid, solid rushes to fluid. There is no wholly masculine man, no purely feminine woman.

This was, and remains, a remarkably modern concept, and it is one of the points in *Woman* that speak most clearly to our own time. Men are only now, with great difficulty, coming to accept the fact that the "feminine" exists in everyone, while women have scarcely less difficulty coping with their own submerged and deflected aggressiveness.

Aside from this recognition of psychological androgyny, and the main theme of self-reliance, the two most effective points in the essay are her discussions of prostitution and vocational freedom. The passage on prostitution is lengthy and forthright. In a society in which women were truly the partners of men and in which marriage included friendship and mutual respect, she argues, prostitution would no longer thrive. She attacks the double standard which allowed men as much sexual freedom as they pleased on the grounds that their sex drives were uncontrollable, while at the same time keeping women in total ignorance of sex and then severely punishing them, by imprisonment or social ostracism, for yielding to those same "uncontrollable" needs of men. It is hardly fair, she says, to expect "purity" in women but not in men, nor is it fair to put on women all the burden of sexual responsibility, especially when they have been carefully protected from knowing what it is they are responsible for:

"You," say the men, "must frown upon vice; you must decline the attentions of the corrupt; you must not submit to the will of your husband when it seems to you unworthy, but give the laws in marriage, and redeem it from its present sensual and mental pollutions."

This seems to us hard. Men have, indeed, been, for more than a hundred years, rating women for countenancing vice. But, at the same time, they have carefully hid from them its nature, so that the preference often shown by women for bad men arises rather from a confused idea that they are bold and adventurous, acquainted with regions which women are forbidden to explore, and the curiosity that ensues, than a corrupt heart in the woman. As to marriage, it has been inculcated on women, for centuries, that men have not only stronger passions than they, but of a sort that it would be shameful for them to share or even understand; that, therefore, they must "confide in their husbands," that is, submit implicitly to their will; that the least appearance of coldness or withdrawal, from whatever cause, in the wife is wicked, because liable to turn her husband's thoughts to illicit indulgence; for a man is so constituted that he must indulge his passions or die!

She is, in effect, asking for sex education for women and sexual restraint in men, and these were strong words in a time when a lady did not go out into the street without a bonnet for fear of being thought a loose woman. A spinster of thirty-four was not supposed to know what prostitution was, nor indeed what sex was, and her frankness no doubt cost her some readers, if not among women themselves then among the men who chose their books for them. Though she stops short of the modern acknowledgment that women have their own sexual needs, her bold indictment of the double standard was well ahead of her time. It remains relevant in its broadest implications, as does her condemnation of the socially sanctioned coquetry, still highly visible in everything from *Playboy* to Barbie dolls, by means of which both sexes are encouraged to think of women primarily as sexual objects.

About vocational freedom she is unequivocal, although she was writing at a time when even the "traditional" female vocations, teaching and nursing, were not yet fully open to women. She did not believe that the achievement of self-reliance depended on what kind of work a woman did, since she was conservative enough to think that most women, if allowed to choose, would remain within the home. But she was adamant in her insistence that the choice itself, whatever it was, be made with absolute freedom, and that the full range of vocations be open to women as to men. What she has to say about vocational freedom is startlingly modern:

> But if you ask me what offices they may fill, I reply—any. I do not care what case you put; let them be sea-captains, if you will. . . . In families that I know, some little girls like to saw wood, others to use carpenters' tools. Where these tastes are indulged, cheerfulness and good-humor are promoted. Where they are forbidden, because "such things are not proper for girls," they grow sullen and mischievous.

Only in the past few years have we seen our first women accepted as students at Annapolis or the U.S. Merchant Marine Academy, and as of this writing none of them has become captain of a ship.

As can be seen, *Woman in the Nineteenth Century* is by no means an uncomplicated declaration of women's rights. Read against the background of Margaret's life it betrays her own conflicts: her struggle to reconcile "Minerva" and "the Muse" in herself, her unsatisfied dependency needs, her doubts as well as her hope for the future of her sex once the barriers were removed. How far woman would go, or in what directions, she would not predict, and for this reason, if for no other, she sometimes seems to take away with one hand what she has given with the other. She was, everyone was (she once wrote) a "mutilated" being,[3] and she saw the future of her sex, as she saw her own life, in terms of constantly changing, organic growth. She was no Cassandra; she would not prophesy. That her own uncertainties over sex roles are not unfamiliar to both men and women a century and a quarter later, that the ideal of womanly self-reliance and the recognition of the complex nature of sexual identity are still meeting strong resistance, testifies to the clarity of her vision and to the difficulty of the personal ordeal out of which the book grew.

XIII

New York

A few months before Margaret came to New York, Horace Greeley and his wife had left their city lodgings and rented an old farmhouse overlooking the East River at Turtle Bay, between Thirty-fourth and Fiftieth streets. Here they might have been in New England, except for the convenience of the Third Avenue stage which ran every half-hour at the foot of the lane. There were no other houses nearby, Manhattan being little more than a cornfield north of the "lamp district," which ended at Union Square. The house itself, though sagging a little here and there, was painted a warm yellow and set off by fine old trees. Approaching down a long, narrow lane, the visitor passed through neat borders of shrubbery and flowers and, entering, found himself in a wide hall which ran the length of the house, opening onto a veranda above the river. From here gravel paths wound down among rocks and trees to the shore. In the spring the myrtle-covered bank near the river was a mass of blue flowers, and Margaret liked to sit there on the rocks in the evening, with the water lapping at her feet, and watch the sailboats gliding against the background of the

Long Island shore. The silence was so deep that Greeley, when he first arrived there, had trouble sleeping at night. Only the cluster of buildings on Blackwell's Island, almost directly opposite, was a somber reminder of the presence of the city.

Indoors the illusion of peace vanished, for the house was kept, as Margaret told Eugene, in "Castle Rackrent style."[1] It was not that there was any physical clutter; the Greeleys were militantly ascetic in their life style, eschewing not only meat, spices, liquor, coffee, and tea, but also such visual superfluities as curtains, rugs, and pictures. But Mary Greeley, a deceptively frail-looking former schoolteacher, was in fact an iron-willed neurasthenic who kept her servants and her husband perpetually on their mettle. Cooks, nurses, and maids were hired and fired every few weeks, and the lion of the *Tribune,* unable to resign as easily as the cook, spent almost all his waking hours in his office. Eight-month-old "Pickie" was still too young to feel the full weight of his mother's regimen, which would later include two baths and at least as many whippings a day, and the prohibition of haircuts, trousers, "dirty" (ordinary) food, and the company of other children—all of which he would resist with some spirit.

At the moment, however, Pickie was a contented, alert baby, and one of Margaret's chief reasons for staying. She had never in her adult life been able to be with small children as much as she wanted to, and Pickie began partly to fill the gap in her affections left by the death of little Waldo Emerson. Nor did the domestic chaos disturb her as much as it might have, for Mary Greeley was unfailingly kind to Margaret personally, and the house and grounds were so large that it was always possible to find a quiet corner.

With Greeley himself she got on slowly. There were several small impediments to their becoming friends, the first being Greeley's strong initial dislike of Margaret's social mannerisms. The sight of her holding court amid a circle of his wife's friends, all of whom seemed to regard her with a "strangely Oriental adoration," only stiffened his resolve to "keep [his] eye beam clear."[2] He deliberately avoided her for some weeks, which was easy enough since he saw her only at breakfast, except for brief encounters at the *Tribune* office. Eventually, however, the breakfast-table Margaret prevailed over the drawing-room Margaret, and Greeley became another unwilling captive in her train:

> As time wore on, and I became inevitably better and better acquainted with her, I found myself drawn, almost irresistibly, into the general current. I found that her faults and weaknesses were all superficial and obvious to the most casual, if undazzled, observer. They rather dwindled than expanded upon a fuller knowledge; or rather, took on new and brighter aspects in the light of her radiant and lofty soul.[3]

Margaret liked Greeley at once, though not unreservedly. She wrote Aunt Mary that Greeley was "a man of genuine excellence, honorable, benevolent, of an uncorrupted disposition, and, in his way, of even great abilities," though Boston gentility prompted her to add that "in modes of life and manners he is the man of the people, and of the *American* people, but I find my way to get along with all that."[4]

In truth Greeley's manners were rough, and his lumberman's vocabulary could match that of any sailor on the New York docks. He cultivated an eccentric image, as befitting the editor of a grass-roots newspaper renowned for its independence. He always wore a cream-colored jacket and trousers, which with his fluffy, tow-colored hair and pale blue eyes made him look rather like an albino, and he took a mischievous pleasure in knowing that people wondered if he wore the *same* suit, year after year. (He didn't.) If Margaret found him too rustic, he found her too finicky. He did not see why a woman who wrote so convincingly on women's rights should lean on a man's arm as she crossed a room or require his protection on a dark street at night. Possibly his teasing on this score had deeper roots, for although he warmly applauded *Woman in the Nineteenth Century*, he professed to be mystified by Margaret's assertion that women's excessive dependence in relationships, particularly in marriage, undermined their development as whole people. In any case, he was quick to taunt her when she expected, as she continued to do, the usual male courtesies from the men around her, and he would fire her own words at her, "Let them be sea-captains!" whenever she made the mistake of waiting for him to open a door.

Both the Greeleys were hydropaths, believing in the application of cold water, both inside and out, for the cure and prevention of ills. They disapproved so strongly of medicine that Margaret felt uncomfortable about keeping it in the house. She would not forego her tea, however, and that became a sore point. The diet at Turtle Bay, as Greeley explains happily in his autobiography, was Spartan enough to discourage all but the most persevering guest: "Usually, a day, or at most two, of beans and potatoes, boiled rice, puddings, bread and butter, with no condiment but salt, and never a pickle, was all [visitors] could abide." [5] Margaret accepted the food without complaint, but she continued to brew up several strong cups of tea a day. Greeley was certain that this misguided practice was the cause of her illnesses, and he undertook to warn her about it one morning when she appeared at breakfast suffering from a raging headache. She replied, with all the graciousness that a migraine can inspire at eight in the morning, that she declined being lectured on the food or beverage she saw fit to take, and the meal proceeded in uncomfortable silence. Eventually some compromise was reached on this subject when Margaret, with the blessing of Mary Greeley, began to see a mesmerist in the city, Dr. Theodore Léger, about the pains in her head and back. Georgianna Bruce Kirby, who knew Margaret from the days of Brook Farm and who visited her in Turtle Bay, describes the mesmeric treatment for the spinal curvature from which she claims Margaret suffered. Having accompanied Margaret on one of her visits to Léger's office, Mrs. Kirby writes that Margaret would sit on a stool with her back exposed, while Dr. Léger held his right hand in the air, with the fingers pointing toward the base of the spine, and slowly moved it upward toward the head. She says Margaret told her it felt "like having a rod of iron worked into her poor spine." [6] However improbable may be the claim of a "cure" thus effected, we may at least give Dr. Léger credit for temporarily protecting Margaret from the regimen of bloodletting, opium, and fasting prescribed by regular physicians.

Aside from his doubts about her health, Greeley had his doubts about Margaret's reliability as a journalist, and these were only gradually allayed. Margaret's visits to the *Tribune* office were perfunctory. She worked at home, as she always had, and only when she was well and in a writing mood. To Greeley, who wrote with great facility and claimed with justice that he could write ten columns to her one, this was incomprehensible, and his impatience with her unprofessional schedule was heightened by his belief that it all came of drinking tea. Only after several months, during which Margaret faithfully produced the agreed-on number of articles (she wrote about 250 in all), did Greeley come to accept those working habits which he termed "fantastic" and "absurd" in print and probably something a good deal stronger in private.[7]

His opinion of her was mellowed, too, by the quality of her writing. Margaret's *Tribune* articles were better than her *Dial* writing from the start and improved as she went along. The wide range of topics they covered and the growing terseness of style show the benefit of a discipline imposed by the newspaper format. She continued to write large numbers of purely literary reviews, but many of the books she reviewed now had to do with social issues, and she used these articles to air her own views about abolitionism, capital punishment, women's rights, hygiene, prejudice against the Irish and the poor, and a variety of other subjects. She also wrote miscellaneous articles from time to time, including the series on city institutions which began with her visit to Sing Sing.

Some biographers have tended to attribute Margaret's apparently new interest in social reform to a sudden enlightenment brought about by Horace Greeley and the squalid realities of the New York streets. What a mercy it was (they imply) that Margaret Fuller escaped from the Never-Never-Land of Boston Transcendentalism into the real world. This is true only to the extent that the massive social problems of the larger city provided a focus for an already developing social consciousness. That consciousness itself was firmly rooted in Transcendentalism, Unitarianism, and her father's Jeffersonian liberalism, and had already found expression in the two books she wrote before she came to New York. Her companion on her visits to city institutions was William Channing, who was not only a passionate socialist and labor reformer but also as pure a Transcendentalist as ever floated out of Boston.

By 1845 New York had already become the fifth largest city in the world. Its population, now over 370,000, had quadrupled since the turn of the century. Technologically it was far in advance of the rest of the country. New Yorkers, most of whom had been born somewhere else, had reason to be proud of the city's carefully planned grid of streets, its admirable system of public transportation, its Croton waterworks and its gaslights, its handsome new buildings, its big money and the way it had been made. They liked to point out that Cornelius Vanderbilt had begun his steamboat fortune by offering ferry service from Staten Island on his own sailboat at the age of sixteen, and that John Jacob Astor had begun his life here as a penniless immigrant orphan. (Astor had recently built a mansion a whole block long, the only building in America with running water above the first floor.) Faith in the rewards awaiting the self-made man was strong. At the same time, New Yorkers took some pride in the provisions they had made for the unfortunate. A large proportion of the city's "sights" were philanthropic institutions, many of which were housed in new buildings, some surrounded by flower beds and designed by well-known architects. Prominently listed in the city's guidebooks were the Bloomingdale Asylum for the Insane (built in 1821); the Institution for the Blind (1839); the Institution for the Deaf and Dumb (1829); the New York Orphan Asylum (1840); the Association for the Benefit of Colored Orphans (1842); and a multitude of older and smaller institutions, including the New York Hospital, several other orphanages, half a dozen sailors' homes, and an Asylum for Respectable Aged Indigent Females. On Blackwell's Island and the nearby mainland the city had constructed an almshouse, an insane asylum, a hospital, an orphanage, and a penitentiary.

But New Yorkers were finding that no matter how many institutions they built the poor were always with them, arriving in ever-increasing numbers from the politically unstable, famine-ridden countries of northern Europe. Conditions in some of the city's slums, especially the notorious Five Points section, rivaled the worst in Dickens's London. This was an uncomfortable truth that people avoided, preferring to admire the exterior design of their institutions rather than think about what went on inside them, or even worse, about what happened to those who never reached them. One measure of the climate of moral indifference in the city has to do not with human beings, but with animals: in *Letters from New York,* Lydia Maria Child describes the gangs of dog killers who were hired by the city to kill stray dogs by beating them to death, sometimes at the rate of 300 a day.[8] Passersby simply averted their eyes. Horses, as everyone knows, were hardly better off. Against the moral apathy which increased with the size of the city Horace Greeley pitted himself and his *Tribune.* The provocative nature of his editorials for Fourierism, abolitionism, and other unpopular causes was a goad with which he prodded the public into realizing it could feel anything at all.

Margaret visited Sing Sing and the Bloomingdale Asylum each twice, and went on to the various institutions on Blackwell's Island and to the city jail, known as The Tombs. She found that the institutions were run at the whim of their administrators, whose tenure was always uncertain. There always seemed to be enough for the inmates to eat; beyond that, conditions varied enormously. Bloomingdale Asylum, under the superintendence of Dr. Earle, was a model of its kind. There were lectures, amusements, and light work for the patients, who were hardly distinguishable from their visitors. Her visit to the other public insane asylum, on Blackwell's Island, revealed many of the horrors of an old-fashioned madhouse: "They crouched in corners; they had no eye for the stranger, no heart for hope, no habitual expectation of light."[9] The other facilities on the island were equally grim, providing no more than the bare physical necessities. At the penitentiary 700 of the 1,200 prisoners were women, but all the guards were male. "Never was prison treated more simply as a social convenience, without regard to pure right, or a hope of reformation," Margaret wrote.[10] Here and there she found grosser abuses, like the overwhelming stench at the city jail or the ophthalmia epidemic at the orphanage. But the dominant theme in these articles is the Transcendentalist concern for the psychological well-being of the individual. Margaret would not, if she could help it, allow the public to congratulate itself on the number of paupers and criminals it kept fed, clean, and off the streets. She saw in the inmates of all these institutions an emotional deprivation which was not much different from that she had seen in the Indian women on Mackinaw.

In her literary criticism Margaret continued to follow the standards set forth in her "Essay on Critics," distinguishing talent from genius, praising whatever deserved praise even in minor writers, but clearly pointing out faults, especially in those who were already secure in the public esteem. This quickly gained her a reputation for waspishness which was undoubtedly related to her personal reputation and which was entirely undeserved. The petty maliciousness that characterized the British reviews was the one thing she tried most to avoid. She belonged, she said, to the "gentle affirmative school," and though her reviews are frank and occasionally even angry, they are free of personal spite. But they betrayed the sex of their writer not at all, and this offense was not easily forgiven. A lady reviewer (supposing such an anomalous creature existed) was expected to praise or be silent, as she would in society; if absolutely driven to find fault, she would have to do so in a timid, self-deprecatory way which could not be taken seriously. Margaret's reviews were based on an assumption of competence which, though it would not have been remarkable in a man, was thought by many to be intolerable in a woman. It roused the witch-hunting instincts of men who were ready to see in any negative comment of Margaret's, no matter how disinterested, evidence of that kind of spitefulness they expected from a woman who "unsexed" herself by writing like men. Hence Poe's revealing observation that humanity could be divided into three classes: "men, women, and Margaret Fuller." [11]

Particularly controversial was Margaret's review of Longfellow. When Greeley asked her to review Longfellow's new book of poems she tried to excuse herself on the grounds that she had no sympathy at all with that school of poetry and could not do justice to it. But Greeley would not be put off and she had to do it. She was reluctant to attack Longfellow, who was a very mild, courteous man, but he had generally been hailed as the first American poet worthy to stand with the great Europeans, and she did not mince words:

We must confess to a coolness toward Mr. Longfellow, in consequence of the exaggerated praises that have been bestowed upon
him. When we see a person of moderate powers receive honors
which should be reserved for the highest, we feel somewhat like as-
sailing him and taking from him the crown which should be reserved
for grander brows. And yet this is, perhaps, ungenerous. . . .

Mr. Longfellow has been accused of plagiarism. We have been
surprised that any one should have been anxious to fasten special
charges of this kind upon him, when we had supposed it so obvious
that the greater part of his mental stores were derived from the work
of others. He has no style of his own growing out of his own experiences and observation of nature. Nature with him, whether human or
external, is always seen through the windows of literature.[12]

There was a minor uproar over this review, and for a while
Margaret found herself in an unlikely alliance with her rival critic
Poe, whose opinion of Longfellow coincided with her own. Her
judgment that Longfellow's was a minor, imitative voice, not truly
American, has long since been confirmed. (Margaret later earned
the undying animosity of James Russell Lowell, who also had
been the subject of a good deal of puffery, when she wrote in her
essay on American literature that he was no more than a clever
versifier, and that his work was "absolutely wanting in the true
spirit and tone of poesy.")[13]

She did not spare writers with whom she had always sympathized. Her review of Emerson's second book of *Essays* praises it
generously but calls attention to Emerson's disjointed, epigramma-
tic style, which she believes is related to a certain discon-
nectedness from life itself:

. . . In no one essay is the main stress so obvious as to produce on
the mind the harmonious effect of a noble river or tree in full leaf.
Single passages and sentences engage our attention too much in
proportion. These essays, it has been justly said, tire like a string of
mosaics or a house built of medals. . . . Here is undoubtedly the
man of ideas, but we want the ideal man also; want the heart and genius of human life to interpret it, and here our satisfaction is not so
perfect. We doubt this friend raised himself too early to the perpen-
dicular and did not lie along the ground long enough to hear the
secret whispers of our parent life.[14]

Her review of Carlyle's *Oliver Cromwell,* one of her best, shows a just perception of the way the healthy rage of *Sartor Resartus* had soured into a semifascistic celebration of might for might's sake. At the risk of being called a "rose-water imbecile" (Carlyle's term for a lily-livered liberal), Margaret refuses to join him in his veneration of Cromwell as one of history's misunderstood benefactors, preferring to "stick to the received notions of Old Noll, with his great red nose, hard heart, long head and crafty ambiguities. . . . To us it looks black for one who kills kings to grow to be more kingly than a king." [15]

As she had in the *Dial,* she continued to try to widen American acquaintance with lesser-known European writers, among them George Sand, Honoré de Balzac, Alfred Tennyson, Elizabeth Barrett, and Robert Browning. Although as a Transcendentalist she felt keenly the necessity for Americans to develop a literature truly their own, her taste in literature remained free of any trace of parochialism. Her review of Browning's *Bells and Pomegranates,* written while the poet was still so obscure she could find no copy of the book in New York and had to send to Boston for it, shows a discerning tolerance for the density and knottiness of Browning's verse, on the grounds that, unlike Longfellow's fluency, these qualities were intrinsic. Her attempts to promote the young and obscure among American writers were not always so fortunate, but she was quick to recognize Poe, Melville, and especially Hawthorne, and in general her view of the still immature state of American literature was sound.

The only other critic of significance writing at the time was Edgar Allan Poe, who also happened to be living in New York. The two were almost exactly opposite in their critical standards, but alike at least in having any at all. They resembled each other too in their condemnation of American literary parochialism and in their moderate opinion of Longfellow. In some ways Poe was keen-sighted where Margaret was myopic: he saw the genius of Keats and Dickens, for example, as she did not. He had, moreover, a refreshing scorn for the moral pieties and reverence for "poetic inspiration" that characterized the New England Romantics, although his hot-blooded southern defensiveness could blur his ability to tell one New Englander from another. (He lumped James Russell Lowell and Margaret together as equally deluded followers of Emerson—a mistake which both of them must have found rather trying.)

But Poe's esthetic standards were too narrow to serve as a useful basis for general criticism, and he was a splenetic, contumelious man whose writing would have been well suited to the *Edinburgh Review*. While Margaret could appreciate a moderate talent for what it was, Poe looked for genius everywhere and was enraged when he did not find it. His individual reviews were often more appealing than Margaret's, on stylistic grounds if no other. But in her search for a comprehensive esthetic framework in which Milton could take his place with the author of "The Raven," Margaret must be acknowledged to have made the more solid contribution to the development of criticism.

During her first few weeks in New York, Margaret saw the proofs of *Woman in the Nineteenth Century* through the press. The book was published in March and sold briskly. In the New York and Boston press notices there were the inevitable sputterings of moral indignation, and over teacups and decanters there was doubtless the kind of nasty-minded speculation that followed the publication of any feminist book, that a woman who could write on such subjects was no better than she ought to be. But no one attacked her to her face, and there were even some favorable reviews, including one by Lydia Maria Child. The book made Margaret a national figure and to her surprise brought her $85, the first money any of her books had earned. By the end of the year she was working on a second edition, and in December the book was paid the distinction of being pirated by an English publisher.

Gradually she made friends in New York, though never as many or as close as those in Boston. She attended the literary gatherings at the home of Anna Lynch. She often visited Mr. and Mrs. Richard Manning, or went to Brooklyn to see Marcus Spring, a wealthy, philanthropic, Quaker merchant, and his wife Rebecca. Several of her old friends, notably Sam and Anna Ward, now lived in New York. Ellery Channing returned to the *Tribune* (though only for a few weeks), and kept her entertained with fatherly little notes full of advice on the conduct of journalism. She saw much of William and Lucy Channing and of Christopher Cranch and his wife, and over the course of the year Elizabeth Hoar, Charles Newcomb, Caroline Sturgis, Waldo Emerson, and Margaret's mother all found their way to New York. Gifts arrived: clothes from the Randalls and Eliza Farrar, a purse from young Anna Loring, a continuous supply of tea from Cary Sturgis, sums of money to buy the small luxuries missing from Turtle Bay. In spite of her distance from the city, she found it easy to travel by bus to the opera or a Philharmonic concert in the evening. The Norwegian violinist Ole Bull was a good friend until he returned to his own country. Later she took under her wing the Danish novelist and revolutionary Harro Harring, rather rashly lent him $500 from her savings, and helped arrange to publish his novel *Dolores* privately after commercial publishers had shied away from it on religious grounds.

Some of Margaret's friendships suffered as a result of her moving to New York. Inundated with letters (she had over sixty correspondents), she wrote her brother Richard rather testily that she had very little time to answer them and that all her writing energies were devoted to her *Tribune* column. She no longer felt inclined to put her best energies into personal relations as she always had, but wished to "share and impel the general stream of thought." [16] In the face of this unwonted coldness only her staunchest friends continued to write. One who apparently did not was Emerson, although they did exchange a short note or two and saw each other when Emerson spent two days in New York in August. In November Margaret visited Massachusetts and stopped in Concord, but the old feeling was missing: "Our moods did not match," she wrote Anna Ward. "He was with Plato, and I with the instincts." [17] This was the perennial difference between them, but it had been magnified by Margaret's new career. Emerson had thought of her going to New York as a kind of martyrdom, observing that "the muses have feet, to be sure, but it is an odd arrangement that selects them for the treadmill." [18] Now he found the muse so far from complaining as to mistake her treadmill for a highway. A coolness settled between them which was to remain.

She renewed her acquaintance with Lydia Maria Child, whom she had known briefly in Cambridge years earlier. Several years older than Margaret, Mrs. Child had become a successful novelist while Margaret was still in Miss Prescott's school. Since then she had written several more books, had become a zealous abolitionist, and had suffered accordingly in the public regard. The first woman newspaper editor in the country, she had come to New York to head the *Anti-Slavery Standard*. Now she had passed on the editorship to her husband, David Lee Child, and was busy with free-lance writing and personal activity in various kinds of social reform. A practical, warm-hearted but rather crisp and ascetic woman, she had never been closely connected with the Transcendentalist circle despite the fact that her brother, Convers Francis, was one of its early leaders. She and Margaret did not become intimate friends, but Margaret's reform articles and the fact that "good" society looked askance at both women created a temporary bond between them now.

In the winter of 1845–46 Margaret left Turtle Bay for a few months and took lodgings in the city. Here she began to go out more frequently than before, and with the help of an obliging landlady she did some entertaining of her own. To "Aunt Mary" Rotch, who had sent her a New Year's gift of money for wine (in the belief that it helped ward off headache), she had to confess that she had another, more pressing need:

> You must not think me disobedient . . . if I turn some of the wine into a new dress. Having been one of the class Mrs. Farrar calls *tightum,* and being much invited out now I am in town, I was grudgingly reflecting on the necessity of getting another; grudgingly, for you have no idea how much, in this dirtiest of cities, it costs for a poor scribe, (what it costs the Pharisees, imagination shrinks from counting,) who is far from all aid of unpaid affection in the line of sewing, getting up clothes etc., even to keep herself neat in the tightum line. Mrs. Child will not go out at all, either to evening party or morning call; she says she can't afford the time, the white gloves, the visiting cards, the carriage hire. But I think she lives at disadvantage, by keeping so entirely apart from the common stream of things. I shall never go out when busy, or to keep late hours,—

but to go sometimes is better and pleasanter for me. I find many entertaining acquaintances and some friends; so I mean to steal from
your money, at least ribbons and lace for the inevitable dress, and
that will leave me more of the grape-juice than I should drink between now and another Christmas.[19]

Aunt Mary seems to have conceded the priority of the *tightum*
dress, and a few weeks later Margaret writes that she has had some
"pleasant times" wearing a light green silk which she has had altered and which she wears with blond lace and fresh flowers
bought with Aunt Mary's wine money. "I wore it at a party which
I myself gave. I asked all those who have asked me, and many
pleasant gentlemen."[20]

Nevertheless, Margaret's social demeanor at thirty-five would
still have been the despair of the Fuller aunts, had they not given
up on her years before. Among the New York literati, with whom
she occasionally mingled, she was regarded with the now familiar
mixture of respect and dislike:

> All persons were curious to see her, and in full rooms her fine head
> and spiritual expression at once marked her out from the crowd; but
> the most were repelled by what seemed conceit, pedantry, and a
> harsh spirit of criticism, while, on her part, she appeared to regard
> those around her as frivolous, superficial, and conventional.[21]

The woman who wrote this was later won over in the usual way,
by seeing Margaret alone in an unguarded moment.

Even those who knew Margaret well did not suspect that there
was an important side of her life at this time which she kept entirely hidden. It is expressed in this letter, written in May 1845:

> Dearest Friend,
>   For such I cannot choose but have thee, oh it was a waste of this
> heavenly day to walk upon that terrace away from the gentle grow-
> ing things and talk about these barriers that keep us apart. Better to
> forget them! better be blest in the affinities while we may!
>   And then you have so much more energy and spirit for the fight! I
> must try not to throw down the poor little silk glove again in de-

fiance of the steel gauntlet. And you, oh set up no mental limits against me; do not, I pray.

Is it not hard on my side? You can think what thoughts of conquest you will, and I cannot disprove them to you. On the other side you must be as the stone, if I give way to feelings of love and reliance, and you have your mysterious reasons against me there. You talk to me with such cold wisdom sometimes, I do not know the brother of my soul, to whom I had but just flown.

Next time we must go to Hoboken—it is not so confined there. You must tell me things, and I will forget myself; that is always the best way. I look up the free and noble river. I feel myself associated with you in the new religion and that suits me, but to-day you put me in the dust, and a hundred miles from you, too.

This afternoon, though, a singular change took place in my feelings. I am curious to know, whether induced by you, or rising in myself, and shall ask you so soon as we meet.

There has been the most glorious thunder-shower. I hope you have enjoyed it. Now the moon is shining queenly. I must be with you one more moonlight evening. She seems to bless so purely. I feel all fears and piques melt as I look upon her. Yet through pain, through pain, sweet Queen, must we come to where thy pale mother's smile calls. As says Novalis:

No angel can ascend to heaven
Till the whole heart has fallen to the earth in ashes.

Might these be the right lines? I cannot remember what they are. Come to-morrow evening without fail.[22]

Margaret wrote this to James Nathan, whom she had met through Mrs. Greeley shortly after she arrived in New York. A year younger than Margaret, Nathan was a German Jew and thus claimed affinity with two peoples she admired. He was employed in an import house, but gave her to understand that he was a poet *manqué,* an unwilling bondsman in the world of getting and spending. Few appeals to her sympathy were more effective, as Sam Ward had already proved. Nathan lacked Ward's intellectual and esthetic gifts, but he played the guitar and possessed in some degree that sensitivity that Margaret valued above all else in her friends. For the rest, a certain air of Wertherian *Weltschmerz,* absorbed more or less by osmosis from German literature, hinted at unplumbed depths. Nathan continued to visit Turtle Bay as often as he could without exciting comment, and between visits he and Margaret met clandestinely in the city, usually after she left Dr. Léger's office. When they could not meet they exchanged letters, and this correspondence continued through June, when Nathan left on an extended trip to Europe and the Near East. In October of the following year Margaret asked him to return her letters, but he (more luck to us, less honor to him) refused.

They never actually became lovers. A few weeks after they met Nathan, misinterpreting the passionate tone of her letters, made some clumsy advances which she took to be a manifestation of his "lower nature." She rebuked him, and he apologized. Thereafter the affair followed the vexed course of the earlier one with Sam Ward, and Nathan, a man of ordinary sensibilities and moral perception, quickly found himself in an extraordinary situation. The fact that he projected qualities he did not have, that he belonged to the nation of her beloved Goethe, and that he felt no need to compete with her and in fact had hardly heard of her, was enough to draw on his head all the suppressed feelings of a woman of great mind, energy, and emotional force. It seems clear that he did not return her love, but to do him justice he did make some ineffectual attempts to warn her that he could not marry her, and to have made a little speech about brotherly affection (Letter XIX), to which she acquiesced:

> You said "What shall our relation be now?" —I say: Most friendly; for we are really dear to one another; only it is like other earthly relations. Poison plants will sometimes grow up in the night. But we will weed them out, so soon as possible, and bear with them, since only perfect love casteth out fear.

It was indeed perfect—in the sense of disinterested—love that Margaret believed she felt for Nathan. She insisted on being absolutely honest with herself and with him, and would not consent to feel less than she was capable of feeling, or express less than she felt, out of what, to her, was a mean sense of caution. Nathan, for his part, continued to behave in a manner that belied his occasional words of "cold wisdom." By early April she knew he was going abroad in June, but he allowed her to believe that he would return, and gave her his dog Josey to look after. He brought her a gift of a white veil, but made her promise not to think about what it might mean. He continued, in short, to suffer himself to be admired and give every indication of admiring in return. When he finally left for Europe, it was with protestations of undying devotion.

All the gentle, dependent, conventionally feminine side of Margaret's nature is expressed in her letters to Nathan, and after being held in check for so long it is, in this first rush of feeling, much exaggerated. The old memories of childhood deprivation now clamored for redress, and though she does not refer directly to her father, she writes of a need, even a right, to be "childish" now as a compensation for never having been a child. She is delighted when Nathan, after the fashion of his country, calls her a "little girl," and a foolish one at that: "It seemed so whimsical that [those words] should be addressed to me, who was called on for wisdom and dignity long before my leading-strings were off, and so pleasant too." (XLI)

In retrospect, after Nathan had gone, she herself wondered at her own passivity. The woman who has so recently insisted in print on the need for women to stand on their own two feet and maintain a firm independence in their relationships with men, writes time and time again of her wish to be supported and guided by this man:

> I am with you as never with any other one, I like to be quite still and have you the actor and the voice. You have enough life for both; you will indulge me in this dear repose. (XVII)

> I have felt a strong attraction to you, almost ever since we first met, the attraction of a wandering spirit towards a breast, broad enough and strong enough for a rest, when it wants to furl the wings. (XIX)

> I seek inspiration from your thoughts, life from your life. I seek repose upon your heart. (XXXI)

Nothing could be further from the image of her dominating social presence in a gathering than the delicacy with which she requests an appointment with her friend: "Are you very busy? If not, walk up through John Street toward the Doctor's about twenty minutes past ten. But if you are busy, don't disturb yourself. I go that way at any rate." (V)

When Nathan sailed, Margaret obtained a letter of introduction for him from George Bancroft (now secretary of the Navy under President Polk), and helped him arrange to send back letters for publication in the *Tribune,* which she tactfully edited as they arrived. For some months after he left she continued to write with undiminished warmth, although he seldom replied.

The fact that no hint of her relationship with Nathan reached Margaret's family or friends until years afterward, when he revealed the existence of her letters, gives some indication of the adeptness with which Margaret separated her intellectual and social life from her emotional life. Much as she disliked "dissembling," something very like it had long ago become habitual to her. As she was not the "whole" Margaret with Nathan, so she was not the "whole" Margaret anywhere else, but she had been used to functioning this way ever since childhood. While the friendship continued even Mary Greeley, who often saw them together, decided her early suspicions were unjustified. And after Nathan sailed, Margaret was so far from visibly pining away that the eye of her mother, who was visiting her for a fortnight or so, could detect nothing unusual. The summer passed without incident; she wrote to Nathan, wrote for the *Tribune,* went out as much as she wanted to, played with Pickie and spent peaceful hours rocking with him in the hammock, walked with Josey and threw sticks into the river for him, and in late fall went home to Massachusetts for a month, on one of her customary whirlwind tours of the homes of her friends.

That winter, as has been mentioned before, she lived in the city, first in Warren Street and later in Amity Place. She lost most of January, traditionally a month of illness for her, to a prolonged siege of headache accompanied by boils. February 1846 found her trying to make up the *Tribune* articles she had missed, ushering the second edition of *Woman* through the press, and beginning to work on a selection of her *Dial* and *Tribune* pieces for a book, to be published by Wiley and Putnam under the title *Papers on Literature and Art*. Beyond all this, and her worry over the coldness and scantiness of Nathan's letters, she had something else to occupy her mind now. As early as the preceding fall, Marcus and Rebecca Spring had tentatively proposed to Margaret that she accompany them on a trip to Europe that summer. It had all been very uncertain, both for the Springs and for Margaret, to whom the sum of money involved ($2,000) looked enormous. But by late winter the Springs were firm in their purpose, and Margaret had arranged to borrow some money from Spring, some from the Mannings, and the rest from Sam Ward, with her brother Richard standing security. She wrote to Nathan, asking him if he planned to return before she left in August and whether she might see him in Hamburg in October. She also asked what was to be done with Josey, who was still at Turtle Bay although the Greeleys too were planning to move. Not until June did he reply, and then he avoided all mention of her coming to Germany and mentioned vaguely that he might, or might not, see her in London. As for Josey, she should try to sell or give him away, or, that failing, simply abandon him to become another of New York's strays: "A kind providence, will have a care of him as of many of his other creatures, who seem forlorn, forsaken, and guiltless." [23]* He goes on to ask her to arrange to have a narrative of his trip to the Holy Land published in the *Tribune*. Margaret's reply, written shortly before she left, is businesslike and coolly civil. She does not mention coming to Germany again.

She prepared for the trip in a subdued frame of mind. Doubtless her disillusionment over Nathan had something to do with this; then too, she was still worried about money and was dickering with Greeley and his partner over publishing reports from overseas. And now that she was to be separated still farther from her family, her anxiety over them once more increased. A disastrous fire at Brook Farm made it necessary to find some other accommodations for Lloyd, and her sister's marriage looked more precarious than ever: Ellery had just left for Europe on donations raised by his

---

* I have not been able to find out what happened to Josey, but Margaret had read Mrs. Child's book, even if Nathan hadn't.

friends, while Ellen awaited with some apprehension the Birth of her second child. The callousness of this particular act aside, it seemed clear that the more responsibility was placed upon Ellery, the more he would flee from it. Margaret dreaded the additional burden this would place on her mother.

But finally the difference between Margaret's attitude toward this trip and the one she had not taken eleven years earlier was that she had few remaining illusions about her career. She no longer saw herself as the American de Staël or the brilliant future biographer of Goethe, although she still believed that the earlier trip "would have given her genius wings." Now she was content with a far less exalted goal:

> I do not look forward to seeing Europe now as so very important to me. My mind and character are too much formed. I shall not modify them much but only add to my stores of knowledge. Still, even in this sense, I wish much to go. It is important to me, almost needful in the career I am now engaged in. I feel that, if I persevere, there is nothing to hinder my having an important career even now. But it must be in the capacity of a journalist, and for that I need this new field of observation.[24]

It was as a journalist (having wrung from the thrifty Greeley a promise of $10 an article, or twice the going rate) that she sailed on the *Cambria* for England on August 1, 1846, with Marcus and Rebecca Spring and their son Eddie.

XIV

Britain and France

The S.S. *Cambria* set a record by crossing the Atlantic in ten and a half days, but very little of that time was needed to convince Margaret that she was no sailor. She fled belowdecks, though the smell and the ceaseless vibration of the engines made the ladies' cabin a doubtful refuge for the queasy. She got no sympathy from the stewardess, who sniffed that "any one tempted God Almighty who complained on a voyage where they did not even have to put guards to the dishes." [1] At least she was able unfeignedly to join the crew in their rejoicing when land was sighted. A short time later she was on the dock at Liverpool.

Margaret's purpose in coming to Europe was threefold: she came as an ordinary tourist, as a literary pilgrim, and as a reporter for the *Tribune*. The contrast between the way she saw Europe in 1846 and the way she might have seen it had she come in 1835 is clear in the *Tribune* letters, in her itinerary and even in her choice of traveling companions: Marcus Spring was a Fourierist, a Quaker, and a philanthropist; Rebecca Spring's family had been among the earliest supporters of William Lloyd Garrison. They were anxious to learn about political and social conditions in the Old World, and they found Europe on the brink of revolution. Throughout Margaret's earnest observations on industrial centers, institutions, and urban slums, interlarded though they are with descriptions of landscapes and ruined castles, there runs a Romantic consciousness that is, for all its bookishness, essentially political.[2] Nor was it possible to dissociate politics from literature, since in Europe as in America the new movements for social and political reform were closely related to the Romantic idealization of the common man. Most of the writers Margaret would meet in Europe—among them Harriet Martineau, Joseph Mazzini, the Howitts, George Sand, Adam Mickiewicz, Pierre Jean de Béranger, and Félicité de Lamennais—had drawn their philosophical nourishment from the earlier generation of Romantics, and several of them would play a significant part in the political history of Europe over the next few years. The writings of the great Romantics, particularly Wordsworth, Carlyle, Scott, and Burns, were constantly evoked in Margaret's mind as a backdrop to contemporary events. The *Tribune* letters are written in a disjointed, dilettantish style, but they do have this underlying unity; to be a Romantic in 1846 was to be more than half a revolutionary.

In Liverpool and Manchester, the largest of the industrial "new towns" in England, she was immediately confronted with a panorama of human wretchedness for which even the New York slums had left her ill-prepared. England by now had gained the unenviable distinction of being the world's most industrialized nation, the only one in which the urban population outnumbered the rural. For half a century workers from the countryside had been streaming into these new textile manufacturing cities, and in 1845–47 their numbers were swelled by some 300,000 refugees from the Irish famine, one-quarter of whom stayed in Liverpool. Wages were pitifully low, and there was not enough work to go around. Workers lived crowded in windowless cellars or in the infamous "back-to-back" jerry-built tenements, often several families to a room, with a single privy and a single water pump serving an entire block. Reeking piles of garbage cluttered the streets, which were often unpaved, while down the center ran a gutter for "household slops." The air was so foul with coal smoke that sometimes the rain itself was black. The suffering resulting from overcrowding, unemployment, malnutrition, drunkenness, prostitution, and disease are vividly described in Elizabeth Gaskell's *Mary Barton* and *North and South,* though delicacy prompts her to understate them a little.

Perhaps Margaret's own nerve failed her for similar reasons, or perhaps she was too conscious of her status as a guest to feel free to describe in detail what she saw. It is also true that she was protected from the worst of it, her hosts being liberal reformers who were anxious that she should see what changes their efforts were bringing about. But even a superficial view of Liverpool and Manchester must have had an impact far beyond what she admits in her *Tribune* letters, where she writes of being mobbed by "squalid and shameless beggars" in Liverpool, and of talking at night to Manchester mill girls who were sauntering through the streets "bareheaded, with coarse, rude, and reckless air," while others could be seen sitting vacantly in the gin-palaces,* "too dull to carouse."[3]

It was these intolerable conditions that had given rise to the Chartist movement with its demand for universal male suffrage. The movement was still alive in 1846, and though it would end in failure two years later the social protest it expressed could no longer safely be ignored. Driven partly by fear of cholera and revolution, and partly by their basic sense of decency, the English were trying in a haphazard way to deal with the enormous problems industrialization had thrust on their green and pleasant land. National efforts were hampered by a deep distrust of central government, though this year did see the repeal of the pernicious Corn Laws and the passage of a Nuisance Removal Act and a Baths and Washhouses Act—the latter an attempt to provide public bathing and laundry facilities to people who otherwise had neither enough

---

* "Right against this end of the factory were the gable ends of the last house in the principal street—a house which from its size, its handsome stone facings, and the attempt at ornament in the front, had probably once been a gentleman's house; but now the light which streamed from its enlarged front windows made clear the interior of the splendidly fitted-up room, with its painted walls, its pillared recesses, its gilded and gorgeous fittings up, its miserable, squalid inmates. It was a gin palace." Elizabeth Gaskell, *Mary Barton* (ch. 5).

water to wash in nor fuel to heat it with. Small efforts in relation to the severity of the problems, they nevertheless gave evidence that the worst was over and that reform was becoming more fashionable. It was only a question of whether it was too little too late.

Manchester and Liverpool were proud of their efforts to make the lives of their working classes less miserable. In Manchester Margaret undoubtedly was made aware of the three new public parks purchased by subscription and opened with much fanfare that year. She probably was told about the Saturday half-holidays which the merchants had granted their employees since 1844. She was shown the new public libraries and taken to the free concerts which were offered in the naive hope of weaning the working man away from his own beloved beer-hall music. She was particularly impressed with the Mechanics' Institutes in both cities—evening schools for workers where they could learn not only the basic skills but such esoterica as French, German, the fine arts and mechanical drawing. Here was something to warm a Transcendentalist's heart, and Margaret wrote glowingly of the "excellent spirit, the desire for growth in wisdom and enlightened benevolence" evidenced by these schools.[4] She probably did not realize that the factory operatives for whom the schools had originally been intended had deserted them in droves, and that the large classes she saw were made up of small tradesmen and artisans. It did not escape her notice, however, that the new women's branch of the Liverpool institute had a woman "nominally, not really, at the head."[5]

In the midst of their visit to the two cities Margaret and the Springs took an overnight excursion to the nearby ancient walled city of Chester. Here they found themselves instantly transported into the timeless, pastoral England they had always known through literature. The old town with its visible reminders of Welsh and Roman invasions and its ivy-covered ruined cathedral was totally insulated from the teeming industrial towns only a few miles away. Returning the next day to Liverpool, they heard Harriet Martineau's famous brother James preach at the Paradise Street chapel, but Margaret thought him a poor second to Parker and the other great New England preachers. ("His over-intellectual appearance,'' she noted tersely in her journal; ''his conservative tendencies, liberality only in spots.'')[6] The next day they set off to visit his sister Harriet in the Lake Country, journeying by canal boat and, briefly, by railroad (which Margaret pronounced a convenient but ''most unprofitable and stupid way of travelling.'')[7]

Harriet Martineau's Ambleside house was already full of guests, but she had arranged for the Americans to rent a cottage with a magnificent view of the mountains, and there they spent what Margaret described as eight happy days. Miss Martineau thought them not so happy, and in her *Autobiography* later complained that Margaret hardly spoke to her and was only content when she could ''harangue the drawing-room party.''[8] The old bitterness over Margaret's criticism of *Society in America* lingered on, and in any case both women had altered since their meeting eleven years before, and Margaret was no longer an admiring disciple but a successful writer. It may be too, as Mason Wade suggests, that Margaret's all-too-evident admiration for Henry Atkinson, the young mesmerist who had recently ''cured'' Miss Martineau of her mysteriously debilitating illness, had something to do with the coolness between them.[9]

At Ambleside Margaret began to meet people from a wide spectrum of British life: two landed proprietors, ''both warmly engaged in Reform measures, anti–Corn-Law, anti–Capital-Punishment,—one of them an earnest student of Emerson's Essays''; a wealthy manufacturer who had written ''many valuable pamphlets on popular subjects''; a chemistry professor from Edinburgh University; and ''a fine specimen of the noble, intelligent Scotchwoman, such as Walter Scott and Burns knew how to prize.''[10] There were boating excursions on the lakes, and walks and drives among the bare, sheep-nibbled mountains long familiar from the poems of Wordsworth and Coleridge. With the Springs she called on Wordsworth himself at Rydal Mount. Like many visitors she found the place itself disappointing, ''the retirement of a gentleman, rather than the haunt of a poet.'' But this was fitting for the seventy-six-year-old Wordsworth, who had long since abandoned both his muse and the passionate liberalism of his youth. He was now an elderly Tory, ''a reverend old man clothed in black, and walking with cautious step along the level garden-path.''[11] Even so he spoke more tolerantly than she had expected of the repeal of the Corn Laws.

From the Lake Country the party traveled north by stages to Scotland. After staying overnight in Carlisle, where they visited the cathedral and castle and ''trod, for the first time, in some of the footsteps of the unfortunate Queen of Scots,''[12] they arrived in Edinburgh. They were disappointed to find the university closed and all the city's intelligentsia fled to the country for the summer, but Margaret did meet de Quincy, now like Wordsworth somewhat slowed down by age, but still capable of ''a real grand *conversazione,* quite in the Landor style.''[13] She also met the famous Scottish preacher Thomas Chalmers and the physician Andrew Combe, popular in America for his books in favor of fresh air and exercise, though American publishers had not rewarded him proportionately. A highlight of the Edinburgh visit was her meeting with William and Robert Chambers, publishers of *The Chambers's Edinburgh Journal,* probably the best of a number of new periodicals published especially for the working classes. The Chambers brothers practiced what they preached; their employees enjoyed working conditions that any *Tribune* reporter might well envy, including their own reading room, a savings bank, and evening courses. Margaret carefully described all this in her *Tribune* letter, primarily for the benefit of her own employer, whose tight-fistedness toward his staff contrasted strangely with the idealism of his editorials. She ended by praising the Chambers's highminded publishing ethic, in which money-making was secondary to bringing ''mental and moral benefit to their countrymen.''[14]

She had ample time to wander around the handsome capital city, with its Georgian squares and its Gothic spires. It was resonant with associations from Scott and Burns, though of the two the novelist was perhaps more beloved than the poet. With difficulty she hunted up Burns's statue in the public library; she thought it ''entirely unworthy of its subject.''[15] Scott's, on the other hand, was seated in the heart of the city, with its back appropriately turned to the site of the new railway terminal. She ventured only briefly into the slums, which lay in the older section of the city; the stench defeated her after a quarter of an hour.

While she was in Edinburgh she was badly shaken by the arrival of a letter from James Nathan, announcing his forthcoming marriage to a Hamburg woman. After his silences and his coldness she should have expected as much, and perhaps on a rational level she did. Nevertheless she was so upset that at first she refused to believe the letter was not a forgery. Later she took to her bed with a headache, but not before she had mustered her pride and fired off a note to Nathan through Thomas Delf, his agent in London, saying that she had received his letter but was too much engaged at the time to give it more than a moment's thought.

In a peculiarly distorted way, the Nathan denouement was a repetition of an old pattern. With both Nathan and Sam Ward, and probably with George Davis, Margaret had allowed herself a passionate emotional involvement in which all the language of love was indulged in while all hope of sexual fulfillment was explicitly barred. It was as close as she could come to a normal sexual relationship without bartering away her freedom, and if it was hard on the men around her it was even harder on Margaret herself. Had she been as sexually repressed as most New England women, or had she been able deliberately to stifle her feelings, her emotional life would have been smoother, if not happier. As it was, all three men found it impossible to disentangle themselves except by a sudden and clandestine engagement to another woman. The comparison ends there, however, for Nathan's duplicity and self-righteousness (which will be amplified presently) in no way invite a comparison with the honest perplexity of Ward and Davis.

Fortunately Margaret and her friends were about to leave on a fortnight's tour of the highlands. Margaret climbed up on the box with the coachman, where she had an unimpeded view of the countryside and where she was away from the solicitous eyes of her companions. She stayed there even through a day of drenching rain and said she enjoyed it immensely. They stopped at Perth, and at the little island of Loch Leven, where Mary Stuart abdicated her throne after the defeat of Boswell; then on to the Trossachs, Loch Katrine and Loch Lomond, where they were rowed up the lake by local boatmen who entertained them with Gaelic songs and rather mechanical recitations from "The Lady of the Lake." Arriving at their inn at sunset, they saw behind it the long, heathered-covered flanks of Ben Lomond and decided they would not be content until they had climbed to the summit on horseback. But the weather was unfavorable the next day, and they went to see some highland dancing up the lake instead. That led to some extra sleep the following morning, and by the time they had breakfasted, another party had beaten them to the stables and hired all the horses. The day was too beautiful to waste, though, and Margaret and Marcus decided to make the ascent on foot. Their hosts, who should have recommended a guide, said nothing for fear of being thought mercenary.

Inexperienced and sedentary tourists though they were, they did reach the top, but not until the shadows were beginning to lengthen across the valley. The view, once gained, was not easily left behind, and they did not start down until about four o'clock. They soon lost the trail, which was casually marked and crossed by sheep tracks. Marcus went to find it while Margaret sat down. In a few minutes he called, but the brow of a hill shut off the sound and she did not hear him. Eventually she started down alone, blundering often into bogs and sliding down the steeper slopes by hanging onto the heather. Dusk found her still far from the inn, though she could see the lights from its windows. She was prevented from going any farther by a stream, the depth of which she could not judge in the growing darkness. Exhausted, she lay down, and when she woke it was completely dark.

She retreated to a small space of firm ground and paced up and down all night to keep warm. She had only a light shawl, and her shoes and skirts were soaking wet. In a couple of hours the mists came down, making her wetter still, and she amused herself by comparing the long, curling shapes around her to Ossianic visions of Celtic heroes and maidens. Although there were twenty men with dogs out searching for her, she heard nothing but the sound of the stream, and now and then a grouse starting up from the heather. At dawn, still surrounded by mist, she followed the sound of the stream back up the hill and crossed under a waterfall, which left her scarcely more drenched than she already had been. A few moments later some shepherds found her and carried her to the inn. For all her history of invalidism, she suffered no ill effects after a day or two in bed. She made light of the adventure afterward, but she had certainly discovered in herself a physical endurance she had no idea she possessed.

They left the highlands by way of the pass of Glencoe and Inverary, and arrived two days later at Glasgow. There they were wrenched abruptly back into their own century. The city, Margaret wrote, more resembled an Inferno than any other they had visited. The squalor of Edinburgh's slums, and even of Lancashire's, was not as terrible as this. "The people are more crowded together, and the stamp of squalid, stolid misery and degradation more obvious and appalling."[16] She saw them huddled in the churchyards, lying on the ground, or sitting against the headstones, apparently having no other place to go. The plight of the prostitutes, of which she heard something while she was there, was later confirmed in a pamphlet she read, in which "the details given, the unimaginable horrors to which are there subjected this most wretched portion of the victims of civilization, shew that my impressions were not too strong. . . ."[17]

But even here the wheels of reform were beginning slowly to turn. The question that haunted many members of the prosperous middle class was whether they could be made to turn fast enough. With ladylike circumspection, Margaret used a blunt metaphor to describe the threat of revolution:

> The manufacturing and commercial towns, burning focuses of grief and vice, are also the centres of intellectual life, as in forcing-beds the rarest flowers and fruits are developed by use of impure and repulsive materials. Where evil comes to an extreme, Heaven seems busy in providing means for the remedy. Glaring throughout Scotland and England is the necessity for the devoutest application of intellect and love to the cure of ills that cry aloud, and, without such application, erelong help *must* be sought by other means than words. Yet there is every reason to hope that those who ought to help are seriously, though slowly, becoming alive to the imperative nature of this duty; so we must not cease to hope, even in the streets of Glasgow, and the gin-palaces of Manchester, and the dreariest recesses of London.[18]

But in spite of the impression the misery of the poor made on her, Margaret was still primarily an observer. Her *Tribune* letters, written in her habitually elevated style and lacking in concrete detail, continued to shift in tone from social indignation to effusive praise of the scenery, sometimes with disconcerting swiftness. To some extent, of course, this was the inevitable result of the diary style imposed on a traveler. A careful rereading of the *Tribune* letters shows that she was moved and changed by what she saw, but on first reading her expressions of pity and anger sound a little hollow. Mason Wade comments with some justice that later in the trip her sympathy with the starving weavers of Lyons did not prevent her from moving on to Avignon the next day, where she made a "sentimental pilgrimage" to the tomb of Petrarch's Laura.[19] A Lydia Maria Child might have moved in with the weavers then and there, but Margaret could go no further than to write about them and leave them. And it may be that all Mrs. Child could have done was starve with them.

Leaving Scotland, the party traveled slowly south, stopping first at Sir Walter Scott's home, Abbotsford, where Margaret saw with regret that the place where he was buried was the only spot thereabouts where grass refused to grow. They went on to York and its great cathedral, York Minster ("Such a church is ruined by Protestantism," Margaret wrote), and to Warwick Castle, where they lingered over a handsome collection of Van Dykes. Stratford, she discovered, was already "hackneyed ground," overrun by tourists a bare forty years after Coleridge had brought the bard the attention he deserved. And there were less pleasurable stops: the dingy industrial towns of Birmingham and Sheffield, where she saw "the sooty servitors tending their furnaces,"[20] and a visit to a coal mine at Newcastle, where she and the Springs descended in the usual way, in a bucket tied to a rope. There they saw and pitied the half-blind horses in their underground stables, but the mud and darkness of the tunnel discouraged their attempt to walk to the miners, a mile and a half away.

She spent the next several weeks in London, where she was quickly welcomed into literary circles. As Emerson and Alcott had already discovered, Transcendentalism was kindly thought of in England. Emerson's essays and the *Dial* were widely read, and recently some journals had printed courteous reviews of

Margaret's new book of essays and *Woman in the Nineteenth Century*. She was invited to contribute to one or two English reviews and was soon "engaged in such a crowd of acquaintance" that she had "hardly time to dress and none to sleep." She wrote that she felt much in her element in English society, which seemed less constrained than American and allowed her "a freer play of faculty." [21] Her rounds of visiting left scant time for sight-seeing, though she did manage to see the National Gallery, the zoo, the British Museum, Hampton Court, and one or two other places of interest. She was glad to find them all open to everyone—public access to such places was by no means taken for granted—though it evidently required a little effort for her to reconcile herself to the reverberating tramp of workingmen's boots in the National Gallery. She toured the new model prison at Pentonville, whose administrators prided themselves on having substituted real employment for the treadmill, and found it, like its American counterparts, clean but bleak. She visited one of the new public laundries and later called on one of the chief movers of the Baths and Washhouses Act and other public health measures, Dr. Southwood Smith. Smith had once been secretary to the great utilitarian philosopher Jeremy Bentham, who in a characteristic gesture had bequeathed his skeleton to his friend. Margaret found it seated in his study, dressed in Bentham's clothes and probably looking much more at home than the visitors who had to endure its company.

While she was in London she became friendly with James Nathan's friend Thomas Delf, and at the same time (perhaps with Delf's encouragement) she wrote to Nathan, asking him to return her letters and bitterly reproaching him for leading her on. This led to a fruitless and humiliating exchange which went on for some weeks. Nathan assumed a tone of injured innocence and reminded her of their agreement to have a platonic friendship—the letter of which they had both observed, while freely violating the spirit. Probably Delf had told Margaret more about Nathan than Nathan found it comfortable for her to know, for he alludes to someone who has told her something unpleasant about him, and wails that she has been "most lamentably wrong informed, hoodwinked, and imposed.''[22] All this would have been difficult enough, but she must have been alarmed as well as enraged when he refused to return her letters, vaguely holding out the possibility of giving them back at some future time, but maintaining that for the present he could not bear to part with them. His promise to do nothing but what was "right, manly and honorable" with them was cold comfort, given the usual worth of his promises.[23]

But her new London acquaintances left her little time for wringing her hands over past indiscretions. Among the people she met were William and Mary Howitt, coeditors of *The People's Journal*, a workingmen's publication similar to *Chambers's Journal*. Another, far more important, new friend was Giuseppe Mazzini, the exiled leader of the Italian republican movement.

Mazzini had been exiled from his native Piedmont in 1830 and for many years had lived frugally in England, where he devoted his time to running an evening school for Italian workingmen and street boys and writing ceaselessly on behalf of the Italian republican cause. A fragile-looking, ascetically handsome man whose gaze burned with saintly intensity, he was in fact a kind of secular saint, and his republicanism was based on an ethical Christianity which was none the less zealous for being free of traditional dogma. Over the years he had led or participated in several abortive risings in Italy and had organized the clandestine group known as Young Italy, cells of which were scattered throughout the peninsula. Republican hopes within Italy were fed by a steady stream of Mazzini's pamphlets, smuggled into the country by sympathetic seamen and eagerly passed from hand to hand. Though every attempt at revolution so far had failed to gain popular support and had been savagely suppressed, among Mazzini's other saintly qualities were indefatigable patience and energy. Frequently subject to fits of depression, he nevertheless kept on writing (in *The People's Journal*, among others) and watching for the first sign of faltering control among Italy's several repressive and corrupt regimes.

In Mazzini's exclusive dedication to his cause Margaret recognized a quality which she had seen before only in Emerson, Alcott, and a few other Americans, but nowhere else in Britain. Here Wordsworth's benign Toryism and Carlyle's bitter celebrations of the aristocracy of force seemed all that remained of a Romanticism whose high point had long since passed. Mazzini was no mere fanatic; he was a skilled political leader. Nevertheless he would not ally himself with any party, no matter how powerful, which would unify Italy under an absolute ruler, be he king or pope. For this he was scoffed at by political realists in Europe; but to American eyes, particularly Transcendentalist eyes, what a European took to be extravagantly visionary nonsense could appear simply as a noble and not unreasonable idealism. In her last few weeks in London Margaret formed with Mazzini another of her intense, accelerated friendships.

To no one did Mazzini appear more quixotic than to his friend Thomas Carlyle. Margaret met Carlyle independently of Mazzini, through an introductory note from Emerson. Their first evening together, which might well have become a classic confrontation between an irresistible force and an immovable object, actually was no contest at all. Margaret wryly conceded the field and listened to Carlyle "singing his great full sentences, so that each was like the stanza of a narrative ballad. He let me talk, now and then, enough to free my lungs and change my position, so that I did not get tired." [24] Carlyle, for his part, pronounced Margaret "a strange lilting lean old maid, not nearly such a bore as I expected." [25] There were two other meetings: one dinner at the Carlyles', when the great man railed against poetry, and one at Margaret's, when he railed against democracy. Margaret did not manage to talk to Jane Carlyle at all until the second meeting, when (being in her own lodgings) she was able to draw her away from the steady torrent of sound in the drawing room. She liked Jane very much, apparently missing the tartness which was evident to those who knew her well: "She is full of grace, sweetness, and talent. Her eyes are sad and charming." [26] Another guest that evening was Mazzini, who grew more and more visibly depressed as Carlyle held forth on his favorite theme, "success the test of right;—if people would not behave well, put collars round their necks;—find a hero, and let them be his slaves, &c." Margaret thought it all "very Titanic, and anti-celestial," but to Mazzini, as Jane Carlyle quietly commented later, it was "a matter of life and death.''[27] He had been imprisoned and exiled for opposing such opinions, and several of his friends had been killed. One of them, Jacopo Ruffini, had committed suicide in prison rather than betray fellow members of Young Italy.

Carlyle's obnoxious opinions did not affect Margaret's judgment of the man himself, whom she saw as possessed by a necessary destructive force. Her belief in the demonic is clearly perceptible in her *Tribune* comments:

> It is the usual misfortune of such marked men . . . that they cannot allow other minds room to breathe and show themselves in their atmosphere. . . . . Carlyle, indeed, is arrogant and overbearing, but in his arrogance there is no littleness or self-love: it is the heroic arrogance of some old Scandinavian conqueror,—it is his nature and the untamable impulse that has given him power to crush the dragons. You do not love him, perhaps, nor revere, and perhaps, also, he would only laugh at you if you did; but you like him heartily, and like to see him the powerful smith, the Siegfried, melting all the old iron in his furnace till it glows to a sunset red, and burns you if you senselessly go too near.[28]

In late November Margaret and the Springs left to spend the winter in Paris. With the French Margaret never did become comfortable; she called them ''slippery'' and complained that the studied urbanity of their manners hid what they were really thinking. More aloof than the British, they did not court her acquaintance and left her to find her way into their houses as best she could. They would not call, as the British did, when they received a letter of introduction. In any case, Margaret lacked the right letters of introduction in France. She found, too, that her reading knowledge of the language would not do for conversation, and so she spent much of her time every day closeted with a tutor.

As a consequence of being thrown more on her own resources, she saw more of Paris than she had of London. She went to the opera a few times, but thought it inferior to the English; the theater was another story, and she saw the great actress Rachel several times. She was presented at court and attended a court ball, noting with satisfaction that the American ladies were the handsomest there. She went frequently to the Chamber of Deputies, where she reverently fingered a Rousseau manuscript and listened with mingled amusement and dismay at the chaotic shouting matches that passed for debate on the floor. She went regularly to lectures at the Academy and twice to discussions at the Athenée. With a male companion, probably Spring, she tried to hear the astronomer Leverrier speak at the Sorbonne, but here she found her way barred by an elderly, supercilious guard, who informed them that "Monsieur may enter if he pleases, but Madame must remain here." After the lecture was over she again tried to enter, just to see the empty hall:

> But the guardian again interfered to deny me entrance. "You can go, Madame," said he, "to the College of France; you can go to this and t'other place, but you cannot enter here." "What, sir," said I, "is it your institution alone that remains in a state of barbarism?" "Que voulez vous, Madame?" he replied, and, as he spoke, his little dog began to bark at me,—"Que voulez vous, Madame? c'est la regle." [29]*

Gradually she did meet people; even in France she was not unknown. Her essay on American literature had been translated and published (although the author was listed as "Elizabeth Fuller"), and she was encouraged to translate *Woman* and to become a correspondent for *La Revue Indépendante*. Her connection with Greeley and Spring drew her into association with the followers of Fourier, whose socialistic goals she applauded though she doubted the efficiency of their means. "They are full of hope," she wrote to another sympathizer, William Channing, "and their propaganda has a real and increasing influence . . . But oh! how far to the harvest!" [30] She was impressed by one innovation she had not seen anywhere but Paris: the *crèches,* where working mothers could leave their children during the day. But in general the conditions among the poor during this famine winter were desperate. Unemployment and the price of bread soared, and among a highly literate population the memories of 1789 were kept alive by an active

* "What can I do, Madame? It is the rule."

proletarian press. Secret societies were thriving under the very nose of Louis Philippe. The government and the middle class continued to pretend that nothing was wrong, and that their own prosperity would benefit everyone in the end, but Margaret sensed an impending explosion:

> While Louis Philippe lives, the gases, compressed by his strong grasp, may not burst up to light; but the need of some radical measures of reform is not less strongly felt in France than elsewhere, and the time will come before long when such will be imperatively demanded.[31]

She misjudged only the time, and the strength of Louis Philippe's "grasp." In fact France would have its revolution the following year, while Louis Philippe was still very much alive.

Among the people she met, four were particularly important to her: the ex-priest and republican Lamennais, the poet Béranger, the novelist George Sand, and the Polish poet Adam Mickiewicz. The first two she met only once, and by a rare stroke of luck she found them together when she called. Mme Sand proved more elusive; she was away at Nohant when Margaret arrived in Paris, and only returned some weeks later. Receiving no answer to a letter of introduction, Margaret called, and was almost turned away because the servant garbled her name. But as she turned to leave Sand realized who she was and entered the room:

> She was dressed in a robe of dark violet silk, with a black mantle on her shoulders, her beautiful hair dressed with the greatest taste, her whole appearance and attitude, in its simple and ladylike dignity, presenting an almost ludicrous contrast to the vulgar caricature idea of George Sand. . . . What fixed my attention was the expression of *goodness,* nobleness, and power, that pervaded the whole,—the truly human heart and nature that shone in the eyes. As our eyes met, she said, *"C'est vous,"* and held out her hand. I took it, and went into her little study; we sat down a moment, then I said, *"Il me fait de bien de vous voir,"* and I am sure I said it with my whole heart, for it made me very happy to see such a woman, so large and so developed a character, and everything that *is* good in it so *really* good. I loved, shall always love her.[32]

She saw Sand again, but not alone, and their acquaintance never progressed further. A few days afterward Margaret met Chopin, who by now was "always ill and frail as a snowdrop." He played exquisitely for her, and she "liked his talking scarcely less."[33] He still lived in the same house with Sand, but was no longer her lover, though she continued to nurse him through his acute attacks.

As before she visited local institutions, focusing on those which seemed to place the individual before *la règle,* and she became thoroughly familiar with the galleries and all the places of cultural interest. But from any real contact with ordinary Parisians, rich or poor, she remained cut off, even after she had been there two months. She felt strongly the need of someone "to initiate me into various little secrets of the place and time,—necessary for me to look at things to my satisfaction,—some friend, such as I do not find here."[34] She found such a friend, but only a few days before her departure, when she met Adam Mickiewicz.

Like Mazzini, Mickiewicz was a political exile whose writings were a rallying cry for his people. Poland too was fragmented and victimized under an assortment of despotic regimes, but the Poles were, if possible, even more wretched than the Italians, having been subjected in the nineteenth century to a program of deliberate cultural obliteration. Their strategic position between Russia and Germany was then, as today, an unhealthy one. They had made a desperate, unsuccessful effort to free themselves in 1830, and Adam Mickiewicz, who had written the epic poem *Pan Tadeusz* celebrating the heroism of his people in that brief struggle, had become the national poet of Poland, although he had not seen his native land since his student days. He now held the chair in Slavonic Languages and Literature at the Collège de France, and Margaret introduced herself by sending him a volume of poems by Emerson, whom she knew he admired.

In some ways Mickiewicz strikingly resembled Mazzini. In Paris he was the center of a revolutionary group composed chiefly, but not entirely, of Polish exiles. Like Mazzini he foresaw a messianic role for his country as a leader in a series of sweeping revolutions which would free Europe; but unlike Mazzini he was a fervent (if irregular) Catholic, a mystic, and a poet. He spoke of

Poland as a crucified Christ among nations, whose revolutionary mission was inextricably tied to her sufferings, and whose "resurrection" would revitalize downtrodden people everywhere. It was remarkable that Margaret's two closest friendships in England and France should be formed with these men, both of whom exerted a profound influence on the course of events in Europe. They helped immeasurably to deepen her imaginative understanding of the festering political ills of the Old World.

As people, Mickiewicz and Mazzini were quite different. It was not the Catholic Mickiewicz, but the humanistic political leader Mazzini, who lived the more Spartan life. In Mazzini, Margaret once observed, "holiness has purified, but somewhat dwarfed the man."[35] He was unmarried, and it was rumored that he was true to his former mistress, a widow who lived in Italy in order to be near her children. But he had been many years separated from her by 1846, and their correspondence had in it far more of friendship than love. He carefully kept the hopeful English mamas at a distance, and in truth seems to have spent all his passion on his work and his cause.

That Mickiewicz was different was evident just from looking at him. He was a big man with a broad, open, Slavic face and a mop of unruly hair. He was married, albeit unhappily (his wife was periodically insane), so his friendship with Margaret was understood from the beginning to be free of any romantic complication. But he was an artist and a forthright European male, and he never made Margaret feel, as American men had, that her sex was a regrettable liability. A staunch believer in political equality for women, Jews, and all oppressed groups, he was no less a staunch admirer of *la différence*. He scolded her for her bookishness and her morbid fits of depression (which his own mysticism helped accentuate). But unlike Greeley and Emerson, who scolded her for similar reasons, he encouraged her search for a real alternative, as is clear from his letters:

> The time is coming when inner beauty, inner spiritual life will become the first and essential quality of a woman. Without this quality woman will not exert even physical influence. Learn to appreciate

yourself as a beauty, and after having admired the women of Rome, say, "And as for me, why I am beautiful!" [36]

And,

> I should be grieved if I had contributed in any way to drive you into the regions of melancholy, from which I hoped Italy would help you emerge. I tried to make you understand that you should not confine your life to books and reveries. You have pleaded the liberty of woman in a masculine and frank style. Live and act, as you write.[37]

By the time she received this letter she was already beginning to do so.

XV

Italy, 1847

"Here at Naples," Margaret wrote in March, "I have at last found *my* Italy." Not until she had been there a week did the Italian spring really arrive, banishing a "villainous, horrible wind, exactly like the worst east wind of Boston." But once the Neapolitan hills were thoroughly warmed by the sun, all hint of northern chill disappeared. Margaret, feeling that "Anglo-Saxon crust" she had long recognized in herself grow thinner by the day, clambered up the sides of her own metaphor and viewed the Bay of Naples from Mt. Vesuvius. She went through the Grotto of Pausilippo and visited Sorrento, Capri, and Cuma; Baiae "had still a hid divinity" for her.[1] Nature, history, and people were all merged in a single whole here; thought and feeling were not artificially opposed. Having felt like a stranger in New England for as long as she could remember, she must have been a little amused to find that she could not shed overnight those Bostonisms she had acquired so painfully over the years. She immediately felt at ease among Italians, but to them she must have seemed a rather stiff and imposing *inglesa*.

On the way to Naples Margaret and the Springs had spent three days in Genoa, where she visited Mazzini's mother, a valiant old lady with melancholy eyes like her son's, who had never wavered in her support of the beliefs which kept him in exile. Margaret sent news of her to Mazzini, along with two leaves from the scented verbena growing on his library windowsill. From Genoa they went to Leghorn, where they boarded an English boat for Naples. But at sea they had a disturbing mishap: a mail steamer collided with their ship, for no discernible reason except that both captains disregarded the rules governing right of way. After a long and complicated parley (neither captain spoke the other's language), the English vessel was ignominiously towed back to Leghorn by the offending steamer, and the departure for Naples was delayed twenty-four hours. Margaret spoke lightly about the incident afterward, but it increased her distrust of the sea. The daily papers often reported fatal shipwrecks resulting from causes as trivial as this.

She arrived in Rome early in April, in time for the Easter observances. She was too moved to describe the city: "Italy is beautiful, worthy to be loved and embraced, not talked about." [2] But in a letter to Aunt Mary Rotch she did describe her own new sense of tranquility:

> All winter in Paris, although my life was rich in novelties of value, I was not well; the climate was too damp for me, and then I had too much intellectual excitement of the same kind as at home. I need a respite, a long leisure of enjoyment, a kind of spring time, to renovate my faculties. But Paris is the very focus of intellectual activity of Europe, there I found every topic intensified, clarified, reduced to portable dimensions: there is the cream of all the milk, but I am not strong enough to live on cream at present. I learned much, I suffered to leave Paris, but I find myself better here, where the climate is so enchanting, the people so indolently joyous, and the objects of contemplation so numerous and admirable, that one cannot pass the time better than by quietly *looking* one's fill. . . ." [3]

She found many Americans and English in Rome, among them two old Brook Farm friends, George W. Curtis and Christopher

Cranch. Curtis was just passing through, but Cranch, having kept the faith from the old days, had renounced the hope (such as it was) of a comfortable living in America and brought his family to join the expatriate artists' colony in Italy. Margaret visited all the studios and did her best to drum up patronage for the arts in the *Tribune,* but on the whole she tried to avoid other Americans, most of whom were casual tourists. Even the British, whom she had lately admired amid their own darker landscape, were all too likely to "chatter and sneer" through the Sistine Chapel, praise St. Peter's as "nice," and talk of "managing" the Colosseum by moonlight.[4] She herself visited the Colosseum by moonlight, but her only companions were the resident owls, in whose hooting she found commentary more fitting than any learned text. She attended the Holy Week services at St. Peter's, but liked best to slip into the cathedral at odd moments, when it was nearly empty except for the "processions of monks and nuns stealing in now and then, or the swell of vespers from some side chapel."[5] She went to the Trastevere, the oldest and poorest section of Rome, to watch the Easter celebrations of the inhabitants, reportedly direct descendents of the ancient Romans, among whom the old semipagan dances and songs were kept alive. She saw the sculpture of Michelangelo and the time-ravaged frescoes of Raphael, and found the one far more, and the other far less, than she had hoped for. She drove and walked in the Campagna and in the grounds of the villas surrounding Rome, opened as public parks by a nobility whose sense of class distinction was among the least developed in Europe.

A few days after she arrived in Rome, Margaret had an adventure that was peculiarly Italian. She had gone with the Springs to hear vespers at St. Peter's, and after the service they separated to explore the cathedral, arranging to meet afterward at a given spot. But when Margaret arrived at the place, the Springs were not there. After waiting for some minutes she began to search for them, peering anxiously around the darkening side chapels with her lorgnette, but there was no sign of them, and she could only conclude that they had gone on without her. It was a little dismaying, even to so self-reliant a woman as Margaret. She neither knew the way home nor how to ask directions.

As she stood there wondering what to do, a young man approached and asked in Italian if he could help her. He was tall and
slightly built, good-looking but with a serious, even brooding
expression when his face was in repose. He wore a mustache but
no beard, and appeared to be about thirty. (He was actually
twenty-six.) For the rest, he looked like a gentleman, and it was
no time for social niceties; she accepted with thanks. They went
out to the piazza to find a cab, but by now they had all been taken,
and so there was nothing to do but walk to Margaret's lodgings on
the Corso, well over a mile away. They conversed haltingly as
they went; he spoke a few words of French, she a few of Italian.
His name was Giovanni Angelo Ossoli, and he belonged to an ancient family of modest fortune which for generations had been in
the service of the papacy. His mother had died when he was six.
His father, the Marchese Filippo Ossoli, had been a Vatican official until recently when he had been stricken with an illness. Two
of his three older brothers were in the papal guards, and a third,
like his father, was a functionary at court. He himself had strong
republican sympathies, and so his relations with his brothers were
strained. He had two married sisters. One lived in Ireland, and the
other, Angela, lived in Rome and was his good friend.

Margaret in turn told him something of her own background,
her long-cherished love for Italy, and her friendship with Mazzini.
When they parted he may have asked if he could call, or possibly—as one more picturesque version has it—he returned a day
or two later and waited on the street until she saw him and came
down. Once they had met again, she seems to have pursued him as
resolutely as she always pursued those she had elected to make her
friends. In a letter addressed simply "Dear Youth" but almost certainly written to Ossoli, she chided him for his habitual reserve in
terms he must have found no less puzzling than startling:

> You are the only one whom I have seen here in whose eye I recog-
> nized one of my own kindred. I want to know and to love you and to
> have you love me. You said you have no friendliness of nature but
> that is not true; you are precisely one to need the music, the recogni-
> tion of kindred minds. How can you let me pass you by, without full
> and free communication.[6]

Having received this unequivocal (to an Italian) invitation, he very soon proposed a liaison, and that failing, marriage. She refused, offering instead her usual chastely ardent terms of friendship, which he must have found patently absurd. But they were much together in the following weeks, and in his company she was able to begin to know Rome as intimately as she wanted to.

As their attachment increased, Margaret's future plans become more confused: originally she and the Springs had planned to leave Rome in June, spend some time in northern Italy, and then proceed to Germany through Switzerland. But by the end of April Margaret was writing wistfully of remaining a whole year in Rome. As if guessing her hesitation, Adam Mickiewicz wrote warning her not to be "too hasty about leaving places where you feel well," and not to "leave lightly those who would like to remain near you. This is in reference to that little Italian you met in the Church." [7]

Another reason for her strong attachment to Rome was her growing identification with the republican cause, which she came to understand better through Ossoli. Dante and Alfieri, and more recently Mazzini, had prepared her for the political climate in Italy, and now that she was here she began to feel that this struggle was in some small measure her own, both as an Italian in spirit and as a republican by birth. Fragmented for hundreds of years, Italy was still crushed under an assortment of despots whose power was medieval in scope. In the beginning of the century, under Napoleon, the Italians had had a taste of what it might be like to be unified; all the more bitter had been the new divisions imposed by the Congress of Vienna. The Austrians occupied Lombardy and Venetia; there were Austrian rulers in the nominally independent states of Tuscany, Parma, and Modena; the corrupt and brutal Spanish Bourbons were restored to the throne of Naples and Sicily; the Pope resumed temporal power over central Italy. In Piedmont the hereditary throne was at least Italian, but the Piedmontese kings never forgot that they ruled by sufferance of their Austrian neighbors. Charles Albert, King of Piedmont, had a reputation as a moderate ruler who had played at being a *Carbonaro* in his youth, but it was Charles Albert who had exiled Mazzini and tortured and executed the members of Young Italy.

The center of Christendom was not any more liberal than the secular Italian states. On the contrary, under the rule of the previous Pope, Gregory XVI, the inhabitants had suffered under a regime that was rivaled in ferocity only by the Kingdom of Naples to the south. The poverty was worse, the illiteracy rate higher, the censorship more severe, the sudden arrests and terrorizing by the police more common in the Papal States than under the Austrians, who had looked positively benevolent in comparison with the Holy Father. But in 1846 Gregory had died, and a new Pope, Pius IX, was elected, a gentle-faced, relatively young man who when notified of his election had reportedly exclaimed, "They want to make a Napoleon of me, who am only a poor country priest!" His first official act was to grant a general amnesty to political prisoners, and this was soon followed by other measures which seemed to promise a constitutional government. The Romans responded with massive, spontaneous demonstrations of joy and gratitude: they wept and cheered when he passed; they unhitched the horses from his carriage and drew it themselves through the streets. A new "Hymn to Pio Nono" was heard everywhere in Rome and quickly spread north to the Austrian provinces, where to sing it became an act of defiance which the Catholic Austrians were powerless to prevent.

In May the people's love for the Pope reached a new height when he promised them a representative council, through which their voice would be heard in the government for the first time. It was a small step toward full democracy, but the Romans received it with great rejoicing. In the evening they formed a huge torchlight procession which wound down the Corso to the Quirinal, passing under Margaret's windows:

> The stream of fire advanced slowly, with a perpetual surge-like sound of voices; the torches flashed on the animated Italian faces. I have never seen anything finer. Ascending the Quirinal they made it a mount of light. Bengal fires were thrown up, which cast their red and white light on the noble Greek figures of men and horses that reign over it. The Pope appeared on his balcony; the crowd shouted three vivas; he extended his arms; the crowd fell on their knees and received his benediction; he retired, and the torches were extinguished, and the multitude dispersed in an instant.[8]

But Mazzini was as distrustful of the Pope as he was of Charles Albert, maintaining that Pius IX's personal liberalism and the secular power of the Church were incompatible. And Margaret, though she wanted to share the optimism of those around her, could not help but be skeptical: "He is a man of noble and good aspect, who, it is easy to see, has set his heart upon doing something solid for the benefit of man. But pensively, too, must one feel how hampered and inadequate are the means at his command to accomplish these ends." [9]

It was very difficult not only to leave Ossoli but to leave Rome at this time. But the Springs were restless, and if she were going north at all she should go during the summer. At some point, perhaps even before she left Rome, Margaret decided to return and stay at least through the autumn. It meant foregoing the trip to Germany, and with it the last faint hope of writing a biography of Goethe (she carried an introductory letter to Eckermann), but at the moment it seemed that the best tribute to Goethe might be to experience for herself the sense of rebirth he had found in his own Italian journey. She went with the Springs to Florence, and thence to Venice, where she remained while they went on to Switzerland. She planned to tour the northern cities, alone except for a servant, and return to Rome in October.

In Florence she met several more American artists, among them the sculptors Horatio Greenough, Joseph Mozier, and Hiram Powers (whose "Greek Slave," shipped home to America, caused a great to-do among those members of the public who still believed that marble ladies should come equipped with marble petticoats). And she was introduced to the Florentine intellectual community by a new friend, the Marchioness Costanza Arconati Visconti, whom she had met briefly in Rome. Mme Arconati belonged to the curious tradition of educated, courageous, politically active women which flourished in Catholic, patriarchal Italy. A Milanese, she came from an old and respected family and had married a Visconti, whose ancestors had once been Dukes of Milan. But at the time of the 1821 uprisings she and her husband had committed themselves to the liberal cause and as a result had been exiled by the Austrian authorities. After an absence of twenty-six years, during which they had been active among the Italian nationalists in

Paris, they had been permitted to return on the wave of goodwill inspired by the Pope. They now lived part of the time in Florence, and part of the time on the Arconati estate near Milan. Mme Arconati was a follower of the Abbot Vincenzo Gioberti, who advocated the unification of Italy under the temporal rule of the Pope. Thus she differed sharply from Margaret and from Mazzini in her immediate political goals. But on the larger question of unity there was no division, and as a friend she became a sisterly confidante such as Margaret had not known since leaving Caroline Sturgis behind in Boston.

New Englanders were drawn to Florence then, as they still are. Margaret's American acquaintances felt much at home there; they said it was just like Boston. So it was, and for that reason Margaret felt all the more nostalgic for disorderly, volatile Rome. No other Italian city was as rich in art as Florence, and she dutifully visited the galleries and museums, but now that she actually could see them the Renaissance masterpieces left her relatively cold, compared with the clumsy copies she had rhapsodized over ten years before. So did the Tuscan fondness for lively but abstract discussion; she thought Florentine society "busy and intellectual." [10] At the same time there was little outward sign of political agitation. The Grand Duke had just relaxed censorship of the press, and his rule had always been relatively moderate. Those who opposed it were silent. Politically the Tuscans appeared "still and glum as death," though Margaret believed the stillness was all on the outside: "within, Tuscany burns." [11]

One great drawback in Margaret's decision to remain in Italy had been the never-distant anxiety about money. This was temporarily relieved while she was in Florence when news arrived of the death of her old nemesis, Abraham Fuller. Antagonistic to the last, he had not named her as a beneficiary, but as one of sixty-three residual legatees she would receive some portion of his large estate. She immediately wrote to Richard asking him to borrow $500 for her against the inheritance, and thus mentally fortified set off on a headlong rush through the north that must have made Adam Mickiewicz, when he heard of it, despair of ever truly Europeanizing his friend.

Her itinerary included two days in Bologna, where she found an anomalous old custom of educational equality for women very much alive. Here the women painters of the sixteenth century had been known throughout Italy, and one of them, Lavinia Fontana, had been palantine painter to Pope Gregory XIII. Margaret saw a memorial to a woman professor of Greek and—still more surprising—one to a woman professor of anatomy. From Bologna she proceeded rapidly through Ravenna, Ferarra, and Padua, reaching Venice in mid-July. Here she parted with the Springs and remained a fortnight, the first week feeling much the worse for heat and fatigue. To Venice, one of the highlights of her Italian journey, she paid the characteristic tribute of refusing to describe it. (Her New York readers by now were learning to gauge her affection for a place by her evasiveness about it.) Privately she confided how much she savored being alone at last with Italy, unrestrained by the whims of her companions. She visited St. Mark's cathedral with an American acquaintance and afterward sipped espresso at Florian's. From the Grand Canal she watched the arrival of sumptuously dressed nobility at a ball given by the Duchesse de Berri, wishing that a few more of the crowned heads of Europe could join that lady in her obviously painless exile. With her boy servant Cecco she shopped at the marketplace every day for the fruit that was her diet staple, carrying it home in a gondola. She was pleasantly surprised at the chivalry of her innkeeper, who on learning that she would not pay the rent he asked for his best rooms, immediately settled for less. (This seems to have been her first and last bargaining triumph in Italy.)

But two weeks was all she would spare for Venice before galloping off again. Her route took her through Vicenza, Verona, and Mantua, to Lago di Garda, and thence to Brescia. Here she came down with a high fever which alarmingly resembled the one she had had years before at Groton, and rather than be dangerously ill so far from friends she ordered a bed made up in a carriage and withstood a cramped and lurching drive to Milan. Having recovered there, probably with the help of friends of Mme Arconati, and having resolved to return, she set off once again via Lake Maggiore to the Swiss Alps ("bracing as a cold bath" after the heat and excitement of Italy).[12] The end of August found her at

Lake Como, where she spent a fortnight with Mme Arconati, sampling the luxurious but somewhat cloying country life of the nobility whose villas were scattered along the shore. From there she went to Lake Lugano, and so back to Milan.

Compared with Venice and Florence, Milan offered little to see, but Margaret had had enough of sight-seeing. The people, on the other hand, were among the most interesting she had met in Italy. She called on the aged poet Manzoni, newly married to a young wife and still much beloved although his advocacy of patience under the Austrian yoke was no longer widely accepted. And she saw much of a group of spirited young radicals, none of them over thirty, whose zeal for overthrowing the invader seemed matched by an unusual level of political maturity. By now, thanks to having had to rely on her knowledge of Italian when she traveled alone, she was rapidly mastering the language and was able to join in a conversation with something resembling her fluency in her own tongue. With Italians of all ranks she felt perfectly *simpatica*. The Italians, as she modestly told her mother, responded in kind:

> The Italians sympathize with my character and understand my organization, as no other people ever did; they admire the ready eloquence of my nature, and highly prize my intelligent sympathy (such as they do not find often in foreigners) with their sufferings in the past and hopes for the future.[13]

It was now September, and throughout Italy the tension had been growing during the summer. In June the Pope had granted permission for the formation of a civic guard, and thousands of young men volunteered. He also announced a plan to form a customs union—a very small and ultimately unsuccessful gesture toward unification which angered the Austrians. Metternich retaliated by occupying Ferarra, in the papal dominions, on a trumped-up excuse that fooled nobody. But the Italians, far from being intimidated, united more firmly behind the Pope. In early September the Grand Duke of Tuscany followed the Pope's lead in granting a national guard, which occasioned a great public *festa* in Florence. In Milan while Margaret was there the Lombards staged a similar celebration in honor of their new archbishop, who unlike his predecessor was Italian. The people poured into the streets, and some young men seized the opportunity to sing the "Hymn to Pio Nono" in the faces of the Austrian police. The Austrians charged the crowd, wounding several people in the back. In the *Tribune* Margaret scolded her compatriots for the callousness which allowed American tourists to shrug off incidents such as this:

> . . . I meet persons who call themselves Americans,—miserable, thoughtless Esaus, unworthy their high birthright, —who think that a mess of pottage can satisfy the wants of man, and that the Viennese listening to Strauss's waltzes, the Lombard peasant supping full of his polenta, is *happy enough*. Alas! I have the more reason to be ashamed of my countrymen that it is not among the poor, who have so much toil that there is little time to think, but those who are rich, who travel,—in body that is, they do not travel in mind. Absorbed at home by the lust of gain, the love of show, abroad they see only the equipages, the fine clothes, the food,—they have no heart for the idea, for the destiny of our own great nation: how can they feel the spirit that is struggling now in this and others of Europe?[14]

In October, after another visit to Florence, she returned to Rome and settled into new lodgings on the Corso, near the Pincian Mount and the Piazza del Popolo. Now began two or three months of undiluted happiness: Margaret and Ossoli became lovers. Possibly this had happened as early as the previous spring; there is a hint of it in a letter to a friend, written in August:

> I believe whatever may be the future developments of my life, you will always prize my friendship. Much has changed since you saw me; my character is not now in what may be called the heroic phase. I have done, may do things that might invoke censure; but in the foundation of character,—in my aims, I am always the same and I believe you will always have confidence that I act as I ought and must, and will always value my sympathy.[15]

Whether she had actually done anything to "invoke censure" or only anticipated doing so is a question no biographer, including this one, has yet resolved. But the change which she recognized in herself was no sudden metamorphosis. She did not in one mad moment abandon a life of puritan spinsterhood, but simply found that in Italy she could allow the person she had been all along to become visible. That Margaret should take a lover was not at all strange. Since the early questionings about Goethe which had embarrassed her clerical friends, and continuing with her admiration of Mme de Staël, Mary Wollstonecraft, and George Sand, her defense of prostitutes and her condemnation of sexual hypocrisy in *Woman in the Nineteenth Century,* she had shown an untrammeled recognition of sexuality which on a personal level is abundantly echoed in her letters and journals. It was the unwillingness of her own society to accept the "masculine" woman as a woman at all that forced her into the exaggerated role of the genderless bluestocking. It was not in itself a false role, but it became so because it expressed only one side of a richly complex, androgynous nature. It is worth noting that the two men who were most frankly attracted to her as a woman, Nathan and Ossoli, were both Europeans who initially at least knew nothing of her as an intellectual. Ossoli respected her mind, but he was apparently never threatened by it, perhaps because it was inseparable from her foreignness. She in turn was less assertive with them than with Americans (and indeed with Nathan fell into a passivity that was as exaggerated in its way as her sometime stridency). Yet with both these men she was basically the same person she had always been: to deny this is to minimize the primary cause of sadness and deprivation in her life.

The belief in Margaret's miraculous "feminization," with the implication that until she reached Italy she had less than the full measure of womanly feelings, is still perpetuated by modern biographers. Mason Wade, for example, says that Margaret became Ossoli's lover because "the Latin concept of woman as mother and wife had appealed to her frustrated femininity and sunk into her consciousness, gradually displacing her notion of herself as a Feminist consecrated to a single life."[16] One cannot help but see the battered but indefatigable shade of Sigmund Freud behind this statement. Of course Wade, like every biographer of Margaret Fuller, had recorded those anguished yearnings for love and children which abound in her journals, and these are clearly what he means by "frustrated femininity." At the same time he seems to take it for granted that Margaret herself found them incompatible with feminism. But what Margaret found incompatible with feminism was never love and children, only the social role of the American wife. Her "consecration" to a single life was a reluctant defense against a society that forced her to choose between living as a woman and living as a thinking, creative person. It was the Italian acceptance of sexuality, a concept distinct from the "Latin notion of mother and wife," that encouraged her union with Ossoli. She had in fact refused to become a wife, and that being the case motherhood was the last thing she wanted at the moment.

The glorious Italian autumn weather favored the lovers, who spent every possible moment out of doors. The debilitating heat of summer had given way to the long, mellow days of the grape harvest. The colors of the countryside were disappointing to Margaret, the fields turning sere and brown rather than gold, but the flowers continued to bloom, and she had fresh roses and violets in her room through December. She and Ossoli spent two days at the spacious grounds of the Villa Borghese, where an autumn *festa* was held with races, balloons, and concerts. They went frequently to hear Mass sung in Rome's innumerable churches, and as in the spring took long excursions into the countryside. In December the new representative council was inaugurated, and at a ball given to celebrate that event they saw again the Trasteverines, dancing the saltarello in brilliant costumes.

On Monday evenings Margaret set an extra bowl or two of flowers in her room and received a few guests, among them Christopher and Elizabeth Cranch, the American painters Thomas Hicks and Jaspar Cropsey, and a Polish Princess Radziwill, "a widow, very rich, one of the emancipated women." [17] In November the lawyer-about-to-turn-sculptor William Wetmore Story arrived in Rome with his wife Emelyn and their baby son. Margaret had known Story slightly in Cambridge and had disliked him; he was one of the circle that formed around James Russell Lowell. Now proximity quickly changed her view, and except for Ossoli the Storys became her closest friends. But she deliberately kept her circle of acquaintances small. She spent her days with Ossoli, and her evenings were devoted to reading about Italian history and politics, writing her *Tribune* letters, and writing to her correspondents, of whom there were now about a hundred. All signs of her summer illness had vanished: "I have not been so well since I was a child, nor so happy ever, as during the last six weeks," she wrote her mother in December.[18]

She lived very frugally. In September a letter of credit for $500 had arrived from Richard. Soon afterward came a letter from Horace Greeley telling her to draw against the *Tribune* when she needed money, but she apparently decided to keep this offer in reserve. Her share of Uncle Abraham's estate turned out to be less than $1,000, of which she already owed several hundred to Marcus Spring. She decided to try to make $400 last for six months, living in one room and subsisting mostly on fruit, bread, and wine. Rome was more expensive than Florence,* but then as she wrote to Richard, she "would not give a pin to live in Florence."[19] Her economical living quarters had the added advantage of privacy, since they gave her a plausible excuse for seeing visitors only on Monday evenings. Her landlady, "a most insinuating creature" but a discreet one,[20] had been the mistress of an elderly Marchese who had married her just before he died, thus conferring on her a tarnished respectability and the improbable title of Marchioness. Her current lover was a member of the civic guard, which Ossoli was about to join, and it was probably through an acquaintance with this man that the apartment was found.[21]

According to Margaret's family and early biographers, she and Ossoli were married in December 1847, but almost all references which might have verified the date have been destroyed. The arguments against this claim are strong. Margaret did not wish to remain permanently in Italy. She was talking of leaving in a year, remaining perhaps another year in Germany, France, and England, and then returning to America. There was no place for Ossoli in

---

* According to Mrs. Browning, one could live "like the Grand Duchess" in Florence for £300 (about $1,500) a year. See *The Letters of Elizabeth Barrett Browning* (New York: The MacMillan Co, 1897), I, p. 373.

these plans. To follow her would totally disrupt his life. Apart from the pain of abandoning his country at this crucial point in her history and going to live in an alien culture, there was the question of vocation. Bred as a gentleman and indifferently educated by an elderly priest, he was fit for no profession but the army, and in America the army was presently engaged in fighting the obnoxious Mexican War, after which it would probably be disbanded. He would be without any occupation, entirely dependent on Margaret for financial support—a situation which would certainly strain their relationship. All help, and indeed all communication, from his family would cease the moment it was known he had married a foreigner (which was bad), a Protestant (worse), and a republican (intolerable). This would be true even if the couple remained in Italy. Moreover, keeping a marriage secret would be very difficult, since a papal dispensation was required and Ossoli's brothers were intimately connected with the papal court. To be married by a Protestant minister was unthinkable to Ossoli, whose spiritual allegiance to the Church was strong, however much he abhorred its secular power.

So they took the simplest course for the time being and simply enjoyed what they had together, while waiting for the gentle, brief Italian winter to set in. But when winter came in December, it settled over them like some Old Testament judgment. A steady, chill rain began to fall in mid-December and continued for three months. The many unpaved streets dissolved into a sludgy mess, and the huge ruins became black and oppressive. On either side of the Corso tall buildings shut out the dim daylight, and Margaret had to keep her lamp and her fire lit all day, which soon ate up the money she had budgeted for oil and fuel. Confined indoors, she was unable to use her time for writing; her old winter bout with headache had begun again. All the bright paeans to Italy had disappeared from the New Year's letter she wrote to Richard:

> I am not well at all this last fortnight. The first two months of my stay in Rome were the best time I have had abroad, though less marked by events and sight of living celebrities than any other. But I thought and drank in the spirit of Rome. I passed all my days in the

open air; my nights were tranquil; my appetite and strength returned. But now 16 days of rain, unhappily preceded by three or four of writing have quite destroyed me for the present. My health will never be good for any thing to sustain me in any work of value. I must content myself with doing very little and by and by comes Death to reorganize perhaps for a fuller freer life.[22]

It was not only headache that made her complain about her health, nor was it just the rain that depressed her spirits. By now she was fairly certain that she was going to have a child.

XVI

~~~

*Spring and
Summer, 1848*

Margaret's private difficulties during the early weeks of 1848 did
not prevent her joining the Italians in celebrating a momentous
change in the fortunes of their country. Italy greeted the New Year
with defiant agitation which quickly changed to hope. On January
1, the Milanese united in a resolution to boycott tobacco, which
was a lucrative source of tax revenue for the Austrian emperor.
The Austrian soldiers responded by lighting cigars in the streets
and blowing smoke in the faces of the citizens—a challenge no
Italian could be expected to ignore. Eighty people were killed in
the resulting riots. Afterward Milan subsided into a temporary and
by no means repentant silence, but the same month saw uprisings
in Genoa and Leghorn, while in Sicily the inhabitants of Palermo
celebrated the birthday of Ferdinand II, the King of Naples, by ex-
pelling his soldiers from the island. Naples itself then rose against
the king, who was forced to placate his remaining subjects by
promising them a constitution. The Grand Duke of Tuscany and
the King of Piedmont followed suit.

In Rome the Pope granted a constitution and a two-chamber,

partially elected government in March, but the fever of enthusiasm for the Pope was not as high as it had been. A series of incidents had shown him increasingly dependent on his conservative advisors, fearful of unleashing popular revolution at home and of alienating the Catholic powers in Europe. New Year's Day in Rome saw angry demonstrations in the streets, set off by the peremptory refusal of the governor to allow the people to assemble at the Quirinal to receive the papal blessing. The Pope, who was ill, apparently knew nothing about it, and the next day tried to mend the error by appearing in the streets. Accordingly, Margaret wrote,

> . . . the next day, though rainy and of a searching cold like that of a Scotch mist, we had all our windows thrown open, and the red and yellow tapestries hung out. He passed through the principal parts of the city, the people throwing themselves on their knees and crying out, "O Holy Father, don't desert us! don't forget us! don't listen to our enemies!" The Pope wept often, and replied, "Fear nothing, my people, my heart is yours." . . . For the moment, the difficulties are healed, as they will be whenever the Pope directly shows himself to the people.[1]

Margaret wrote two *Tribune* dispatches in January, relating in detail the reasons for the half-hopeful, half-distrustful mood of the city. Her own tribulations can be inferred only from a new impatience with small annoyances, which she attributes plausibly to the weather. She has no appetite and has given up wine, coffee, and meat. The "horrible cabbage, in which the Romans delight" especially repels her. The ordinary noises and smells of Rome are magnified out of all proportion: the street singers wail "atrocious *arias*" till noon, when they are replaced by the "wicked organ grinder." Her friends troop in to see her, looking for some relief from the universal ennui, and at every ring of the bell the landlady's three yappy dogs set up an earsplitting din, while the maid, too lazy to open the door, yells from the bowels of the house, "Who is it?" Once, encouraged by the maid's negligence, a street pedlar lets himself into Margaret's apartment, "poisoning me at once with the smell of the worst possible cigars, not to be driven out, insisting I shall look upon frightful, ill-cut cameos, and worse-designed mosaics, made by some friend of his, who works in a chamber and will sell *so* cheap."[2]

Her letters home began to allude to some vague calamity hanging over her and show her mood settling into that fatalism with which she had always faced difficult trials in her life. Occasionally she would try to explain these passages in terms of her health or her fear of running out of money, but a letter to Cary Sturgis written in January hints at burdens no sum of money could lighten:

> I have known some happy hours, but they all lead to sorrow; and not only the cups of wine, but of milk, seem drugged with poison for me. It does not *seem* to be my fault, this Destiny; I do not court these things,—they come. I am a poor magnet, with power to be wounded by the bodies I attract. . . . With this year, I enter upon a sphere of my destiny so difficult, that I, at present, see no way out, except through the gate of death. It is useless to write of it; you are at a distance and cannot help me;—whether accident or angel will, I have no intimation. I have no reason to hope I shall not reap what I have sown, and do not. Yet how I shall endure it I cannot guess; it is all a dark, sad enigma. The beautiful forms of art charm no more, and a love, in which there is all fondness, but no help, flatters in vain.[3]

The last sentence may be the only bitter reference she ever made to her liaison with Ossoli, which in general she never regretted. But the isolation of her position and Ossoli's powerlessness to help was all too clear at the moment. Emelyn Story, looking back at this winter afterward, remembered Ossoli as looking pale and dejected for several weeks, and concluded that Margaret must have saved him from pining away altogether by marrying him. But the real explanation was quite different. Ossoli's interesting pallor was undoubtedly caused both by Margaret's pregnancy and by anxiety for his father, who was seriously ill. In February, while Margaret and Ossoli were trying to think of a way out of their predicament, the old count died. This meant that the existing objections to their marrying were increased, since the family estate passed into the hands of Angelo's antagonistic elder brother, Giuseppe. Under the circumstances Margaret reconciled herself to bearing her child out of wedlock. They agreed she would leave Rome for the summer and go away to the mountains, ostensibly for a rest. If either she or the baby died, Ossoli would be better off free; if both survived, and if the liberal tide in Italy continued to rise, it might be possible to marry later on.

Beset by nausea, fear, headache, and a whole legion of imaginary Yankee devils come to punish her for her transgression, Margaret wrote no *Tribune* letters in February. Perhaps more than anything, she dreaded being disowned by her family and friends. Letters from her family urging her to return took on a new poignancy. Her brother Richard offered to make a home for her in the country, the kind of pastoral bower she would willingly have flown to had she been able. She could only tell him that she must wait until autumn to decide, since "there are circumstances and influences now at work in my life, not likely to find their issue till then." [4] The unluckily timed arrival in Rome of Henry Hedge must only have made her more miserable. Ironically, Margaret had brought her affliction upon herself by adhering to the Transcendentalist faith in the inner voice at the expense of defying society. It is a little droll to imagine her justifying her pregnancy—as she no doubt could have—to Emerson or Thoreau with quotations from their own writings. Now here was Hedge, for whom even the *Dial* had been too bold, forcing her to realize how great a distance now divided her from friends whose ideals she still shared. She saw little of him, concentrating when they did meet on one common interest the idealism of both had led them to, the liberation of Italy.

But she had, besides Ossoli, European friends who helped bolster up her courage. One was the Princess Cristina Trivulzio Belgiojoso, like Costanza Arconati a recently returned political exile and a member of a distinguished old Milanese family. She too had spent many years in Paris, but Mme Arconati disapproved of the princess's bohemian life style, and the two women were not on friendly terms. A celebrated beauty, Princess Belgiojoso was also a writer and a committed republican who once remarked that she had spent her youth "like a rat in the library when she was allowed to do as she chose, and like a doll in the parlor when she was not." In Paris she had numbered among her friends most of the political and artistic celebrities of the time, including Sand, Chopin, Rossini, Hiene, Hugo, and Mazzini. Since returning to Italy she had organized the tenant farmers on her estates into a co-operative community and had built new housing, a school, and a recreation center for them. Now she was traveling around Italy mustering support for the republican cause. Margaret, who saw much of her in January, described her to Richard as "a woman of gallantry," adding that although she had undoubtedly had several lovers, her public life had been "truly energetic and beneficent." [5] By example, if nothing else, her friendship was a valuable support at the moment.

No sooner had Princess Belgiojoso left Rome for Naples than Adam Mickiewicz arrived, taking lodgings not far from Margaret. Believing that war would certainly break out against the Austrians, he had come to raise a legion of Polish exiles to fight beside the Italians. Of all Margaret's friends none was so likely to listen sympathetically to a confession of her plight, and he did not disappoint her. His common-sense attitude must have done much to help her overcome her guilt. He saw in her situation a certain amount of awkwardness and (though he minimized it) a certain amount of physical danger, but warned her against the kind of self-recrimination that could sink her into a morbid melancholy.

He was still there when a series of events began which helped Margaret momentarily shake off her depression and set all Europe rejoicing. It was the end of Carnival week, which the Romans celebrated under the same drenching rain that had fallen all winter. Ignoring the weather, they thronged the Corso dressed in gaily colored, lightweight clothes, singing and pelting one another with flowers while Margaret, wrapped in a shawl and boa, watched shivering from her window. Then came the scarcely believable news of simultaneous revolutions in Paris and Vienna: the shaky regime of Louis Philippe had been toppled, and Metternich had been forced to resign and flee the country. Austrian dominance in Europe appeared to be destroyed, while France seemed once again ready to live up to her reputation as friend of the oppressed. In Rome the people wept and embraced in the streets, crying, *"Mira-*

colo! Providenza!'' The Carnival celebrators lit the *moccoletti*, long candles that are traditionally snuffed in a rambunctious Carnival game, and leaving them lit marched through the streets in a joyous candlelight procession. Other demonstrations followed, more hostile but not violent. The Austrian arms were dragged through the streets and burned. Margaret stood with Mickiewicz, looking on, while "Polish women, exiled too, or who perhaps like one nun who is here, had been daily scourged by the orders of a tyrant, brought little pieces . . . and threw them into the flames.'' [6]

Then came the news that all Italians were hoping for: the Milanese had risen against the Austrians and in five days of desperate street fighting had driven them from the city. Conspicuous in the new provisional government now set up were Margaret's young friends of the previous autumn. Simultaneously came word that Venice had expelled its Austrian garrison and proclaimed itself a republic under the leadership of Daniel Manin, and that the tiny duchies of Parma and Modena had overthrown their Austrian rulers as well. King Charles Albert of Piedmont, appealed to by the Milanese, announced he would lead an army to their aid. So he did, albeit with all deliberate speed, so that by the time he reached Lombardy the Austrians were entrenched in a strongly fortified area known as "the Quadrilateral." But Charles Albert vowed to drive them over the border, and men from all over Italy flocked to join him. Tuscany sent both regular soldiers and volunteers, as did the Pope. The Princess Belgiojoso, now in Naples, chartered a ship and organized a volunteer regiment of 200 men, with whom she set off for Lombardy. Even the Neapolitan King Ferdinand sent 16,000 troops, though he soon recalled them to put down his rebellious subjects at home.

In the Colosseum at Rome young men enlisted by the thousands while people of all ranks, from princes to street vendors, donated what they could to equip them. The English and American residents gathered on the fringes of the crowd and watched, some sympathetically, most with a languid skepticism born of a solid conviction of Anglo-Saxon superiority. Margaret heard with indignation the prediction of one Englishman that the volunteers would never reach the front, since the Italians were too lazy to walk that far. In fact, she reported, the Romans marched two days before they reached food and bedding, and had strength left over for "dancing and vivaing Pio Nono in the piazza till after midnight." [7]

The nationalistic slurs cast on the Italians were a continual sore point with Margaret, and she answered them hotly several times in the *Tribune*. They roused her finally to a full sympathy with the American abolitionists, as she recognized in the condescending arguments against Italian liberation the same words that were used to oppose the emancipation of the blacks. But the issue went further: the remarks were not only heard among Anglo-Saxons, but later became (as will be seen) a handy prop for the Gallic ego; even Italians were not above using them against other Italians. This prejudice, rooted in the ancient distrust of the practical, logical temperament toward the emotionally susceptible, was not very different from the Boston merchant's dislike of the *Dial,* Timothy Fuller's distrust of novels, or certain beliefs about women which Margaret had answered at length in *Woman in the Nineteenth Century*. Rome's critics said that a people so quick to love or anger and so fond of creature comforts were "childish" or "womanish," and were incapable of sustained courage or self-discipline. Margaret, who found her own sensibilities mirrored in those of Rome and who by now referred to the Romans as *"my* people," was defending more than just the Romans when she lashed back at this sort of criticism. She had the advantage of knowing that the classical qualities of courage and perseverance were strong in her own nature; that they were strong in the citizens of modern Rome was just beginning to be evident. For Margaret this was a familiar battle joined again.

With the good news from the north came the end of the rain, and nature made amends for the three months of gloom she had visited on Rome. The Campagna was blue with violets, to be succeeded by poppies, cornflowers, and wild roses. The fountains of the city, which before had only added to the general feeling of dampness and tedium, again became pleasantly cool oases in the wide piazzas of sun-warmed stone. Her spirits much restored, Margaret resumed her daily outings, accompanied sometimes by

Ossoli but usually by other friends, since to help meet their joint expenses Ossoli had taken a modest job with an uncle. From Lombardy came encouraging news, beginning in April with the report of a victory at Goito. Adam Mickiewicz took his Polish Legion to Florence, to be greeted with cheers as the "Dante of Poland," while Milan gave a triumphant reception to Giuseppe Mazzini, home in Italy after seventeen years. "He returns, like Wordsworth's great man, 'to see what he foresaw,' " Margaret wrote, "and yet Mazzini sees not all: he aims at political emancipation; but he sees not, perhaps would deny, the bearing of some events, which even now begin to work their way." [8] She meant socialism, a subject in which Mazzini showed little interest. Margaret herself was now "as great an associationist as W. Channing himself," believing that the next form society would take would be small voluntary communities. [9] Perhaps she had in mind the Princess Belgiojoso's cooperative estate in Lombardy; presumably she was thinking of something more efficient than Brook Farm. But the socialism to which she had been strongly attracted in France and England had now become a settled belief, though she adopted it only in a gentle, unstructured, Transcendentalist sense.

As her pregnancy advanced, the prospect of childbirth at the age of thirty-eight, in a mountain village with only the local doctor to help, must occasionally have hit her with cold waves of fear. But the state of her mind was discernible to neither her friends nor her *Tribune* readers, and one wonders again at the skill with which she could conceal her emotional life when she needed to. Her money worries at least were reduced by a letter from Horace Greeley, saying he was sending a bill of exchange for $500 he owed her plus $100 from the *Tribune*—enough to see her through the summer. Moreover, she had a new project to occupy her mind: she had decided to write a history of the revolutionary movement in Italy as it unfolded. This did not mean she was confident of the outcome (for one thing, she shared Mazzini's contempt for the King of Piedmont), but regardless of military developments she saw that Italy already had been permanently transformed in ways she could not adequately explain in the *Tribune* letters, and that sooner or later the present struggle would gain Italians their freedom. She intended to work on the book during her absence from Rome, and now set about gathering the research materials she would need.

Meanwhile, in Rome the strained faith of the people in the Pope as political leader finally collapsed, and he proved himself, as Margaret had predicted, a well-intentioned but limited man who was unequal to the demands placed upon him. On April 29 word arrived in Rome that the Austrians at Ferrara had seized and executed a well-known Roman artist who was a member of the civic guard. An angry crowd marched to the Quirinal to demand that the Pope declare war. The Pope refused, as of course in the end he had to. He had put off the decision as long as possible, and only a fortnight before had blessed the banners of the troops marching to Lombardy. Now he said that he had never meant those troops to pass the papal frontier. "[He] wound up," Margaret wrote, "by lamenting over the war . . . as if it was something offensive to the spirit of religion, and which he would fain see hushed up, and its motives smoothed out and ironed over." [10] In short, he spoke as a spiritual leader when the people expected him to speak as a temporal prince. In that afternoon he lost his remaining political support, although religious loyalty to him remained unchanged. A few days later his ministers resigned under pressure, and he unwillingly appointed a new group headed by the liberal Cardinal Mamiami. There were no more "Viva Pio Nonos" heard in Rome.

In May, as the Romans expressed their resolution to unite Italy with the Pope or without him, and as Charles Albert pursued an inconclusive contest with the Austrian army in the north, Margaret completed arrangements for leaving Rome. The hideaway she and Ossoli had chosen was the village of Aquila, about fifty miles northeast in the Abruzzi mountains, just over the Neapolitan border. It was near enough for Ossoli occasionally to visit her, but far enough away to insure privacy. She told no one where she was going. It was arranged that her overseas mail would be forwarded from Paris to a Rome bank, where Ossoli would collect it for her. He promised too to send her the leading liberal journals, the *Epoca* and Mazzini's new *Italia del Popolo*.

There remained the distasteful task of explaining her actions to her family and old friends. She wrote to Horace Greeley saying she must cease writing for the *Tribune,* pleading ill health. To Emerson, who was in France and who, disturbed at the despondent tone of her last letter, now urged her to sail home with him, she sent an explanation which was true as far as it went: "I am deeply interested in this public drama, and wish to see it *played out.* Methinks I have *my part* therein, either as actor or historian." [11] She gave the American painter Thomas Hicks a packet of letters to be given to her family in the event of her death, apparently without explaining to Hicks himself the cause of her fears. She asked him to

> say to those I leave behind that I was willing to die. I have suffered in life far more than I enjoyed, and I think quite out of proportion with the use my living here is . . . to others. I have wished to be natural and true, but the world was not in harmony with me— nothing came right for me. I think the spirit that governs the Universe must have in reserve for me a sphere where I can develope more freely, and be happier—on earth circumstances do not promise this before my forces shall be too much lavished to make a better path truly avail me. [12]

When she applied for a passport to leave Rome, she gave her name simply as Margherita Ossoli, her birthplace as Rome, and her age as twenty-nine—lies intended to mislead the curious. (Joseph Jay Deiss, who discovered the passport in Rome, concludes from it that she still was not married, which seems true, and goes on to wonder if it implies that Margaret lied to Ossoli about her age. But surely this does an injustice to a woman who in adolescence had squarely faced the prospect of being "bright and ugly.") [13]

On May 29 she set off, accompanied by Ossoli and two woman servants who would remain with her. They spent the night at Tivoli, where Margaret managed to write a breezy letter to Mary Rotch, discussing the news from Rome and from Waldo in England, and explaining at some length the details of Uncle Abraham's legacy, since by now she is "rather sore" at being congratulated on her nonexistent wealth. A single sentence betrays the apprehension that was constantly on her mind: "You must always love me *whatever* I do. I depend on that."[14] She sent a similar appeal to Costanza Arconati.

The next day she arrived at the hamlet of Aquila, rich in evocations of pagan and Christian myth. Pastel-colored houses were scattered along a hillside, here and there overshadowed by some decaying baronial manor. The hours were told by bells from two neighboring monasteries, and from her window Margaret could watch the monks pacing up and down the paths. The fields were brilliant with summer flowers, and the olive and grape were cultivated by workers dressed in the traditional picturesque costume of the Abruzzi. Keeping to her Roman schedule, Margaret worked several hours a day on her book, but the remaining hours she spent roaming around the countryside, sometimes on foot and sometimes riding on a donkey. For a week or two she allowed herself to be carried away by idyllic visions of maternity amid the vineyards and the sheep: the Aquilans are a "simple race," honest tillers of the soil who "never ask for money" and bless her as she passes. She confesses with some pride that she has no more need of the Anglo-Saxon tongue and now thinks "wholly in Italian." With a characteristic blend of snobbery, naïveté, and love of her fellow man, she writes Emerson:

> The ignorance of this people is amusing. I am to them a divine visitant,—an instructive Ceres,—telling them wonderful tales of foreign customs, and even legends of the lives of their own saints. They are people whom I could love and live with. Bread and grapes among them would suffice me.[15]

But soon enough the real, wearisome world caught up with her. It did not take her long to discover that the Aquilans were as venal as anyone else. And from Mme Arconati arrived a prompt answer to the hint she had slipped into her Tivoli letter: "What mystery is there in your last lines? Yes, I am faithful and capable of sympathy, even when opinions do not agree. But what is it? You make me uneasy. People have told me that you had a lover at Rome, one of the Roman Civic Guard."[16] Clearly Ossoli's attentiveness had not gone unobserved and was thought worthy of mention even in

Milan. Adam Mickiewicz had spent the previous month as Mme Arconati's guest, but Margaret must have instantly dismissed any suspicion that he could have betrayed her. Whatever the source, the only possible answer was silence, and she ignored the subject in her next letter. But it must have cost her at least one sleepless night.

She was upset too by the delay of letters to and from Ossoli, which had to pass through the Neapolitan censors. In spite of the fact that they kept their correspondence brief and personal and were very guarded in their allusions to politics, they were being watched. Letters were held up for days, and the journals disappeared altogether for three weeks. Suffering from toothache and the heat and feeling more and more isolated, Margaret gave way to fear and depression. Her head began to throb and for the first of several times she was bled. "I feel myself wholly alone, imprisoned, too unhappy," she wrote her lover. "Do not fail to come on Saturday. I shall die to be left so." [17] On June 29 her spirits were lifted by the arrival of a deluge of newspapers and letters, and shortly thereafter by the promised visit. After Ossoli left she wrote more cheerfully:

> Your letter, caro, has arrived this morning. I am comforted as always, by getting news of you. But you are not "tristissimo," do not grow so thin. We must hope that destiny will at last grow weary of persecuting.—
>
> You know well that if ever it is possible for me to open any path for you, I shall do it. Now all seems dark, but the sun may shine again.
>
> Your visit though too short, has done me good. I am more tranquil, except that I suffer often from my teeth. The nurse says that I must have patience and expect now to suffer this, that it is a common thing in these circumstances. To hear these women, one must think that this condition is a real martyrdom. [18]

But "destiny" continued to be unkind. The arrival of some long-delayed letters from her family depressed her with the urgency of their entreaties that she come home. Money again became a pressing worry: Horace Greeley wrote, accepting with rather testy goodwill her decision not to write for the *Tribune*, and adding that he trusted she had received the $600 he had sent in April. But she had not, and she was running very short of funds. She sent off a call of distress to Richard, but it would be two months before she could receive an answer, and in the meantime she was forced to beg an emergency loan from her banker. She found some relief from loneliness in an acquaintance with the di Torres brothers, two elderly members of the local nobility, who showed her family archives containing manuscript letters by Tasso. But even this diversion brought some shade of worry, since they might let some word drop to their Roman friends about this obscure foreign woman who went by the Ossoli name. Most of all, she worried about the transient Neapolitan soldiers who swaggered about the town and sat up late at night roistering in her lodging house. They were on their way back from Lombardy to help put down the liberals in Naples, and presently they began warming up for this by arresting six in Aquila.

It was the soldiers and the censors that made her finally decide to leave Aquila and move closer to Rome. At the end of July she went to Rieti, still in the Abruzzi but inside the papal frontier. Here she rented an upper suite of rooms in a quiet, airy house overlooking the busy little river Nera. The floor was paved with cool brick, and on the river side was a long wooden terrace where she could walk in the evening. Her window on the other side looked out on a vineyard, where, she wrote Richard, the *contadini* worked a little, sang and played more.[19] Beyond the vineyard was an ancient villa with cypress plantations, and above that the snow-capped peaks of the Abruzzi. Her expenses were $9 a month rent, with all the fruit and salad she could eat for a few cents a day. On Sundays a well-to-do *contadina* with whom she became friendly would call in her holiday dress of red silk bodice, embroidered skirt and coral necklace, bringing a pair of live chickens which she insisted Margaret accept *"per amore mio."*

Here there were no soldiers, and though overseas mail continued to be maddeningly delayed and even lost, her correspondence with Ossoli suffered only from the inefficiencies of the post. Their simply worded letters, often left unsigned, reflect under the mundane patter about daily details a steady depth of concern for each other: she scolds him for telling her nothing about himself and threatens him with silence if he does not mend his ways; he begs her to write every day, and to ask the landlord to write if she is too tired.

Ossoli's accounts of the state of affairs in Rome were sobering. Early in August he wrote that word had come of a decisive victory in the war, causing bells to be rung all over the city. Margaret replied with a cautious thanksgiving, wondering why she had seen no notice of this in the *Epoca*. In fact it soon developed that the joyously welcomed victory was a defeat. Charles Albert had surrendered Milan to the Austrians and gone home to Piedmont, followed by streams of refugees. Soon afterward the Austrians attacked Bologna, in the papal dominions. There was speculation that the Pope would send the civic guard to help defend the city, throwing Ossoli into an agony of indecision about whether to go with them or remain near Margaret. Apparently resolved to behave in a manner befitting a Roman matron, Margaret told him to go if his honor required it. But he knew very well how much she counted on having him nearby, and four days later he wrote agitatedly that he was no closer to a decision. Margaret wrote again that he must do as he thought best, but she was fortified by the suspicion that the Pope would do nothing at all, and she was right: in place of orders to go to Bologna, he gave the guard a benediction. Ossoli was now free to come to Rieti, provided he could obtain a week's leave from his uncle, an irascible and mercenary man who seems to have been the Roman counterpart of Uncle Abraham. This dragon overcome, he arrived in Rieti on the last Sunday of the month and was with Margaret when their son was born September 5, though he had to leave immediately afterward. If Margaret ever overcame discretion enough to describe her ordeal, that description was later destroyed.

The baby was named Angelo Philip Eugene after his father, grandfather, and uncle, but the Rietians soon shortened that to Angelino ("little angel"). Like every baby he was a perpetual revelation to his mother, for a while excluding everything else from her universe. "I thought the mother's heart lived in me before," she later wrote, "but it did not;—I knew nothing about it." [20] The first few days were trying: first Giuditta, one of the Roman servants, was found to be treacherous in some way, and Margaret fired her on the spot. She departed muttering threats about making trouble in Rome, which she was well able to do. Partly as a result of this, Margaret came down with a fever which caused her milk to sour, and the baby refused to nurse. A search for a wet nurse followed, and luckily the landlord found one—a not quite disinterested kindness, as it later turned out. From then on, Angelino's rapid improvement helped Margaret reconcile herself to the disappointment of not nursing him herself. Besides, it was perfectly clear to her where his preference lay: "He is so dear, loves so much to sleep in my lap—he knows well that no one else can take as good care of him as I." [21] Though still in bed after three weeks, she writes happily to Ossoli that she and the baby are beginning to be really well. But she adds, "He is always so charming, how can I ever, ever leave him? I wake in the night, I look at him, I think, ah! it is impossible to leave him." [22]

But she could not remain in Rieti much longer, both because she needed to be in Rome to resume her *Tribune* letters and because her friends would begin to wonder about her. She tried to persuade Ossoli to bring both the baby and the nurse to Rome, but he thought the risk too great. So gradually Margaret resigned herself to leaving the baby with the nurse, Chiara, and her family. But she warned her lover, who was apartment-hunting for her, not to sign any lease that would force her to stay in Rome:

> It seems to me often that I cannot stay long—without seeing the baby. He is so dear, and life seems to me so uncertain, I do not know how to leave my dear ones. . . . O, love, how difficult is life! but you, you are good, if it were only possible for me to make you happy. [23]

Even now, some perverse fate seemed to be hovering over their lives: Margaret was shaken by receiving word of the sudden death of Mary Rotch, who had written cheerfully a few weeks earlier; the landlord tried to seduce Chiara, who threatened to go home if he did not leave her alone; an outbreak of smallpox sent Margaret into a flurry of maternal panic, and the smiling local doctor promised to inoculate the baby. He continued to smile and promise for another two weeks before finally admitting that he had no vaccine. ("[He is] faithless like the rest," Margaret fumed. "All about are dying with smallpox.")[24] The baby was vaccinated only after Ossoli had sent vaccine by coach from Rome.

A formidable problem in these last weeks was the need to baptize the baby. A baptismal certificate was a necessity in the Roman state; if they left Rieti without obtaining it there would certainly be an investigation. But they knew of no one whom they could trust as godfather except Adam Mickiewicz, who had disappeared after the defeat in the north. Finally they had to confide in a nephew of Ossoli's, who did not betray them, and under a very cumbersome and rather shady arrangement the baby was baptized with only the parents present, Ossoli standing in for the godfather by proxy. With the baptismal certificate a second document was prepared, certifying that Angelino was indeed his father's son and entitled to inherit his property.

The journey to Rome was hardly a restful conclusion to all this. A sudden torrential rain flooded the countryside, and a coach which they would have boarded, except for a last-minute change of plans, was swamped at a river crossing and the passengers nearly drowned. Margaret, who saw all these events by now as part of a malignant pattern, took this to mean at least that it was "not the will of Heaven that [my life] should terminate very soon."[25] Venturing out several days later, she and Ossoli reached the outskirts of Rome safely but found the meadows and roads completely flooded, spread out in the moonlight like a vast sheet of silver. Through this supernaturally beautiful and rather perilous lake the coach was drawn, depositing at the gates of Rome, like passengers entering another world, a weary-looking member of the civic guard and his equally weary fellow traveler: Margaret Fuller, American spinster journalist, back from a refreshing summer in the country.

XVII

The Siege of Rome

Margaret's new apartment on the Piazza Barberini had a view that seems especially fitting for anyone writing on the Rome of 1849. On one side of the piazza was the Quirinal Palace, where Pius IX wrestled with the consequences of his own liberalism, surrounded by conservative advisors and increasingly remote from the needs of his subjects. On the other side, representing the secular wealth protected by the Church, was the Palace Barberini, owned by an ancient, noble family and presided over by grim portraits of the Cenci. The square between them was crowded with ordinary people, taking the sun or going about their daily affairs. Thus the apartment offered a historian's view of the protagonists in the current struggle. In addition it had an interesting past (it had once been occupied by Hans Christian Andersen) and a superior chimney. The landlady and her husband, an elderly couple, clucked occasionally but never intruded. Margaret shared a floor with a middle-aged Prussian peasant sculptor who had educated himself and made a career in art against enormous odds; the more expensive quarters below were occupied by a Russian princess with a mustache and a wealthy English lady who, in keeping with the endearing custom of her nation, kept her terrace filled with flowers. On the top floor lived a priest, who took it upon himself to see that Margaret's fire was always well lit, though in return he asked a great many questions. At first she may even have been tempted to tell him everything and ask his help; but he obviously did not have the mettle of a Friar Lawrence, and no ordinary son of the Church would do.

Word arrived by every post from Rieti that Angelino was well, and Margaret took some comfort, if not much cheer, from this evidence that he could get along perfectly well without her. She told herself she could best help him by finishing and publishing her book, but even for Angelino she would not give up her daylight hours outdoors, and writing was saved for the evening. To help meet present needs she resumed her letters to the *Tribune.* Her schedule resulted in a rather solitary life, but few of her non-Italian friends were in Rome now anyway, the majority of the resident foreigners having scented revolution in the air: "Most of the English have fled in affright,—the Germans and French are wanted at home,—the Czar has recalled many of his younger subjects; he does not like the schooling they get here." [1] She missed the Storys and the Cranches, who were in Florence, but solitude at least relieved her of the need to keep up a constant masquerade. The burden of her secret, with the addition of Angelino, had become almost insupportable, and heavy innuendos kept finding their way into her letters. To her mother she wrote: "Were you here, I would confide in you fully . . . these most strange and romantic chapters in the story of my sad life"; [2] to Marcus Spring: "I have no hope, unless that God will show me some way I do not know of now"; [3] and finally to the entire readership of the New York *Tribune:* "Indeed, I left [in the mountains] what was most precious, but which I could not take with me." [4] A challenge on any of these might have afforded as much relief as alarm, but by now she could play such games with impunity, her friends in America having thrown up their hands over someone so obviously demented as to linger in damp, unhealthy Rome ("the region of the dead," Horace Greeley called it), [5] all the while complaining bitterly about her health. Her Italian life and her motives for remaining in Italy were so puzzling to those at home that one more question here or there escaped comment even from her mother. In December, needing very much to confide in someone at home, she wrote to Caroline Sturgis, saying she was married and had a child. It was not the whole truth, of course, but it was as much as she dared tell any American.

No sooner had Margaret arrived in Rome than public events began to accelerate. Elsewhere the forces of reaction had grown stronger over the summer, not only in the north but in the south, where Ferdinand of Naples had battered the Sicilians into submission—and past it—with artillery, thereby earning himself the nickname of "King Bomba." Now the Pope appointed as his chief minister Pellegrino Rossi, a moderate of the Guizot school who was hated by liberals and conservatives alike and whose fortune it was (as Carlyle once said of the Unitarians) to be hunted as a rat among cats and a cat among rats. On November 15, as Rossi arrived at the Chamber of Deputies, he found a crowd of glowering, hissing onlookers gathered outside the door. Smiling, he stepped from his carriage and pushed his way to the steps; but as he reached them someone jostled him, then stabbed him fatally from behind. The assassin melted silently into the crowd, while the papal guard, called back from the countryside by Rossi because he did not trust the civic guard, remained at their posts and did nothing. Reporting the murder in the *Tribune,* Margaret would go no further in her condemnation than to quote some unnamed philosopher: "I cannot sympathize under any circumstances with so immoral a deed; but surely the manner of doing it was great." [6]

The next day a huge crowd, including both the civic and the papal guards in military order, marched on the Quirinal to demand reform. Margaret, watching from the Pincian Mount, thought that "nothing could be gentler than the disposition of those composing the crowd. . . . All felt that Pius IX had fallen irrevocably from his high place as the friend of progress and father of Italy; but still he was personally beloved, and still his name, so often shouted in hope and joy, had not quite lost its *prestige.*" [7] Somehow this continued regard failed to communicate itself to the Pope, who refused to see a delegation. The crowd became excited and tried to force the palace doors. Margaret, who had hurried home to her apartment, heard shouts and a drum roll, while her landlady ran up and down in terror, crying "Jesu Maria, they are killing the Pope! O poor Holy Father!" They were not killing the Pope, but they did kill his confessor, who had fired on them from an upper window, and one of the crowd was killed by the Swiss guard. The demonstrators remained outside the palace through the evening, and eventually they tried to burn down the doors. The Pope, badly frightened, finally saw their delegates and agreed to their demands. But ten days later, dressed in a plain cassock and spectacles, he fled to Gaeta, where he put himself under the protection of King Bomba. The Romans looked around in some surprise and found themselves alone and free. "In a few days," Margaret wrote, "all began to say: 'Well, who would have thought it? The Pope, the Cardinals, the Princes are gone, and Rome is perfectly tranquil, and one does not miss anything, except that there are not so many rich carriages and liveries.'"[8]

At Christmas time Margaret went alone to Rieti. She found Angelino well, though he had caught a "pox" of some kind, perhaps only chickenpox. He had come through it unscarred, but he was smaller than she had expected. The mild weather turned bitterly cold just as she arrived, and she shivered in her brick-paved, unheated room in Chiara's house. But she preferred being upstairs alone with her son to sharing her hours with him with the large and obstreperous family in the kitchen. She sat watching him sleep, with feelings she later tried to describe to Caroline:

> When I first took him in my arms he made no sound but leaned his head against my bosom, and staid so, he seemed to say how could you abandon me. . . . You speak of my being happy; all the solid happiness I have known has been at times when he went to sleep in my arms. . . . I do not look forward to his career and his manly life: it is *now* I want to be with him, before [illegible] care and bafflings begin. If I had a little money I should go with him into strict retirement for a year or two and live for him alone. This I cannot do; all life that has been or could be natural to me is invariably denied. God knows why, I suppose.[9]

She returned to find the Romans preparing to elect, by universal franchise,* a Constituent Assembly. A warning from the Pope, threatening all who voted with excommunication, heightened the anger against him and may even have contributed to the heavy turn out on election day. When the warning arrived, the people took all the copies they could find and deposited them in privies; for good measure, they pulled the symbolic cardinals' hats from the hatters' shop doors and threw them into the Tiber. The elections were duly held, with Mazzini and Garibaldi (Italy's great guerilla leader, now returned after long exile) elected *in absentia* as deputies. On February 5 the Assembly was opened, following a soberly triumphant parade through the streets, to the strains of the "Marseillaise," which made up in spirit for what it lacked in old-fashioned spectacle. After three days of debate, rather trying to the republic's more impetuous supporters, the Roman Republic was officially declared. Almost simultaneously, word arrived that Tuscany too was free, the Grand Duke having found it expedient to join the Pope at Gaeta.

Carnival soon followed, under clear skies that promised no repetition of the previous year's wetting. Margaret entered into it all, enjoying nothing so much as the candle-snuffing horseplay of the *moccoletti,* which had been omitted in 1848 in honor of the Viennese revolution. Now the taunts of *"Senza moccolo, senza mo"* rang out constantly above the general Carnival hubbub, and in this very old but truly republican game the nobleman's candle was no more sacred than the ragamuffin's. To Margaret it was all part of "that wild, innocent gayety of which this people alone is capable after childhood. . . . The Roman still plays amid his serious affairs, and very serious have they been this past winter." [10]

The young republic gained in strength and confidence, while casting a nervous eye on the Catholic powers, to whom the Pope had appealed for help. The Austrians were still busy putting down their own revolution, and with luck would remain so. The Romans

---

* The term "universal," used by Margaret and by later historians, was—as might be expected—not quite accurate. It is curious that the author of *Woman in the Nineteenth Century* did not comment on this, given the fact that Mazzini and Adam Mickiewicz both advocated political equality for women. Ironically, though radicalized in so much else, she may never have overcome her doubts about woman suffrage.

scorned any threat from Naples. France alone could be dangerous if she chose, but she still called herself a republic and might reasonably be expected to leave a sister republic alone. As for the larger republic across the Atlantic, she folded her arms and was silent, in spite of repeated appeals from Margaret and other sympathizers with the Roman cause. Warm expressions of support came from the American press, but the government only made the equivocal gesture of sending an envoy (Lewis Cass, Jr.) who was instructed not to recognize the republic. The few Americans in Rome, as well as the other foreigners, continued to sneer.* The English told Margaret they "hoped to see all these fellows shot yet." (The English clergy she met, out of Christian charity, only hoped to see them hung.) An American told her "he 'had no confidence in the Republic.' Why? Because he 'had no confidence in the people.' Why? Because 'they were not like *our* people.' " [11]

All winter the sun continued to shine, in an extension of autumn that melted imperceptibly into spring. Margaret felt physically strong and well. Expecting the rains of the previous year to return, she resolved *"never* to make my hay when the sun shines: *i.e.,* to give no fine day to books and pens," [12] and she spent many days on the Campagna, sometimes alone but usually with Ossoli. "We got out in the morning, carrying the roast chestnuts from Rome; the bread and wine are found in some lonely little osteria; and so we dine; and reach Rome again, just in time to see it, from a little distance, gilded by the sunset." [13] If from habit she took a book along, she seldom opened it. The double influence of nature and the past was too compelling. The very stones spoke:

> There is nothing like it in America—the old genius of Europe has mellowed all its marbles here. Earth is so full of it that one cannot have that feeling of holy virgin loneliness as in America. I cannot feel alone here. The spirits of dead men crowd me in the most apparently solitary places. I have no genius at all, I am all the time too full of sympathy. [14]

But she felt an emotional fatigue, a permanent loss of mental resilience as the result of the past year's ordeal. She worried over

---

* An exception was the artist Thomas Crawford, who joined the civic guard.

her own future, over that of her lover and child, and over the future of Rome. Her earlier Christian stoicism, the belief that she would always be tested by a loving God, had been tempered into a fatalism that in its darker moments resembles Thomas Hardy's. "Dark or bright," she wrote in an otherwise determinedly cheerful letter to her mother, "life goes on and men and women are decoyed or hunted up the hill." [15] Poverty seemed to be the rod chosen by her own personal chastising fate. She could not go on forever begging loans from her brothers and friends, though she sent out an appeal in January which was soon answered by Eugene and Richard. But her book would not be finished for another year at least, and the *Tribune* letters barely paid the rent. She was oppressed too by a growing alienation from those at home. Partly, of course, this was caused by her having concealed so much from them; partly it was caused by letters having been lost, so that when she finally heard from home there were references to important events that she knew nothing about. Two close friends, Mary Rotch and Ellen Sturgis Hooper, had died in her absence, as had Eugene's baby son. She was hurt to discover that both her brother Richard and Caroline Sturgis had been married without her knowledge, and that Cary had even written to her after the event without mentioning it. Her pique at her friend was soon softened, partly by the news that Cary was pregnant; but her cool congratulations to her brother (notwithstanding her reticence to him about her own life) have in them some of the old paterfamilias tone. A letter from a group of friends headed by Eliza Farrar, arriving in the middle of a sunny but hungry January, informed her that she would be assured of an annuity of $300 if she would only come home. She was, she said, "unspeakably grateful," [16] but the condition (which was later withdrawn) stung, with its implication that her friends felt her to be under some wicked enchantment, to be broken only by what they knew was a potent charm. Related to this was the news that Mary Rotch had left her entire fortune of $150,000 to be divided between her lawyer and one friend. Just $5,000 of this would have given the little Ossoli-Fuller ménage a long respite, and it was hard not to believe that the elderly, staid Quaker lady had expressed her disapproval of Margaret's Italian sojourn in a most telling way—and without half-knowing what there was to disapprove of.

Another vibration, distinctly unpleasant, reached her from across the Atlantic. James Russell Lowell, whose merits as a poet Margaret had lightly dismissed in print, had retaliated in his 1848 "Fable for Critics," copies of which now arrived in Italy. Like Poe and Hawthorne, Lowell had no love for Transcendentalists in general (he had once taken a gratuitous shot at Emerson, but later apologized). But his attack on Margaret in the "Fable" was disproportionately keen, considering the moderate tone of the piece as a whole. All her Fuller-esque mannerisms and pomposities were inflated and tricked out for public view. As for her oft-lamented lack of a vocation, Lowell suggested that she was ideally suited to be "Tiring-woman* to the Muses." William Story, who in the old days had probably more than once joined Lowell in some schoolboy snickering at Margaret's expense, wrote to rebuke his friend, though with a trace of the schoolboy still:

> . . . You drove your arrow too sharply through Miranda. The joke of "Tiring-woman to the Muses" is too happy; but because fate has really been unkind to her, and because she depends on her pen for her bread-and-water (and that is nearly all she has to eat), and because she is her own worst enemy, and because through her disappointment and disease, which [things] embitter every one, she has struggled most stoutly and manfully, I could have wished you had let her pass scot-free.[17]

All this, plus doubts over whether the Roman republic would be allowed to survive, cast a pall over her spirits in early March. Help arrived in the form of the Storys, who had been persuaded to return by her frequent assurances that republican Rome was perfectly safe, if socially a little dull. With Margaret as their guide, apartment-hunting was dispensed with in a single morning, followed by lunch with the Crawfords and vespers at St. Peter's. In the following days there were walks and picnics, and in the eve-

---

* Ladies'-maid. Lowell later made handsome amends by defending Margaret's behavior during the siege of Rome.

ning opera at the Argentina. Ossoli joined them when he was not drilling with the guard, the Storys being, of all Margaret's American friends, the ones he was most comfortable with. March brought another familiar face: Mazzini had lingered in Florence for some weeks after being elected to the Roman assembly, but now suddenly he appeared, arriving by night so as to avoid the embarrassing huzzas that had greeted him in Milan. Margaret heard that he had come, and a few evenings later, as she sat writing in her apartment, there was a late knock at the door. She heard the sound of his voice in the hall, and he was in the room before she could lay down her pen. "He enters to defend Italy, if any man can, against her foes. Can any?—I feel no confidence: they are so many. [Mazzini's] life has known one hour of pure joy, but I fear, I fear the entrance into Jerusalem may be followed by the sacrifice."[18]

But March passed calmly in Rome, the only agitation being caused by news that Charles Albert of Piedmont was preparing to march once more against the Austrians. Many republicans still believed he had betrayed Italy, and though the Assembly voted to send troops, there was no repetition of the massive enlistments of the previous year. At the end of the month Margaret left for another visit to Rieti, whence she wrote Ossoli on March 27:

> I found our treasure in the best health, and now so good! He goes to sleep all alone in bed, day or night —He is asleep now, sucking his little hand. He is very fat, but strangely small, his hair does not grow at all—and he still wears those horrid black caps. At first all talked so loud he looked at me all surprised, and cried a little — But when he was alone with me, he seemed to recollect me, and leaned and rubbed his forehead as in the first days.[19]

But this visit did not pass as quietly as the last. Garibaldi and his legion were quartered in Rieti, and sensational rumors about them were circulating in the town. They were said to be murdering priests and citizens and even one another (though there was no mention of babies), and Margaret was afraid to go outside with Angelino. Then one day, sitting as usual upstairs with the baby, she heard a great uproar below, and running into the kitchen found

Chiara's two brothers facing each other in fury, one brandishing a knife and the other a club, while the women of the house tugged frantically at their arms. Neighbors ran in and separated them, but Margaret was much alarmed and sent for Ossoli to come and help her decide whether to bring Angelino to Rome. He did come, but they knew that if Rome were attacked, even Rieti would be safer. In the end they left Angelino where he was, no doubt after extracting many remorseful promises from the brothers.

On the way to Rome they traveled separately, and according to Emelyn Story, Margaret actually encountered at an inn a group of the legionnaires she had successfully avoided at Rieti. She was at lunch when they arrived, and rising as they trooped through the door, she directed the terrified *padrone*—no doubt in accents fully worthy of Timothy Fuller's daughter—to "give these good men wine and bread on my account." The legionnaires, whose reputation for ferocity far oustripped their exploits, accepted with great courtesy and afterward ceremoniously handed her into her carriage.[20]

In Rome Mazzini, at the head of a triumvirate, was virtually running the city and had instituted a series of democratic reforms. But the news from Lombardy was ominous: Charles Albert had been defeated at Novara after only a few days of fighting, and the Austrians seemed ready to turn their attention elsewhere. The Florentines, perceiving they would be next, invited their Grand Duke to return. The Neapolitans were massing on the Roman frontier. Then came the gravest news of all: A French force of several thousand men, commanded by General Nicolas Charles Oudinot, landed at Civita Vecchia on April 24 and announced they had come to "liberate" Rome from the reign of terror which they seemed genuinely convinced existed there. The assembly voted to resist any French attempt to enter Rome, and Garibaldi hurried down from the mountains with his legion. Soon afterward a brigade of Lombard Bersaglieri, seasoned veterans from the north, arrived to strengthen the Roman defense. The populace turned to the task of building wooden barricades and earth fortifications to supplement the ancient city walls. Meanwhile the French, marching toward Rome through the deserted countryside, entertained one another with pointed remarks on the renowned valor of the Italians.

Princess Belgiojoso returned to Rome in these last days of April and began organizing hospitals for the care of the expected casualties. She had no money, her estates having been confiscated, but several of the abandoned ecclesiastical buildings were given over to her, and she enlisted large numbers of women to nurse and make bandages, and fitted out the hospitals with funds begged from door to door. Each hospital needed a director, however, and on the morning of April 30, as the tense and silent city awaited the French attack, Margaret received a note appointing her director of the hospital of the *Fate Bene Fratelli.* It was none too soon: gunfire was heard from the direction of the Janiculum Wall shortly afterward, and it continued all afternoon. By evening Garibaldi had routed the French, but at a heavy cost, and Margaret's hospital was full.

A month-long interval of quiet followed, broken only by a successful Roman sortie against the Neapolitans. Oudinot sent an envoy, Ferdinand de Lesseps, to negotiate a treaty. It was an oddly threatening, oddly peaceful period. Margaret visited Ossoli at his post on the Vatican Wall, accompanied by the Storys and carrying a basket of provisions. He showed them where the wall was spattered with blood, and where, on the battlefield below, bands of monks hunted for the unburied dead. It was one of the few times in the month Margaret saw him, since he would not leave his men and her schedule at the hospital was irregular and fatiguing. When she did go she could not talk to him alone. In odd moments at home she sent him notes assuring him of her safety; she also composed a letter for the *Tribune,* and, doubtless with her family in mind, sat for a portrait by Thomas Hicks. It is pitilessly faithful, showing her sitting with bent head and slumped shoulders, staring fixedly before her. Her eyes are puffy and her hands lie listlessly in her lap. The whole figure is expressive of bone-weariness.

Meanwhile the Storys and the other remaining Americans passed the time in forced amusements, concocting salads and listening to bad music, and trying to take their accustomed walks on streets that had been sprinkled with gravel for the cavalry. Early in the month they had all been asked to move to the Casa Dies, a substantial building where it was hoped they would be safe under a prominently displayed American flag. Margaret went there as well, taking her meals with the Storys when she was not at the hospital. She awaited the end of the month with few illusions, mourning over the disfigurement the city was already suffering. All the trees in Rome had been cut down to build barricades, and foreseeing worse to come, she felt for the first time that she might some day be willing to leave Rome. Hoping to be proved wrong, she believed the French and Austrians were capable of bombarding Rome, for reasons undignified by any high ideal. "Say to all," she wrote to Richard, "that should any accident, possible to these troubled times, transfer me to another scene of existence, they need not regret it. There must be better worlds than this,—where innocent blood is not ruthlessly shed, where treason does not so easily triumph, where the greatest and best are not crucified." [21]

Communications from Rieti were infrequent, although sometimes a courier would manage to dodge through the French cavalry patrols. One such man brought word from Chiara, demanding money for Angelino's board and warning that unless it was soon forthcoming she would not be responsible for him. Margaret found a way to smuggle the money out of Rome, and she afterward heard that it had arrived, but her feelings toward the nurse, whom she had trusted until now, may be imagined. In her anxiety over what might happen to Angelino if she and Ossoli were killed, she decided to risk telling one more person about him. She chose Emelyn Story, who, in answer to a message asking her to come, found Margaret lying exhausted on her bed after a day at the hospital. After making her friend promise not to repeat what she was about to say, Margaret told her that she and Ossoli were married and that they were worried about the welfare of their child, who was in the mountains. She gave Emelyn a packet of papers to give to her family in case anything happened to her, and she asked her to see that Angelino reached America. Overcoming her amazement like the warm and sensible person she apparently was, Emelyn agreed and took the papers. She glanced at one or two with Margaret, but afterward remembered only the document certifying that Angelino was his father's heir—a document which, had she thought about it, strongly implied his illegitimacy. On her assertion that there was also a marriage certificate, which she did not see, rests the claim that Margaret and Ossoli were married in 1847 or 1848.

As it turned out, the Storys left Rome soon after this. Margaret herself, torn between loyalty to Rome and her lover and loyalty to her child, briefly considered leaving but decided against it. Having returned the papers, Emelyn and William safely passed through the French lines on May 24, and went to Florence. The big, echoing house was now empty except for Margaret and the *padrone,* and in her loneliness she turned for companionship to Lewis Cass, Jr., the American envoy. She had been disposed to dislike him at first, since his very presence in Rome angered and embarrassed her as an American; but since the battle of April 30, he had proved steadily kind and solicitous of her welfare, and apart from his official function he was discovered to be a gentle, rather pensive young man. They spent several evenings talking by a hearth which was now kindled more for morale than for heat.

Events took a hopeful turn at the end of May, when de Lesseps and the triumvirate reached an agreement that would have saved the city and guaranteed French protection against the Austrians. But Oudinot would not sign it, and as de Lesseps went off to Paris to plead his cause there, Oudinot announced that he was preparing to attack on June 4. Inexplicably, the Italians took this to mean he would attack the city itself, and two strategic villas outside the walls were lightly manned. These the French attacked before dawn on June 3; by evening, despite repeated, suicidal acts of heroism by Garibaldi's men and the Lombards, the villas had been taken. The French now were in a position from which they could freely shell the city and systematically demolish portions of the Janiculum Wall.

From this time on defense was useless, but Mazzini at least had expected this all along, knowing that even a useless defense could be an inspiration to Italians in the years ahead. It was not a remarkable view for a man who, even to look at him, seemed made for martyrdom. What was remarkable was that the whole city shared it. In two *Tribune* letters which she somehow managed to write during the siege, Margaret related instances of an almost universal courage and endurance among these people who, until the year before, had been politically ignorant and lethargic. As the French began to shell the city, Italian bands played the "Marseillaise" at them from the walls. The Italian soldiers picked up the French bombs and tossed them back at the enemy, while the women in Trastevere ran around with pans of wet clay, extinguishing the fuses. But such evidences of pluck and daring were entirely lost on the French, who kept up their cannonade throughout the month of June, often at night as well as during the day. The face of Rome was permanently changed, the worst damage being inflicted on the historic villas which were used as fighting stations by both sides. "Rome is being destroyed," Margaret wrote to Emerson after a week of shelling:

> Her glorious oaks,—her villas, haunts of sacred beauty, that seemed the possession of the world for ever,—the villa of Raphael, the villa of Albani, home of Winckelmann and the best expression of the ideal of modern Rome, and so many other sanctuaries of beauty,— all must perish, lest a foe should level a musket from their shelter. I could not, could not!
>
> I know not, dear friend, whether I shall ever get home across that great ocean, but here in Rome I shall no longer wish to live. O Rome, *my* country! could I imagine that the triumph of what I held dear was to heap such desolation on thy head![22]

She was forced to realize what she had suspected about herself even before the bombardment began: if she had had the power, she would have given up the republic in order to save the city. It was a major failure in her own eyes such as she had not had to admit before. When she measured herself against Italian women—Mazzini's mother, Princess Belgiojoso, or the wife of Mazzini's friend Modena—she found she was lacking in precisely that moral courage she had always prided herself on. She was no Plutarchian matron, and that discovery was one private, very painful bit of damage inflicted by the French.

She was, however, something of a Florence Nightingale, though limited in how much she could do by her total lack of training. In the same letter to Emerson she says,

Since the 30th of April, I go almost daily to the hospitals, and though I have suffered, for I had no idea before how terrible gunshot wounds and wound-fevers are, yet I have taken pleasure, and great pleasure, in being with the men. There is scarcely one who is not moved by a noble spirit. Many, especially among the Lombards, are the flower of the Italian youth. When they begin to get better, I carry them books and flowers; they read, and we talk.

The palace of the Pope, on the Quirinal, is now used for convalescents. In those beautiful gardens I walk with them, one with his sling, another with his crutch. The gardener plays off all his water-works for the defenders of the country, and gathers flowers for me, their friend.[23]

But the largest part of what she did could hardly have been so picturesque, and neither to Emerson nor to anyone else did she describe the grimmer details of her work. The wounded of April 30 had been exposed to musket shot; the wounded who came in now had been exposed to explosive shells as well, and there were many deaths and many amputations, as well as a high incidence of gangrene. The spirit of the men was such that whatever help she brought them was more than reciprocated. "You say I sustained them," she wrote later to Channing,

Often have they sustained my courage; one, kissing the pieces of bone that were so painfully extracted from his arm, hanging them round his neck to be worn as the true relics of to-day; mementoes that he also had done and borne something for his country and the hopes of humanity. One fair young man, who is made a cripple for life, clasped my hand as he saw me crying over the spasms I could not relieve, and faintly cried "Viva l'Italia." "Think only, *cara bona donna,*" said a poor wounded soldier, "that I can always wear my uniform on *festas,* just as it is now, with the holes where the balls went through, for a memory." "God is good; God knows," they often said to me, when I had not a word to cheer them.[24]

On June 22, after a night of particularly heavy shelling, the French finally succeeded in breaching the Janiculum and gaining entrance to the city. Even now the Italians did not surrender, but retreated to a second line of defense, which against all probability they held for another eight days. But the shelling was now heavy all over the city. On the night of June 28, more than thirty shells fell on or near the Hotel Russie, where Cass lived, and a comparable number fell around the Casa Dies. The following day Cass received a message from Margaret, and on going to see her found her, as had Emelyn Story before him, lying pale and exhausted on a sofa, holding a packet of papers. She told him she and Ossoli were married and had a child. Ossoli, now commanding a battery on the Pincian Mount, did not expect to survive another night like the last, and she had decided to join him at his post. She asked Cass to see that the papers reached America if anything happened to her. Like Mrs. Story, Cass later said that Margaret had told him a marriage certificate was among the documents, but he did not see it. He took the packet and afterward saw her walking with Ossoli toward the Pincian Mount.

But the siege was already over. That afternoon, possibly while Margaret and Cass were talking, Mazzini, Garibaldi, and the Assembly were debating whether to surrender, fight in the streets, or take the army and the government into the mountains. Mazzini and Garibaldi favored the last course, but the assembly voted to cease all resistance and remain in their seats. Garibaldi sent out a message that he was leaving the city, and that anyone who wanted to follow him was welcome, though he offered them only "hunger, thirst, forced marches, battles and death."[25] Several thousand accepted this bleak (and later amply fulfilled) promise, and on July 2, Margaret and Ossoli watched as the men assembled with their families, who would be left behind, near the Porta San Giovanni:

> They had all put on the beautiful dress of the Garibaldi legion, the tunic of bright red cloth, the Greek cap, or else round hat with Puritan plume. Their long hair was blown back from resolute faces; all looked full of courage. They had counted the cost before they entered on this perilous struggle; they had weighed life and all its material advantages against liberty, and made their election; they turned not back, nor flinched, at this bitter crisis. I saw the wounded, all that could go, laden upon their baggage cars; some were already pale and fainting, still they wished to go. I saw many youths, born to rich inheritance, carrying in a handkerchief all their worldly goods. The

women were ready; their eyes too were resolved, if sad. The wife of Garibaldi followed him on horseback. He himself was distinguished by the white tunic; his look was entirely that of a hero of the Middle Ages,—his face still young, for the excitements of his life, though so many, have all been youthful, and there is no fatigue upon his brow or cheek. Fall or stand, one sees in him a man engaged in the career for which he is adapted by nature. He went upon the parapet, and looked upon the road with a spy-glass, and, no obstruction being in sight, he turned his face for a moment back upon Rome, then led the way through the gate. Hard was the heart, stony and seared the eye, that had no tear for that moment.[26]

Mazzini remained behind. He deliberately walked the streets after the French had entered, so as to leave them no fragment of their old argument that the republicans were hated by the majority of Romans. They did not dare arrest him. Margaret, who had not seen him in some time, visited him at the house of his friend Modena and found that ''he had grown old; all the vital juices seemed exhausted; his eyes were all blood-shot; his skin orange; flesh he had none; his hair was mixed with white; his hand was painful to the touch; but he had never flinched, never quailed; had protested in the last hour against surrender; sweet and calm, but full of a more fiery purpose than ever; in him I revered the hero, and owned myself not of that mould.''[27] Through Cass she obtained a passport for him, but he could not use it without a French visa. Finally he made his way out of Italy alone, with the help of a loyal sea captain. He eventually returned to England and lived there twenty more years, surviving—as did Garibaldi—to see Italy united and free.

Margaret and Ossoli remained in Rome until mid-July, partly because there seemed to be no place for them to go and partly so that Ossoli could try to obtain some part of his inheritance. Margaret tended the wounded as long as the French would allow her—which apparently was not long—and sent one more *Tribune* letter. Finally, when it seemed that to remain longer would be to risk being imprisoned in the city, they left for Rieti. Margaret wrote to Channing, asking him to assure her mother that she was safe:

Say, she need feel no anxiety, if she do not hear from me for some time. I may feel indisposed to write, as I do now; my heart is too full. Private hopes of mine are fallen with the hopes of Italy. I have played for a new stake, and lost it. Life looks too difficult. But for the present I shall try to wave all thought of self and renew my strength.[28]

Their plans beyond the next few weeks were unsettled and depended entirely on whether they would be allowed to stay in Italy over the winter. Thanks to the money sent earlier from home, plus help from some friend in Rome, possibly Story, they had enough to live on while Margaret finished her book. After that, they would have to trust themselves to the chilly havens of New England.

XVIII

~~~~~

Rieti and Florence

It was not difficult to leave Rome. Not only the ruined buildings and bomb-pitted streets, but the sight of the jaunty French soldiers and the sullen, apathetic faces of the people who had so recently been willing to die in defense of the city sickened and depressed Margaret. Leaving the wounded, now about to be transported from hospitals to prisons, was another thing:

> I cannot tell you what I endured in leaving Rome, abandoning the wounded soldiers. . . . Some of the poorer men, who rise bereft even of the right arm,—one having lost both the right arm and the right leg,—I could have provided for with a small sum. Could I have sold my hair, or blood from my arm, I would have done it. Had any of the rich Americans remained in Rome, they would have given it to me; they helped nobly at first . . . but they had all gone.[1]

But anxiety for Angelino drew her toward Rieti, and she and Ossoli were thankful for the carriage and horses Lewis Cass was able to procure for them (at a cost of well over a month's rent).

The placid face of Rieti, that "little red-brown nest, which those we call the aborigines of Italy made long before Rome was,"[2] promised refuge, as it had the year before. Implicit in the slow, never-changing rhythms of the life there was the sense that even the bombardment and capture of Rome was no more than a flick of the lash on the tough and wrinkled hide of this ancient country. Ossoli, like most other republicans, was already calculating that in two or three years Italy might be ready for another revolution. Margaret's first letter to Cass from Rieti begins with an elaborately picturesque description of the town, lying "tranquil amid the network of vineyards. Its casinos and convents gleam pleasantly from the hillsides, the dirt accumulates undisturbed in its streets, and pigs and children wallow in it, while Madonna-veiled, bare-legged women twirl the distaff at every door and window." Even the presence of a troop of Spanish soldiers (for Spain, not to be out-done, had dispatched her own small force to Italy) seems not to worry her. She enjoys the "noble sounds of their language," though she hopes they will leave soon, since they "eat everything up like locusts."[3]

But after this self-consciously literary introduction she comes to her real preoccupation, which is her son. Again Rieti's charm had proved illusory, and she had found Angelino dangerously ill, apparently of malnutrition. Chiara no longer had milk enough for both Angelino and her own son, and having no money to buy milk, and probably doubting that the *inglesa* would ever escape from Rome, she had been nursing her own child and feeding Angelino on bread soaked in wine. Margaret's accusation that Chiara had "betrayed him for the sake of a few *scudi*"[4] may not have been quite true, but he was indeed "worn to a skeleton, all his sweet childish graces fled; he is so weak it seems to me he can scarcely ever revive to health. If he cannot, I do not wish him to live; life is hard enough for the strong, it is too much for the feeble. Only, if he dies, I hope I shall, too. I was too fatigued before, and this last shipwreck of hopes would be more than I could bear."[5] Eleven days later he is still so ill that she cannot invite Cass to visit them, and she and Ossoli are taking turns sitting up all night with him.

By the end of August he was over the worst of it, and even his anxious mother could admit he was no longer in any danger. But then she was profoundly shaken by a letter from Horace Greeley that echoed all her own worst fears: the irrepressible Pickie, now five years old, had been stricken with cholera and had died fifteen hours later. Margaret's grief was keen, compounded by her own child's narrow escape and by her still largely unexpressed mourning for Rome. Even the death of her father had not unloosed such a flood of tears: shattering though that had been, it had not seemed part of a larger pattern. "I have never wept so for grief of my own, as now for yours," she wrote Greeley. "No child, except little Waldo Emerson, had I ever so loved. . . . The conditions of this planet are not propitious to the lovely, the just, the pure; it is these that go away; it is the unjust that triumph."[6]

But no more thunderbolts fell. Angelino recovered steadily, with the help of a new wet nurse, and tentatively Margaret and Ossoli began to savor the novelty of living together as a family for the first time. Except for one disturbing incident—Ossoli wandered over the Neapolitan border one day and was arrested, but with Margaret's help he was released the following morning—the hot, slow days succeeded one another with reassuring monotony. Ossoli's serene temper was a balm to Margaret, who had never been with him for long enough at a time to appreciate it fully. Stoical and pious, affectionate, chivalrous toward her as her father had been toward her mother, he was never ebullient but never depressed either, and under his calming influence Margaret began to regain some of her own strength and plan for the future. They decided to go to Florence as soon as the baby could travel and stay there for the winter. With luck their reputation as radicals would not have preceded them and the Austrians would leave them alone. The following summer they would probably go to America, but Ossoli left that decision to Margaret and she did not feel able to cope with it yet.

Early in September Ossoli went to Rome to exchange some money and to try to persuade his brothers to buy out a share of his inheritance. While he was gone, on Angelino's first birthday, Margaret received a letter from the London publishers of Chapman and Son, rejecting her book both because it was unfinished and because a new English copyright law had made the publication of foreign authors more complicated. She had already been warned of this by Thomas Carlyle, who had made inquiries for her, but the disappointment was hard to swallow. "It has been my fate," she wrote bitterly to Cass, "that when I worked for others I could always succeed; when I tried to keep the least thing for myself, it was not permitted. Must this schooling be life-long?" [7] Attempts to follow up on some earlier, casual offers of journalistic assignments also came to nothing. Like most offers of that kind, they had chilled with age. Meanwhile Ossoli's brother Giuseppe, who had had to hide in his own cellar during the days of the republic, let it be known that he would make things as difficult as possible for Angelo.

So their attempts at breadwinning were checked for a while, but fortunately, thanks to the American annuity and the friend in Rome, they had enough money to see them through the winter. Meanwhile Margaret set about one more difficult task. Since it was pointless to hide Angelino's existence any longer—all Florence would know about it soon enough—she wrote to her mother, her brothers and sister, and a few of her friends, telling them that she was married and had a child. It took the usual two months for their replies to reach her, but when they came they were, on the whole, comforting. Her mother's letter, warm with sympathy, sent the first real pang of homesickness through her: "I send my first kiss with my fervent blessing to my grandson. I hope your husband will understand a little of my English, for I am too old to speak Italian fluently enough to make him understand how dearly I shall love him if he brings you safe to me." [8] Other letters followed, all generous and understanding, though Richard was silent for some time. She heard nothing at all from Horace Greeley, to whom she had communicated her news with tactless abruptness at the end of her letter about Pickie.

If Greeley did disapprove, he was not alone, and it was just as well that Margaret was far out of range of the delicious little shock waves that rippled through Boston and New York. Her friends were sometimes hard pressed to defend her, especially since she had flatly refused to give them specific dates with which to arm their rebuttals. People who had been offended by *Woman in the Nineteenth Century,* or who had been stung by her criticism in person or in print, or who just couldn't abide her imperial air, felt themselves vindicated in their opinion that strong, intellectual women were "masculine" and "coarse" and would sooner or later come to a bad end. Intellectual and sexual "forwardness" were inescapably linked in women, and wasn't it a pity that this one came from a decent American family? The wickedly condescending remark with which Hawthorne closed the journal entry quoted earlier is probably representative of what many people said in 1849, although Hawthorne himself did not write it until much later: "I do not know but I like her better for it; because she proved herself a very woman after all, and fell as the weakest of her sisters might."[9] There was a malicious triumph in deciding that Margaret was, after all, just another frail and licentious daughter of Eve. Her sexual transgression relieved many people of the necessity to take her seriously.

In Europe, too, the scandal spread rapidly as far as the tables d'hôte in Venice, where William Story unluckily heard it for the first time, his wife having kept her word to Margaret. Emelyn Story, Caroline Sturgis Tappan, and William Channing all discreetly warned her of what she might have to face at home, but with more than a hint of her old hauteur she announced her defiance of the scandalmongers of Boston and New York:

> I feel a good deal of contempt for those so easily disconcerted or reassured. I was not a child; I had lived in the midst of that New England society, in a way that entitled me to esteem, and a favorable interpretation, where there was doubt about my motives or actions. I pity those who are inclined to think ill, when they might as well have inclined the other way. However, let them go; there are many in the world who stand the test, enough to keep us from shivering to death.[10]

Braced for the worst, she arrived in Florence with her new family in October after a leisurely trip through Perugia and the Tuscan vineyards. But the way she was received by the American community there made it plain that in Italy at least she had nothing to fear.* Soon she was involved in a round of calls and concerts, and regularly attending the evening soirees at which the Americans assembled. "What you say of the meddling curiosity of people repels me," she wrote Caroline in December:

> It is so different here. When I made my appearance with a husband and a child of a year old nobody did the least thing to annoy me. All were most cordial, none asked or implied questions. Yet there were not a few that might justly have complained that when they were confiding to me all their affairs and doing much to serve me, I had observed absolute silence to them. Others might for more than one reason be displeased at the choice I made. All have acted in the kindliest and most refined manner. An Italian lady with whom I was intimate who might be qualified in the court Journal as one "of the highest rank sustained by the most scrupulous decorum"!! when I wrote "Dear friend, I am married. I have a child. There are particulars as to my reasons for keeping this secret I do not wish to tell. This is rather an odd affair, will it make any difference in our relations?" She answered "What difference can it make, except that I shall love you more now that we can sympathize as mothers?" Her first visit here was to me; she adopted at once Ossoli and the child to her love.[11]

The lady was Costanza Arconati, whose strict sense of propriety might easily have been offended, especially in view of the rumors she had heard.

Margaret had not been able to meet the Brownings in her previous visits to Florence, though she had corresponded with Mrs. Browning from Rome. Now that she did meet them, Mrs. Browning hardly knew what to make of her. Her rather tart comments on their much-postponed introduction suggest that there may have been more eyebrows raised in Florence than Margaret was aware of:

---

* If Julian Hawthorne can be believed, not all her friends were as hospitable as they seemed. Joseph Mozier supposedly told Nathaniel Hawthorne some years later that Angelo Ossoli was "half an idiot" and that Margaret's book on Italy did not exist. *Nathaniel Hawthorne and His Wife*, pp. 259–62.

The American authoress, Miss Fuller, with whom we had had some slight intercourse by letter, and who has been at Rome during the siege, as a devoted friend of the republicans and a meritorious attendant on the hospitals, has taken us by surprise at Florence, retiring from the Roman field with a husband and child above a year old. Nobody had even suspected a word of this underplot, and her American friends stood in mute astonishment before this apparition of them here. The husband is a Roman marquis, appearing amiable and gentlemanly, and having fought well, they say, at the siege, but with no pretension to cope with his wife on any ground appertaining to the intellect. She talks, and he listens. I always wonder at that species of marriage; but people are so different in their matrimonial ideals that it may answer sometimes.[12]

The irregularity of Margaret's marriage was a point on which Mrs. Browning was understandably prepared to be tolerant. Margaret's socialism may have been a more serious impediment, since throughout the events of the previous year Mrs. Browning's sympathies had remained with the Pope, the Grand Duke, and the London *Times*. But common maternal concerns and Margaret's early recognition of the Brownings' poetry prevailed, and they became friends. Margaret was less at ease with Robert Browning than with his wife, finding her attempts at intimacy blocked by a reserve which, like Thomas Carlyle's, was all the more impenetrable because it took the form of conversation rather than silence. Browning was exasperatingly hearty and witty, and her acquaintance with him was "singularly external. I know not that I ever had such with any person of substance."[13] Kept thus at bay, she nevertheless was drawn strongly to both of them, and they to her. "A very interesting person she is," Mrs. Browning wrote when she had grown to know Margaret well, "far better than her writings —thoughtful, spiritual in her habitual mode of mind; not only exalted, but *exaltée* in her opinions, and yet calm in manner."[14]

Socially, then, Florence was a snug haven. Politically it was full of shoals. Margaret did observe that, unlike the French in Rome, the Austrians were "wonderfully discreet," though "both [officers and soldiers] feel the knife not infrequently, and they would gladly at this moment put even cowardly Florence in state of siege."[15]

But discretion did not rule out a keen nose for imported radicals, and immediately after Ossoli arrived the police began to question his improbable American passport. For about two weeks he and his family were threatened with expulsion, until Lewis Cass and Horatio Greenough (who had a highly placed Italian friend) managed to convince the Austrians that he was not an agitator. After that they were left in peace. Margaret, for one, had no heart at the moment for political intrigue:

> Weary in spirit with the deep disappointments of the last year, I wish to dwell little on [the past] for the moment, but seek some consolation in the affections. My little boy is quite well now, and I often feel happy in seeing how joyous and full of activity he seems. Ossoli, too, feels happier here. The future is full of difficulties for us; but having settled our plans for the present we shall set it aside while we may—"Sufficient for the day is the *Evil* thereof"—and, if the *good* be not *always* sufficient, in our case it is; so let us say grace to our dinner of herbs.[16]

Ossoli's sole gesture of defiance while he lived in Florence was to wear the brown uniform of the Roman civic guard while he was at home. Luckily they had no Austrian callers.

That winter, from which both past and future were firmly excluded, was an interval of almost pure gold. Margaret and Ossoli took an apartment on the Piazza Santa Maria Novella, with a view of the picture-book church of that name, and beyond it the delicate, pale gold tower of the Campanile. A casual visitor later remembered spending several evenings with them in their dining room, "a small square room, sparingly, yet sufficiently furnished, with polished floor and frescoed ceiling,—and, drawn up closely before the cheerful fire, an oval table, on which stood a monkish lamp of brass, with depending chains that support quaint classic cups for olive oil."[17] The "cheerful fire" made this the most popular room in the otherwise unheated apartment, though as long as the weather permitted Margaret spent about three hours every morning in a separate *sala,* working on her book while the baby slept. Otherwise she allowed her days to arrange themselves around his schedule, concentrating on being with him during the short, intimate period of his infancy, which was almost gone and of which she had been largely cheated. In a long letter to Caroline Sturgis Tappan she described a domestic life which she still could hardly believe was her own:

> In the morn g [*sic*], so soon as dressed, he signs to come into our room, then draws our curtain, kisses me, rather violently pats my face . . . stretches himself and says *bravo,* then expects as a reward to be tied in his chair and have his play things. These engage him busily, but still he calls to us to sing and drum to enliven the scene. Sometimes he calls me to kiss his hand; he laughs very much at this. Enchanting is that baby laugh, all dimples and glitter, so strangely arch and innocent. Then I wash and dress him; that is his great time. He makes it as long as he can insisting to dress and wash me the while; kicking, throwing the water about full of all manner of tricks that I think girls never dream of. Then is his walk; we have beautiful walks here for him. . . .[18]

She felt herself to be much changed even since the previous year and mentioned it to several people, among them the Springs: "Say to my dearest William [Channing] not to feel anxious about people's talk concerning me. It is not directed against the real Margaret, but a phantom. . . . People when they see me will not generally be inclined to injure me, for they will see the expression of a heart bettered by experience—more humble and tender, more anxious to serve its kind than ever before." [19] The change, if over-emphasised, can be taken to imply that motherhood was all Margaret ever wanted or needed out of life, and that having borne a child she had (to put it bluntly) gone a little soft in the head. Again Mason Wade is representative:

> Margaret no longer needed a cause, now that her prayer of many years before for "a bud on my tree of life, so scathed by the lightning and bound by the frost," had been answered. . . . Her subjugation of herself to a man in the marriage act, and the bearing and rearing of a child, had made her nature soft and gentle and feminine at last. The psychological change is clearly evident in her writing, particularly in the letters to her friends and family about the silly little doings of her child. She had found happiness in being a woman

and in fulfilling a woman's natural duties, and the long struggle between her masculine and feminine traits was ended at last.[20]

If we pass over the term "subjugation" (which in itself requires
a whole book in reply), we can begin by agreeing that motherhood, like her love for Ossoli, had brought out that latent warmth
and tenderness which had always been apparent to those who knew
her. And it is clear that during this period of closeness with her
child her writing came in a poor second. But she knew very well
how short this time would be, and that knowledge lent it intensity.
And even now she wrote, in answer to a remark of Rebecca
Spring's, "In answer to what you say, that it is still better to give
the world this living soul than a portion of my life in a printed
book; it is true; and yet of my book I could know whether it would
be of some worth or not, of my child I must wait to see what his
worth will be."[21] It is a mild enough reply, but it does show that
even at the height of her maternal preoccupation Margaret thought
of herself as having two things to contribute to the world, her child
and her work. Once they arrived in America she expected to support all three of them by writing and by giving lessons in Italian
history, and though she knew that the writing at least would be
grub-work, there was no question in her mind that this was still her
vocation. She had by no means withdrawn from the world; it is not
even clear that, despite her gentler demeanor, a few encounters
with her critics in Boston might not have revived her old Amazon-
ian spirit.

Nor is it true that she "no longer needed a cause." In the same
letter to the Springs she reaffirms her commitment to socialism: "I
have become an enthusiastic Socialist; elsewhere is no comfort, no
solution for the problems of the times." And to revolution: "What
you say is deeply true about the peace way being the best . . .
[but] I am not sure that I can keep my hands free from blood." She
had not ended the "struggle between her masculine and feminine
traits" by suppressing one in favor of the other; she had ended it by
finally being able to give expression to both.

Another factor in her new mildness was the tremendous psychic
toll taken by the revolution. The physical horrors she had wit-

nessed and been helpless to relieve, her separation from her child, and especially the brutal extinction of the hope that *this* time the Good and the True would win—all had drained her of the energy and confidence she had once had in superabundance. In particular she was tormented by the memory of her own failure as a revolutionary. She could not square her belief in the Roman cause with her revulsion at the war it caused. Arguing against Marcus Spring's pacifism, she acknowledged that she herself was ''consistent no way. . . . The agonies of that baptism of blood I feel oh how deeply in the golden June days of Rome . . . I felt I should have shrunk back. I could not have had it shed.'' [22] To Channing, just after the fall of Rome, she had written,

> You say truly, I shall come home humbler. God grant it may be entirely humble! In future, while more than ever deeply penetrated with principles, and the need of the martyr spirit to sustain them, I will ever own that there are few worthy, and that I am one of the least. [23]

All of this contributed to a change that would have been evident in her letters even if she herself had not remarked on it. She had indeed ''found happiness in being a woman.'' She was also nearly forty and had been through a series of experiences that would have exhausted a much younger person, and having measured herself against her own standards and found herself wanting, she was just plain tired.

Christmas was the high point of that winter in Florence. Margaret, having had no childhood experience of a holiday which in early Boston days was regarded as half-pagan, half-popish, discovered it through her son's eyes. On Christmas morning three large stuffed animals arrived for him. She wrote to Caroline:

> It almost made me cry to see the kind of fearful rapture with which he regarded them. . . . He was different with all the three, loving the bird, very wild and shouting with the horse, with the cat pulling her face close to his, staring in her eyes, and then throwing her away. . . . You would laugh to know how much remorse I feel that I never gave children more toys in the course of my life. I regret all

the money I ever spent on myself or in little presents for grown people, hardened sinners. . . . I am sure if Jesus Christ had given, it would not have been little crosses.[24]

Christmas also brought snow, blurring and simplifying the stone tracery of the buildings and muffling the sounds of passing carriages. Christmas Eve Margaret and Ossoli went to hear midnight mass at the Annuziata, afterward visiting the vast, empty Duomo, dark except for two candlelit altars and silent except for the chanting of invisible priests. Then they walked home through the snow:

. . . There is snow all over Florence in our most beautiful piazza. Sta. Maria Novella with its fair loggia and bridal church is a carpet of snow and the full moon looking down. I had forgotten how angelical all that is, how fit to die by. I have only seen snow in mountain patches for so long. Here it is the even, holy shroud of a desired peace. God bless all good and bad tonight and save me from despair.[25]

With the snow came a cold spell which lasted two months. In January Margaret and Ossoli both caught the flu, and afterward Margaret had to abandon her *sala* and spend her days, along with everyone else including her very bored and restless little boy, in the dining room near the fire. There was no question of writing here, so she read books on contemporary history by Lamartine and Louis Blanc, and one or two on earlier times, including Macaulay's history of the James II period, which she thought were relevant to the present. She continued to see much of the Brownings, the Arconatis, and the Greenoughs, and when she and Ossoli spent the evening at home they were joined by young Horace Sumner, brother of the abolitionist Charles Sumner, Jr. and, as Margaret wrote her mother (she was continually surprised at how many childhood associations kept turning up in Florence), son of "father's Mr. Charles Sumner."[26] Recently recovered from a serious illness, Sumner was a solemn young man, strangely old in his ways, who remembered Margaret and Lloyd from Brook Farm. He was their most faithful visitor, bringing Margaret flowers daily and exchanging lessons in Italian and English with Ossoli.

Toward the end of February the cold dissolved into another incredibly soft Italian spring. "This has been a divine day," Margaret wrote on March 5. "The most glorious sunshine, and gently flowing airs, crows cawing and searching in gay bands; the birds twittering their first notes of love; the fields enameled with anemones, cowslips and crocuses—the Italian spring is as good as Paradise." But into this Eden intruded the realization that they could no longer postpone leaving Italy: "How dreadful it will be hereafter to shiver and pine up to the middle of May; yet I must go brave that and many an ugly thing beside."[27] They had already explored the possibility of sailing from France on a steamer, since on the baby's account this shorter and safer route was much to be preferred. But it was too expensive, and they reluctantly decided to wait for a good merchant sailing-ship to dock at Leghorn.

The future was grim, but Margaret and Ossoli both looked forward to returning to Italy in a few years. In the interval they envisioned living in some rural retreat, perhaps just outside of New York so that Ossoli could be near an Italian settlement. Their survival as a family depended on whether Margaret would be able to earn a living. After receiving Chapman's refusal she had sent an inquiry to Wiley and Putnam, who were interested, but not enough to offer her favorable terms. She hoped to bring them around with the help of some business-wise friend, and to this end Emerson had offered his services. If she could accomplish this much, and find some regular writing to do for periodicals, she and Ossoli could afford to ignore the worst that was said about them.

Margaret hoped her mother would come and live with them, feeling sure that in her Ossoli would find a companion and ally. Of all the difficulties that lay ahead, none disturbed her so much as the fear that her friends would not understand or accept him. Her love for him was not unique in her life; it resembled her love for her mother, Ellen Kilshaw, Anna Barker, and several other friends in its nonintellectual quality and its reliance on shared experiences and feelings which did not need to be communicated verbally. But it was not the sort of tie people accepted between a man and a woman, let alone a husband and wife, unless the two were intellectually equal or the man was superior. To Ossoli, Margaret's intellectual attainments were incidental. Their relationship, in spite of its dramatic beginning, was based on shared sympathies and domestic affection rather than grand passion, and it involved a rare degree of mutual independence. Reserved and self-sufficient to begin with, Ossoli simply went his own way and allowed Margaret to go hers. When she went out in the evening he often left her at the door and called for her later, though if she were visiting the Arconatis or anyone else with whom he would be comfortable he would remain. If she had evening callers and the conversation lapsed into English he would excuse himself and go to a café; Margaret explained that he did not wish to put a constraint on the company by his presence, but to this we can probably add the less altruistic excuse of boredom. In any case, none of her friends ever detected the slightest sign of jealousy or irritation in his thus excluding himself.

But in America he would have no cafés and no political discussions to withdraw to, and he would be more dependent on Margaret than ever before. She foresaw that this might put an unbearable strain on their relationship, especially if her friends could not find it in themselves to make Ossoli feel welcome. Time after time she approached the subject gingerly in her letters, in fact conveying the essence of Ossoli's personality much better than she thought she did. To Ward she wrote,

> You are among the very few of my friends who I think may be able to see why we can live together, and may appreciate the unspoiled nature and loveliness of his character: he is entirely without what is commonly called culture, educated by a tutor and that tutor an old priest . . . I think he never used to go through with a book; nature . . . he has spelled thoroughly. To me the simplicity, the reality, the great tenderness and refinement of his character make a domestic place in this world and as it is for my heart that he loves me, I hope he may always be able to feel the same, but that is as God pleases.[28]

And to the Springs, who now admitted they had hoped when she left them in Venice in 1847 that she was returning to her "Giovanni attachment":

I have expected that those who cared for me chiefly for my activity of intellect would not care for him, but that those in whom the moral nature predominates would gradually learn to love and admire him and see what a treasure his affection must be to me. But that would be only gradually, for it is by acts, not words, that one so simple, true, delicate and retiring can be known.[29]

She was afraid that the strangeness and isolation Ossoli would have to face in America, plus the fact that he was much younger than she, might cause him to drift away from her. She had long ago faced and accepted the fact that the boundaries of their love were finite. She hinted as much to her mother and sister, and to Sam Ward. She spelled it out plainly to her fellow radical William Channing in a letter that shows she had retained and broadened the view of marriage she had expressed in her 1842 Concord journal:

My love for Ossoli is most pure and tender, nor has anyone, except little children or mother, ever loved me as genuinely as he does. . . . Our relation covers only a part of my life, but I do not perceive that it interferes with anything I ought to have or be; I do not feel any way constrained or limited or that I have made any sacrifice. Younger I might, because I should have been exposed to love some other in a way that might give him pain, but I do not now feel apprehensive of that. There is more danger for him, as he is younger than I; if he should, I shall do all that this false state of society permits to give him what freedom he may need.[30]

It may have been this letter, or one like it, that made Channing wonder if Margaret and Ossoli were married at all.[31] But there is strong indirect evidence that they were legally united shortly before they sailed for America. Deiss points to a hitherto overlooked letter from Ossoli's sister Angela to Ellen Channing, in which she says the couple were married while they lived in Florence.[32] And in the spring of 1850 Margaret suddenly sent Emelyn Story a new address using the title Marchesa, though she had not used it before. A few weeks later she wrote Mme Arconati that though it seemed "silly for a radical like me, to be carrying a title," she was inclined to do so for the sake of affirming Ossoli's right to it.[33] In

October she had asked to be addressed simply as "Margaret Ossoli." Now, after six months, she rather lamely explains that without the title letters might go astray.

Early in April Margaret and Mrs. Mozier went to inspect the American bark *Elizabeth,* anchored at Leghorn. It was a new, stoutly built vessel, commanded by one Seth Hasty from Maine, who had had enough confidence in his ship and his own seamanship to bring his wife Catherine along on the voyage. Afterward the Hastys came to Florence to visit the Moziers, and everything Margaret saw of them increased her liking for them both. The Ossolis arranged to sail on the *Elizabeth* in May, and in the intervening weeks, while the vessel took on a mixed cargo that included 150 tons of Carrara marble and Powers's statue of John Calhoun, Margaret busied herself with packing and planning for the voyage. A two-month voyage with a child not yet weaned required a great deal of planning. By the time she had bought a goat, a small flock of poultry, oranges, lemons, hard biscuit, extra baby linen, and a well-stocked medicine chest, the expense of the voyage (financed chiefly by a note drawn on Marcus Spring) began to approach that of the previously rejected steamer.

She went about these preparations under a cloud of apprehension which brought on a ten-day attack of headache. She had always been nervous about the sea, but now she saw evil omens everywhere. She read in the newspapers of the wreck of the *Westmoreland,* which was carrying another of Powers's sculptures. Two weeks later she read of the sudden death of a Paris acquaintance who had borrowed a muff of Margaret's and had just been about to return it; on the next page was a notice of the wreck of the *Argo,* the steamer they had wanted to take from France. Also wrecked were another steamer and a sailing packet, though both steamers and packets were supposedly safer than merchant ships like the *Elizabeth.* "Thus, as it seems, safety is not to be found in the wisest calculation," Margaret wrote Mme Arconati:

> I shall embark more composedly in my merchant ship; praying, indeed, fervently, that it may not be my lot to lose my babe at sea, either by unsolaced sickness, or amid the howling waves. Or, that if I should it may be brief anguish, and Ossoli, he and I go together.[34]

They spent their last evening in Florence with the Brownings, who teased Ossoli about an old prophecy that he should fear death by water. Margaret smiled and replied that the name *Elizabeth* must bring them good luck. But Mrs. Browning was a little shaken to see, in a Bible they had brought as a gift from Angelino to the Browning's son, the inscription, "In memory of Angelo Eugene Ossoli." [35]

XIX

Voyage of the Elizabeth

The *Elizabeth* sailed on May 17, 1850, carrying five passengers: the Ossolis and their son; Horace Sumner; and a young Italian girl, Celeste Paolini, who had agreed to help look after Angelino (now usually called Nino in honor of undeniably being more little boy than angel). After a rainy spell which delayed loading, the weather had turned mild and sunny, and despite a heavy, last-minute reluctance to board, once the vessel was under way Margaret appeared to be in high spirits. All the changes she had requested in her stateroom had been faithfully carried out, and nothing seemed lacking for her child's comfort. Nino himself was delighted with his white nanny goat and spent much of his time minutely inspecting the workings of the ship in the company of Captain Hasty or one of the crew. Not every two-year-old has a goat and a full-sized sailing vessel as his own personal playthings, and it is not surprising that everyone remarked on his happy disposition.

The sea was calm, and Margaret escaped headache and seasickness after the first day. She settled down to enjoy the voyage, working in the morning and spending the afternoon on deck. Evenings were given over to singing and playing music in the main cabin. Ossoli's and Sumner's language lessons were extended to include the captain and his wife, and it began to seem more likely that Angelo would learn enough English before he reached America at least to exchange small talk with his in-laws.

After a week at sea Captain Hasty felt feverish and complained of pains in his head and back. He went to his room to lie down, but there seemed to be nothing serious the matter. Like all active people he was bored with being sick, and Margaret took Nino in to play with him in the evening. But the next day he was much worse, too sick to play with Nino even if Margaret had been willing to bring him back. In the absence of a doctor no one had any idea of what to do, aside from the standard fever remedies of cold cloths and plenty of liquids. After a few days they could only use one of these since the patient's face and throat were grossly swollen and he could not swallow. His wife nursed him continually for ten days, but soon after the ship anchored at Gibraltar Hasty died. The British authorities refused to allow a doctor on board, but the disease was guessed to be confluent smallpox.* Margaret wrote of the captain's death and burial at sea to Marcus Spring:

> I have seen since we parted great suffering but nothing physical to be compared to this, where the once fair and expressive mould of man is thus lost in corruption before life has fled. He died yesterday morning and was buried in deep water, the American consul's barge towing out one from this ship which bore the body about six o'clock. It was Sunday. A divinely calm soft glowing afternoon had succeeded a morning of bleak cold wind. You cannot think how beautiful the whole thing was—the decent array and sad reverence of the sailors—the many ships with their banners flying, the stern pillar of Hercules all veiled in roseate vapor, the little angel white sails diving into the blue depths with that solemn spoil of the poor good man—so still who had been so agonized and gasping as the last sun stooped. —Yes! it was beautiful but how dear a price we pay for the poems of this world. We shall be now in Quarantine a week, no

---

* A form of smallpox in which the lesions coalesce and cause severe swelling and abcesses, especially around the head and extremities.

person permitted to come on board till it is seen whether disease may break out in other cases. I have no great reason to think it will *not,* yet do not feel afraid. Ossoli has had it, so is safe; the baby is of course subject to injury. . . . It is vain by prudence to seek to evade the stern assaults of Destiny. I submit.[1]

While the *Elizabeth* lay in the harbor no one else showed any signs of illness, and on June 9 she sailed under the command of Mr. Bangs, the first mate. Two days later Nino came down with a fever.* The disease progressed rapidly, with severe swelling of the face, closing both the child's eyes. His parents worked ceaselessly to save him, though Ossoli told Catherine Hasty that he did not see how Nino could recover and that he was resigned to losing him. But Margaret, in spite of her habitual fatalism, refused to admit that she could not single-handedly keep him alive. On the morning of the ninth day she burst into Mrs. Hasty's room to announce that Nino could see. From then on he recovered steadily, and once again he seems not to have been scarred, although confluent small-pox can be particularly vicious in its disfigurement. But Margaret must have found cause for reflection in the fact that of all those who had been exposed to infection, only Nino had caught it.

The rest of the voyage was peaceful, though hampered by a persistent westerly wind. Having slept off the fatigue of that desperate week, Margaret felt unusually well except for an occasional pain in the back. June merged pleasantly into July, and the morning of June 18 found the *Elizabeth* 4° east of Bermuda, her sails finally taut with a fresh southeast wind. By nine that night the wind had increased to gale force, but Mr. Bangs said there was no cause for alarm and asked the passengers to bring their trunks to the main cabin, promising to have them safely docked at New York the following morning.

At 2:30 A.M. the *Elizabeth* was ploughing through very heavy seas, her sails closely reefed. Mr. Bangs, having taken a sounding that showed twenty-one fathoms, decided that the danger of being blown onto the New Jersey shore—apparently the only danger he

---

* This is puzzling, in view of his earlier inoculation. Evidently it provided only temporary immunity.

imagined—was nil. He left some orders with the watch and turned in. An inexperienced navigator, he had underestimated the speed with which they were being driven north. In fact they were only a little south of Long Island, and had already been caught in the powerful current that sweeps west along its shore.

For eons the surf has been dumping sand on the Long Island beaches and snatching it back again, building a wall of sand bars, one of which is Fire Island. Beyond this first line a second one is forming, too young to be more than a line of proturberances on the sea floor, over which the whitecaps foam but do not break on a calm day. The *Elizabeth* struck one of these bars, off Fire Island beach, at around 3:30 A.M. on July 19. The passengers, thrown out of their bunks at the first shock, felt the next wave pick up the stern of the vessel and slam it broadside against the bar; the violence of the blow drove the cargo of marble through the ship's side, flooding the hold. There the vessel stayed, entirely helpless, canted half on her side and pounded by the surf.*

Catherine Hasty, picking herself up from the floor, heard a scream from the direction of Margaret's room, followed by a muffled shout of "Cut away!" from the deck, where the crew was trying to free the ship from a tangle of broken masts and rigging. She felt her way to the main cabin, where she found the Ossolis and the other passengers safe. The lights had been doused by the first wave, which had smashed in the skylight and torn the cabin door from its hinges. Water continued to pour rhythmically through these openings, but there was a relatively dry place next to the windward wall, now tilted at a crazy angle. They leaned back against it, bracing their feet against a large table. Convinced that the ship would soon sink, they exchanged messages to family and friends in case anyone should survive. Margaret, dressed in a long white nightgown with her wet hair loose around her shoulders, tried to quiet her screaming son. Ossoli did his best to comfort the hysterical Celeste, and as the only other Catholic on board finally

---

* Accounts of what followed differ in details but agree in essentials. The description here given, which makes no claim to be definitive, is drawn from the published account in *At Home and Abroad,* New York *Tribune* articles in Boxes A and B, Houghton Library, and letters written by Catherine Hasty and Caroline Sturgis Tappen (HL XVII).

succeeded in persuading her to pray with him. After the first shout from the crew they heard nothing more, and they supposed everyone else had been swept overboard; the crew, safe in the forecastle, supposed the same about them.

Sometime after dawn Mrs. Hasty made her way to the door and peered out. About a quarter of a mile away and half-obscured by the rain she made out the irregular outline of what she took to be rocks (in fact they were only dunes). The deck between the cabin and the forecastle was regularly submerged by huge waves, but the forecastle lay above water, and to her surprise she made out the figure of a sailor standing near the door. She waved and shouted but he was looking toward shore and could not hear her. But presently Davis, the second mate, noticed her and made his way across the deck, doubled over and clinging to the rail. A sailor followed him, and one by one they conducted the passengers back to the forecastle. Nino was carried in a bag slung around the sailor's neck. Mrs. Hasty, crossing with Davis, was knocked down and would have been washed away if he had not grabbed her by the hair. Later Davis returned to the cabin three times: once to fetch Captain Hasty's watch for his widow, once for some wine and figs for breakfast, and once for some money and jewelry of Margaret's. Still in the wrecked cabin was the trunk containing her manuscript, but she could not ask him to go back again.

In the forecastle, wrapped in coats and blankets and strengthened by the food, the passengers began to think there was some chance of rescue. As the light grew stronger figures could be seen on the beach—beachcombers, looking for debris from the wreck— but they seemed oblivious to any sign of life on board. It was decided that someone would try to bring help. The ship's boats were all smashed or lost, but Margaret had brought two life preservers, one of which was still usable, and a sailor took it and dived in. He was carried far up the beach by the current but eventually was seen to reach shore. Another sailor followed with a spar. Encouraged by their example, Horace Sumner took a plank and jumped in, but he sank almost immediately. After that, numbed and sickened, the others sat down to wait for help.

But although the activity on the beach increased, none of it seemed directed at rescue. Carts were seen to arrive, but only to be loaded with the scraps of exotic cargo which were already being tossed on the beach: bolts of silk and wool, flasks of oil, boxes of almonds and juniper berries, Leghorn hats. To those aboard it appeared that no one intended to help them, although in fact a lifeboat and a mortar gun with a line were on their way from a lifesaving station two miles or more away. Meanwhile the tide, which had ebbed at nine, was coming back in, and the officers urged the passengers to trust themselves to planks, each rigged with ropes and propelled by a swimming sailor. Celeste refused, and Margaret insisted she would not be separated from her son and husband. Finally Mrs. Hasty and Davis, in order to prove it could be done, jumped in together. After a long struggle during which the plank was overturned twice, they were dragged half-conscious from the surf some distance up the beach, but it is not certain whether those on board saw them. Bangs now turned again to Margaret, offering to take Nino himself, but she again refused to let him go. Having seen Sumner drown so quickly she must have realized that a very young child would have no chance at all, and with the beach only a few hundred yards off she still hoped for rescue. And in fact the carts carrying the lifeboat and mortar did finally arrive, but no one was willing or able to launch the boat in a hurricane surf. The mortar, which had to be fired against the wind, was found to be useless. For another two hours or more the lifesaving team stood around on the beach and stared at the wreck and the survivors stared back, while the scavengers went about their business. Bangs renewed his arguments, but the passengers would not listen to him. Finally, exasperated, he shouted, "Save yourselves!" and jumped overboard, followed by most of the crew. Four stayed on board: the steward Bates, who had a son Nino's age home in England; the carpenter; the cook; and a very old, sick sailor.

About three o'clock the ship began to break up. The cabin had been swept away, and now the forecastle was flooded and the last remaining mast was beginning to loosen, prying the deck up with it. The eight people on board gathered around it, and Bates made a last desperate effort to persuade Margaret to part with Nino. Even as he succeeded, Ossoli was washed overboard, but Margaret, intent on her child, did not see him go. A moment later a last, mountainous wave broke over the vessel, carrying off the mast and everyone remaining on board. The cook and the carpenter, thrown clear, saw Ossoli and Celeste cling for a moment to the rigging, then disappear. There was no sign of Margaret. The bodies of Nino and the steward were washed up on the beach a few minutes later.

EPILOGUE

When news of the wreck reached Massachusetts, Ellery Channing and Thoreau went to Fire Island to help search for the personal effects of the Ossolis. The body of Nino, buried by the grieving sailors among the dunes, was brought back to Massachusetts and buried at Mt. Auburn cemetery in Cambridge. Celeste's body was recovered, but the bodies of Margaret and Ossoli never were found. There is one unsubstantiated story, told many years later by a man who was a child on the island at the time of the wreck, that the unidentified bodies of a man and woman were washed up several days later and that Horace Greeley, being notified, refused to claim them. The informant said they were then surreptitiously buried on Coney Island by the sea captain who found them, who for some reason thought he had violated the law.[1] The story is probably apocryphal (Why should Greeley refuse? Why wasn't the family notified?), but it does raise the merest shadow of a question that will never be answered. Of the Ossolis' possessions only a trunkful of letters and some of Nino's clothes were found. The manuscript of Margaret's book, which would have made a significant contribution to the study of modern Italian history, was lost.

Among her friends, shock and grief were tinged with relief that she would not have to face what seemed to them to be a hopelessly uphill struggle. Emerson, Channing, and the Springs had all urged her at the last minute to stay in Italy, but by then it was too late. "She died in a happy hour for herself," Emerson wrote Carlyle. "Her health was much exhausted. Her marriage would have taken her away from us all, and there was a subsistence yet to be secured, and diminished powers, and old age."[2] But in his own journal he was more optimistic:

> The timorous said "What shall she do?" . . . But she had only to open her mouth and a triumphant success awaited her. She would fast enough have disposed of the circumstances and the bystanders. . . . Here were already mothers waiting tediously for her coming, for the education of their daughters.[3]

Within weeks after the tragedy Emerson, William Channing, Ward, and a few others were collecting Margaret's papers with the intention of publishing a memoir. Emerson no more wanted to edit this than he had the *Dial,* but he was maneuvered into taking the leading role. Ward soon withdrew, and Channing and James Freeman Clarke were coeditors. The resulting volumes, published in 1852, represent a conscientious attempt to draw an honest portrait, but they are colored by an overriding anxiety not to offend anyone and by the editors' own prejudices. Responsibility for the mutilation and suppression of a great deal of material must be shared by Margaret's family and many of her friends. The editors subjected the papers that did reach them to further heavy censorship, rearranging and rewording passages that were written at quite different times in order to deliberately obscure the context or make them conform to some thematic pattern. If there was anything relating to George Davis, it disappeared, along with almost all the Ward material. The Nathan letters no doubt would have gone as well had they been available. All evidence of her love affair with Ossoli is suppressed, so that she is made to seem less of a social rebel than she was. There is no adequate idea given of her political beliefs and activities in Europe, partly because the editors were so far removed from her during those years; accounts written by Mazzini and the Brownings were somehow lost. The Negative allusions to people are excised, so that although we are often told about Margaret's famous wit, we are left with precious few examples of it. Her less attractive traits, including her self-important airs and her tendency to morbid depression, are given full weight. Her balanced judgment, which was expressed mostly in her published writings, is not well presented. The picture that emerges from the *Memoirs* is of a tender-hearted, passionate woman, fitfully strong but very much at the mercy of her emotions and subject to frequent attacks of the vapors. There is heavy emphasis on the romantic and religious side of her nature, but little on the classical side, to which she owed not only the shrewdness of her criticism but the stoical toughness that kept her idealism from shattering completely in its repeated collisions with reality.

Although the public eulogizing continued for some time after her death, so did the more outrageous local anecdotes about her, polished into little gems of social history to be passed to the next generation. In America the "Margaret Myth" was given a seal of authenticity by the publication of Hawthorne's journal notes in 1895. Harriet Martineau's *Autobiography,* published in 1877, had much the same effect in England, but there the printed attacks on Margaret had begun much earlier, soon after the publication of the *Memoirs.* In a discussion of the British reviewers' comments on the *Memoirs,* Frances M. Barbour points out that the reception of the book ranged from patronizing to hysterically hostile. The reviewers generally ignored Margaret's stature as a critic, but there was a good deal of righteous fuming over her personal life and her unwomanly abundance of pride. Barbour concludes, "It is strange . . . that only two reviews out of more than twelve arrived at anything like a just estimate of her work. . . . It was Margaret Fuller Ossoli, wife and mother, not Margaret Fuller, woman of letters, who interested English critics in 1852." [4]

In justice to the reviewers, it should be remembered that the *Memoirs* itself neglects Margaret's work in favor of her personality. But most of the English critics used the book as an excuse for expressing their personal views about Margaret. Of particular interest is a passage Barbour quotes from a *Westminster Review* piece, which turns out to have been written by the young George Eliot, still Mary Ann Evans and silent coeditor of the journal: "From the time she became a mother till the final tragedy . . . [Margaret Fuller] was an altered woman, and evinced a greatness of soul and heroism of character so grand and subduing, that we feel disposed to extend to her whole career the admiration and sympathy inspired by the closing scenes." [5] This is meant to be complimentary, and the rest of the review is generous. But the inference that before she had a child Margaret was not capable of "greatness of soul" and so on, is unfair, and more than a little incongruous considering its source.

A stronger, more mischievous version of this theme showed up in the *Prospective Review*. Here the writer recoils from Margaret's socialism and finds her tolerance of George Sand's amours "unspeakably shocking," but waxes poetic about the wonders wrought by marriage and maternity. In terms which Queen Victoria and Sigmund Freud alike would have found admirable, he rhapsodizes about Margaret's salvation through the miracle of biology. She becomes "a new creature, a thorough woman." She "flowers like a rhododendron, or an azalea taken from a clay soil." [6]

The damage done by such well-meaning friends was subtle and oblique; but for a forthright example of antifeminist bias we can turn to the *New Quarterly* reviewer, whose frenzied invective matches Hawthorne's. Even given the British tradition of *ad hominem* reviews, it was a rather remarkable performance:

> Margaret Fuller was one of those he-women, who, thank Heaven! for the most part figure and flourish, and have their fame on the other side of the Atlantic. She was an intellectual Bloomer of the largest calibre. She was an Encyclopedia in cerulean stockings. She understood Socrates better than Plato did, Faust better than Goethe did, Kant Philosophy better than Kant did . . . but alack the difference between an encyclopedia bound in calf and an encyclopedia moving in blue stockings. Every fact, word, thought, idea, theory, notion, line, verse, that crowded in the cranium of Margaret Fuller was a weapon. They shot from her like pellets from a steam gun. She bristled all over with transcendentalism, assaulted you with metaphysics, suffocated you with mythology, peppered you with

ethics, and struck you down with heavy history. . . . We need
hardly say that we do not recommend this book to English family
reading . . . we think it is not a nice book for English ladies, and
not an entertaining book for English gentlemen.[7]

The *New Quarterly* reviewer went on to sneer that she actually
did very little, and stripped of its malice, the comment is not
without foundation. The question "What did she *do?*" is still
often asked, and a mechanical recitation of the various hats she
wore is unsatisfying. She shares with Poe the distinction of being
our first major literary critic; she was our first woman foreign correspondent; she contributed much to the feminist movement and to
the rise of American Romanticism. She went further than any
other woman of her time in forcing an unwilling public to accept
the idea of a woman as a major intellectual figure. The effect she
had on women's ability to believe in themselves is immeasurable,
and her thinking on androgeny and vocational equality is still vital
today. She brought a unique journalistic perspective to mid-cen-
tury revolutionary Europe, where she was put in the position—the
irony of which she fully understood—of seeing the Old World
transformed by early American ideals, even while America itself
began to turn away from them.

But ultimately she should be remembered for what she was
rather than what she did. Her achievement cannot be measured except in terms of the handicaps under which she gained it. She wrote
relatively little as compared with the giants of her century, and
though she had broader insights than most, by no stretch of the
imagination can she be called a first-rate writer. But in carving a
niche for herself on the enormous wall of resistance that faced her,
she left a foothold for others. In this respect she may more closely
resemble someone like the self-educated black abolitionist leader
Frederick Douglass than she does any of her white male contemporaries. The psychological burdens of a white woman were similar
in kind, if not in degree, to those of a man born into slavery. They
took their toll, particularly during the last two years of her life, but
even then she did not mistake her personal exhaustion for the
defeat of the ideals in which she believed. Given the circumstances
of her life, it took an uncommon variety of strength and courage to
continue to accept the Universe, warts and all.

NOTES

ABBREVIATIONS

HL: Houghton Library, Harvard University; general reference #fMS Am 1086 unless otherwise indicated. Numerals refer to volume numbers, letters to one of three boxes (A,B,C) of miscellaneous materials. Each volume contains its own index, and there is also a master index of Fuller papers. Serious scholars are urged to obtain a copy of Robert N. Hudspeth's "Calendar of the Letters of Margaret Fuller" (*Studies in the American Renaissance,* 1976) for a definitive dating of letters.

Mem.:   *Memoirs of Margaret Fuller Ossoli,* ed. Ralph Waldo Emerson, William Henry Channing, and James Freeman Clarke (Boston: Phillips, Sampson, 1852; reprinted by Burt Franklin, 1972).

BPL: Boston Public Library, Department of Rare Books and Manuscripts. References are in item numbers, general reference #MS Am 1450.

MHS: Margaret Fuller Commonplace Book, 1844; MS journal at the Massachusetts Historical Society, on deposit by Mrs. Lewis F. Perry.

INTRODUCTION

1. Hoyt, "Glimpses," p. 98. 2. Mem. I, p. 132.

CHAPTER 1

1. Howe, *Reminiscences,* p. 24.
2. HL II.
3. Ibid.
4. Ibid.
5. Ibid.
6. Ibid.
7. Ibid.
8. Ibid.
9. Ibid.
10. Ibid.
11. HL I.

CHAPTER 2

1. HL III.
2. Mem. I, pp. 13–14.
3. Ibid., p. 14.
4. Higginson, *Ossoli,* p. 17.
5. Fuller, *Recollections,* p. 10.
6. HL II.
7. Mem. I, p. 15.
8. Ibid., pp. 17–18.
9. Ibid., p. 18.
10. Ibid., p. 20.
11. Ibid., p. 20.
12. Ibid., p. 22.
13. Ibid., p. 28.
14. Ibid., pp. 27–28.
15. HL III.
16. Ibid.
17. Mem. I, p. 25.
18. Ibid., p. 30.
19. HL III.
20. Mem. I, p. 23.
21. Ibid., pp. 35, 38–39.
22. HL II.
23. Ibid.
24. Ibid.
25. See especially HL II, 1/18/19. 2/17/19.
26. HL II.
27. Ibid.
28. Ibid.
29. HL III.
30. Ibid.
31. Ibid.
32. Ibid.
33. Ibid.
34. Ibid.
35. Ibid.
36. HL V.
37. HL III.
38. HL V.
39. HL IX.
40. Ibid.
41. HL IV.
42. HL X.
43. HL IX.

CHAPTER 3

1. HL IX.
2. Mem. II, p. 5.
3. HL VIII.
4. HL IV.

5. HL X.
6. HL V.
7. HL IV.
8. Higginson, *Ossoli,* p. 23.
9. HL WORKS III.
10. HL IV.
11. Mem. I, p. 229.
12. HL IV.
13. Ibid.
14. Ibid.
15. Ibid.
16. Ibid.
17. Ibid.
18. Ibid.
19. Ibid.
20. HL X.
21. HL V.
22. Ibid.
23. HL IX.
24. HL V.
25. Ibid.
26. Miller, *Fuller,* p. 5.
27. Quoted in full in Mem. I, pp. 42–52.
28. Mem. I, p. 57.
29. HL V.

CHAPTER 4

1. Brown, *Always Young,* p. 153.
2. Ibid., p. 136.
3. Mem. I, p. 286.
4. Ibid., p. 75.
5. Ibid., p. 95.
6. HL, WORKS I.
7. Mem. II, pp. 6–7.
8. Ibid., pp. 7–8.
9. Clarke, *Letters,* p. 15.
10. Ibid., p. 17; see also pp. 18, 26.
11. Higginson, *Ossoli,* p. 36.
12. Ibid., p. 37.
13. Ibid., p. 37.
14. [Farrar], *Friend,* p. 193.
15. Ibid., p. 33.
16. Mem. I, pp. 52–53.
17. Ibid., p. 56.
18. Higginson, *Ossoli,* p. 25.
19. Brown, *Always Young,* p. 107.
20. Mem. I, p. 114.
21. HL, WORKS I.

CHAPTER 5

1. HL X.
2. Fuller, *Recollections,* p. 30.
3. HL WORKS I.
4. Child, *Housewife.* These two extracts are taken from pp. 16, 78–79.
5. HL X.
6. Clarke, *Letters,* pp. 73–74.
7. HL WORKS I.
8. Ibid.
9. Mem. I, p. 136.
10. Ibid., pp. 139–41.
11. HL WORKS III.
12. HL WORKS I.
13. HL X.
14. Ibid.
15. Chevigny, *Woman,* p. 179.
16. Jones, "Fuller's Attempt."
17. Mem. I, p. 154.
18. HL WORKS III.
19. HL WORKS I.
20. Mem. I, pp. 157–58.
21. Ibid., p. 161.

CHAPTER 6

1. Emerson, *Journals,* IV, p. 237.
2. Emerson, "The American Scholar."
3. Emerson, *Journals,* VI, p. 366.
4. BPL 273.
5. Miller, *Fuller,* p. 52.
6. Strauch, "Repulsions."
7. Mem. I, p. 202.
8. Ibid., p. 202.
9. Ibid., p. 214.
10. Emerson, *Journals,* IV, p. 460.
11. Ibid., p. 216.
12. Ibid., p. 9.
13. Ibid., p. 81.
14. Emerson, *Letters,* II, p. 36.
15. Peabody, *Record,* p. 14.
16. HL IX.
17. Mem. I, p. 175.
18. HL WORKS I.
19. Ibid.
20. Fuller, *Recollections,* p. 65.
21. Mem. I, p. 229.
22. HL Box A, in a letter to Higginson.
23. Kirby, *Years,* pp. 213–14.
24. HL, Tappan papers, 3/13/45.
25. Mem. I, pp. 172–73.
26. Ibid., p. 175.
27. Shepard, *Progress,* pp. 195–96.
28. Emerson, *Letters,* II, pp. 61–62.
29. Higginson, *Ossoli,* p. 78.
30. Shepard, *Progress,* p. 208.
31. Mem. I, pp. 193–94.
32. BPL 79.

CHAPTER 7

1. Emerson, *Journals,* IV, p. 216.
2. Emerson, *Letters,* II, p. 168.
3. Emerson, *Journals,* IV, p. 238.
4. Ibid., pp. 126–27.
5. Mem. I, p. 281.
6. Ibid., p. 294.
7. BPL 160.
8. Johnson, "Margaret Fuller" (HL Box A).
9. BPL 181.
10. BPL 161.
11. Emerson, "The American Scholar."
12. Crowe, *Ripley,* p. 75.
13. HL IX.
14. Mem II, p. 93. He notes that Margaret used the same term to describe Mme de Staël.
15. Mem. I, p. 219.
16. Ibid., p. 229.
17. Ibid., p. 227.
18. Ibid., p. 232.
19. Ibid., p. 297.
20. Emerson, *Letters,* II, p. 143.
21. Mem. I, pp. 183–84.
22. Ibid., pp. 185–86.
23. HL IX.
24. BPL 88.
25. Higginson, *Ossoli,* p. 90.
26. Cooke, *Dial,* 2, p. 60.
27. Emerson, *Letters,* II, p. 143.
28. BPL 122.
29. Mem. I, p. 237.
30. Ibid., pp. 291–92.
31. HL WORKS I.

CHAPTER 8

1. BPL 68.
2. Emerson, "The Divinity School Address."
3. Emerson, *Letters,* II, p. 202.
4. Mem. II, pp. 20–21.
5. Mem. I, pp. 332–33.
6. Ibid., pp. 326–37.
7. Dall, *Margaret.*
8. Emerson, *Letters,* II, pp. 384–85.
9. Dall, *Margaret,* p. 156.
10. Mem. I, p. 281.
11. Ibid., pp. 280–81.
12. Ibid., p. 340.
13. Martineau, *Autobiography,* II, pp. 71–72.
14. Higginson, *Ossoli,* p. 127.
15. BPL 37.
16. Ibid., 38.
17. Higginson, *Ossoli,* p. 150.
18. BPL 37.
19. Emerson, *Correspondence,* p. 332.
20. Cooke, *Dial,* I, p. 170.
21. Emerson, *Correspondence,* p. 287.
22. Cooke, *Dial,* I, p. 78.
23. Ibid., p. 75.
24. Emerson, *Correspondence,* pp. 312–13.
25. HL WORKS II.
26. [Ripley], *Dial,* 2, (January 1841), "Woman," pp. 364–66.
27. Fuller, *Dial,* 4, "Lawsuit," pp. 14, 43–44, 47.

CHAPTER 9

1. Frothingham, *Transcendentalism,* p. 126.
2. Emerson, *Journals,* VI, p. 82.
3. Mem. I, p. 236.
4. Ibid., p. 234.
5. Miller, *Fuller,* p. x.
6. HL WORKS I.
7. Mem. I, p. 279.
8. Mem. II, p. 96.
9. Ibid., p. 58.
10. HL WORKS I.
11. HL IX.
12. Ibid.
13. Emerson, *Journals,* V, pp. 279–80.
14. Mem. II, p. 107.
15. Ibid., pp. 38–39.
16. Mem. I, p. 309.
17. BPL 73.
18. Ibid., 120; Mem I, p. 293.
19. Mem. I, p. 295.
20. Emerson, *Journals,* VI, p. 361.
21. Ibid., p. 369.
22. Ibid., p. 134.
23. Mem. I, pp. 295–96.
24. Emerson, *Journals,* IV, p. 333.
25. BPL 119.
26. Mem. I, p. 213.
27. BPL 46.
28. Emerson, *Journals,* VI, p. 166.
29. Emerson, *Letters,* III, p. 35.
30. Ibid., pp. 79–80.
31. Emerson, *Letters,* II, p. 336.
32. Ibid., p. 340.

33. Ibid., p. 455.
34. Myerson, "1842 Journal." (The original is in HL Box A.)
35. Ibid., p. 331.
36. Ibid., p. 332.
37. N. Hawthorne, *American Notebooks,* p. 160.
38. Myerson, "1842 Journal," p. 325.
39. Ibid., p. 336.
40. Emerson, *Letters,* III, p. 89.
41. HL WORKS I.

CHAPTER 10

1. Emerson, *Letters,* II, p. 364.
2. Rusk, *Life,* p. 291.
3. Wagenknecht, *Hawthorne,* p. 164.
4. James, *Hawthorne,* p. 80.
5. Wagenknecht, *Hawthorne,* p. 18.
6. Emerson, *Letters,* III, p. 72.
7. MHS.
8. Ibid.
9. Ibid.
10. As quoted in Frothingham, *Transcendentalism,* pp. 171–72.
11. Frye, *Anatomy,* p. 101.
12. N. Hawthorne, *American Notebooks,* pp. lix–lxi.
13. J. Hawthorne, *Hawthorne,* I, p. 261.

CHAPTER 11

1. All quotations in this chapter, unless otherwise indicated, are from Fuller, *Summer on the Lakes in 1843,* in *At Home and Abroad* (Boston: Crosby, Nichols & Co., 1856).
2. BPL 51.
3. Emerson, *Letters,* III, pp. 200–1.
4. Ibid., p. 177.
5. HL WORKS I.
6. HL WORKS, V.
7. Emerson, *Letters,* III, p. 221.
8. MHS.
9. Ibid.

CHAPTER 12

1. All quotations in this chapter, unless otherwise indicated, are from Fuller, *Woman in the Nineteenth Century* (Boston: John P. Jewett & Co., 1855).
2. BPL 52.
3. Mem. I, p. 235.

CHAPTER *13*

1. HL WORKS II.
2. Mem. II, p. 156.
3. Ibid., pp 156–57.
4. HL WORKS I.
5. Greeley, *Recollections,* p. 104.
6. Kirby, *Years,* p. 214.
7. Mem. II, p. 155.
8. Child, *Letters,* I, p. 23.
9. *N.Y. Daily Tribune,* 19 March 1845.
10. Ibid.
11. Miller, *Fuller,* p. 192.
12. *N.Y. Daily Tribune,* 10 December 1845.
13. Fuller, *Papers,* II, p. 132.
14. *N.Y. Daily Tribune,* 7 December 1844.
15. Ibid., 19 December 1845.
16. HL WORKS II.
17. HL, Ward-Barker Papers, 11/16/45.
18. Emerson, *Letters,* III, p. 268.
19. HL WORKS I.
20. Ibid.
21. Mem. II, p. 166.
22. Fuller, *Love-Letters,* XXX. All subsequent quotations from this book will be indicated in the text by numerals.
23. HL X.
24. HL, Ward-Barker papers, 3/3/46.

CHAPTER *14*

1. Fuller, *At Home,* p. 119.
2. For a good discussion of the development of Margaret Fuller's political consciousness see Allen, ''Impassioned Yankee.'' I disagree, however, with her conclusion that Margaret's idealism made her incapable of compromise.
3. Ibid., p. 124.
4. Ibid., p. 121.
5. Higginson, *Ossoli,* p. 221.
6. Ibid., p. 221.
7. Fuller, *At Home,* p. 128.
8. Martineau, *Autobiography,* II, p. 252.
9. Wade, *Fuller,* p. 176.
10. Fuller, *At Home,* pp. 129–30.
11. Ibid., pp. 131–32.
12. Ibid., p. 136.
13. Mem. II, p. 184.
14. Fuller, *At Home,* p. 144.
15. Ibid., p. 140.
16. Ibid., pp. 159–60.
17. HL WORKS I.
18. Fuller, *At Home,* p. 160.
19. Wade, *Fuller,* p. 199.
20. Fuller, *At Home,* pp. 165–66.
21. Mem. II, p. 184.
22. HL X.
23. Ibid.
24. Mem. II, p. 185.
25. Froude, *Carlyle,* I, p. 401.
26. Mem. II, p. 187.
27. Ibid., pp. 187–88.
28. Fuller, *At Home,* p. 184.
29. Ibid., p. 193.
30. BPL 101.

31. Fuller, *At Home,* p. 205.
32. Mem. II, pp. 195–96.
33. Ibid., p. 198.
34. Ibid., p. 201.

35. Ibid., p. 173.
36. Wellisz, *Friendship,* p. 18.
37. Ibid., p. 23.

CHAPTER *15*

The footnotes for the Italian chapters do not adequately reflect my debt to *The Roman Years of Margaret Fuller,* by Joseph Jay Deiss, which provided many details previously unknown by scholars. I relied on it for corroboration and explanation of primary source materials.

1. Fuller, *At Home,* pp. 217–18.
2. Ibid., p. 220.
3. HL IX.
4. Fuller, *At Home,* p. 221.
5. Ibid., p. 224.
6. HL IX.
7. Wellisz, *Friendship,* p. 20.
8. Fuller, *At Home,* p. 225.
9. Ibid., p. 224.
10. Mem. II, p. 216.
11. Fuller, *At Home,* p. 231.

12. Ibid., p. 238.
13. HL IX.
14. Fuller, *At Home,* p. 240.
15. HL WORKS I.
16. Wade, *Fuller,* pp. 216–17.
17. Mem. II, p. 222.
18. Ibid., p. 223.
19. Ibid., p. 221.
20. HL IX.
21. Deiss, *Roman Years,* p. 84.
22. HL IX.

CHAPTER *16*

1. Fuller, *At Home,* pp. 280–81.
2. Ibid., pp. 296–97.
3. Mem. II, pp. 231–33.
4. HL IX.
5. Ibid.
6. Fuller, *At Home,* p. 306.
7. Ibid., p. 308.
8. Ibid., p. 320.
9. HL IX.
10. Fuller, *At Home,* p. 323.
11. Mem. II, p. 239.
12. BPL 82.
13. Deiss, *Roman Years,* pp. 211–12.

14. HL IX.
15. Mem. II, p. 244.
16. HL XI.
17. HL WORKS II.
18. Ibid.
19. HL IX.
20. Mem. II, p. 278.
21. HL WORKS II.
22. Ibid.
23. Ibid., translation slightly modernized.
24. HL WORKS II.
25. Mem. II, p. 248.

CHAPTER *17*

1. Fuller, *At Home,* p. 337.
2. Mem. II, p. 245.
3. Ibid., p. 254.
4. Fuller, *At Home,* p. 336.
5. Stoddard, *Greeley,* p. 118.
6. Fuller, *At Home,* p. 338.
7. Ibid., p. 340.
8. Ibid., p. 343.
9. HL IX.
10. Fuller, *At Home,* pp. 346–48.
11. Ibid., p. 358.
12. Mem. II, p. 256.
13. Ibid., p. 257.
14. BPL 106.
15. HL IX.
16. Ibid.
17. James, *Story,* I, p. 171.
18. HL IX.
19. HL WORKS II.
20. Mem. II, p. 287.
21. HL WORKS I.
22. Fuller, *At Home,* p. 436.
23. Ibid., pp. 434–35.
24. Mem. II, p. 270.
25. Trevelyan, *Garibaldi's Defence,* p. 231.
26. Fuller, *At Home,* p. 413.
27. Mem. II, p. 268.
28. Ibid., p. 267.

CHAPTER *18*

1. Fuller, *At Home,* pp. 437–38.
2. Higginson, *Ossoli,* p. 266.
3. Ibid., pp. 266–67.
4. BPL 30.
5. Higginson, *Ossoli,* p. 268.
6. Cleveland, *Story,* pp. 244–45.
7. BPL 171.
8. HL VIII.
9. J. Hawthorne, *Hawthorne,* pp. 261–62.
10. Mem. II, pp. 318–19.
11. HL IX.
12. Browning, *Letters,* I, p. 428.
13. HL WORKS I.
14. Browning, *Letters,* I, p. 445.
15. BPL 172.
16. HL IX.
17. Mem. II, p. 326.
18. HL IX.
19. Ibid.
20. Wade, *Fuller,* p. 257.
21. HL IX.
22. Ibid.
23. Mem. II, pp. 268–69.
24. HL IX.
25. Ibid.
26. Ibid.
27. BPL 81b.
28. HL, Ward-Barker Papers, 10/21/49.
29. HL IX.
30. BPL 109.
31. Emerson, *Journals* (ed. Gilman, et al.), XI, p. 463.
32. Deiss, *Roman Years,* pp. 291–92.
33. Emerson, *Journals* (ed. Gilman, et al.), XI, p. 462.
34. Higginson, *Ossoli,* p. 275.
35. Browning, *Letters,* I, pp. 459–60.

CHAPTER *19*

1. HL IX.

EPILOGUE

1. HL Box A.
2. Emerson, *Correspondence,* p. 462.
3. Emerson, *Journals,* VIII, p. 116.
4. Barbour, "British Reviewers," p. 625.
5. *Westminster Review,* April 1852, p. 353; Barbour, "British Reviewers," p. 622.
6. Barbour, "British Reviewers," pp. 622–23.
7. Ibid., pp. 623–25.

BIBLIOGRAPHY

PRIMARY SOURCES

Most important have been manuscripts and other materials in the possession of the Houghton Library at Harvard University and the Boston Public Library. I have also consulted manuscripts from the Massachusetts Historical Society, the New York Public Library, Wellesley College Library, Princeton University Library, and Pennsylvania State University Library.

WORKS BY MARGARET FULLER

At this writing (September 1976), reprints are available of *Life Without and Life Within, Love-Letters of Margaret Fuller, Papers on Literature and Art, At Home and Abroad* (including *Summer on the Lakes*), and *Woman in the Nineteenth Century*. An anthology edited by Joel Myerson, *Margaret Fuller: Essays on American Life and Letters,* will be published soon by the College and University Press of New Haven. Myerson has also prepared two bibliographies of Margaret Fuller's writings, both to be published soon by Burt Franklin: *Margaret Fuller: A Descriptive Primary Bibliography* and *Margaret Fuller: An Annotated Secondary*

Bibliography. A complete collection of Margaret Fuller's letters is being edited by Robert N. Hudspeth, who is also editing the *Tribune* writings in collaboration with Wilma Ebbitt. Hudspeth's "A Calendar of the Letters of Margaret Fuller," an exhaustive list of existing manuscript letters, will appear in the 1976 volume of *Studies in the American Renaissance.*

ORIGINAL EDITIONS

Conversations with Goethe in the Last Years of His Life, Translated from the German of Eckermann. Boston: Hilliard, Gray, 1839.

Günderode: A Translation from the German. Boston: E. P. Peabody, 1842. Completed by Minna Wesselhoeft and published as *Correspondence of Fräulein Günderode and Bettina von Arnim.* Boston: Burnham, 1861.

"The Great Lawsuit: Man vs. Men. Woman vs. Women." *Dial,* 4 (July 1843), pp. 1–47.

Summer on the Lakes, in 1843. Boston: Charles C. Little & James Brown; New York: Charles S. Francis, 1844.

Woman in the Nineteenth Century. New York: Greeley & McElrath, 1845. Reprinted by W. W. Norton.

Papers on Literature and Art. New York: Wiley & Putnam, 1846. Reprinted by AMS Press.

At Home and Abroad, ed. A. B. Fuller. Boston: Crosby, Nichols; London: Sampson Low, Son & Co., 1856. Reprinted by Kennikat Press.

Life Without and Life Within, ed. A. B. Fuller. Boston: Brown, Taggard, & Chase; New York: Sheldon; Philadelphia: J. B. Lippincott; London: Sampson Low, Son & Co., 1860. Reprinted by Gregg Press.

Love-Letters of Margaret Fuller, 1845–1846. New York: D. Appleton, 1903. Reprinted by Greenwood Press.

THREE ANTHOLOGIES OF MARGARET FULLER'S WRITINGS ARE NOW AVAILABLE:

Chevigny, Bell Gale. *The Woman and the Myth: Margaret Fuller's Life and Writings.* New York: The Feminist Press, 1976.

Miller, Perry. *Margaret Fuller: American Romantic.* New York: Doubleday, 1963. Reprinted by Cornell University Press, 1970.

Wade, Mason. *The Writings of Margaret Fuller.* New York: The Viking Press, 1941.

BIOGRAPHIES OF MARGARET FULLER

Anthony, Katharine. *Margaret Fuller: A Psychological Portrait*. Darby, Penn.: Darby Books, 1920.

Bell, Margaret. *Margaret Fuller*. New York: Albert & Charles Boni, 1930.

Braun, F. A. *Margaret Fuller and Goethe*. New York: Henry Holt, 1910.

Brown, Arthur W. *Margaret Fuller*. United States Authors Series. New York: Twayne Publishers, 1964.

Chipperfield, Faith. *In Quest of Love*. New York: Coward-McCann, 1957.

Deiss, Joseph Jay. *The Roman Years of Margaret Fuller*. New York: Thomas Y. Crowell, 1969.

Fuller, Margaret. *Memoirs of Margaret Fuller Ossoli,* ed. Ralph Waldo Emerson, William Henry Channing, and James Freeman Clarke. Boston: Phillips, Sampson, 1852. Reprinted by Burt Franklin, 1972.

Higginson, Thomas Wentworth. *Margaret Fuller Ossoli*. American Men of Letters Series. Boston: Houghton Mifflin, 1884. Reprinted by Haskell House, 1968.

Howe, Julia Ward. *Margaret Fuller*. Boston: Roberts Bros., 1883.

Stern, Madeleine B. *The Life of Margaret Fuller*. New York: E. P. Dutton, 1942.

Wade, Mason. *Margaret Fuller: Whetstone of Genius*. New York: The Viking Press, 1940. Reprinted by Augustus M. Kelley, 1973.

SECONDARY SOURCES

Allen, Margaret V. "This Impassioned Yankee." *Southwest Review,* 58 (1972), pp. 162–71.

Barbour, Frances M. "Margaret Fuller and the British Reviewers." *New England Quarterly,* 9 (Dec. 1936), pp. 618–25.

Beecher, Catherine E. *A Treatise on Domestic Economy*. Boston: Thos. H. Webb, 1842.

Bolster, Arthur S., Jr. *James Freeman Clarke*. Boston: Beacon Press, 1954.

Brooks, Van Wyck. *The Flowering of New England*. New York: E. P. Dutton, 1936.

Brown, Arthur W. *Always Young for Liberty: A Biography of William Ellery Channing*. Syracuse: Syracuse University Press, 1956.

Browning, Elizabeth Barrett. *The Letters of Elizabeth Barrett Browning*, ed. Frederic G. Kenyon. New York: MacMillan, 1897.

Child, Lydia Maria. *The American Frugal Housewife*. New York: Samuel S. and William Wood, 1860.

————. *Letters from New York*. New York: C. S. Francis, 1845.

Clarke, James Freeman. *Autobiography*. Boston: Houghton Mifflin, 1892.

————. *The Letters of James Freeman Clarke to Margaret Fuller*, ed. John Wesley Thomas. Hamburg: Cram, de Gruyter, 1957.

Cleveland, Cecilia. *The Story of a Summer*. New York: G. W. Carleton, 1874.

Commager, H. Steele. *Theodore Parker*. Boston: Little, Brown, 1936.

Cooke, G. W. *An Historical and Biographical Introduction to Accompany the DIAL*. New York: Russell & Russell, 1961.

Crowe, Charles. *George Ripley: Transcendentalist and Utopian Socialist*. Athens, Ga.: University of Georgia Press, 1967.

Dall, Caroline Healey. *Margaret and Her Friends*. Boston: Roberts Bros., 1895.

Detti, Emma. *Margaret Fuller Ossoli e i suoi Correspondenti*. Firenze: Felice Le Monnier, 1942.

Emerson, Ralph W. "The American Scholar." In *Selections from Ralph Waldo Emerson*, ed. Stephen E. Whicher. Cambridge: Riverside Press, 1957.

————. *The Correspondence of Emerson and Carlyle*, ed. Joseph Slater. New York: Columbia University Press, 1964.

————. "The Divinity School Address." In *Selections from Ralph Waldo Emerson*, ed. Stephen E. Whicher. Cambridge: Riverside Press, 1957.

————. *Journals of Ralph Waldo Emerson*, ed. Edward Waldo Emerson and Waldo Emerson Forbes. Boston: Houghton Mifflin, 1910.

————. *Journals of Ralph Waldo Emerson*, ed. William H. Gilman, et al., Vol. XI. Cambridge: Harvard University Press, 1975.

————. *The Letters of Ralph Waldo Emerson*, ed. Ralph L. Rusk. New York: Columbia University Press, 1939.

[Farrar, Eliza]. *The Young Lady's Friend*. Boston: American Stationers', 1836.

Frothingham, Octavius B. *Transcendentalism in New England*. Boston: American Unitarian Assn., 1903.

Froude, James Anthony. *Thomas Carlyle: A History of His Life in London*. London: Longmans, Green, 1885.

Frye, Northrup. *The Anatomy of Criticism*. Princeton: Princeton University Press, 1971.

Fuller, Arthur Buckminster. *Historical Notices of Thomas Fuller and His Descendents*. Cambridge: 1902.

Fuller, Richard F. *Recollections of Richard F. Fuller*. Boston: 1936.

Greeley, Horace. *Recollections of a Busy Life*. New York: J. B. Ford, 1868.

Hawthorne, Julian. *Nathaniel Hawthorne and His Wife*. Boston: Houghton Mifflin, 1895.

Hawthorne, Nathaniel. *The American Notebooks,* ed. Randall Stewart. New Haven: Yale University Press, 1932.

———. *The Blithedale Romance*. New York: Dell Publishing, Laurel Edition, 1962.

Holt, Edgar. *The Making of Italy, 1815–1870*. New York: Atheneum, 1971.

Howe, Julia Ward. *Reminiscences*. Boston: Houghton Mifflin, 1899.

Hoyt, Edward A., and Brigham, Loriman S. "Glimpses of Margaret Fuller: The Greene Street School and Florence." *New England Quarterly,* 29 (Mar. 1956), 87–98.

Hudspeth, Robert N. *Ellery Channing*. United States Authors Series. New York: Twayne Publishers, 1973.

James, Henry. *Hawthorne*. New York: Harper & Bros., 1901.

———. *William Wetmore Story and His Friends*. Boston: Houghton Mifflin, 1903.

Johnson, Harriet Hall. "Margaret Fuller as Known by Her Scholars." *Christian Register,* April 21, 1910.

Jones, Alexander. "Margaret Fuller's Attempt to Write Fiction." *Boston Public Library Quarterly,* 6 (April 1954), pp. 67–73.

Jones, Louis C. "A Margaret Fuller Letter to Elizabeth Barrett Browning." *American Literature,* 9 (Mar. 1937), pp. 70–71.

King, Bolton. *Mazzini*. London: J. M. Dent, 1902.

Kirby, Georgianna Bruce. *Years of Experience*. Reprinted from 1887 edition. New York: AMS Press, 1971.

Martin, Willard E., Jr. "A Last Letter of Margaret Fuller Ossoli." *American Literature*, 5 (Mar. 1933), pp. 66–69.

Martineau, Harriet. *Autobiography*. (2 vol.) London: Smith, Elder, 1877.

———. *Society in America*. New York and London: Saunders & Otley, 1837.

McGill, Frederick T. *Channing of Concord*. New Brunswick, N.J.: Rutgers University Press, 1967.

McMaster, Helen Neill. "Margaret Fuller as Literary Critic." *University of Buffalo Studies*, 7 (Dec. 1928).

Miller, Perry. *The American Transcendentalists*. New York: Doubleday, 1957. Reprinted by Cornell University Press, 1970.

———. "I Find No Intellect Comparable to My Own." *American Heritage*, 8 (Feb. 1954), pp. 96–99.

Myerson, Joel. "Margaret Fuller's 1842 Journal: At Concord with the Emersons." *Harvard Library Bulletin*, 21 (July 1973), pp. 320–340.

Orr, Evelyn W. "Two Margaret Fuller Manuscripts." *New England Quarterly*, 11 (Dec. 1938), pp. 794–802.

Peabody, E. P. *Record of a School*. Reprinted from 1836 edition. New York, Arno Press, 1969.

Randel, W. P. "Hawthorne, Channing, and Margaret Fuller." *American Literature*, 10 (Jan. 1939), pp. 472–79.

[Ripley, Sophia]. "Woman." *Dial* 2 (Jan. 1841), pp. 362–66 (signed *W.N.*).

Rostenberg, Leona. "Mazzini to Margaret Fuller, 1847–1849." *American Historical Review*, 47 (Oct. 1941), pp. 73–80.

Rusk, Ralph L. *The Life of Ralph Waldo Emerson*. New York: Columbia University Press, 1949.

Shepard, Odell. *Pedlar's Progress*. Boston: Little, Brown, 1937.

Stern, Madeleine B. "Margaret Fuller's Schooldays in Cambridge." *New England Quarterly*, 13 (June 1940), pp. 207–22.

BIBLIOGRAPHY

Stoddard, Henry Luther. *Horace Greeley: Printer, Editor, Crusader*. New York: G. P. Putnam's Sons, 1946.

Strauch, Carl F. "Hatred's Swift Repulsions: Emerson, Margaret Fuller, and Others." *Studies in Romanticism,* 7 (Winter 1968), pp. 65–103.

Trevelyan, George M. *Garibaldi's Defence of the Roman Republic*. London: Longmans, Green, 1907.

Wagenknecht, Edward. *Nathaniel Hawthorne: Man and Writer*. New York: Oxford University Press, 1961.

Warfel, Harry R. "Margaret Fuller and Ralph Waldo Emerson." *Publications of the Modern Language Association,* 50 (June 1935), pp. 576–94.

Wellisz, Leopold. *The Friendship of Margaret Fuller D'Ossoli and Adam Mickiewicz*. New York: Polish Book Importing Co., 1947.

BACKGROUND READING

Alcott, Bronson. *The Journals of Bronson Alcott,* ed. Odell Shepard. Boston: Little, Brown, 1938.

Belden, E. Porter. *New York: Past, Present and Future*. New York: G. P. Putnam, 1849.

Best, Geoffrey. *Mid-Victorian Britain*. New York: Schocken Books, 1972.

Cornelius, Mrs. *The Young Housekeeper's Friend*. Boston: Tappan, Whittemore & Mason, 1850.

Fasel, George. *Europe in Upheaval: The Revolutions of 1848*. Rand McNally European History Series. Chicago: Rand McNally, 1970.

Hale, Edward Everett. *Recollections of a New England Boyhood*. New York: Cassell Publishing, 1893.

Hammond, J. F. and Hammond, Barbara. *The Age of the Chartists*. London: Longmans, Green, 1930.

Higginson, Thomas Wentworth. *Cheerful Yesterdays*. Cambridge: Riverside Press, 1898.

———. *Old Cambridge*. New York: MacMillan, 1899.

Howe, M. A. de Wolfe. *Boston, the Place and Its People.* New York: Mac-Millan, 1903.

Marraro, Howard R. *American Opinion on the Unification of Italy, 1846–1861.* New York: Columbia University Press, 1932.

Mazzini, Giuseppe. *Letters to an English Family, 1844–1854,* ed. E. F. Richards. London: John Lane, 1920–22.

A Picture of New York in 1846. New York: Homans & Ellis, 1846.

Robertson, Priscilla. *Revolutions of 1848: A Social History.* Princeton: Princeton University Press, 1952.

Smith, Matthew Hale. *Sunshine and Shadow in New York.* Hartford: J. B. Burr, 1869.

Swift, Lindsay. *Brook Farm.* New York: MacMillan, 1900.

Talmon, J. L. *Romanticism and Revolt: Europe 1815–1848.* New York: Harcourt, Brace & World, 1967.

Tharp, Louise Hall. *The Peabody Sisters of Salem.* Boston: Little, Brown, 1950.

Whitridge, Arnold. *Men in Crisis.* New York: Charles Scribner's Sons, 1949.

Young, G. M. *Early Victorian England.* London: Oxford University Press, 1934.

INDEX

Books and articles are by Margaret Fuller unless otherwise indicated

abolitionism, 9, 53, 109, 112, 152-153, 160, 164, 237, 286
acceptance, doctrine of, 1, 67-68, 86-87, 342
Adams, John, 50
Adams, John Quincy, 54, 66, 70-71, 72
Aids to Reflection (Coleridge), 66
Alcott, A Bronson: controversy over, 105-106, 114-116, 141; and *Dial,* 153-155, 157, 158; and MF, 105-106, 111-116, 141; idealism of, 99-100, 120; and Millerites, 165; retirement of, 143; as Transcendentalist, 124-126
Alfieri, Count Vittorio, 77, 268
American Frugal Housewife, The (Child), 79-80
American Indians, MF on, 203-207
American literature, MF essay on, 259
"American Scholar, The" (Emerson address), 122-123, 140
Anatomy of Criticism, The (Frye), 193-194

Anti-Slavery Standard, 237
Arconati, Mme (Marchioness Costanza Arconati Visconti), 270-271, 272, 283, 290, 319, 325
Ariosto, Lodovico, 109
Astor, John Jacob, 230
Atheneum (Boston), 134-135
At Home and Abroad, 334n
Atkinson, Henry, 249
Austen, Jane, 57
Autobiography (Martineau), 152, 249, 340

Balzac, Honoré de, 234
Bancroft, George, 49, 50, 66, 81, 154, 192, 242
Barbour, Frances M., 340-341
Barlow, Almira, 76, 87, 95, 138, 148, 187, 193
Bartol, Cyrus, 125
Beecher, Catherine, 78-79, 80, 216
Beecher, Lyman, 52
Beethoven, MF on, 160

Belgiojoso, Princess Cristina Trivulzio, 283-285, 306
Bells and Pomegranates (Browning), MF review of, 234
Béranger, Pierre Jean de, 246, 260
Berri, Duchesse de, 272
Beyond God the Father (Daly), 220n
Bible, the, 86, 88, 96, 107-108
Biographia Literaria (Coleridge), 66
Blanc, Louis, 325
Blithedale Romance (Hawthorne), 187, 190-191, 193-195
Bloomingdale Asylum, 230, 231
Boston Quarterly Review, 125
Boston Times, 157
Brentano, Bettina, 175
Brontë, Emily, 193n
Brontë sisters, 57
Brook Farm, 125, 161, 165, 177-178, 187-189, 243, 287
Brown, Arthur W., 67
Browne, M. A., 57
Browne, Sir Thomas, 66, 101
Browning, Elizabeth Barrett, 113, 234, 319-320, 325, 330, 340
Browning, Robert, 234, 320, 325, 340
Brownson, Orestes, 114, 125, 128, 154, 157
Bruce, Georgianna, *see* Kirby, Georgianna Bruce
Bull, Ole, 236
Bulwer-Lytton, Edward, MF article on, 82
Burns, Robert, 246, 249, 250
Byron, George Gordon, Lord, 25n, 85

Calvinism, 51-52, 67, 124
Cambridgeport Private Grammar School, 64n
Carlyle, Jane, 257-258
Carlyle, Thomas: and *Dial*, 154, 157-158; and Emerson, 100, 101; and MF, 66, 85, 87, 96, 234, 246, 256-258, 317, 320; psychosomatic illnesses of, 113
Cass, Lewis, Jr., 301, 308, 311, 312, 314-315, 321
Catlin, George, 205
Century of Struggle (Flexner), 109n
Cervantes, Miguel de, 24, 25

Chalmers, Thomas, 250
Chambers, William and Robert, 250
Chambers's Edinburgh Journal, 250
Channing, Edward Tyrrel, 49
Channing, Ellen Kilshaw Fuller: as member of Fuller household, 28, 34, 76, 94, 106, 138, 140; as wife of W. E. Channing, 178-179, 184, 192, 209, 210, 243-244, 328
Channing, Lucy, 236
Channing, Margaret, 192, 209
Channing, Mary, 148
Channing, Susan, 36-37
Channing, Dr. William Ellery, 5, 9, 22, 51-53, 110-112, 116, 124, 142-143, 176, 185-186
Channing, William Ellery: and *Dial*, 155-157; and MF, 111, 167, 181, 235-236, 338; and Hawthorne, 193; marriage of, *see* Channing, Ellen Kilshaw Fuller; on Tribune, 210-211, 235
Channing, William Henry: in Cincinnati, 71, 138; and *Dial;* 154-155; MF's friendship with, 40, 55, 111, 138, 167, 192, 208, 210, 211, 318, 339; quoted, 37, 58-59, 128, 145-146; Transcendentalism of, 125, 229
Charles Albert, King of Piedmont, 268, 280, 285, 287, 288, 304, 305
Chartist movement, 247
Chaucer, Geoffrey, 101
Chevigny, Bell Gale, 1
Chiara (Angelo's nurse), 294, 299, 307, 315
Child, David Lee, 237
Child, Lydia Maria, 55, 79-80, 111, 148, 153, 159, 237; MF compared to, 3, 254; *Letters from New York*, 208, 231; *Woman in the Nineteenth Century* reviewed by, 235
Chopin, Frédéric, 284
"Christabel" (Coleridge), 193-194
Christian Examiner, The, 82, 124
Christian Register, 154
Cicero, 32, 35, 43
Cincinnati Gazette, 178
Clapp, Eliza Thayer, 159
Clarke, James Freeman: and Alcott, 114; attitude toward women, 190; and *Dial*,

Clarke, James Freeman (Cont.)
150, 155, 156, 157; education of, 22; MF's
friendship with, 59-61, 66-69, 81, 82-83,
86, 88, 90, 95, 102, 129, 339; occult
interests of, 127-128; quoted, 4, 55, 60,
66, 69, 196, 204; as Transcendentalist,
124-126, 165
Clarke, Sarah, 55, 81, 107, 118, 143, 146,
159, 196-208 passim, 219
Clarke, William, 196, 200
Coleridge, Samuel Taylor, 53, 66, 68, 84,
101, 110, 124, 193, 221, 249
Combe, Andrew, 250
Conversations (1839-42), 108, 144-153,
166, 175, 186, 208
Conversations with Children on the Gospels
(Alcott), 107, 114
Conversations with Goethe (Eckermann),
MF translation of, 89, 117, 143
Cooke, G. W., 133
Correspondence of Günderode and Bettina
von Arnim, MF's translation of, 175
Crabbe, George, MF article on, 82
Cranch, Christopher, 157, 165, 187, 188,
210, 236, 265-266, 276, 297
Cranch, Elizabeth, 236, 276, 297
Crane, Margarett, see Fuller, Margarett
Crane
Crane, Major Peter, 13
Crane family, 13, 18, 32, 38
Crawford, Thomas, 301n, 303
Critique of Pure Reason (Kant), 67, 124
Cropsey, Jaspar, 276
Curtis, George W., 265-266

Daily Advertiser, 81, 114
Dall, Caroline Healey, 113, 150, 151
Daly, Mary, 220n
Dana, Judge Francis, 54
Dana, Richard Henry, 64n, 112, 131, 141
Dana, Judge Samuel, 74
Dante, 109-110, 268
Davis, George, 55, 71, 86, 92, 135, 339
Deiss, Joseph Jay, 2, 289, 328
Delf, Thomas, 251, 255-256
de Quincy, Thomas, 250
Dial: Emerson and, 179-180, 208; in Eng-
land, 254; MF and, 134, 154-162, 166,
172, 176, 185, 229; goals of, 88, 153-158,
286
Dickens, Charles, 234
Dickinson, Emily, 57
Disraeli, 118
Divine Comedy (Dante), 109-110
"Divine Presence in Nature and the Soul,
The" (Parker), 157
"Divinity School Address" (Emerson), 140,
153, 165
Dr. Park's School, Boston, 34, 36-38
Dolores (Harring), 236
Dwight, John Sullivan, 125, 157, 187, 188

Eckermann, Johann Peter, 89, 117, 143, 270
Edgeworth, Maria, 20
Edinburgh Review, 2, 235
Edwards, Jonathan, 51
Eliot, George, 341
Emerson, Charles, 99, 101
Emerson, Edward, 99
Emerson, Ellen (baby), 141
Emerson, Ellen Tucker, 99, 155
Emerson, Lydia Jackson ("Lidian"), 98,
101-102, 105, 124, 126, 148, 157, 177,
182-183
Emerson, Mary Moody, 104, 105
Emerson, Ralph Waldo: and Alcott, 99-100,
114; Christianity challenged by, 140; on
consistency, 110-111; controversy over,
140-141; and Dial, 154-159, 179-180,
208; dislike of laughing, 103, 118; dualism
of, 99-100; Essays, 156, 233; and Hiram
Fuller, 120-121; MF compared with, 4; on
MF's conversation, 146, 150-151, 166,
167, 176; on MF's death, 339; MF's debt
to, 101-105, 184-185, 215, 219; MF's dif-
ferences with, 87, 181-185, 192, 209-
210, 236; MF's early interest in, 41, 87-
88; MF's first meeting with, 101, 102-103;
MF's friendship with, 98-105, 180-185;
MF's influence on, 118-120; Goethe and,
89; Hawthorne and, 191; influence of, 5,
50, 53, 98-100, 178, 249, 254; journals of,
3-4; marital problems of, 182-183; Mazzini and, 256-257; Poe and, 235; stoicism

Emerson, Ralph Waldo (Cont.)
of, 180; Transcendentalism of, 124-125, 165-166, 188; views on friendship, 119, 122, 181-185; on self-realization, 141; on self-reliance, 5, 119, 215; on women, 104-105, 119-120, 174, 190
Emerson, Waldo, 141, 180, 316
Emerson, William, 208
Epoca, 288, 293
"Essay on Critics," 157, 158, 232
Essays (Emerson), 156; MF review of, 233
Everett, Edward, 49, 66, 154

"Fable for Critics" (Lowell), 303
Faerie Queene (Spenser), 193-194
Farrar, Eliza, 3, 61-64, 102, 104, 146, 236, 237, 302
Farrar family, 70, 74, 84, 90-92, 180
Fate Bene Fratelli hospital, 306
Fay, Harriet, 42, 61
feminist movement, 2-3, 53, 161-162, 221, 235, 276
Ferdinand II, King of Naples, 280, 285
"Festus" (Bailey), MF essay on, 159
Fichte, Johann Gottlieb, 67
Fielding, Henry, 24, 25
Flexner, Eleanor, 109n
Fontana, Lavinia, 272
Fourier, Charles, 188, 259
Francis, Convers, 124, 125, 237
Francis, Lydia Maria, see Child, Lydia Maria
Freeman, Dr. James, 60
Friend (Coleridge), 66
Frye, Northrop, 193-194
Fuller, Abraham (uncle), 34, 40, 43, 69, 94, 106, 127, 179, 271, 277
Fuller, Arthur (brother), 38, 75, 76, 106, 138, 140, 177, 185, 200
Fuller, Edward (brother), 76
Fuller, Elisha (uncle), 10-11, 18, 32, 34, 42
Fuller, Ellen Kilshaw (sister), see Channing, Ellen Kilshaw Fuller
Fuller, Eugene, 19, 20, 31-41 passim, 65, 74, 93-94, 106, 138, 139, 177, 179, 302
Fuller, Hiram (head of Greene St. School; no relation), 117, 120-121, 138
Fuller, James Lloyd (brother), 65, 76, 94, 138, 144, 177-178, 179, 187, 210, 243

Fuller, Julia Adelaide (sister), 18-19
Fuller, (Sarah) Margaret, see Ossoli, Margaret Fuller
Fuller, Margarett Crane (mother): background of, 13-15; character and personality of, 17-20, 26, 27, 34, 37, 39, 74, 93-94, 177; health of, 65-66, 77, 113; influence on MF, 19-20, 126, 317
Fuller, Richard (brother), 43, 94, 106, 140, 179, 184, 185; and MF, 138, 177, 243, 271, 283, 292, 302, 317; quoted, 20, 76, 96, 113
Fuller, Sarah Williams (grandmother), 8, 13, 25, 32, 77
Fuller, Thomas (ancestor), 7
Fuller, Timothy (father): affectionate nature of, 10, 14, 17, 18, 28, 30-31; attitude toward women, 11-13, 40-41, 110, 190; character of, 9-10, 19-20, 26; death of, 93; early life of, 9-15; educational views of, 3, 5, 11, 17-32 passim, 40-47 passim, 161, 286; financial methods of, 94; influence on MF, 17-24, 30-34, 40-42, 77, 92-93, 101, 104, 161, 229; political career of, 12-13, 15, 30, 32, 34, 38, 54, 70-72; religious views of, 9-10, 24, 52; rural retirement of, 73-75
Fuller, Timothy (grandfather), 7-9
Fuller, William Henry (brother), 31-34 passim, 74, 94, 138, 177, 179
Fuller, William Williams (uncle), 200
Fuller family, history of, 7-15

Garibaldi, Giuseppe, 300, 304-305, 306, 311-312
Gaskell, Elizabeth, 247
Gioberti, Abbot Vincenzo, 271
God, concepts of, 52-53, 67-68, 86-87, 124-126
Goethe, Wolfgang von: concepts of, 4, 66-69, 81, 85, 89; conversations with Eckermann, 89, 117, 143; Dana's view of, 112; demonology of, 128; MF's projected biography of, 89-90, 95-96, 114, 117, 143-144, 153, 159, 270; Hermann und Dorothea, 69; influence on MF, 66-69, 101, 109, 128, 136, 275; Jungfrau von

Goethe, Wolfgang von (Cont.)
  Orleans, Die, 69; New England view of,
  25; *Tasso,* 69, 82, 88
Gone with the Wind (Mitchell), 193
"Great Lawsuit, The," 160-162, 185, 186,
  208, 209, 213
"Greek Slave" (Powers sculpture), 270
Greeley, Horace: and Ellery Channing,
  210-211; and MF, 208-210, 225-232, 243,
  244, 250, 277, 287, 291-292, 316, 338; on
  Rome, 297
Greeley, Mary, 208, 225-226, 228, 242
Greene Street School, Providence, 117, 120,
  138
Greenough, Horatio, 270, 321
Gregory XIII (Pope), 272
Gregory XVI (Pope), 269
Grimké sisters, 109
Günderode, Caroline von, 175
Gurney, Joseph John, 131

Hale, Nathan, 50-51, 114
Hardy, Thomas, 193-194
Harring, Harro, 236
Hartley, David, 51
Harvard Library, MF's "invasion" of,
  196-197, 208
Hasty, Catherine, 329, 332-336
Hasty, Seth, 329, 331
Hawthorne, Julian, 319n
Hawthorne, Nathaniel: attitude toward
  women, 2, 190, 195; and Brook Farm,
  189; and Emerson, 191; and MF, 2,
  144-145, 180, 184, 187-195, 209, 234,
  318, 319n, 340
Hawthorne, Sophia, 184, 190, 191, 209
Hawthorne, Una, 192
Hedda Gabler (Ibsen), 193-194
Hedge, Frederick Henry: education of, 22;
  MF's friendship with, 55-58 passim, 66,
  75, 81, 86, 87-88, 114-115, 150, 283; on
  New England people, 112; as Transcen-
  dentalist, 88, 123-125, 153-156; as Uni-
  tarian, 71, 142
"Hedge's Club" (original Transcendentalists), 123-124
Hedge, Levi, 22

Hegel, Georg, 67
Heine, Heinrich, 95, 284
Herbert, George, 101
Hermann und Dorothea (Goethe), 69
Hicks, Thomas, 276, 289, 306
Higginson, T. W., 19, 22, 39, 62, 66
Hoar, Elizabeth, 99, 100, 105, 124, 143,
  148, 184, 219, 236
Holmes, Abiel, 52
Holmes, Oliver Wendell, 39-40, 46, 49-50,
  64n
Homer, 128
Hooper, Ellen Sturgis, 146, 155, 157, 159,
  302
Howe, Julia Ward, 9, 22
Howitt, Mary and William, 246, 256
Hugo, Victor, 284

Illustrations on Political Economy (Mar-
  tineau), 90-91
Irving, Washington, 205
Italia del Popolo, 288
Italian revolution: MF's experiences in, 274,
  281, 293, 296-313; MF's projected history
  of, 287, 316-317, 319n, 321, 338-339
Italians, MF's rapport with, 273, 286, 290

Jackson, Andrew, 50, 71, 72
Jackson, Marianne, 148
James, Henry, 190-191
Jefferson, Thomas, 77, 229
Jonson, Ben, 101
Jungfrau von Orleans, Die (Goethe), 69

Kant, Immanuel, 67, 124
Keats, Emma, 178
Keats, George, 82
Keats, John, 234
Kilshaw, Ellen, 27-34 passim, 46, 62, 71,
  219
Kirby, Georgianna Bruce, 113, 189, 211,
  228
Knapp, J. J., 58
Kneeland, Abner, 141

Lamartine, Alphonse de, 325
Lamb, Charles, 66
Lamennais, Félicité de, 246, 260
Léger, Theodore, 113, 228
Leicester Academy, 11, 12, 106
Lesseps, Ferdinand de, 306, 308
Lessing, Gotthold, 109
Letters from New York (Child), 208, 231
Letters from Palmyra (Ware), MF review of, 129
Leverrier, Urbain, 259
Literary Remains (Coleridge), 101
Literature of the South of Europe (Sismondi), 64
"Lives of the Great Composers," 159, 160
Locke, John, 51
London Monthly Review, 154
Longfellow, Henry Wadsworth, 46, 50;
    MR criticism of, 232-233, 234
Loring, Anna, 236
Loring, Louisa, 148, 153
Louis Philippe, 284
Lowell, James Russell, 2, 4, 48-49, 50, 233, 235, 276, 303
Lynch, Anna, 235

Macaulay, Thomas B., 325
Macintosh, Sir James, 95
Manin, David, 285
Mann, Horace, 144-145
Manning, Richard, 235, 243
Manzoni, Alessandro, 273
Margaret Fuller: Whetstone of Genius (Wade), 2-3
"Margaret Myth," 1-4, 340
"Mariana," 44-45, 54, 217-218
Martineau, Harriet, 22, 113, 246; and MF, 90-91, 96, 102, 115-116, 126, 152-153, 249-250, 340
Martineau, James, 248
Mary Barton (Gaskell), 247
Mather, Cotton and Increase, 51
Mazzini, Giuseppi: MF friendship with, 246, 256-258, 262, 268, 312, 340; role in history, 246, 256-258, 268, 270, 287, 288, 300-312 passim
Melville, Herman, 234

Memoirs, 2-5 passim, 45, 58, 134, 148, 339-340
Metternich, Klemens von, 273, 284
Michelangelo, 134
Mickiewicz, Adam, 246, 260-263, 268, 284-285, 287, 291, 295
Mill, John Stuart, 23
Miller, Perry, 44, 102, 166
Miller, William, 165
Milton, John, 101, 235
"Miranda," 215-218
Miss Prescott's School for Young Ladies, Groton, 41
Mr. Dickinson's School, Cambridge, 32, 34
Mr. Frost's School, Cambridge, 38-39
Mitchell, Margaret, 193n
"Modern Drama, The," 208
Molière, 24, 25
Monotti, Carlo, 134
More, Hannah, MF article on, 82
Mozier, Joseph, 270, 319n, 329
Munroe, James, 159
Myerson, Joel, 182

Nathan, James, 238-244, 251, 255-256, 275, 339
Nature (Emerson), 123
Neal, John, 132, 214
necessitarianism, 52, 68
Newcomb, Charles King, 128, 142, 143, 187, 236
Newcomb, Mrs. Charles, 148
New Quarterly, 341-342
New York Tribune: account of MF's death in, 334n; MF's articles for, 208, 226-232, 242; MF's letters to (from abroad), 245, 250, 253-254, 258, 274, 277, 281, 286, 287, 297-300, 302, 306, 308-309, 311-312
North American Indians (Catlin), 205
North American Review, 81, 154
North and South (Gaskell), 247
Norton, Andrews, 140-141, 165
Novalis, 67, 239
Nuisance Removal Act, 247

Oberon (Wieland), 25
"Ode to Dejection" (Coleridge), 84

"Ode to Immortality" (Wordsworth), 105
Oliver Cromwell (Carlyle), MF review of, 234
Ossoli, Angela (sister-in-law), 267, 328
Ossoli, Angelo Philip Eugene ("Angelino"; "Nino") (son): birth and baptism of, 293-295; death of, 334-338; illnesses of, 314-316, 333; legitimacy of, 295, 307-308; Mozier's comment on, 319n
Ossoli, Marchese Filippo (father-in-law), 267, 282
Ossoli, Giovanni Angelo (husband): Elizabeth Browning on, 320; death of, 330, 334-337; family problems of, 282-283, 316, 317; MF's first meeting with, 266-268; MF's relationship with, 270, 274-278, 282-283, 287, 288-294, 297, 304, 316, 320, 326-330; military service of, 267, 292, 293, 306, 311, 320; as revolutionary, 315, 320-321; as teacher, 325, 332
Ossoli, Giuseppe (brother-in-law), 282, 317
Ossoli, Margaret Fuller (chronological): birth, 15; early years, 16-35; enters Dr. Park's school, 34; enters Miss Prescott's School, 41; at Temple School, 105-116; at Greene Street School, 117-138; begins Conversations, 144; edits *Dial*, 154-186; travels West, 196-208, accepts *Tribune* job, 210; arrives Britain, 245; arrives France, 258; arrives Italy, 263; meets Ossoli, 266-268; birth of child, 293-295; marriage, 328; death, 337
Ossoli, Margaret Fuller (topical): achievement of, 1-6, 342; activist temperament of, 5, 23, 155; adulation of, 151-152; ambition of, 3, 4, 44, 59, 64; on androgyny, 111, 162, 175, 221-222; as art critic, 134, 135, 158, 160, 271; biographies of, 1, 2-3, 59, 277; bluestocking qualities of, 1, 130, 137, 275; on celibacy, 4-5, 71, 135-138, 171, 218-219, 275-276; on censure directed against herself, 57-58, 274-275, 317-323; conversation of, 37, 43-44, 55-57, 75, 101, 103, 122, 145-153; on death, 18, 95, 278-279, 282, 289, 307; as editor, 154-155, 158; education of, 3, 5, 17-25, 30, 34-35, 40, 60, 61-62; on educational equality, 160-162; emotional problems of, 1-6, 43-47, 70, 120, 129-131, 137-138, 166-167, 199, 236, 242, 287, 297-303; fame of, 1-6, 56, 87, 338-342; family life, as daughter and sister, 38, 66, 70, 77-80, 93-97, 138, 140, 144, 177, 185, 243-244; as mate and mother, 277-279, 282-283, 287-299, 304, 315, 320-330, 333, 334, 336; fatalism of, 282, 295, 302, 333; "feminization" of, 3, 28, 35, 40-43, 275, 322-325; friendship pattern of, 37, 54-56, 60, 62-63, 102, 119, 122, 181-183; on giving presents, 324-325; health of, 21, 45, 66, 71, 107, 112-114, 140, 179, 210, 278-279, 283; homosexual element in, 62-63; as hospital director, 306, 309-312; income of, 108, 146, 179-180, 208, 277, 287, 289, 292, 302, 313, 329; intellect of, 4, 18, 23, 27, 54, 55, 103, 104, 132-133, 166-167, 175, 184-185, 320; isolation of, 3-4; as journalist, 229, 244, 245-246, 253-254, 281-282, 309; as literary critic, 88-89, 111, 160, 232-235; love pattern of, 62, 251, 326-327 (*see also* Davis, George; Nathan, James; Ossoli, Giovanni; Ward, Samuel Gray); male attitudes toward, 40, 59-60; manners and mannerisms of, 4-5, 26-40, 43-47, 54-59, 103-104, 152, 167, 236, 238, 286; on marriage, 162, 214, 219-220, 328; marriage of, *see* Ossoli, Giovanni; on mental solitude, 75; as music critic, 158, 160; mystical experience of, 86; name changes of, 13n, 15, 27, 33, 289, 328-329; and nature, 25-26, 27, 42, 83-84, 126, 201; occult interests of, 127-129; physical appearance, 32-40 passim, 45, 61-62, 102-103, 152-153, 237-238, 252-253; political consciousness of, 5; portraits of, 61, 306; on prostitution, 222-223; reading habits of, 20-25, 31-32, 64-69, 76-77, 86, 101; religious views of, 85-86, 96, 125-126, 132-133, 171-172; as revolutionary, 246, 268, 286, 309, 323-324; Roman code of, 23, 293, 309; as Romantic, 5-6, 246; self-doubts of, 4, 95, 174-175, 224, 309, 324; on self-reliance, 215-218; sexual conflicts of, 1-6, 102, 173, 224, 251, 275, 323-324; as social

Ossoli, Margaret Fuller (topical) (Cont.)
   critic, 188-189, 198-207, 211-224, 229,
   245-248, 254; socialism of, 287, 320, 323;
   on vocational equality, 160-162, 222-224;
   on womanhood, 129-131, 147, 160-162,
   172-175, 221-222; on woman suffrage,
   132, 214, 300n; as writer, 46, 60, 75,
   88, 92, 120, 160, 162, 173-174, 185,
   220, 229, 272, 323
Oudinot, Gen. Nicolas, 305, 306, 308
Ovid, 23
Owen, Robert, 188

Paolini, Celeste, 331-338 passim
Papers on Literature and Art, 243
Parents' Assistant (Edgeworth), 20
Parker, Theodore, 53, 112, 125, 143,
   155-159, 165, 180, 190
Parker, Mrs. Theodore, 148
Peabody, Elizabeth, 55, 102, 106, 114, 125,
   144-147, 152, 159, 175, 219
Peabody, Sophia, *see* Hawthorne, Sophia;
   Peabody sisters
Peabody sisters, 107, 146, 150
People's Journal, The, 256
Petrarch, 109
Philip Van Artevelde (Taylor), 200; MF
   article on, 82, 88
Phillips, Jonathan, 112
"Philosophy of History" (Emerson), 111
Pilgrim's Progress (Bunyan), 108
Pius IX (Pope), 269, 273-274, 280-281, 288,
   298-300
Plutarch, 23, 26, 309
Poe, Edgar Allan, 2, 233-235
Powers, Hiram, 270, 329
Prescott, Susan, 43, 45-46, 64-65, 74
Prospective Review, 341

Quarterly Review, 154
Quincy, Mrs. Josiah, 148

Rachel, Mlle, 221, 258
Radziwill, Princess, 276
Randall, Elizabeth, 55, 61, 70, 81

Randall family, 74, 94, 236
Raphael, 134
Récamier, Jeanne, 62, 170
Record of a School (Peabody), 106n
Return of the Native (Hardy), 193-194
Revue Indépendante, La, 259
Richter, Jean Paul, 66, 67, 109
Ripley, Ezra, 105
Ripley, George: and Emerson, 102; and MF,
   111, 117, 143, 150, 177; and Transcenden-
   talism, 124-125, 154-155, 157, 158, 165,
   187, 188; and Unitarianism, 53, 111, 112
Ripley, Sarah Alden, 104, 109, 124, 148
Ripley, Sophia, 102, 128, 143, 146, 147,
   161, 187
"Romaic and Rhine Ballads," 180
Roman Republic, 300, 304-313
Romanticism, 53, 67-69, 246, 256-257
Roman Years of Margaret Fuller, The
   (Deiss), 2
Romeo and Juliet (Shakespeare), 24
Rossi, Pellegrino, 298
Rotch, Mary, 176, 237-238, 265, 289,
   294-295, 302-303
Ruffini, Jacopo, 258
Russell, Harriet, 92

Sand, George, 25, 101, 146, 220, 234,
   260-261, 275, 284, 341
Sartor Resartus (Carlyle), 234
Schelling, Friedrich Wilhelm von, 67
Schiller, Johann Christoph von, 66-67, 109
Scott, Sir Walter, 25, 246, 254
"self-culture" concept, 4, 64, 89
Shakespeare, 23-26 passim, 101, 110,
   193-194, 254
Sing Sing, 211, 229, 231
Sismondi, Jean Charles de, 64
Smith, Dr. Southwood, 255
Smollett, Tobias, 24, 25
Society in America (Martineau), 115; MF
   review of, 249
Sotheby, William, 25
Spenser, Edmund, 193-194
Spring, Eddie, 244
Spring, Marcus, 235, 245, 277, 297, 324,
   329

Spring, Rebecca, 235, 245, 323
Spring family, MF's travels with, 243-244, 248-259 passim, 265-272 passim, 327, 337
Staël, Mme de, 46, 62-63, 220, 275
Stewart, Randall, 193-194
Stories for Children (Hawthorne), MF's review of, 180
Story, Emelyn, 276, 282, 297, 305, 307-308, 318-319
Story, William Wetmore, 150, 276, 297, 303-308 passim, 318
Sturgis, Caroline, *see* Tappan, Caroline Sturgis
Summer on the Lakes, 44-45, 196-209, 217-218
Sumner, Horace, 325, 331, 332, 335
"Sympathy" (Thoreau), 157

tabula rasa concept, 52, 67
Tappan, Caroline Sturgis: in Conversation group, 146; description of, 133; and *Dial*, 155, 159; and Emerson, 100, 102, 133, 181; and MF, 100, 133, 143, 176, 210, 211, 236, 302, 318
Tasso, Torquato, 109, 292
Tasso (Goethe), MF translation of, 69, 82, 88
Taylor, Henry, 82, 200
temperance movement, 53, 164
Temple School, 105-116
Tennyson, Alfred, 234
Thackeray, William Makepeace, 193-194
Thoreau, Henry David, 125, 142, 155, 157, 158, 177, 179, 181, 208, 209, 338
Ticknor, George, 49, 66
Tieck, Johann Ludwig, 109
Tombs (NYC jail), 231
Transcendental Club, 123-125, 144-146, 153-154
Transcendentalism: and abolitionism, 152-153; basic beliefs of, 67, 124-127, 141-142, 165-166, 283; beginnings of, 112, 123-125; in England, 254-255; feminism and, 160-162; MF and, 3, 124-129, 144-146, 186, 215, 229, 231-232, 283; idealism of, 257; influence of, 5, 160-161; socialism and, 287

Treatise on Domestic Economy, A (Beecher), 78-79
Tuscany, Grand Duke of, 271, 273, 280, 300, 305
Twice Told Tales (Hawthorne), MF's review of, 180
"Two Agonies" (Browne), 57
Tuckerman, Jane, 148

Unitarianism, 9, 24, 29, 60n, 112; contributions of, 160; controversy over, 51-53; MF and, 67, 68, 85-86, 229

Vanderbilt, Cornelius, 230
Vanity Fair (Thackeray), 193-194
Very, Jones, 141-142, 150
Vindication of the Rights of Women (Wollstonecraft), 11
Virgil, 20-21, 32, 35
Visconti, Marchioness Costanza Arconati, *see* Arconati, Mme
Vivian Gray (Disraeli), 118

Wade, Mason, 2-3, 249, 254, 275-276, 322-323
Ward, Anna, 62-63, 81, 84, 100, 102, 119, 128, 143, 146, 169-172, 235
Ward, Samuel Gray; and *Dial*, 157; and Emerson, 100, 181; and MF, 92, 133-137, 143, 144, 167-172, 235, 243, 327, 328, 339
Ware, Elizabeth, 42
Ware, William, 129
Western Messenger, 88, 129
Westminster Review, 341
Wheeler, Charles Stearns, 150
White, Maria, 148
Whitman, Walt, 5, 178
Wieland, Christoph, 25
Williams, Susan, 34, 37
Wilson, H. D., 157
Wollstonecraft, Mary, 11, 25, 220, 275
"Woman" (Ripley), 161
Woman and the Myth, The (Chevigny), 1

Woman in the Nineteenth Century: discussion of, 213-224; in England, 254-255; in France, 259; Greeley's reaction to, 227-228; public indignation at, 318; significance of, 5, 108, 136, 224, 275, 286; writing of, 209, 210
women: in abolitionist movement, 109; as artists, 4, 120, 162, 172-175, 221; attitudes toward, 40-41, 59, 104-105, 110-111, 119-120, 174, 190; education of, 11, 108-111, 116, 160-162, 203, 216, 223-224, 271-272; emancipation of, 153; as homemakers, 77-80; image of, 186; intellectual equality of, 4; legal status of, 214-215; as pioneers, 200-207; as prostitutes, 211-212, 222-223; in social reform, 160-162; status of, 28-29, 147, 207. *See also* feminist movement
Wordsworth, William, 25, 66, 68, 105, 246, 249-250, 256
World Anti-Slavery Convention, 161

Young Lady's Friend, The (Farrar), 62-64

"Zenobia," *see Blithedale Romance*
Zinzendorf, Countess, 219-220